INTERPRETIVE AND SUPPORTIVE
Psychotherapies

MATCHING THERAPY AND PATIENT PERSONALITY

INTERPRETIVE AND SUPPORTIVE
Psychotherapies

MATCHING THERAPY AND PATIENT PERSONALITY

William E. Piper
Anthony S. Joyce
Mary McCallum
Hassan F. Azim
John S. Ogrodniczuk

American Psychological Association
Washington, DC

Copyright © 2002 by the American Psychological Association. All rights reserved. Except as permitted under the United States Copyright Act of 1976, no part of this publication may be reproduced or distributed in any form or by any means, or stored in a database or retrieval system, without the prior written permission of the publisher.

Published by
American Psychological Association
750 First Street, NE
Washington, DC 20002
www.apa.org

To order
APA Order Department
P.O. Box 92984
Washington, DC 20090-2984
Tel: (800) 374-2721,
 Direct: (202) 336-5510
Fax: (202) 336-5502,
 TDD/TTY: (202) 336-6123
Online: www.apa.org/books/
E-mail: order@apa.org

In the U.K., Europe, Africa, and the
 Middle East, copies may be ordered
 from
American Psychological Association
3 Henrietta Street
Covent Garden, London
WC2E 8LU England

Typeset in Goudy by World Composition Services, Inc., Sterling, VA

Printer: Data Reproductions Inc., Ann Arbor, MI
Cover Designer: Naylor Design, Washington, DC
Production Editor: Catherine Hudson
Editor/Project Manager: Debbie K. Hardin, Charlottesville, VA

The opinions and statements published are the responsibility of the authors, and such opinions and statements do not necessarily represent the policies of the American Psychological Association.

Library of Congress Cataloging-in-Publication Data

Interpretive and supportive psychotherapies : matching therapy and patient personality / William E. Piper ... [et al.].—1st ed.
 p. cm.
 Includes bibliographical references and indexes.
 ISBN 1-55798-831-5 (alk. paper)
 1. Psychodynamic psychotherapy. 2. Supportive psychotherapy. 3. Psychotherapy—Differential therapeutics. 4. Personality assessment. 5. Psychoanalytic interpretation. 6. Brief psychotherapy. 7. Insight in psychotherapy. I. Piper, William E.

RC489.P72.I58 2001
616.89'14—dc21
                                                                            2001035704

British Library Cataloguing-in-Publication Data
A CIP record is available from the British Library.

Printed in the United States of America
First Edition

To the many patients whose willingness to share their experience
in psychotherapy for the benefit of future patients
made this research possible.

To my family, Martha, Emily, and Hannah,
and the wise Margarets in our lives.
—William E. Piper

To my wife, Martha, for her grace and our life together.
—Anthony S. Joyce

To my husband, Don:
"How deep is the ocean; How high is the sky?"
—Mary McCallum

To my wife, Francisca, and to my children,
Ramsey, Omar, Samir, and Dominique.
—Hassan F. Azim

To my wife, Jennifer, and my daughter, Mikayla,
for all their support and encouragement.
—John S. Ogrodniczuk

CONTENTS

Acknowledgments ix

Introduction 3

PART I. THE DEVELOPMENT OF DYNAMIC SHORT-TERM THERAPIES 11

1. Defining Dynamically Oriented, Short-Term Interpretive Psychotherapy and Determining Good Candidates 13

2. Defining Dynamically Oriented Supportive Psychotherapy and Determining Good Candidates 33

3. Interpretive and Supportive Dimensions of Psychotherapy 49

PART II. EMPIRICAL FINDINGS 59

4. Optimal Matching of Patients and Short-Term Psychotherapies 61

5. Quality of Object Relations and Psychological Mindedness: Predictive Patient Characteristics in Time-Limited Therapies 77

6. Interaction of Interpretive and Supportive Forms of Psychotherapy and Patient Personality Variables 91

7. Determining the Role Gender Plays as a Patient Aptitude for Therapy 121

| | 8. | Relationships Among Therapy Process, Outcome, and Dropping Out .... 133 |

PART III. CASE STUDIES: MATCHING PATIENTS AND THERAPIES 151

| | 9. | Clinical Illustrations of Dropping Out From Interpretive Psychotherapy: The Importance of Flexibility .... 153 |
| | 10. | Relationships Between Patient Personality Variables and the Process of Psychotherapy: Clinical Illustrations of Successful and Unsuccessful Cases .... 173 |

PART IV. MANUALS AND MONITORING SCALES 207

| | 11. | Therapy Manuals for Interpretive and Supportive Forms of Psychotherapy .... 209 |
| | 12. | Use of the Interpretive and Supportive Technique Scale .... 221 |

PART V. CONCLUSION 233

| | 13. | Themes and Future Directions .... 235 |

Appendix I.   Manual for Time-Limited, Short-Term Interpretive Individual Therapy 249

Appendix II.   Manual for Time-Limited, Short-Term Supportive Individual Therapy 259

Appendix III. Rater Manual for the Interpretive and Supportive Technique Scale 269

References 281

Author Index 301

Subject Index 307

About the Authors 315

ACKNOWLEDGMENTS

Conducting a methodologically complex psychotherapy clinical trial over a five-year period requires the collaboration of a large number of people. To those directly involved in the research project, we wish to give our thanks for their many contributions. First, we wish to express our appreciation to the eight therapists who each provided both the interpretive and supportive therapies that were studied. Their tolerance of such research requirements as random assignment of patients, therapy manuals, tape recording of sessions, adherence checks and feedback, and repeated rating forms to complete was more than admirable. Despite the many research requirements, they managed to be clinically sensitive to the patients' needs and to provide treatment in a skillful manner. The therapists were J. Fyfe Bahrey, Satwant K. Duggal, Andrea Duncan, Scott C. Duncan, Dianne R. Kipnes, William J. M. Nickerson, John G. O'Kelly, and B. Jill Spaner. We also wish to thank Douglas R. Ginter, John S. Rosie, and David Shih, who served as interview assessors of quality of object relations.

In regard to research personnel, the project would not have been possible without the daily vigilance and efforts of an experienced research coordinator. Hillary Morin skillfully served that role. She was assisted by a team of research assistants who performed a number of diverse functions. They included Shellene A. Greer, Jennifer Michel, Claire Leighton-Morris, Corey Mackenzie, Ward S. Nicholson, Tamara Schuld, Tara Simpson, and Stan Tubinshlak.

The success of clinical research projects is very much dependent on departmental administrative support. We wish to thank the chair of the Department of Psychiatry of the University of Alberta, Roger C. Bland, who provided support and encouragement for the current project as he has for many others that we have completed. We are also appreciative that the project was funded by a federal grant from the National Health Research and Development Program of Health and Welfare Canada.

We also wish to thank three people who helped with the preparation of the book itself. Shannon Hancock was responsible for coordinating the preparation of the entire manuscript. Linda Deng and Christine Stoochnoff assisted her. Their careful work was very helpful.

We believe that it is worth noting that each investigator on our team—with the exception of the research assistants—has been either a researcher–clinician or a clinician–researcher. The clinical setting has been in continuous operation since 1973. The rate of attrition of clinicians, researchers, and administrators has been low. A deliberate policy of intermingling of the offices of clinicians, researchers, and administrators, which facilitated "rubbing shoulders" on a daily basis, was instituted early on in organizing the clinic. We believe that this has facilitated a climate of trust and collaboration. This climate has also been facilitated by weekly staff–staff relations meetings in the clinic and weekly research meetings that focused on the specific project. Both were attended by clinicians and researchers. The therapists who provided the therapies in the project were included at multiple stages of the project, from the proposal to participation to the interpretation of findings. Therapists in the clinic who did not provide the therapies but who referred patients were invited to attend the weekly research meetings, and many did. They also attended group supervisory sessions in which the treatment of patients in the project was discussed. Overall, we tried to include as many staff of the clinic as possible as participants of the project, whether participation was extensive or minimal. We believe that the sense of mutual participation, collaboration, and ownership produced a higher quality research project and a higher quality clinical service to the patients who participated.

INTERPRETIVE AND SUPPORTIVE
Psychotherapies
MATCHING THERAPY AND PATIENT PERSONALITY

INTRODUCTION

At the beginning of the twenty-first century, systems of heath care delivery in many countries remain in a state of transition. In countries such as the United States, which favor privately operated managed care systems, and countries such as Canada, which favor publicly funded systems, there has been much turmoil and unrest. Of primary concern is the continuing escalation of costs for health care in the absence of evidence that the quality of care is improving. The same concerns that have preoccupied the general field of health care have preoccupied the mental health field. There has been strong pressure to decrease the length of stay for psychiatric inpatients and to reduce the number of sessions for outpatients. In the case of outpatients, who represent a large and diverse population with problems typically related to depression, anxiety, low self-esteem, and interpersonal conflicts, the charged climate has provided strong impetus for the development and use of time-limited, short-term therapies. *Time-limited* means that both the patient and the therapist know the total amount of time and number of sessions is limited. In its strictest sense, the amount of time and number of sessions are known before the onset of therapy. *Short-term* is a relative word that ranges from a few weeks to a year, or from approximately 5 to 50 sessions. Most short-term therapies discussed in the literature are 20 sessions or fewer. In addition to economic factors, recognition of certain advantages to time-limited, short-term therapies and emergence of favorable evidence from outcome studies have encouraged the development and use of such therapies.

Although there has been a general shift toward eclecticism in the field of psychotherapy during the past 20 years, as well as a shift toward short-term therapies, a large proportion of therapists have maintained their allegiance to the psychodynamic theoretical model. Despite their common theoretical basis, dynamically oriented forms of therapy differ widely in their primary objectives and in their techniques, especially short-term therapies. In regard to objectives, forms that are considered to be interpretive (or expressive) in nature give primary emphasis to enhancing insight about repetitive conflicts and traumas that underlie the patient's problems. In contrast, forms that are considered to be supportive in nature give primary emphasis to improving the patient's immediate adaptation to his or her environment. In regard to techniques, a distinguishing feature of dynamic long-term therapy has been therapist interpretation, in particular transference interpretation. Nevertheless, in short-term therapy some dynamic therapists actively provide interpretations (including transference interpretations), and others do not. The former therapists are considered to be practicing a more interpretive (or expressive) form of short-term dynamic psychotherapy and the latter a more supportive form. The terms *interpretive* (or expressive) and *supportive* have come to represent two general classes of dynamic therapies that encompass a variety of specific forms.

Historically, dynamic therapists first modified their long-term forms of interpretive therapies to create short-term forms of interpretive therapies. More recently, recognition of the usefulness of supportive techniques has led to the development of short-term forms of supportive therapies. In addition to the therapist technique of interpretation per se, a number of other features, some referring to therapist techniques and some referring to session objectives, differentiate the various forms of dynamic psychotherapies. Each feature can be identified as either interpretive or supportive in nature—in other words, as being part of an interpretive approach or a supportive approach to psychotherapy. At the same time, each feature can be viewed as a continuous dimension. The more that the therapist's emphasis is toward the interpretive end of interpretive dimensions and the less it is toward the supportive end of supportive dimensions, the more the therapy is interpretive in nature. Conversely, the more that the therapist's emphasis is toward the supportive end of supportive dimensions and the less it is toward the interpretive end of interpretive dimensions, the more the therapy is supportive in nature. Because there are multiple dimensions, many combinations are possible.

For interpretive therapy, distinguishing features include pressure on the patient to talk, exploration of uncomfortable emotions, and focus on past figures. For supportive therapy, distinguishing features include gratification, praise, guidance, structured problem solving, and therapist disclosure. Because of the impact of these different features, the process of interpretive therapy is regarded as more depriving and anxiety-arousing than the process of supportive therapy. One of the objectives of this book is to present a set of supportive and interpretive dimensions that can be used to clearly distinguish different forms of dynamic psychotherapies. Fourteen features (seven interpretive and seven supportive) are defined. We believe that this set will assist clinicians, trainers, and researchers in conceptualizing and distinguishing the many different forms of short-term dynamic therapies. We have found that the features are useful in constructing therapy manuals and a treatment adherence scale, components that have become required methodological components of contemporary psychotherapy research.

Similar to others in the field, our clinic and research teams first began developing and studying a form of time-limited, short-term therapy that emphasized interpretive features. It most closely followed approaches developed by Malan (1976a) and Strupp and Binder (1984). In 1990, we published findings from a large-scale, controlled trial of our interpretive therapy that supported its efficacy (Piper, Azim, McCallum, & Joyce, 1990). The sample consisted of a diagnostically mixed group of outpatients who presented with difficulties related to depression, anxiety, low self-esteem, and interpersonal conflict. The study also provided evidence that a particular patient personality characteristic was directly related to the strength of the working relationship (also known as the therapeutic alliance) between the patient and the therapist, and to favorable outcome. The characteristic was the patient's quality of object relations (QOR), which in general refers to the quality of the patient's lifelong pattern of relationships with significant others. Patients with higher QOR scores were believed to be more able to tolerate and benefit from the relatively depriving and anxiety-arousing features of interpretive therapy. Patient characteristics such as QOR have been regarded as important determinants of treatment outcome by many of the developers of short-term interpretive therapies.

Later in the 1990s, our clinic and research teams developed a form of time-limited, short-term therapy that emphasized supportive features. Following positive experiences with supportive therapy in our clinic, we became interested in comparing the interpretive and supportive forms of therapy that we had developed. At the same time, we were also interested in learning more about the importance of certain patient characteristics. The possibility of identifying optimal patient–treatment matches intrigued us. Previous research by other investigators suggested that certain patient characteristics were related to better outcome with some therapies and poorer outcomes with other therapies. Such characteristics are clinically important because of their potential to serve as differential selection criteria.

In the research literature, the optimal matching of patients and treatments has been conceptualized in terms of aptitude–treatment interactions (ATIs; Cronbach, 1957; Snow, 1991). *Aptitudes* refer to a broad class of patient and environmental variables that include patient personality characteristics. Advocates of the search for ATIs in the field of psychotherapy believe that important differential treatment effects may be discovered if research is guided by theory (Beutler, 1991), sound methodology (Dance & Neufeld, 1988), and appropriate statistical analyses (Howard, Krause, Saunders, & Kopta, 1997). Accordingly, we designed and conducted an ATI study that attempted to meet these requirements. The study and its findings represent the centerpiece of this book. The hypotheses that involved ATIs were guided by psychodynamic theory and previous research. The study used a large sample, a randomized design, experienced therapists, therapy manuals, technical adherence checks, and multiple outcome criteria. We were also interested in whether the effects persisted during the year following the termination of therapy.

In addition to QOR, we were also interested in the importance of a second patient personality characteristic that we had studied in previous research, psychological mindedness (PM). In general, PM refers to a person's ability to understand people and their problems in psychological terms. On the bases of our own and other investigators' research findings, we hypothesized that for each of the two personality characteristics (QOR, PM), we would find an interaction with the form of therapy (interpretive, supportive). More specifically, we hypothesized that higher levels of QOR (or PM) would be associated with more favorable outcome in interpretive therapy, and lower levels of QOR (or PM) would be associated with more favorable outcome in supportive therapy.

A number of interesting findings emerged from the study. Some were evident from statistical analyses involving the entire sample of patients. Others were evident from examining individual cases. In regard to the central ATI hypotheses and the entire sample, an interaction with form of therapy was found for QOR but not for PM. In contrast, PM was directly related to favorable outcome in both forms of therapy. Both of these general findings confirm the importance of patient personality characteristics in time-limited, short-term dynamic therapies.

Consider the differing experiences of Robin and Patricia, who both participated in interpretive therapy and whose cases are presented in chapter 10. Robin was a 33-year-old man who was hospitalized overnight for suicide precautions after he was devastated when his live-in girlfriend and his former wife decided to sever their relationships with him on the same day. From his assessments, he received a high QOR score and a very high PM score. Despite these promising attributes, he got off to a rocky start with his female therapist. Out of his first four sessions, he missed two and was late for a third. However, he soon settled down and slowly began expressing his mixed feelings toward his many parental figures (natural and step-parents) and his difficulties in tolerating such conflicts. His high PM enabled him to appreciate and understand the phenomena of intrapsychic conflict, ambivalence toward lost persons, and defense mechanisms. His high QOR seemed to provide him with the confidence and resourcefulness to explore painful themes and relationship patterns in short-term therapy. His more mature qualities permitted an exploration of some of his more primitive qualities. His outcome was among the most favorable in the study.

Patricia was a 44-year-old woman who reported feeling out of control and depressed after losing her job and breaking up with her boyfriend during the past few months. From her assessments, she received a low QOR score that revealed a primitive pattern of relationships. Her PM score was also quite low. She dutifully attended her therapy sessions, where she lamented the many losses in her life and her inability to find a caring male partner. However, she experienced considerable difficulty in working with her female therapist's interventions. Attempts by the therapist to explore the patterns and meanings of her conflicts were met with puzzlement and passive indifference, which reflected her low PM. Similarly, her low QOR interfered with her ability to benefit from the interpretive approach. Rather than acknowledge negative transference, she seemed intent in seeing the therapist as only a benign figure. Her reaction to termination was to immediately join a support group (Adult Children of Alcoholics). Overall, her outcome was among the least impressive of the patients who were treated with interpretive therapy. Chapter 10 also includes presentations of a successful case and an unsuccessful case in supportive therapy.

In general, both interpretive therapy and supportive therapy were associated with favorable outcome. The dropout rate was significantly lower in supportive therapy than in interpretive therapy. A careful examination of the process of therapy revealed that dropping out in interpretive therapy was associated with a weak alliance, low levels of patient work, and a frequent use of transference interpretations by the therapist. Consider the case of Ian, a 53-year-old man who complained of work stress and a general lack of motivation. Recently, he had experienced a nasty altercation with his two daughters that led to estrangement, and he had received a farewell letter from his father in Europe who was dying of cancer. He received a moderate QOR score and a high PM score, which should have served him well in interpretive therapy. However, that was not the case. His therapy began and continued as a battle of wills with his male therapist. Ian expressed displeasure about having to convey his background and history once again in the therapy sessions. The therapist's interpretations about Ian's resentment toward the therapist appeared to be valid but ineffective. The therapist persisted with transference interpretations, and the patient persisted with resistance. Alliance ratings provided by the two were low. Finally, Ian requested a change of therapist. Further interpretations only led to passive submission and termination by Ian at session 6. Unfortunately, the therapist had been unable to extricate himself from an unproductive power struggle with the patient. This case is presented in greater detail in chapter 9, as well as a different case in which the therapist *was* able to avoid continuation of a power struggle and retain the patient for productive work and a positive outcome.

In addition to investigating the effects of patient characteristics and therapist technique, we conducted a set of exploratory post hoc analyses that revealed several gender effects. Men had stronger alliances and better outcome in interpretive therapy, and women had stronger alliances and better outcome in supportive therapy. These are a sample of findings that are presented, illustrated, and discussed in this book. Throughout, we have attempted to indicate the potential clinical implications of the research findings. Two chapters of the book (chapters 9 and 10) are devoted entirely to clinical illustrations. We have also included the therapy manuals for the two forms of therapy and the adherence rating scale as appendixes, so that they may be more accessible to those who may wish to use them.

ORGANIZATION OF THE BOOK

Part I (chapters 1–3) of the book deals with the historical and theoretical foundations of dynamically oriented short-term psychotherapies. The first two chapters provide the historical background regarding the origins and development of the two forms of time-limited, short-term individual therapy that were studied in the central research project that is presented later in this book. Chapter 1 focuses on the development of short-term therapies in general and interpretive short-term therapies in particular. It makes comparisons between the particular form of interpretive therapy that we developed and forms developed by others. Chapter 2 focuses on supportive therapy in general. It indicates that short-term forms of supportive therapy are a relatively recent development, and makes comparisons between the particular form of supportive therapy that we developed and forms developed by others.

Chapter 3 identifies factors that have contributed to lack of clarity and difficulty in specifying the defining features of interpretive and supportive therapies. To assist clinicians, trainers, and researchers in conceptualizing and distinguishing the many forms of interpretive and supportive therapies, the set of 14 features (dimensions) that guided much of our work is presented. The content of the features is closely associated with the content of the therapy manuals and the adherence scale that we constructed for use in our research project. These are presented at the end of the book in the appendixes.

Part II (chapters 4–8) focuses on the empirical findings of other researchers and our own research team. In chapter 4, we address the general topic of matching patients and therapies, with special emphasis on the ATI research paradigm. To provide examples, we review ATI research in the problem areas of substance abuse and depression. Chapter 5 presents the two patient personality characteristics that were investigated in the central

ATI research project of the book. We present findings for QOR and PM as predictors of important clinical events from a series of previous, psychotherapy clinical trials that we conducted. These findings and our conceptual understanding of them form the basis of our rationale for including QOR and PM in the ATI research project.

Chapter 6 presents the central ATI research project of the book and its main outcome findings. Chapter 7 presents findings concerning patient and therapist gender. Both chapters 6 and 7 emphasize the importance of considering interaction effects involving patient characteristics and forms of therapy in psychotherapy research. Chapter 8 continues with an additional set of research findings that emerged from the research project. It addresses relationships among therapy process variables (e.g., the therapeutic alliance and therapist transference interpretation), treatment outcome, and dropping out. In the case of dropping out, certain risk factors are identified and suggestions for prevention are provided.

Part III (chapters 9 and 10) provides case studies and clinical illustrations of some of the main findings of the research project. Chapter 9 focuses on two case examples, both of whom received interpretive therapy. One dropped out and one completed therapy. The role of the therapist's style of intervention is emphasized as instrumental in both cases. Chapter 10 focuses on four case examples. They represent successful and unsuccessful cases from each of the two forms of therapy. The importance of the match between the patient's personality characteristics and the form of therapy is emphasized. In addition, the importance of therapist flexibility is highlighted as a crucial factor.

Part IV (chapters 11 and 12) focuses on the use of manuals and monitoring scales for training, research, and practice. Information about the manuals and adherence scale that we used in our study is presented in chapter 11 and 12, respectively. Chapter 11 also addresses potential problems associated with the use of manuals and the specific dilemma that is created for dynamic therapies. The type of manuals that we used is offered as a possible solution to the problems and dilemma. Chapter 12 highlights the psychometric properties of the adherence scale and its potential use for training, research, and practice.

Finally, Part V consists of a single chapter (chapter 13) that highlights and integrates themes that emerge from the preceding chapters of the book. Chapter 13 also considers future clinical and research directions.

READERSHIP

This book is primarily addressed to the wide range of trainees, trainers, practitioners, and researchers who are interested in providing short-term individual psychotherapies to outpatients who present with a variety of psychological problems. Psychotherapy trainees—psychiatric residents; graduate students in counseling or clinical psychology, education, social work, or nursing—will find the arrangement of the technical features of interpretive and supportive approaches into multiple continua a useful framework for conceptualizing different approaches to the craft. Instructors and therapy supervisors will find that the clinical vignettes offer useful examples of a number of critical in-session phenomena. The interpretive and supportive therapy manuals, and the associated adherence rating scale, can also be easily adapted for classroom role-play or practicum activities. Based on the empirical findings of the comparative trial, we have attempted to formulate recommendations for therapy practice that can be readily adopted by clinicians working on their own or in public clinic, health care center, or hospital settings. In addition, administrators who are responsible for providing efficient and effective treatment to large numbers of patients in the current era of health care reform may find the book to be relevant to their work. Most directly, this book is addressed to those practitioners and researchers who value and believe in the possibility of optimal patient–treatment matching. It is clear that effective psychotherapy practice in the future will rely on the results of ATI studies and the development of pragmatic treatment guidelines. We hope this book is a useful step toward that future.

I

THE DEVELOPMENT OF DYNAMIC SHORT-TERM THERAPIES

1

DEFINING DYNAMICALLY ORIENTED, SHORT-TERM INTERPRETIVE PSYCHOTHERAPY AND DETERMINING GOOD CANDIDATES

In beginning this volume, we wish to introduce and describe the two forms of dynamically oriented, short-term individual psychotherapy (interpretive and supportive) that our team has articulated since 1980. We will emphasize the contrasting features and objectives associated with the two forms of therapy and indicate how each approach occupies a distinct position on multiple continua of therapeutic technique and strategy. In later chapters, we will review the findings from clinical trials that studied the two forms of therapy and we will attempt to integrate the findings conceptually and clinically. In this chapter, we focus on short-term, interpretive psychotherapy (STI), sometimes referred to as expressive therapy. We consider its historical roots and its development throughout the past century as evidenced by the emergence of a number of different approaches to STI therapy. We use the term *approach* to encompass a broad set of characteristics associated with any particular form of therapy. The characteristics include the therapy's theoretical bases (model), clinical procedures (selection of patients, preparation of patients, formulation of patients), and basic features (objectives, technique). Each approach has been identified with a particular person or team of people. After reviewing the different approaches, we present our team's approach and consider the degree to which its characteristics are shared with others' approaches. In the next chapter, we address short-term supportive psychotherapy in a similar way.

SHORT-TERM INTERPRETIVE PSYCHOTHERAPY

A number of identifying characteristics of STI therapy have been highlighted in the literature (Magnavita, 1993; J. Marmor, 1979a, 1979b; Mendelsohn, 1978). These include (a) careful patient selection; (b) an emphasis on limited time for treatment; (c) a consistent focus on a circumscribed problem area; (d) an active therapist stance; and (e) a technical emphasis on the interpretation of recurrent conflict across past relationships, current relationships, and the transference relationship with the therapist. The theoretical underpinnings and technique of all approaches to STI therapy are based on the psychoanalytical perspective. Many of these characteristics were advocated by early theorists, often to negative reactions from the psychoanalytical community, and "rediscovered" years later by clinicians interested in shortening the duration of dynamic therapy. It was not until the 1970s that the various characteristics could be found combined within distinct, short-term, dynamic therapy approaches. The history of STI therapy is thus the story of how these different characteristics became woven into a coherent whole.

Levenson and Butler described short-term dynamic psychotherapy as a treatment "of limited duration during which the therapist is active in maintaining a circumscribed focus with limited goals, using a framework of analytically-derived concepts and techniques" (1999, p. 1144). The active focus on limited goals for a limited period requires that the therapist be selective about the patients who are offered STI therapy. The "time-limited attitude" also requires that the therapist actively promote a therapeutic relationship based on collaborative engagement. The circumscribed focus implies that brief therapy does not offer a "cure" for what ails the patient. Instead, STI therapy affords an opportunity for the patient to foster changes in behavior and thinking that will result in more adaptive coping and an improved sense of self. In effect, STI therapy aims for the patient "to initiate a process of change which will carry on long after the therapy itself has ended" (Mendelsohn, 1978, p. 148). The theme that cuts across many approaches to STI therapy is the importance of maintaining a realistic view of what is possible in the time available.

BEGINNINGS: FREUD AND THE EARLY PSYCHOANALYSTS

Several of Freud's early analyses were completed within short time durations and in retrospect can be considered short-term treatment. Jones (1957) reported that Freud's earliest analyses ranged from several months to about one year. The conductor Bruno Walter had a successful six-session therapy in 1906; Gustav Mahler, the composer, was relieved of an impotence problem following a single four-hour session in 1908. However, the goals of psychoanalysis soon became more ambitious: to examine and understand the dynamics of conscious and unconscious mental functioning. The development of the free association method and the encouragement of a full transference neurosis led to greater passivity on the part of the analyst and a dramatic lengthening of the treatment. As is well-known, Freud (1937/1962) later became pessimistic about the interminable nature of certain psychoanalytical treatments.

The first advocates of a shorter psychodynamic treatment took as their starting point the relative inactivity of the psychoanalyst. Sandor Ferenczi (1920/1980) argued for an "active therapy" and other technical modifications designed to shorten the duration of psychoanalysis. Some of these innovations were restrictive and pressuring—for example, directing the patient to face a present feared situation—and others were loving and indulgent, based on making amends for the experience of parental rejection or abuse. Freud soundly chastised Ferenczi for promoting recommendations to hug and kiss patients (Jones, 1957). Ferenczi subsequently abandoned these techniques without giving up his efforts to develop a more active, brief analytical approach.

These efforts reached fruition in Ferenczi's collaboration with Otto Rank, *The Development of Psychoanalysis* (1925/1986). The authors stressed three important principles. First, establishing a focus for the treatment was held to encourage patient autonomy and responsibility. Second, the therapist actively attended to the immediate analytical situation and its transference implications. Third, a time limit on treatment was used to stimulate issues associated with separation and individuation. Ferenczi and Rank argued that the here-and-now working through of these conflicts as revealed in the transference relationship was the curative mechanism of treatment. Ferenczi and Rank thus initiated a move beyond Freud's one-person psychology of intrapsychic functioning toward the two-person psychology of the patient–therapist relationship that is now more dominant in analytical theory (J. R. Greenberg & Mitchell, 1983; Messer & Warren, 1995). In addition, Rank's later discussions of "will therapy" (1929/1978) underscored the importance of patient motivation, defined as the willingness to actively participate in therapy, to attempt self-understanding, and to change. Rank's views on these issues set the stage for the development of selection criteria that proved central to the first wave of brief psychodynamic therapies developed by Malan (1976a), Sifneos (1972), and Davanloo (1980).

Though he was not a proponent of shorter treatments, Wilhelm Reich's (1933) work on character analysis identified another important selection criterion for STI therapy: The patient should possess an appropriate degree of ego strength to tolerate the level of anxiety aroused by an intensive, focused-therapy approach (Magnavita, 1993). Reich's forceful use of persistent confrontation to penetrate character resistances and address conflictual aggressive feelings presaged Davanloo's (1980) development of broad-focused, short-term dynamic therapy.

The work of Franz Alexander and Thomas French, *Psychoanalytic Therapy* (1946), is commonly regarded as the first manual of STI therapy (Eisenstein, 1986). Based on clinical research involving 292 cases at the Chicago Institute for Psychoanalysis, these authors are best known for experimenting with control or manipulation of the transference relationship to suit the particular psychodynamics of the patient. The patient's experience of the therapy relationship as a "corrective emotional experience" was emphasized. Based on a careful dynamic formulation, the therapist's "transference role" was defined—in other words, to be unlike how the damaging parent was with the patient. This role playing was intended to help the patient achieve mastery of his or her conflict by action rather than by insight, and was regarded as a "rehearsal for life." It is now evident that this deliberate manipulation of the transference could give rise to further problems such as retraumatization of the patient or defensive idealization of the therapist (M. J. Horowitz, Marmar, Krupnick, et al., 1984). Nonetheless, this work demonstrated the curative power of a here-and-now focus on transference feelings in the therapy relationship, or "emotional re-education." Alexander and French (1946) also varied the frequency of sessions to prevent patient dependency and implemented long or short interruptions of treatment to assess the patient's autonomy in preparation for termination. They considered the patient's ego adaptive capacity, ability to engage in the therapy process, and response to "trial interpretations" that addressed conflict across relationships in the past, present, and the transference. All these innovations were aimed at contesting the presumed relationship between the duration and effectiveness of analytical therapy. The essential element in their formulations was the flexibility of the therapist and the need to avert patient regression during abbreviated therapy.

French (1958) also coined the term "focal conflict" to describe a situation in which an impulse, in conflict with values, expectations, or prohibitions, leads to a specific defensive compromise and symptom. By addressing the focal conflict, a more adaptive position on the part of the patient could be encouraged. Balint, Ornstein, and Balint (1972) developed a short-duration "focal psychotherapy" that relied on this principle. The advent of STI therapy had arrived.

POST-WORLD WAR II TO THE 1970S: THE FIRST WAVE

Two social factors accelerated the development of brief dynamic therapy in the United States and elsewhere following World War II. The first was the challenge posed by the thousands of veterans who returned from the battle lines in need of mental health services and, in the United States, with Veterans Administration entitlement to such treatment. At the same time, Grinker and Spiegel (1944) reported on the development of short-term therapy for war neurosis, or in current parlance, symptoms of posttraumatic stress disorder. Lindemann (1944) was also developing a brief crisis intervention model, based in part on his work with relatives and friends of the victims of the Coconut Grove fire, which was a tragic fire that claimed the lives of many people in a Boston nightclub. Similar brief-crisis models were developed by Bellak and Small (1965) and Harris, Kalis, and Freeman (1963, 1964). These interventions stimulated greater interest in developing more active approaches to psychodynamic therapy.

The second influential factor was the impact of American legislative initiatives on providing mental health services. The Joint Commission on Mental Illness and Health (1961) was quickly followed by the Community Mental Health Centers Act in 1962, which mandated the universal availability of psychotherapy services. The subsequent high demand for treatment, coupled with staff shortages in community clinics, resulted in extended waiting periods for patients seeking psychotherapy. These pressures added impetus to the development of coherent approaches to STI therapy. During the 1960s and 1970s, models of brief dynamic therapy were presented in rapid succession by Malan (1963), Sifneos (1972), Davanloo (1980), and Mann (1973). In each case, many problems of patient resistance were bypassed through a careful selection process (Worchel, 1990). Together, these approaches represented the first wave of fully articulated, brief, dynamic psychotherapies.

The approaches of Malan, Sifneos, and Davanloo all focus on a circumscribed problem formulated in psychodynamic terms and address the transference manifestations of this conflict as it emerges in the sessions. The therapies differ along a dimension of confrontation, with Sifneos and Davanloo each making a greater use of anxiety-provoking interventions than is seen in Malan's approach. Messer and Warren (1995) have grouped these approaches together as exemplars of a drive–structural model of STI therapy, given their emphasis on the interplay of the triangle of conflict (impulses, anxiety, and defenses) and triangle of insight (recognition of patterns across past, present, and the transference). These models are descendents of the classical analytical model of Freud, Ferenczi, Rank, and Reich. Mann's approach, with attention to the existential issues of loss, separation, and finite time, is distinctively different. In Messer and Warren's (1995) typology, Mann's time-limited therapy represents an integrative approach and a bridge between the drive–structural approaches and the more recent relational approaches (M. J. Horowitz, Marmar, Krupnick, et al., 1984; Luborsky, 1984; Strupp & Binder, 1984; Weiss, Sampson, & the Mount Zion Psychotherapy Research Group, 1986).

David Malan

Malan's (1963, 1976a, 1976b) focal therapy was developed as a form of applied psychoanalysis and evolved out of Balint's application of his earlier clinical work with Ferenczi to his later work at the Tavistock Clinic in London. Malan emphasized the therapist's choosing and maintaining a narrow focus on a particular conflict, dealing with this conflict before a predetermined date of termination, and approaching this focal conflict strictly with interpretive activity (Malan, 1976b). This strictly interpretive focal approach requires that the patient both rapidly engage in a therapeutic alliance and terminate therapy without developing unexpected serious symptoms. As a consequence, Malan regarded the balance between the patient's motivation and the focality of the conflict to be critical. Clear selection criteria were central to his approach. Appropriate patients are "fast learners" (Burke, White, & Havens, 1979) of high intelligence and ego strength, strong motivation for change, and good interpersonal skills. Ideally, the patient presents with a focal complaint and responds to trial interpretations regarding the underlying conflict. Commonly, the patients Malan studied were considered to have had issues with dependency and depression.

In contrast to writers advocating a fixed number of sessions for brief therapy, Malan argued that setting a date for termination reduces the time devoted to examining possible motivations underlying patient absences from sessions and encourages a higher level of engagement and involvement with the therapist. In practice, the therapist assumes the role of a concerned but objective doctor. He believed that interpretations addressing the triangle of insight (Menninger, 1958)—conflictual relationship patterns in the past, in the present, and in the transference relationship—were the principal mechanism of change. He advocated the use of transference interpretations early in the therapy process. The therapies Malan studied had an average duration of 20 sessions. Malan offered empirical support for the assertion that a greater use of interpretations linking the patient's response to the therapist with the patient's earlier responses to parental caretakers (the therapist–patient or T–P linking interpretation) was directly associated with therapy benefit (Malan, 1976a, 1976b). In subsequent studies of stronger methodology, Malan's findings received moderate (Marziali, 1984; Marziali & Sullivan, 1980) or no support (Piper, Debbane, Bienvenu, de Carufel, & Garant, 1986). More recently, Malan (1986) has speculated that interpretation alone can only reach a small minority of patients, and he has brought his approach more in line with the technique of Davanloo (1980).

Peter Sifneos

At the same time Malan was conducting his research in London, Sifneos (1972) developed his short-term anxiety-provoking psychotherapy at the Massachusetts General Hospital in Boston. Sifneos specifically addressed Oedipal conflicts with his approach, believing that a good outcome was not possible in dealing with other areas (Ursano & Hales, 1986). However, this focus on Oedipal conflicts has been for the treatment of patients with physical symptoms and phobic or mild obsessional neuroses (Sifneos, 1984b, 1985). Sifneos emphasizes selecting patients who are able to tolerate the intensity of treatment and develop a mature relationship with the therapist. Sifneos is even more stringent in patient selection than is Malan, and has developed specific criteria for assessing motivation. In the second edition of the therapy manual (Sifneos, 1987), the following criteria are presented: The patient (a) has the capacity to identify a circumscribed chief complaint; (b) reports evidence of a meaningful give-and-take relationship with another person during childhood; (c) is able to relate flexibly to the evaluator during the initial interview and to experience and express feelings freely; (d) has above-average intelligence and can conceptualize problems in psychological terms; and (e) is motivated for change and not just symptom relief. Using these criteria substantially limits appropriate patients to those with fewer severe neurotic disorders. Patients with narcissistic disorders, extreme passivity or dependence, and impulse control problems are commonly excluded. Sifneos himself estimated that short-term anxiety-provoking therapy was applicable to only 2 to 10% of the outpatient population.

Before therapy begins, the therapist and patient agree on a psychodynamic formulation of the patient's problems, which becomes the focus of treatment. Sifneos's technique relies heavily on early and repeated use of confrontative interpretations, analysis of resistance and ambivalence, and increasing anxiety by attention to defenses and transference patterns (Magnavita, 1993). Characterological problems are actively avoided. The therapist's role is that of an empathic and provocative teacher. The therapy process generally follows a recurrent cycle of progression, resistance, interpretation of resistance, and further progression. A termination date is often set during therapy once there has been evidence of patient change. Therapies have generally spanned 12 to 16 sessions, and have rarely exceeded 20 sessions (Flegenheimer, 1982). "The aggressive confrontational style of this treatment underscores the importance of excluding preoedipal problems and the importance of the therapist's countertransference reactions related to being aggressive" (Ursano & Hales, 1986, p. 1509). The empirical support Sifneos (1984a, 1987) has offered for his approach is largely anecdotal. More rigorous studies that support the efficacy of the model have recently presented positive findings (Svartberg & Stiles, 1994).

Habib Davanloo

Davanloo (1979) refined a broad-focused, short-term dynamic therapy based on his tutelage by Malan and the systematic study of patients seen over a 20-year period at McGill University in Montreal. The approach is the most confrontative of the drive–structural models. According to anecdotal reports, the therapy does appear to be effective with obsessional and phobic neuroses and more severe character problems. Unfortunately, Davanloo's research findings have not been presented in any systematic fashion in the literature. It has been argued that the technique relies a great deal on the personal charisma of the therapist, as the Montreal videotapes of Davanloo demonstrating the approach attest. Broad-focused, short-term dynamic therapy is a demanding treatment approach for both therapist and patient. The importance of extensive training in the method cannot be underestimated. For therapists who feel comfortable with aggressively challenging the patient's defensive resistance, Sifneos's method may be the easier of the two to master.

Given the patient problems Davanloo targets with his method, it is not surprising that he dismisses severity and duration of emotional problems as exclusion criteria. Instead, Davanloo relies on the patient's response to "trial therapy," a single session where the focal conflict is kept rigorously in the foreground and the patient's defenses to examining the conflict are unceasingly challenged by a "relentless helper." The aim during the session is to achieve an "unlocking of the unconscious feeling" associated with the focal conflict. The selection questions Davanloo considers through the trial therapy are quite similar to Malan's, although Davanloo places more emphasis on the patient's response to interpretation and quality of object relations. The therapy process commonly focuses on chronic difficulties with anger. During treatment, a strong alliance is critical. In the opening phase (the first five sessions), the therapist continues to "gently but relentlessly" confront the patient about defenses against feelings in the present (i.e., the transference) and in the past. Signs of resistance are brought to the patient's attention immediately. Defensive maneuvers against this confrontation are also challenged until the patient is able to express anger directly to the therapist. The feelings associated with the "core neurotic structure" can then be accessed and are then addressed during the midphase of therapy. During this phase, the therapist makes frequent interpretations of the central conflict. The end of treatment occurs when there is a cessation of the initial symptoms. The average duration of broad-focused therapy is 15 to 25 sessions, with shorter durations for the patients with Oedipal problems (similar to those seen by Sifneos) and longer durations for patients with severe or multiple problems.

Davanloo (1980) and Flegenheimer (1982) have offered anecdotal evidence regarding the effectiveness of the model, including follow-up at two to seven years after therapy. The Beth Israel Psychotherapy Research Program has studied Davanloo's approach as one of four forms of brief therapy for personality disorders (Winston et al., 1991). The Davanloo approach was found to be of equivalent effectiveness with the other treatments and more effective than a control condition, and there was evidence that the method had a more beneficial effect in relieving depression.

James Mann

Mann (1973) developed his distinct approach to STI therapy at the Boston University School of Medicine. Time-limited therapy (TLP), which Mann advocates, reflects Mann's emphasis on the finite duration of treatment as the central feature of the approach. Mann is consistent with Rank (1929/1978) in recommending a clear focus on the issues of separation–individuation and loss that are stimulated by his firm 12-session time limit. "Mastery of separation anxiety becomes the model for the mastery of other neurotic anxieties" (1929/1978, pp. 24–25). TLP has been regarded as most appropriate for young adults in a developmental crisis associated with early life transitions (M. J. Horowitz, Marmar, Krupnick, et al., 1984). However, the four "basic universal conflict situations" Mann describes—independence versus dependence, activity versus passivity, adequate versus diminished self-esteem, and unresolved or delayed grief—would appear to be central to a larger range of patient presentations. Relative to the drive–structural models, Mann is more inclusive in selecting patients for brief therapy. He does emphasize the patient's ego strength as reflected by work performance and past relationships. He also places a premium on the patient's "capacity for rapid affective involvement and equally rapid disengagement" (Mann, 1991, p. 19). Patients with mild borderline disorder and other forms of preoedipal pathology are among those depicted in the case studies of TLP (Mann, 1973, 1991; Mann & Goldman, 1982).

In three or four assessment sessions, Mann frames the focal conflict as a feeling state, the "present and chronically endured pain," which incorporates a particular conception of the self. Presentation of the central focus conveys the therapist's empathic understanding to the patient and solidifies a therapeutic alliance. The focal conflict is seen as a "paradigm of the transference" that is expected to emerge in therapy. The time limit creates a clearly demarcated beginning of the therapy, a distinct middle, and an unavoidable ending. The patient's emotional reactions to termination also follow a distinct progression through stages: (a) a sense of timelessness and idealization of the therapist as helper, usually associated with symptom relief; (b) disillusionment with the therapist and anxiety about dealing with the central problem in the time available; and (c) the expression of feelings of loss and separation and efforts to manage ambivalence. In contrast with the drive–structural approaches, Mann does not advocate confrontation. The therapist's task is to empathize with the patient's feelings of grief, sadness, anger, and guilt reactivated by the unavoidable loss of the ambivalently valued therapy relationship. Mann therefore regards the termination as the crucial stage of treatment. The objective is to have the patient internalize a "good enough" therapist and experience "a genuine maturational event" in contrast to the conflictual separation from early caretakers.

Two studies of Mann's approach have been conducted by independent investigators. In a small uncontrolled study of 14 patients, Joyce and Piper (1990) reported significant pre- to posttherapy change on measures of symptomatology and role functioning. At pretherapy, the sample proved to be significantly different from a nonpatient normative sample on 19 of 20 outcome variables. Following treatment, the sample differed from the nonpatient normative sample on only 4 of the 20 variables. A wait-list controlled trial of time-limited psychotherapy was conducted by Shefler, Dasberg, and Ben-Shakhar (1993), who reported statistically and clinically significant improvement across diverse measures of outcome. Gains were maintained at 6- and 12-month follow-up. The patients were highly selected, however, constituting only 11% of those screened.

THE 1980s AND 1990s: THE SECOND WAVE

Dramatic social change was also associated with a second wave of brief therapy approaches that emerged during the 1980s and 1990s. Growing concern for the costs of medical treatment, and the consequent development of third-party payer systems, were distinguishing features of the past two decades. Insurance providers reduced coverage of psychotherapy as part of the overall effort to offset the rising costs of health care. Practitioners are now required to justify the need for extended therapy, establish treatment plans with specific goals, and make clear-cut predictions of the anticipated duration of contact with the patient. Providing effective treatments to meet patient demands within fee constraints have made expertise in brief therapy a practical necessity for many mental health professionals.

Third-party payers have also become more demanding of empirical evidence regarding the effectiveness of the psychotherapy treatments they cover. During this same period, evidence for the effectiveness of psychotherapy, including STI therapy, began to accumulate. In a landmark study that introduced the concept of meta-analysis, M. L. Smith, Glass, and Miller (1980) reported that patients treated with psychotherapy were better off than 80% of an untreated sample at termination. Because most of the therapies included in the studies they reviewed were short, averaging 15 sessions, these findings support the effectiveness of brief therapy (Messer & Warren, 1995). Studies comparing time-limited versus time-unlimited therapy generally found the two approaches to be equivalent in effectiveness (see reviews by Koss & Butcher, 1986; Koss & Shiang, 1994; Luborsky, Singer, & Luborsky, 1975; Orlinsky & Howard, 1986). In a comparative study of four forms of dynamically oriented therapy (short-term individual, long-term individual, short-term group, long-term group), short-term individual and long-term group therapy were rated as more effective and cost-effective by therapists and patients (Piper, Debbane, Bienvenu, & Garant, 1984). Investigations comparing STI therapy with other theoretical approaches (e.g., cognitive–behavioral) have generally reported equivalent outcomes (Cross, Sheehan, & Khan, 1982; Sloane, Staples, Cristol, Yorkston, & Whipple, 1975; Shapiro et al., 1994; Strupp & Hadley, 1979; Thompson, Gallagher, & Breckenridge, 1987). These findings have received support from a meta-analysis that had stringent methodological requirements for study inclusion (Crits-Christoph, 1992; see also Diguer et al., 1993).

The second wave of brief dynamic therapies included (a) supportive–expressive psychotherapy (Luborsky, 1984); (b) the brief therapy of stress-response syndromes (M. J. Horowitz, Marmar, Weiss, 1984); (c) the approach based on control–mastery theory (Weiss et al., 1986); and (d) time-limited dynamic psychotherapy (Strupp & Binder, 1984). These approaches are characterized by two features. The first was the development of each approach as a treatment manual for a program of research on psychoanalytical therapy. Messer and Warren (1995) pointed out that "none of these groups of theorists intentionally set out to develop or promote a model of brief therapy" (p. 116). The approaches maintained a lesser focus on issues of duration and patient selection than earlier approaches, in contrast to a greater emphasis on the formulation of patient problems and the techniques of dynamic therapy. The concept of focality is central, and each group recommends the formulation of a therapeutic focus. As a result, clinical foci are more diverse, rely less on monolithic analytical constructs (e.g., the Oedipal conflict), and are more experience-near—in other words, the patient–therapist transaction is a key technical element. The methods of problem formulation associated with these approaches tend to be highly specialized and at the same time highly applicable to clinical practice.

The second defining feature was theoretical. The newer approaches moved away from intrapsychic models of theory and practice to more interpersonal, or relational, models. The works of Klein, Fairbairn, Winnicott,

Sullivan, and Bowlby provided the theoretical base for the new approaches. Stylistically, the therapist's stance changed from the role of objective observer to that of an active participant–observer. This shift assigns more influence to the therapist's personality than with previous models. Greater attention is paid to manifestations of transference and countertransference in the patient–therapist transaction. Technically, there has been much less emphasis on the confrontation of defenses and resistance and more emphasis on interpersonal collaboration and emotional contact. The interpretation of transference remains central but has been reconceptualized. The focus is now on the particular patient's internalized object relations and the reenactment, examination, and change of these "scripts" in the therapy setting. In a relational approach, the aim of STI therapy is the corrective interpersonal experience.

Finally, each approach has marshaled compelling empirical evidence of effectiveness. The research focus of each group has recently shifted to address the treatment of specific disorders and the relationships of technical and process variables to outcome. Brief summaries of each of the models follow. The summaries touch on the view of internalized object relations central to each approach, the implications for problem formulation and therapy technique, and the findings from the respective research investigations.

Supportive–Expressive Psychotherapy

Members of Lester Luborsky's research group from the University of Pennsylvania (Luborsky, 1984; Luborsky et al., 1980; Luborsky, Crits-Christoph, Mintz, & Auerbach, 1988) originally developed supportive–expressive (SE) psychotherapy as an open-ended analytical treatment. The approach places emphasis on the development of the "helping alliance" and accuracy in the interpretation of the patient's central interpersonal conflict. Supportive and expressive interventions are regarded as "elements of all therapeutic interactions" (Messer & Warren, 1995, p. 151). A greater use of supportive techniques is advocated for patients of lower functioning, meaning that patient selection for SE therapy is quite broad. Exceptions include patients with borderline or antisocial disorders and those with suicidal impulses who have difficulty with dependence and separations. The average duration of cases in the Penn Psychotherapy Project was between 20 and 40 sessions. Descriptions in the past 10 years (Luborsky & Mark, 1991) have focused solely on the short-term model of SE therapy and its application to the treatment of opiate addiction and depressive disorders comorbid with personality disorder. Evidence for the effectiveness of the SE therapy approach is provided in Luborsky et al. (1980) and Luborsky et al. (1988).

The "core conflictual relationship theme" (CCRT) serves as the guiding construct for the SE therapist and the Penn research. The CCRT is a model of the patient's central interpersonal conflict, developed from the review of "relationship episodes" provided by the patient in assessment or therapy sessions. Each CCRT consists of (a) a wish, need, or intention, invariably relational in form; (b) a response from the other persons involved in the conflict; and (c) a response of the self (see Luborsky & Crits-Christoph, 1990). Formulation of the CCRT determines the therapy focus and guides the therapist's technique; interventions are aimed at explicating the patient's CCRT and its action both in and outside of the therapy situation. Luborsky (1984, pp. 120–141) provided clear guidelines for working with the CCRT focus in SE therapy. The Penn group has provided evidence that the accuracy of the therapist's interpretation relative to the CCRT contributes to a healthy therapeutic alliance and independently predicts treatment outcome (Crits-Christoph, Barber, & Kurcias, 1993; Crits-Christoph, Cooper, & Luborsky, 1988).

Brief Therapy of Stress Response Syndromes

Mardi Horowitz's group at the Center for the Study of Neuroses in San Francisco (M. J. Horowitz, Marmar, Krupnick, et al., 1984) have blended cognitive and object relations theory in their approach to the STI therapy of stress-response syndromes. Internalized object relations are conceived of as "role relationship schemas" or working models of interpersonal transactions. Psychopathology is viewed as the result of persistent inappropriate applications of rigid or inadequate role relationship schemas. The patients targeted for the 12-session treatment are not of any particular diagnosis but tend to present with neurotic-level problems associated with traumatic loss and related stress reactions. Patients with "excessively conflictual or deficient personality structure" (M. J. Horowitz, 1991, p. 168) are excluded. Formulations of the interpersonal schemas associated with the individual's stress reaction are developed using a method called configurational analysis (M. J. Horowitz, Marmar, Krupnick, et al., 1984). Configurational analysis is a qualitative method of articulating the patient's "role relationship models"—in other words, the views of self and other and the nature of the interpersonal transactions that determine the patient's experience of dreaded, neutral, or desired states of mind (M. J. Horowitz, 1994). Horowitz's approach resembles the CCRT method but allows for substantially greater complexity in the formulation.

Horowitz recommends different interventions as appropriate to the corresponding phase of the stress response syndrome (see M. J. Horowitz, 1986, p. 131). During the initial intrusive–repetitive stress response phase, interventions are largely supportive and ameliorative. The therapist assists the patient in reducing the intensity of overwhelming affective states. In the later denial–numbing phase, the emphasis shifts to a broader exploration of emotional experience and self-expression. The focus of the therapy also changes, moving from the immediate stress-related symptoms to the patient's schemas of interpersonal relationships. The stress event remains central, but attention to the transference relationship is heightened as therapy progresses (M. J. Horowitz, 1991). Termination of therapy is considered a critical opportunity to work through the experience of loss in a more adaptive fashion.

Support for the effectiveness of brief therapy for stress response syndromes is reported in a number of publications (M. J. Horowitz et al., 1981; Horowitz, Marmar, Krupnick, et al., 1984; Horowitz, Marmar, Weiss, et al., 1984). Statistically and clinically significant change was demonstrated at posttreatment, particularly on theoretically relevant measures of stress-response symptomatology. Changes in the quality of the alliance have been identified as a combined function of patient pretherapy characteristics (e.g., quality of interpersonal relations) and therapist actions (Horowitz, Marmar, Weiss, et al., 1984).

Brief Analytical Therapy Based on Control–Mastery Theory

Joseph Weiss, Harold Sampson, and the Mount Zion Psychotherapy Research Group (1986), also in San Francisco, developed an STI therapy based on control–mastery theory. Although definitely psychoanalytical in perspective, the theory has a distinctive cognitive orientation. Internalized object relations are a function of the system of underlying beliefs that determine the individual's relationship to interpersonal realities and define the individual's experience of control and mastery of these realities. The theory asserts that unconscious beliefs are based on early interpersonal experience and serve as guides to individual adaptation. Unconscious beliefs therefore function as organizing principles for perception, personality, and psychopathology ("pathogenic" beliefs). For example, the patient may believe that asserting her independence would be damaging to her mother's well-being. Beliefs also underlie the "tests" posed to the therapist by the patient. The aim of the patient's test is to disconfirm a pathogenic belief associated with interpersonal experiences of anxiety, shame, and guilt. To continue with the example, the patient might announce her intention to take a vacation and miss the next therapy session, with an interest in the therapist's response to this declaration. "Passing" the patient's test is a form of corrective interpersonal experience and held to be associated with therapeutic benefit. To pass the patient's test in the running example, the therapist could respond by being glad for the patient's opportunity to take a holiday and wish her a good time.

The patient's central pathogenic belief is identified through the plan formulation method (Silberschatz, Curtis, & Nathan, 1989). Like the CCRT, the plan consists of four components: the patient's goals (e.g., to be more autonomous), the obstacles to attaining these goals (i.e., the pathogenic belief), the tests that will confront the therapist (i.e., the unconscious enactment of the belief), and the required insights (e.g., the therapist is not damaged by the patient's autonomous action). The "plan compatibility" of the therapist's interventions—that is, how well the intervention functions in passing the patient's test—are regarded as critical to disconfirming the pathogenic belief and facilitating the required insight.

The Mount Zion group has adopted an intensive case study approach to understand the impact of technique on the therapy process. This research perspective has precluded the development of clear selection criteria, but it can be assumed that the Mount Zion samples would overlap with those studied at Penn. The case study approach has documented strong evidence of improvement in time-limited control-mastery therapy (Silberschatz & Curtis, 1986). The "plan compatibility" of interpretations was found to be directly associated with in-session progress, whereas the transference–nontransference designation of interpretations had no clear effect (Silberschatz, Fretter, & Curtis, 1986).

Time-Limited Dynamic Psychotherapy

Hans Strupp developed time-limited dynamic psychotherapy (TLDP) at Vanderbilt University, following years of groundbreaking research on the elements of effective treatment. The approach (Strupp & Binder, 1984) aims at integrating classical and interpersonal analytical theory and technique. The interpersonal basis of TLDP is explicit (Benjamin, 1982; Sullivan, 1953). More than the approaches reviewed earlier, TLDP places a greater emphasis on the therapist's awareness and use of countertransference reactions. Few diagnostic categories are excluded from treatment. Instead, the therapist formulates an interpersonal diagnosis, based in part on his or her own response to the patient. Selection criteria include the presence of emotional discomfort, basic trust, a willingness to consider conflicts as interpersonal, a willingness to examine feelings, and the capacity for mature relationships. As a result, few diagnostic categories are excluded from treatment.

A date of termination, rather than a set number of sessions, is decided on at the initiation of TLDP. The primary goal of TLDP is to improve interpersonal functioning by addressing the "cyclical maladaptive pattern," or CMP, as it emerges in the therapy relationship. The CMP specifies four categories of information: acts of self, expectations of others' reactions, perceived acts of others toward self, and subsequent acts of the self toward the self (affective experience). The CMP therefore addresses components similar to the CCRT. In each session, the therapist works to identify a theme that is related to this central focus and based on observations of the patient–therapist interaction. Early transference interpretations are encouraged. Interpretations linking the theme to relationships outside therapy are also offered. Once the patient can observe and understand the pattern in each context, the focus turns to an exploration for origins of the pattern. Unlike Sifneos or Davanloo, Strupp and Binder (1984) have emphasized gauging the patient's moment-to-moment receptivity to interpretation before intervening.

The Vanderbilt research provided the first strong evidence of the importance of the therapeutic alliance. The Vanderbilt I study found that therapy provided by lay counselors or experienced therapists had greater benefit than a wait-list control condition. The benefits of therapy were directly associated with the quality of the therapy relationship (Strupp & Hadley, 1979), an effect that was evident regardless of therapist experience. A series of case studies examined the factors responsible for variation in therapy outcome (Strupp, 1980a, 1980b, 1980c, 1980d). Poorer outcomes or a more difficult course of therapy were associated with patients who displayed attitudes of distrust and hostility and who had chronic interpersonal problems and poor motivation. In this regard, the treatment for personality disorders developed at Beth Israel Hospital in New York (Pollack & Horner, 1985) bears mention. Brief adaptive psychotherapy (BAP) is very similar to TLDP, but adds the use of confrontative interventions for managing characterological resistances. BAP was found to be more effective than a control condition and equivalent in effectiveness relative to a Davanloo-based approach (Winston et al., 1991).

The Vanderbilt II study found that therapists trained in TLDP showed strong adherence to the model but were less sensitive and more hostile toward the patient following training (Henry, Strupp, Butler, Schact, & Binder, 1993). This unexpected effect was associated with a weaker therapeutic alliance and poorer outcome. The Vanderbilt II study clearly demonstrated that there are limitations associated with strict adherence to therapy manuals, if not deterioration in the therapist's skill and effectiveness. This finding may in fact have far-reaching implications about the dangers associated with doggedly adhering to manuals and reifying theory into dogma.

APPROPRIATE PATIENTS FOR INTERPRETIVE THERAPY

In the case of short-term interpretive therapies, appropriateness is defined primarily in terms of specific capacities of the individual patient. This reflects the focus of these approaches on intrapsychic or interpersonal functioning as opposed to particular symptom clusters or diagnostic profiles. The selection criteria emphasized within each therapy approach have been addressed in previous sections of this chapter. In general, advocates of the earlier drive–structural approaches placed much greater emphasis on specific patient-selection criteria than the later approaches based on a relational model. The earlier approaches also narrowed the definition of appropriateness to patients dealing with particular dynamic conflicts—for example, dependency or Oedipal concerns—whereas the later methods were regarded as applicable to a broader range of pathology. However, most, if not all, approaches exclude patients with substance abuse problems, patients with severe personality pathology, patients likely to decompensate in response to an interpretive focus, and patients with a tendency toward the acting-out of intense affect. These patients are regarded as unable to work productively within an intensive, short-term, interpretive therapy approach.

A number of patient characteristics are addressed as good prognostic indicators by proponents of all brief interpretive approaches. The most important of these is the patient's capacity for basic trust or ability to establish a collaborative working relationship with the therapist. As an indication of this capacity, the patient should be able to describe at least one meaningful give-and-take relationship during the initial history. A second important characteristic is the patient's capacity to formulate his or her difficulty in terms of a focal complaint. The patient's ability to agree with the therapist on a circumscribed focus for the treatment allows the work to proceed readily and with clarity, and is regarded as indicative of some maturity in ego functioning. A related strength is the patient's capacity to have a realistic view of what STI therapy can provide—in other words, the patient is willing to acknowledge that an important goal of treatment is not "cure" but the initiation of a process of understanding and change that can continue after termination. The patient's motivation is frequently mentioned as an important characteristic, although providing a clear definition of this construct has proven elusive. In general, motivation is reflected by the patient's willingness to actively participate in the tasks of therapy, to attempt self-understanding even when this proves painful, and to attempt change beyond the level of symptom relief.

Additional characteristics more specifically concern the patient's ability to engage in the process of interpretive therapy. These include the patient's intelligence and appreciation that intrapsychic and interpersonal conflicts are associated with the experience of problems. The patient's capacity to tolerate the anxiety aroused by the interpretive method is often evaluated by his or her response to trial interpretations during the initial assessment process.

Barber and Crits-Christoph (1991) offered a comparative summary of the inclusion and exclusion criteria associated with a range of brief interpretive therapy approaches. Davanloo (1980) and Sifneos (1987) have both written extensively on the characteristics required of the patient and their assessment.

SHORT-TERM INTERPRETIVE THERAPY: SHARED CHARACTERISTICS

This historical review provided capsule descriptions of the many STI therapy approaches that emerged since the 1970s. Each of these varied approaches can be assigned, generally speaking, to one or the other of the two major psychoanalytical models, the drive–structural or the relational models (Greenberg & Mitchell, 1983; Messer & Warren, 1995). The approach to STI therapy that we have studied in Edmonton draws from approaches that have followed both analytical models. In our previous work (Piper, Azim, McCallum, & Joyce, 1990; Piper, Joyce, McCallum, & Azim, 1998), we have described our approach as a blend of the approaches of Malan (1976a, 1976b) and Strupp and Binder (1984). In truth, the Edmonton approach to STI therapy shares characteristics that cut across many of these approaches. Table 1-1 provides an overview of the characteristics embodied in STI therapy and shared with other approaches. The particular characteristic is associated with the approach or approaches that assign it the greatest degree of emphasis.

The STI therapist has the goal of explicating, through interpretive activity, the triangles of conflict and insight. The primary focus is on the interpersonal enactment of transference patterns in the here-and-now relationship. The therapist's style is flexible, ranging from the concerned, objective doctor (Malan), to the empathic helper (Mann), to the analytical collaborative partner (Luborsky, Strupp, and Binder). In our research projects, the treatment has a fixed 20-session time limit, and there is a focus on termination throughout therapy (Mann). In our analyses, we have frequently segmented the therapy into beginning, working, and termination phases, each of approximately seven sessions. Patient selection for STI therapy is broad-based; patients with mild to moderate character disorders are included. Assessment for STI therapy addresses the motivation for treatment and is based in part on the assessing therapist's response to the patient's interpersonal style. A key variable in our research is the patient personality characteristic we describe as quality of object relations, or QOR (Azim, Piper, Segal, Nixon, & Duncan, 1991). The QOR construct has proven to be a strong predictor of the quality of the therapeutic alliance, the patient's response to technique, and outcome. QOR refers to a person's internal enduring tendency to establish certain types of relationships that range from primitive to mature.

Table 1-1
Short-Term Interpretive Therapy: Shared Characteristics

Characteristic	Approach Sharing Characteristic
General clinical approach	
Primarily interpretive focus on triangles of conflict, insight	Malan, Sifneos, Davanloo
Importance of here-and-now interpersonal focus	Strupp, Mt. Zion
Therapist style	
• concerned objective doctor	Malan
• empathic helper	Mann
• analytic collaborative partner	Strupp, Luborsky
Phasic segmenting of therapy	Mann, Horowitz
20-session time limit; fixed	Malan, Sifneos, Strupp; Mann, Horowitz
Patient selection	
Broad-based, including character problems	Davanloo
• issues with dependence, depression	Malan
• Oedipal issues	Sifneos
• borderline and other preoedipal disorders	Mann
Based in part on therapist's use of self	Strupp
Importance of patient motivation	Sifneos
Importance of patient pretherapy characteristics (e.g., QOR)	Davanloo, Strupp, Horowitz
Formulation	
Choice of focus by therapist	Malan
Central focus = cyclic, maladaptive interpersonal pattern that acts as a heuristic paradigm of transference enactment	Mann, Strupp, Luborsky, Horowitz, Mt. Zion
Technique	
Development and maintenance of strong alliance critical	Luborsky, Strupp
Therapist applies understanding of countertransference reactions	Strupp
Interpretive accuracy relative to formulation important	Luborsky, Mt. Zion
Patient receptivity to interpretation monitored	Strupp, Mt. Zion
Early transference interpretations appropriate	Malan, Strupp
More focus on transference in later sessions	Davanloo, Horowitz
Focus on termination throughout therapy	Mann
Use of supportive techniques as needed to further process	Luborsky

Therapy addresses a central maladaptive pattern specific to the individual patient that may or may not reflect universal conflicts—for example, Oedipal concerns. The maladaptive pattern is formulated by the therapist following the initial sessions of the therapy contract, and is used as a template for the transference pattern expected to emerge during treatment. During therapy, the therapist's deliberate attention to and use of countertransference responses illuminates the nature of the transference pattern enacted by the patient. Interpretive accuracy—that is, consistency with the problem formulation—is viewed as a technical goal. Emphasis is also placed on a judicious use of transference interpretations, provided at junctures when the patient is receptive and able to work in response. Establishing the therapeutic alliance in the early phase of therapy is critical, and the strength of the alliance is monitored throughout. Early transference interpretations are seen as appropriate if well-timed; in the later phases of therapy, a greater focus on transference can be implemented. Finally, the use of supportive techniques is regarded as suitable if required in particular situations or by particular patients. Supportive techniques are applied to further the interpretive focus.

The guidelines embodied in the STI therapy manual (appendix I) have been based on these shared characteristics. The manual provides a framework for the approach; the specific implementation of the therapy has been deliberately left as a matter of the individual therapist's empathy, creativity, and flexibility. In this way, the hope has been to strike a balance between a clear application of the model and to preserve the naturalistic ecology of the treatment environment. Later chapters will flesh out this initial sketch of STI therapy. The next chapter offers a review of the different approaches to dynamically oriented, short-term supportive therapy, and provides a similar sketch of the identifying characteristics of the Edmonton approach to short-term supportive therapy.

2

DEFINING DYNAMICALLY ORIENTED SUPPORTIVE PSYCHOTHERAPY AND DETERMINING GOOD CANDIDATES

We begin this chapter with a brief introduction and historical overview of the emergence of supportive therapy as a distinct treatment. We then present consensus opinions on identifying characteristics of supportive therapy and appropriate patients. Then we highlight the characteristics of contemporary approaches. We conclude this chapter by considering the characteristics that have been incorporated in the short-term supportive therapy approach that we developed and studied in Edmonton.

INTRODUCTION TO SUPPORTIVE PSYCHOTHERAPY

The approaches to short-term interpretive therapy that were reviewed in the previous chapter were grouped into drive–structural or relational models based on their theoretical underpinnings. In contrast, there has been no unifying theory that provides a conceptual basis for the practice of supportive psychotherapy. For many years, supportive therapy was defined as interpretive therapy that deemphasized certain components (e.g., a passive–receptive stance, a focus on transference and resistance). As an extreme example of this viewpoint, Crown (1988) declared that "if it's supportive, it cannot be psychotherapy" (p. 269). As a consequence, there has been relatively little attention paid to supportive therapy in the literature or in clinical training programs. This has remained the case despite the frequent observation that supportive therapy is "a ubiquitous treatment modality" (Buckley, 1986, p. 515) used by a majority of clinicians and offered to a majority of patients seen in clinical practice. Only in the past decade has supportive therapy come into its own as a truly distinct and effective treatment.

In general terms, supportive therapy is a treatment principally focused on strengthening mental structures that are acutely or chronically deficient, in contrast to the focus on facilitating insight in interpretive therapy. Dewald (1969), Pine (1976), Werman (1988), and Appelbaum (1989) have commented on the parallel between supportive therapy and good parenting. Like the effective parent with a developing child, the supportive therapist is accepting and offers guidance to facilitate the patient's growth. Holmes (1988) suggested the overriding task is "to cure sometimes, relieve often, and comfort always" (p. 829). Although certain therapeutic techniques can be considered to be specifically supportive (Hellerstein, Pinsker, Rosenthal, & Klee, 1994; Rockland, 1993), the therapist relies predominantly on common factors (e.g., the therapeutic relationship) to bring about change. The therapist is consistently caring and positive in his or her behavior, and provides a "holding environment" both to protect the patient from external dangers (e.g., involvement in bad relationships) and to set explicit limits on the patient's more problematic impulses. Most important, the therapy relationship is used to illustrate principles about other relationships in the patient's life.

Throughout treatment, the therapist explicitly orients interventions toward the attainment of goals associated with improved adaptation. According to Novalis, Rojcewicz, and Peele (1993), these goals include (a) reducing behavioral dysfunctions; (b) decreasing subjective mental distress; (c) supporting and enhancing the patient's strengths, coping skills, and capacities to use environmental supports; (d) maximizing the patient's autonomy; and (e) achieving the best possible independence from psychiatric illness. The therapist's approach is essentially "pedagogical and personal" (Werman, 1988, p. 156)—that is, teaching and guidance are offered in the context of a supportive relationship.

A Brief Historical Overview

The value of supportive strategies such as education and emotional catharsis has been recognized since the time of the ancient Greeks (Novalis et al., 1993). The German physician Johann Reil (1759–1813) achieved the first systematic organization of supportive methods. For restoring health, Reil emphasized security, stimulation, and comfort accomplished through talking, appropriate physical labor and rest, education, music and art therapy, and occupational therapy. Reil gave as much priority to verbal methods of cure as to other forms of medical care. A similar perspective was taken by Benjamin Rush (1745–1813), the founder of American psychiatry, who recommended direct advice, education, employment, and moderation. These early contributions served as the base for current approaches to supportive therapy.

Psychoanalysis came into existence when Freud abandoned hypnosis and touching the patient's forehead in favor of the "talking cure." Early psychoanalysts such as Jones (1913), Ferenczi (1916), Rado (1925), and Abraham (1926) examined the transference relationship in treatments that relied on suggestion or the use of hypnosis. A primary role was ascribed to the patient's childlike transference to an idealized, powerful parent–therapist. Benefit in these treatments was regarded as a form of transference cure—that is, the patient manifested improved functioning in an unconscious effort to secure the approval of the therapist. The powerful influence of the therapy relationship, now central to supportive practice, was established early in the development of psychotherapeutic techniques.

In 1931, Glover suggested that "inexact" interpretations could offer therapeutic benefit in certain instances. An inexact interpretation addresses the patient's intrapsychic conflicts in a partial or derivative way, thereby deflecting the patient's attention away from the actual sources of his or her anxiety. The application of the inexact interpretation by the patient in "understanding" his or her difficulties leads to increased repression and symptomatic improvement. Schilder (1938) and Levine (1945) listed additional supportive interventions to define the beginnings of an overall treatment strategy. The techniques they considered included benevolent hospital care and verbal methods (e.g., advice and persuasion, ventilation). They also addressed supportive means of dealing with intrapsychic difficulties—for example, a stance of authoritative firmness and provision of outlets for aggressiveness, reassurance in the face of fears and feelings of inferiority, and opportunities for healthy identification. Alexander and French (1946) highlighted many characteristics of supportive therapy in their efforts to shorten the length of psychoanalysis. They stressed a focus on present life problems, the importance of the patient's actions in attempting change, and the necessity of preventing regression during therapy sessions. In their view, therapy ought to be aimed at promoting more productive efforts at problem-solving. The patient's ability to handle new experiences was regarded as a crucial measure of outcome. By the end of World War II, then, many of the strategies that are now identifying characteristics of supportive therapy had been articulated.

In the subsequent decade, emphasis was placed on the distinction between interpretive and supportive therapy approaches and the technical implications of this differentiation. Bibring (1954) offered definitions of five essential therapeutic techniques: suggestion, abreaction, manipulation, clarification, and interpretation. He asserted that supportive and interpretive approaches could be easily differentiated because the former used the first four techniques but avoided the use of interpretation. Gill (1951) was the first to spell out the fundamental strategy of supportive therapy in terms of three basic guidelines. First, the therapist should support and praise ego activities in which adaptive defenses are combined with gratifications, while at the same time discouraging or criticizing activities using maladaptive defenses. Second, defenses that are absolutely necessary to the patient's continued equilibrium are never undermined. Third, inexact interpretations can be used to achieve some discharge of problematic impulses. This strategy was in contrast to the traditional interpretive approach aimed at weakening the patient's defenses so that a full experience of the intrapsychic conflict could be manifested and interpreted in the transference. Knight (1954) argued that patients who could not tolerate these demands in interpretive therapy might achieve greater benefit from a supportive approach. It was soon accepted that the aim of supportive therapy was not insight but instead the patient's achievement of a more effective adaptation to the demands of daily life (Bloch, 1977).

Alexander's (1961) concept of the corrective emotional experience and his strategy of varying session frequency also became applicable to supportive therapy. Extending the time between sessions can be used to reinforce the patient's growing sense of mastery and independence. The relationship with a benign helper can promote the patient's internalization of a "good enough" parental figure. For many patients, this might be the very first such experience. Tarachow (1963) emphasized the therapist's "realness" in facilitating a corrective emotional experience—in other words, the supportive therapist does not interpret the transference but responds to it as if it were an actual relationship. Tarachow also introduced the techniques of benign projections and introjections to complement Glover's (1931) inexact interpretations. Benign projections attributed the patient's difficulties to significant others, and benign introjections ascribed problems to physical influences outside the patient's control—for example, "a chemical imbalance."

The literature on supportive therapy began to increase between 1970 to 1990, particularly regarding the treatment of serious disorders of ego functioning (e.g., narcissistic and borderline character disorders, schizophrenia), and the adjunctive treatment of medical disorders (e.g., ulcerative colitis, chronic bronchitis, and emphysema). Dewald (1969) stated unequivocally that supportive therapy aims at symptom relief and overt behavior change without attempting to modify personality or resolve unconscious conflict. In his view, supportive therapy aims to help the individual adjust as optimally as possible to the limitations imposed by his or her disorder. Dewald followed Goldman (1956) in viewing supportive therapy as a reparative (as opposed to restructuring) treatment. In the first textbook devoted explicitly to supportive therapy, Werman (1984) highlighted the approach as "a substitutive treatment which supplies those psychological elements that (the patient) either lacks entirely or possesses insufficiently" (p. 8). Supportive therapy could therefore also be differentiated from interpretive therapy in terms of its goals and strategies. By the mid-1980s, supportive psychotherapy had an established identity.

The increased interest in supportive approaches during this period could in part be attributed to the impact of the findings from the Menninger Psychotherapy Study (Wallerstein, 1986, 1989). Supportive therapy was compared with supportive–interpretive psychotherapy, analytical psychotherapy, and psychoanalysis, as these treatments were implemented with 42 patients of the Menninger Clinic in Topeka, Kansas. The patients represented a range of pathology, from moderate to severe. The therapies ranged in duration from one to several years. In some cases, patient follow-up spanned periods of up to 30 years. Wallerstein's conclusions included the following: (a) The results obtained using supportive therapy were more impressive than expected, whereas the results of analytical treatments were less impressive. (b) All treatments tended to become more supportive over time. (c) In all treatments, substantial change was attributable to the supportive more than the interpretive strategies of the therapist. By the close of the 1980s, supportive therapy had become an identifiable approach with some empirical validation. Developments since have further articulated the identity of supportive therapy and promoted a clearer theoretical rationale for the treatment approach.

Resistance to accepting supportive therapy as a distinct treatment has been stubborn. According to Pinsker (1994), the American Psychiatric Association's (1984) Commission on Psychiatric Therapies provided "a very limited" definition (p. 531) of supportive therapy. The treatment was held to use the "simple" techniques of ventilation, abreaction, reassurance, clarification, advice, and limit-setting, and was seen as suitable only for more impaired or lower functioning patients. In contrast to this restricted view, Pinsker (1994) followed Wallace (1983) and Werman (1984) in emphasizing that supportive therapy is a suitable treatment for a wider range of problems associated with acute crisis or more chronic conditions. This broader applicability has also been promoted by Luborsky (1984), Pinsker, Rosenthal, and McCullough (1991), Rockland (1989b, 1992), and Novalis et al. (1993). These approaches share many of the same characteristics but differ in terms of certain technical or conceptual emphases. Like the interpretive approaches reviewed previously, supportive therapy can now be regarded as a distinct treatment encompassing a number of established approaches.

Shared Characteristics of Supportive Psychotherapy

Consensus on many of the key characteristics of supportive therapy has been evident in the literature over the past decade. This section outlines the therapist's supportive orientation and interventions that cut across different approaches, using a format originally proposed by Hollis (1964).

Focus on Reflection and Adaptation

In broad terms, the therapist's objective is to maximize the patient's adaptation to current life circumstances. In therapies of shorter duration, the therapist narrows the focus to a circumscribed life problem and offers an approach of rational problem-solving. The goals are to resolve present life concerns and improve the patient's reality testing and coping capacity for the future. Supportive therapy is therefore both ameliorative and preventative. The therapist encourages rational reflection on the problem and potential solutions while minimizing anxiety in the session. There is less focus on the patient–therapist interaction and more on problematic relationships outside of treatment. The patient's identification with the therapist and the tools of treatment is encouraged.

Ventilation and Containment

The therapist is warmly encouraging and accepting of ventilation by the patient. The therapist offers reassurance and takes a stance of realistic hopefulness regarding the patient's experience and problems. The therapist engages in active listening, or tracking (Pinsker et al., 1991), to convey that understanding the patient is important and taken seriously. The therapist conveys the message that the problems being faced are not uncommon for most people (universalizing) and confronts distortions and exaggerations by references to the reality of the patient's life situation (decatastrophizing; Pinsker et al., 1991).

Sustaining Procedures

The therapist encourages a problem-oriented collaboration with the patient. Methods of facilitating collaboration include (a) encouraging a "we bond"—in other words, referring to the tasks of therapy as a joint endeavor; (b) conveying respect for the patient; (c) conveying recognition of the patient's growing ability to do what the therapist does in using the basic tools of the treatment; (d) referring to experiences that the patient and therapist have been through together; and (e) engaging in a joint search for understanding of the problem and formulation of a strategy for problem resolution (Luborsky, 1984).

The emphasis is on the patient taking action to resolve difficulties, particularly those involving other people. When circumstances require, the therapist can use or return to a crisis intervention perspective. If necessary, the therapist prescribes medications and describes the rationale and likely effects (Pinsker, 1997). The therapist prevents regression during and between sessions by maintaining a focus on present concerns, and counters the development of an overly dependent relationship by encouraging mastery. A mild positive transference—in other words, the therapist as a benevolent and knowledgeable authority—is maintained but not addressed. The positive transference provides greater leverage for the therapist's attempts at direct influence.

The therapist offers praise for the patient's efforts toward more adaptive behavior. Most authors stress that praise be provided appropriately—that is, when the patient progresses toward greater adaptation. The patient's questions, unless serving as a maladaptive resistance to the therapy, are answered promptly and clearly. The therapist explains the import of questions so they are not perceived as attack or criticism. Immediate feedback is provided in response to the patient's stated intentions or chosen actions. The therapist is open and disclosing about coping strategies and values and frames these comments in terms of healthy adaptation. The style of the therapy dialogue is conversational but always with a purpose and focus (Winston, Pinsker, & McCullough, 1986). The therapist conveys the impression of a disciplined professional with a specific task (Winston et al., 1989).

Direct Influence Procedures

The therapy has a decidedly educational slant. The patient is introduced to effective problem-solving by considering alternative strategies and plans for goal attainment. The patient practices the techniques of anticipatory preparation and role rehearsal. The therapist advises on the basis of expert knowledge of mental health and human behavior. Focusing on the patient's behavior in his or her environment, the therapist uses suggestion, persuasion, limit-setting, and, if required, direct prohibitions. Interventions in the environment—for example, organizing subsidized care for health concerns or family interviews—are implemented if the therapist and patient agree that they could be useful.

Adaptive defenses in the patient's repertoire—in other words, those that are effective, noninjurious, and gratifying to the patient and others—are accepted and strengthened (Gill, 1951). Mature defenses (sublimation, reaction formation) are reinforced. Maladaptive defenses, particularly more primitive mechanisms such as splitting and projection, are challenged and undermined. The therapist remains oriented to enhancing and reinforcing the patient's ego functions and strengthening reality testing and decision-making.

MODIFICATIONS OF INTERPRETIVE TECHNIQUES

Most often, the therapist addresses comments to the patient's conscious or preconscious processes and rarely to unconscious processes. As Karasu

(1986) put it, "The wisdom of supportive therapy is knowing what to overlook" (p. 522). For the most part, the patient's resistances are bypassed, except those that are maladaptive and that threaten the treatment. "The major resistance that must be dealt with is the resistance to staying in therapy" (Werman, 1988, p. 161). Clarification and confrontation are used freely, but the use of interpretation is generally not recommended. There is an attempt to meet the patient's need to feel understood rather than the patient's need to acquire self-understanding. The same approach is used in addressing projective processes and other maladaptive defenses (e.g., rationalizing, massive denial). Patient attitudes of entitlement are confronted. Negative or intensely positive (erotic, idealized) transferences are addressed promptly to the extent necessary to prevent interference with treatment and to demonstrate that the therapist is comfortable with negative or intense feelings (Dewald, 1994). Such distorted perception is met with skepticism and the patient is confronted with the reality of the therapy relationship. When appropriate, an "upward" interpretation can direct the focus away from the treatment relationship by drawing parallels to the patient's dealings with significant others (Rockland, 1989a). On occasion, the therapist may clarify the patient's interpersonal style and facilitate limited insight into character problems. Supportive therapy demands a high level of therapist activity and skill in judging the adaptive–maladaptive balance of specific behaviors and deciding whether to support, ignore, or undermine them (Rockland, 1989a). There is thus an increased danger of countertransference enactment. The therapist must maintain an awareness of countertransference reactions, particularly those associated with impulses to direct the patient's life or engage in sadistic denigration.

APPROPRIATE PATIENTS FOR SUPPORTIVE THERAPY

A wide range of patients is appropriate for supportive therapy. *Selection criteria* refer less to the capacities of the individual patient and more to various broad categories of pathology. The general categories include (a) previously well-functioning patients in acute crisis; (b) patients with a clear medical condition requiring adjunctive support (e.g., Rosser et al., 1983); and (c) chronic patients, including those with phobic (Zitrin, Klein, & Woerner, 1978), schizophrenic (Stanton et al., 1984), or severe borderline and narcissistic (Kernberg, 1986) conditions. The treatment is also appropriate for (d) patients who are not introspective or curious about themselves—for example, with primary or secondary alexithymia (Freyberger, 1977) or a "psychosomatic character pattern" (Karasu, 1986).

Patients in Crisis

Supportive therapy, usually of short-term duration, is frequently offered to patients experiencing stressful circumstances that overwhelm their coping capacities. Commonly, patients present after being exposed to significant and unresolved trauma, grief reaction, or other disruptive interpersonal event (Dewald, 1994). Alexander (1961) encouraged direct interventions in the patient's environment to alleviate the immediate crisis. Lindemann (1944) emphasized focusing on defining or redefining the coping task and using strategies closest to the patient's available repertoire to achieve resolution. For the patient in crisis, the therapist offers a model of "thinking first and acting after" (Steinberg, 1989, p. 1141). Treatment objectives include the amelioration of distress, a return to homeostatic functioning and better adaptation, or simply to prevent further regression.

Physical Conditions

Supportive therapies are often used as adjunctive treatments for adapting to the risk, diagnosis, or management of many medical illnesses. These include diabetes, acute leukemia, breast cancer, renal disease, respiratory illness, coronary artery disease (Razin, 1982), ulcerative colitis and peptic ulcer disease (Sjödin, Svedlund, Ottosson, & Dotevall, 1986), herpes simplex viral infection, and opiate addiction (Woody et al., 1983). Most of the literature on the medical uses of supportive therapy comprises case studies. Controlled studies have been plagued with methodological problems that likely contribute to the inconsistencies in the findings. In general, however, the value of supportive interventions in decreasing morbidity and length of stay for medical and surgical patients is impressive (Rockland, 1993).

Rosser and colleagues (1983) studied the outcome of psychotherapy for patients disabled by chronic obstructive airways disease. Sixty-five patients were randomly allocated to one of three types of therapy or to an untreated control group, and followed up six months later. The analytical group received a form of transference-focused interpretive therapy; the supportive group received a similar therapy without transference interpretations; and the nurse group met with an experienced medical nurse who focused on practical realities in the patient's life. The latter condition actually resembled supportive treatment but without a focus on interpersonal difficulties. Patients in the treatment conditions showed greater benefit than the untreated control patients. The group treated by the medical nurse experienced sustained relief from breathlessness but showed less psychodynamic change than the two therapy groups. Psychiatric symptoms were reduced in those receiving supportive but not analytical therapy.

Sjödin et al. (1986) studied the effect of short-term, ten-session therapy in combination with medical care compared with medical care alone for 103 outpatients with chronic peptic ulcer disease. The therapy was described as similar to that of Malan (1976a), although with an emphasis on coping with stress and emotional problems. At times, a more didactic strategy was used to draw attention to associations between stressful life events and abdominal symptoms. Patients in both groups had improved to a similar degree after three months. However, at 15-month follow-up, there were significant differences in favor of the supportive therapy condition, which maintained improvement. The control group deteriorated. The short-term therapy was believed to have stabilized the improvement resulting from medical care.

Woody et al. (1983) compared drug counseling alone or drug counseling plus either supportive–expressive (S–E) therapy or cognitive–behavioral treatment for opiate-dependent patients. All three treatment groups showed significant improvement on self-report measures, observer ratings, and records of drug use at seven-month follow-up. The S–E group exhibited the greatest change, particularly in the areas of symptoms and employment. These changes were attributed to the supportive relationship between patient and therapist.

Chronic Patients

Supportive therapy is indicated for characterological or functional disorders when reality testing is flawed; when primitive defenses such as projection and denial predominate; when object relations are impaired and characterized by a poor capacity for mutuality and reciprocity; when there is a failure to modulate affect (especially aggression) and impulses; and when there is overwhelming anxiety around issues of separation and individuation (Buckley, 1986; Werman, 1988). Supportive therapy may also be indicated for notable superego problems—in other words, a failure to maintain society's moral standards (Werman, 1988). Patients for whom medication is central to the treatment plan (Rockland, 1987) or who are too fragile or unmotivated to participate in interpretive therapy (Hellerstein et al., 1994) are frequently offered supportive therapy. These forms of ego deficit are typically of lifelong duration and cut across virtually every diagnostic category. Treatment objectives are to achieve the best adjustment possible for the individual patient and to encourage some degree of autonomy (Bloch, 1977).

Controlled studies investigating the efficacy of supportive therapy have been conducted with phobic and schizophrenic patients. Zitrin and colleagues (Zitrin et al., 1978; Zitrin, Klein, Woerner, & Ross, 1983; see also Klein, Zitrin, Woerner, & Ross, 1983) found that supportive therapy and behavior therapy were equivalent in effectiveness for agoraphobic, mixed, or simple phobic patients. Studies of supportive therapy with schizophrenic patients have a long history but have been criticized for having small samples of only chronic patients, poorly defined treatments, poor regulation of different medication regimens, inadequate control conditions, and inexperienced therapists (Carpenter, 1984). Stanton et al. (1984) and Gunderson et al. (1984) attempted to remedy these methodological problems in a two-year multihospital investigation of the relative benefits of a reality–adaptive, supportive therapy and an exploratory, insight-oriented therapy for non-chronic schizophrenic patients. The supportive therapy focused on augmenting the patient's current reality testing. Both therapies proved to have many supportive techniques in common. The differences between the two treatment groups were minimal across a comprehensive set of outcome variables. Measures of recurrence and role performance favored the supportive therapy, particularly at two-year follow-up. Supportive therapy patients spent more time functioning independently, had a much shorter initial hospitalization, made fewer job changes, and assumed more household responsibilities than insight-oriented therapy patients. The latter patients showed better outcomes in the areas of ego functioning and cognition. In terms of time outside the hospital and full-time employment, the supportive therapy—offered at only a third of the frequency of interpretive therapy—emerged as the more cost-effective treatment.

Alexithymic Patients

Karasu (1986) characterized patients with a "psychosomatic character pattern" as having distorted object relationships, an impoverished use of language, an inability to use regression or dream-type functioning, and a marked lack of neurotic symptoms. Sifneos (1972–1973) added to this list a constriction of emotional understanding, an inability to verbalize feelings, and the absence of a self-reflective capacity. With the alexithymic patient, advice and guidance regarding work, family situations, leisure activities, and other environmental and reality issues are offered. The patient begins to rely on the therapist as a teacher or ally. The goal is to have the patient experience positive feelings toward the therapist without the emergence of somatic symptoms.

Freyberger (1977; Freyberger, Küsebeck, Lempa, Wellman, & Avenarius, 1985) anecdotally reported on the use of supportive therapy in managing primary alexithymia (ulcerative colitis patients) and alexithymia secondary to the development of medical illness (e.g., myocardial infarction and hemodialysis patients). The therapy process develops across three phases: (a) ventilating regarding the patient's hypochondriac concerns; (b) encouraging a more differentiated verbalization of the feelings; and (c) helping the patient see the relationships between bodily symptoms and past and present conflict situations. The therapies ranged from one to seven years, with the average length being approximately three years. Relative to standard medical care, therapy resulted in greater reductions in psychiatric symptoms.

CONTEMPORARY APPROACHES TO SUPPORTIVE THERAPY

Contemporary approaches to supportive therapy make use of most or all of the identifying characteristics discussed previously. The various approaches differ in terms of emphasizing certain strategies or in outlining a conceptual framework for practice. In this section, the unique contributions of particular approaches are briefly considered.

Dewald (1969, 1994), Werman (1984), and Luborsky (1984) have developed Schlesinger's (1969) idea of a continuum of psychodynamically oriented therapy, with supportive therapy occupying one pole and interpretive therapy occupying the other. The two modalities are distinguished in terms of their goals and strategies at particular stages of treatment. In practice, supportive and interpretive therapies tend to overlap and "pure" forms of either approach are considered to be unlikely (Pine, 1976). These authors offer guidelines for determining the relative emphasis on supportive and interpretive interventions for a given patient at a given point in the treatment process. According to Luborsky (1984, p. 74), the guiding questions are, "What in the patient needs support? How should the support be provided? When is this support likely to be the most necessary?" The therapist's integration of the patient's presenting symptomatology, ego strength, motivation, and personality structure allows an estimate of the desired ratio of supportive and interpretive techniques for the planned therapy. From this perspective, the therapist is primarily oriented to providing interpretive therapy and only incorporates supportive techniques as required by the particular patient.

Rockland (1989b, 1992) has developed an approach of psychodynamically oriented supportive therapy (POST). Rockland also endorses the concept of a supportive–interpretive dimension but suggests that POST provides a conceptual framework for the supportive pole of the continuum. Rockland first articulated the "generic" version of supportive therapy (1989b) and then addressed the supportive treatment of patients with borderline personality disorder (1992). He argued that the therapist must have a good understanding of the patient's core conflicts, characteristic defenses, ego function, superego organization, and object relations regardless of whether the therapy approach is oriented toward support or toward interpretive work. The focus of POST is always on the improvement of ego functioning, via direct or indirect methods. Rockland defined the following direct methods of strengthening ego functions:

1. Reality testing is improved by clarifying, confronting, and undermining primitive defenses.
2. Drive regulation is strengthened by discouraging impulsivity and encouraging delay and sublimations.
3. Object relations are improved by encouraging and praising healthier modes of relatedness and discouraging unhealthier modes, both in and outside of therapy.
4. Thought processes are improved by confronting vague and idiosyncratic speech.
5. Defensive functions are strengthened by supporting adaptive defenses while undermining and discouraging those that are maladaptive.
6. The synthetic function of the ego is improved by clarifying, confronting, and undermining splitting operations.

Among the indirect methods, Rockland refers to the following:

1. Pressure on the ego from drive demands is decreased by relative gratifications (e.g., appropriate praise and encouragement).
2. Pressure from an overly punitive superego is decreased by undermining perfectionism or by the therapist sharing more realistic values.
3. External stressors are decreased by the use of environmental interventions.

Rockland has identified supportive techniques that can be used by nondynamically trained clinicians—for example, encouraging the therapeutic alliance, furnishing hope, giving suggestions, and furnishing a model for identification. In contrast, techniques that require psychodynamic knowledge and skills include reinforcing adaptive and undermining maladaptive defenses; supplying inexact interpretations, benign introjections and projections; and determining the style of intervention in accord with the patient's character style.

Kernberg (1986) also addressed the supportive treatment of patients with severe personality disorders. He has been critical of the view that supportive therapy is based on simple common sense; "supportive psychotherapy begins where the effectiveness of common sense ends" (p. 153). He defined the approach in terms of technique: Supportive therapy does not use interpretation, partially uses clarification and abreaction, and mostly uses suggestion and environmental manipulation. In his view, the latter techniques eliminate any question of the therapist's technical neutrality. Kernberg has recommended that the therapist concentrate on primitive defenses and negative transferences as they manifest themselves in the here and now of the therapeutic interaction. Primitive defenses are identified and addressed, not by interpretation but by demonstrating their self-defeating and ego-weakening effects.

Pinsker (1994, 1997) and members of the psychotherapy research team at the Beth Israel Hospital in New York (Hellerstein et al., 1994; Pinsker et al., 1991; Winston et al., 1989) described an approach based on a specific therapeutic strategy and a related set of rules and techniques. The explicit objectives of supportive therapy are encompassed by their definition: "Individual dynamic supportive therapy is a dyadic treatment characterized by the use of direct measures to ameliorate symptoms and *to maintain, restore, or improve self-esteem, adaptive skills, and ego function*" (Pinsker et al., 1991, p. 221). Whereas Rockland (1989b, 1992) has described the self-esteem change as resulting from appropriate transference gratifications (e.g., praise), the Beth Israel group has described specific techniques to bolster the patient's self-esteem as well as to target better adaptation and strengthen ego functioning. To the extent necessary to achieve these objectives, the Beth Israel approach also stresses the examination of relationships, whether these are real or transferential, as well as past and current patterns of emotional response or behavior. Thus facilitating insight is not regarded by the group as a contaminant of the supportive approach but rather used as required to promote the attainment of the three strategic objectives.

> Even the most supportive treatment has the objectives of increasing the patient's awareness of the relationship between his behavior and the responses of other people, his ability to sort out cause-and-effect relationships, and his appreciation on a manifest level of the connection between past and current patterns. (Winston et al., 1986, p. 1113)

The techniques recommended by the Beth Israel group covers a broad range: reducing anxiety (including the supportive provision of interpretations); enhancing self-esteem; respecting defenses (unless maladaptive); clarification, confrontation, and interpretation (incomplete interpretations or interpreting "upward"); rationalization and reframing; encouragement and reassurance; advising and modeling; rehearsal or anticipation; and responding to ventilation. The Beth Israel group has argued that supportive therapy represents the "default" model of individual therapy, a treatment that should be mastered before incorporating more interpretive techniques and strategies. Pinsker (1994) has described supportive therapy as a "shell program," with interpretive approaches regarded as elaborations on this basic model of treatment.

The consensus view of supportive technique suggests that interpretations should be deemphasized. In contrast, Pine (1984, 1986) has argued that interpretations do have a place in the supportive approach. From his perspective, the therapist's work to support the patient's best possible level of functioning minimizes vulnerability and makes interpretive intervention possible. Certain modifications are implemented to accommodate providing interpretation in supportive therapy. These include (a) indicating that the patient is not expected to provide an immediate response to the interpretation, but can respond when comfortable; (b) "striking when the iron is cold" (Pine, 1986, p. 528)—in other words, providing the interpretation when the particular conflict is less active and the patient is more receptive; (c) encouraging the patient's activity in articulating the interpretive content—for example, increasing the patient's readiness for the interpretation or being tentative in delivering the intervention; or (d) increasing the "holding" aspects of the therapeutic environment—for example, providing reassurance that the therapist and patient will work together to deal with the patient's conflict. Rather than a differentiation between supportive and interpretive forms of therapy, Pine (1984) argued that a better distinction is between interpretations given in the context of support versus interpretations given in the context of abstinence. From his perspective, "insight is one of the best forms of support" (p. 66). Pine's recommendations may be best suited for patients receiving supportive–interpretive psychotherapy; others (Pinsker, 1997; Rockland, 1989b, 1992) would argue that these techniques are not appropriate when providing the distinctly supportive therapy outlined in this section.

SHORT-TERM SUPPORTIVE THERAPY: SHARED CHARACTERISTICS

In developing a short-term, time-limited supportive therapy, our Edmonton team used many of the same structural characteristics as our short-term interpretive approach. In our research projects, both therapies are offered for 20 weekly sessions and both address a circumscribed goal for treatment. Both use broad selection criteria and emphasize the assessment of patient motivation. Both treatment manuals provide general guidelines, thus encouraging the therapist's individual application of the characteristics. The supportive therapist's interventions are expected to be consistent with a psychodynamic formulation of the patient's core conflicts, as in the interpretive approach, but focus more on the maladaptive interpersonal outcomes of these conflicts and the development of alternative coping strategies. In effect, the therapist's focus is on the patient's adaptation to circumstances in the present and less on promoting insight into the link between past circumstances and current behavior. Said another way, the focus in supportive therapy is on the patient's behavior with others in his or her life now, and not on the unconscious meanings of behavior in light of past experiences.

The Edmonton short-term supportive treatment also uses many of the characteristics described by the previously mentioned authors. The goal is resolving a circumscribed problem in the patient's current situation. The objectives are to strengthen the patient's ego functions and improve adaptation to present circumstances (Rockland, 1989b). The therapist's style of conducting brief supportive therapy is given particular emphasis in our treatment manual, which is presented in appendix II. The provision of a "holding environment" is translated into an emphasis on giving the patient a feeling of security in the therapy relationship. The therapist works at conveying to the patient that his or her feelings and predicaments are accurately understood. The therapist makes a greater "use of self" in the transaction, and more readily offers personal values, advice, and suggestions regarding environmental change than in the interpretive approach. The focus is on outside relationships, and transference reactions are discouraged. Clarifying the reality aspects of the therapy relationship is used when needed to dispel intense or negative transference manifestations.

Our short-term supportive therapy relies primarily on the techniques of support (i.e., communicating interest in, liking for, and understanding of the patient), advice, education, problem-solving, clarification, and confrontation. Interpretations are generally deemphasized. Occasionally, they may be used as required to provide limited insight or undermine less healthy resistances. In these instances, the therapist can offer interpretive comments in a supportive manner. Pine (1986) offered a number of suggestions for how this can be accomplished. Alternatively, the therapist can rely on "partial" interpretations (Gill, 1951)—that is, offering interpretive clarifications of the patient's conflict that fall short of a complete representation of the dynamics involved. For example, the therapist may address the paranoid patient's discomfort about a growing friendship with another man given the patient's early victimization by the father, without raising the patient's intense fear of the expression of homosexual impulses. The therapist considers the patient's capacity to assimilate and work with observations regarding his or her conflict, and the capacity to tolerate the anxiety that may result, in determining the "completeness" of the interpretation.

Both forms of short-term therapy that were developed in Edmonton share a common, psychodynamic theoretical orientation, but emphasize distinctly different treatment objectives, session objectives, and techniques. We believe that each of the two forms of therapy is an effective treatment for certain types of patients, and that each has some unique therapeutic factors associated with it. To represent the different basic features conceptually, we believe that more is needed than a single supportive–interpretive continuum of dynamic therapy. The following chapter outlines a more complex conceptual representation of our two forms of therapy. The representation involves multiple supportive–interpretive continua, which can be used with many forms of interpretive and supportive therapies.

3

INTERPRETIVE AND SUPPORTIVE DIMENSIONS OF PSYCHOTHERAPY

As the previous two chapters indicate, many different forms of interpretive psychotherapy and supportive psychotherapy are described in the literature. Because of the many varieties, it is difficult to specify the essential and defining features of either interpretive psychotherapy or supportive psychotherapy. As we have defined the term, *features* refer to the overall therapy objectives, session objectives, and therapist techniques (behaviors) associated with a particular form of therapy. Although some features are shared among the different forms of interpretive psychotherapy or among the different forms of supportive psychotherapy, there are numerous unique features that distinguish specific forms. Sometimes, authors have offered concise definitions that include a few primary features for interpretive psychotherapy or for supportive psychotherapy, but inevitably they exclude other important features. More often, authors have provided complex definitions for interpretive psychotherapy or supportive psychotherapy, which include lengthy lists of features (objectives, techniques) with accompanying descriptions. Examples include the books of Malan (1979) and Sifneos (1987) in the case of interpretive psychotherapy and the books of Pinsker (1997) and Rockland (1989b, 1992) in the case of supportive psychotherapy. Such books devote a number of chapters to the features of interpretive psychotherapy or supportive psychotherapy. In the process, they successfully convey the complexity of the therapies. However, sometimes the attempt to be comprehensive creates its own problems such as overinclusion.

An example of overinclusion is the book by Novalis et al. (1993) on the topic of supportive psychotherapy. The authors divided supportive psychotherapy techniques into explanatory and directive categories. They then noted that explanatory techniques include several types, including interpretation. Although the authors explain that the level of interpretation

---

Parts of this chapter have been taken, verbatim or adapted, from "Psychodynamic Psychotherapy," *American Psychiatric Press Review of Psychiatry, 15,* 109–128, 1996. Copyright 1996 by American Psychiatric Press, Inc. Adapted by permission of the publisher and author.

in supportive psychotherapy is superficial and used infrequently, we believe that it is conceptually confusing to define a technique (supportive) in terms of low levels of what it is not (interpretive). The authors introduce some confusion in their definition of the goals of supportive psychotherapy. They include both resolving intrapsychic conflicts and restructuring personality as infrequent goals of supportive psychotherapy, goals that traditionally have been associated with interpretive psychotherapy. The conceptual difficulties may be a consequence of the authors' particular position that supportive psychotherapy is not dependent on any overriding concept or theory. Unfortunately, this atheoretical eclecticism contributes to conceptual confusion in an otherwise useful manual for practitioners of supportive psychotherapy.

Another contributor to conceptual confusion in the literature is the failure of authors to distinguish between the nature of features (objectives, techniques) and the nature of therapies. A feature can be categorized as purely interpretive or purely supportive, whereas a therapy cannot. For example, the technique of interpreting transference can be categorized as purely interpretive, just as the technique of offering praise can be categorized as purely supportive. In contrast, therapies cannot be categorized as purely interpretive or purely supportive, because they consist of combinations of both interpretive features and supportive features. Although a therapy may primarily use interpretive features or supportive features, it never uses only interpretive features or supportive features. Despite this fact, the terms *interpretive therapy* and *supportive therapy* are commonly used as if they represented homogeneous entities. At times, this results in their being regarded as mutually exclusive. Most clinicians and researchers understand that this is not the case. Instead, they use the terms to indicate emphasis, not exclusivity.

Rather than conceptualizing a dichotomy consisting of purely interpretive psychotherapy and purely supportive psychotherapy, some authors place the two pure psychotherapies on the ends of a single continuum. Combinations of the two therapies are placed along the continuum. For example, Pinsker (1997) presented a continuum that ranges from psychoanalysis at one end to expressive–supportive therapy to supportive–expressive therapy to supportive therapy at the other end. The hyphenated therapies indicate relative emphasis. Although the concept of a continuum is more complex than a dichotomy, it too is an oversimplification. This is evident if one tries to specify the nature of the dimension that defines the single continuum. It quickly becomes clear that the therapies on the "continuum" differ on many features. Thus, there are actually many continua, one for each feature. This multidimensional perspective is conceptually more cumbersome than a dichotomous perspective or a unidimensional perspective, but it is much more accurate in representing the complexity of the therapies. It is also more useful for research investigations.

Consistent with the multidimensional perspective, we have defined *features* as including overall therapy objectives, session objectives, and therapist techniques (behaviors). Some authors, such as Dewald (1969), use the terms *strategies* and *tactics* to refer to objectives and techniques, respectively. Regardless of the terminology, failure to distinguish clearly between objectives (strategies) and techniques (tactics) has also contributed to conceptual difficulties.

In an attempt to reduce conceptual difficulties, we suggest the following definitions and formulations. *Overall objectives* refer to the general or ultimate aims of therapy. Although helping patients solve their presenting problems is an overall objective of both interpretive and supportive forms of psychotherapy, the pathways differ. In supportive psychotherapy, presenting problems are addressed directly. In interpretive psychotherapy, they are addressed indirectly. Sometimes the terms *primary objectives* versus *secondary objectives* are used to make this distinction.

From our viewpoint, the *primary (or direct) objective of supportive psychotherapy* is to improve the patient's immediate adaptation to his or her life situation. To restore the patient's equilibrium, symptoms must be reduced, self-esteem boosted, and stressors reduced. There is a focus on the immediate needs of the patients. In many cases, there is a crisis–intervention orientation, even if the "crisis" is relatively minor and repetitive. Thus, there is an attempt to initiate restorative procedures as soon as possible and strengthen them as therapy proceeds. The *secondary (or indirect) objective of supportive psychotherapy* is to teach the patient problem-solving skills that can be used in the future. This includes such skills as learning how to define problems, consider alternative solutions, consider the advantages and disadvantages of solutions, try out solutions, and evaluate the outcomes of attempted solutions. In psychodynamic theory, this is referred to as *building ego strength*.

From our viewpoint, the *primary objective of interpretive psychotherapy* is to enhance the patient's insight about repetitive conflicts (intrapsychic and interpersonal) and trauma that serve to underlie and sustain the patient's presenting problems. This is part of a process of achieving self-understanding and control that continues beyond the termination of psychotherapy, which in psychodynamic theory is achieved through the process of working through. In long-term forms of interpretive psychotherapy, the primary objective would also include character change. The *secondary objective of interpretive psychotherapy* is to help the patient successfully adapt to and, when possible, alleviate the presenting problems that brought the patient to the therapist.

Considering the primary and secondary objectives for both interpretive psychotherapy and supportive psychotherapy, it is evident that both short-term and long-term objectives are included for each. To some extent, what is primary for interpretive psychotherapy tends to be secondary for supportive psychotherapy and vice versa. During each therapy, there is an oscillation between working on primary and secondary objectives, which tests the skills of the therapist.

Session objectives are general goals that indicate what the therapist is trying to achieve during individual sessions. They do not represent the specific techniques (behaviors) the therapist uses to achieve such objectives. For example, a session objective in interpretive psychotherapy is to create a state of tolerable deprivation and provoke anxiety during the session. Faced with the same material in supportive therapy, the objective would be to create a state of gratification and decrease anxiety. How the therapist actually brings about the desired results depends in part on the specific techniques the therapist uses. In interpretive psychotherapy, the technique of interpreting transference can lead to a state of deprivation and anxiety. In supportive psychotherapy, the technique of offering praise can lead to a state of gratification. Table 3-1 provides a list of features (i.e., session objectives and techniques) that have been used in the literature to differentiate

Table 3-1
Features of Interpretive Psychotherapy and Supportive Psychotherapy

Interpretive Features	Supportive Features
Create a state of tolerable deprivation and anxiety in the session.	Create a state of gratification in the session.
Create pressure on the patient to talk by being nondirective.	Relieve pressure on the patient to talk by being directive and conversational.
Provide interpretations.	Provide noninterpretive interventions—for example, reflections, questions, clarifications.
Focus on the patient–therapist relationship.	Focus on patient relationships that are external to therapy.
Explore and interpret positive and negative transference.	Facilitate positive transference and redirect negative transference.
Focus on early relationships.	Focus on current relationships.
Explore the patient's subjective impressions of others.	Focus on realistic impressions of others.
Focus on unconscious processes.	Focus on conscious processes.
Explore the meaning of uncomfortable emotions.	Allow the expression of uncomfortable emotions.
Explore and interpret mature and immature defenses.	Facilitate mature defenses and discourage immature defenses.
Internalize responsibility for difficulties.	Externalize responsibility for difficulties.
Make links among therapist, parental, and significant other relationships.	Engage in structured problem-solving.
	Provide guidance and advice.
	Offer praise.
	Provide self-disclosures about personal information, opinions, and values.

interpretive therapy from supportive therapy. Although each is identified with one or the other form of therapy, each may be viewed as representing a continuum. For each continuum, the more the therapist emphasizes the feature, the more he or she is working interpretively or working supportively.

If there is considerable emphasis on interpretive features or supportive features, a therapy session is regarded as interpretive or supportive, respectively. For example, a therapist who mainly focuses on unconscious transference manifestations in the context of parental relationships, through the use of interpretations that arouse tension in the patient, is conducting an interpretive session. In contrast, a therapist who mainly focuses on alternative ways to relate to a current partner, through the use of questions, guidance, and praise of the patient's past efforts, which is gratifying, is conducting a supportive session.

Most sessions are composed of a mixture of interpretive features and supportive features. Some sessions have substantial proportions of both. On the one hand, this may represent indecisiveness, inconsistency, or incompetence on the part of the therapist. Observation of the patient's immediate responses (e.g., confusion, withdrawal, or active resistance) and the pattern over the session should allow the therapist and supervisor (if involved) to determine if a significant problem exists. On the other hand, the presence of both interpretive and supportive features may reflect a deliberate and useful effort to shift emphasis during certain phases of the session. Rockland (1989b) has made the suggestion that, depending on the patient, certain areas of conflict, such as pre-Oedipal, can be handled supportively, and others, such as Oedipal, can be handled interpretively. Conceivably, both may be required during the same session.

Similar considerations may apply to the entire therapy. If the therapy is mainly composed of interpretive sessions or supportive sessions, it would be regarded as interpretive psychotherapy or supportive psychotherapy, respectively. In contrast, some therapies are composed of substantial proportions of both interpretive sessions and supportive sessions. This, too, may represent a plan on the part of the therapist to shift emphasis during different phases of treatment. A supportive phase of therapy (e.g., the beginning sessions), which allows for establishing a strong working relationship, may be followed by an interpretive phase. Rockland (1993) noted that this sequence has been used successfully with survivors of incest (Stone, 1989), patients with dual diagnoses (Kaufman, 1989), and patients presenting with psychosomatic symptoms (Karasu, 1986).

In interpretive psychotherapy, shifts toward more supportive features during a session or more supportive sessions during therapy are common and at times essential. In general, it is the therapist's intention to use supportive interventions to remove particular obstacles to progress at different stages of therapy or to assist the patient in better tolerating the interpretive approach. Four particular situations will be considered: (a) strengthening the alliance early in therapy, (b) reducing strains in the therapeutic alliance later in therapy, (c) reducing resistance to transference exploration later in therapy, and (d) maintaining a focus on termination issues late in therapy.

(a) The patient may be frightened or intimidated by the process. A strictly interpretive approach can exacerbate the patient's anxiety or defensiveness and perhaps prompt the patient to flee. Inquiring sensitively about current concerns (rather than historical determinants of conflicts) and encouraging ventilation or catharsis can provide the patient with the experience of validation and increase feelings of safety with the therapist. Some patients are very sensitive to criticism and react negatively to early use of interpretations. The therapist can minimize this impact by using reflection, clarification, and encouragement for the patient's efforts to be revealing. Some patients have considerable difficulty being in touch with their feelings. Empathic acknowledgment, slowing the pace, and tracking the patient's immediate affective state can serve an important educative function early in therapy. Finally, the therapist can encourage greater self-focus by showing active curiosity and acceptance of the patient's subjective experience.

(b) Strains in the therapeutic alliance later in therapy are nearly inevitable as the work of interpretive therapy proceeds. This is usually related to the patient's fear of further confronting intrapsychic or interpersonal conflicts. Confrontation and interpretation are usually the first approaches to address patient resistance. However, decreased receptivity or increased defensiveness to the therapist's interventions may indicate that a more supportive strategy is required. The therapist's attitude of curiosity, acceptance, and interest in understanding the patient should be emphasized before offering additional interpretive comments. Again, greater use of reflection, restatement, and clarification are called for in this situation. Educative interventions about the nature of the therapy process may be useful. Similarly, acknowledgement and praise for the patient's progress and encouragement to continue the joint work of treatment may serve to strengthen the alliance and allow the work of therapy to proceed. The return to a primarily interpretive approach should be gradual.

(c) Addressing the patient's recurrent interpersonal dynamics in the here and now relationship is one of the more useful and powerful strategies of interpretive therapy. Sometimes, however, patients become frightened and resistant to further exploration in response to transference interpretation. The use of supportive techniques can help soften the delivery of transference interpretations and encourage the patient to work with them. Providing acknowledgments of the patient's resilience in surviving abuse and deprivation earlier and perhaps currently in their lives as related to the content of the interpretation, and highlighting the costs of defensive compromises in an educative manner can be helpful in facilitating further exploration of the transference. Finally, inquiring about the immediate and subsequent (between sessions) reactions of the patient to transference work can reassure the patient that affective reactions are normal and provide further material for productive work.

(d) The impending termination of therapy can be associated with the patient's experience of a return of symptoms or increased anxiety about the loss of the therapist. Supportive interventions (e.g., education about the termination process, acknowledgment of the gains made by the patient, and reassurance about availability of assistance after therapy should the patient require it) can be useful in maintaining a focus on termination issues.

As we have indicated, sometimes the use of supportive features during an interpretive session or the use of a supportive session during interpretive therapy is part of a treatment plan. Other times it simply represents an intuitive shift on the therapist's part during a session or during therapy. In either case, *therapist flexibility* is required. Studies that investigate the most appropriate match between patient personality and form of therapy, such as the one featured in this book, provide information about the general emphasis of therapy that is likely to be most effective with particular patients. This does not preclude the need to flexibly adapt the approach to a particular patient's needs as a function of the stage of therapy and specific obstacles that arise.

In this chapter, we have highlighted a number of factors that have contributed to a lack of clarity and difficulty in being able to specify the defining features of interpretive therapy and supportive therapy. These have included the large number of features associated with each form of therapy, attempts to be concise, attempts to be comprehensive, failure to distinguish between the nature of features and the nature of psychotherapies, and failure to distinguish between objectives and techniques. There are several additional factors that have contributed to the difficulties. They concern attitudes and perceptions about the nature of supportive psychotherapy and its relationship to interpretive psychotherapy.

The review of the development of interpretive psychotherapy and supportive psychotherapy in chapters 1 and 2 indicates that, historically, interpretive psychotherapy has been regarded as the much more valuable form of therapy. Certain of its features—for example, the interpretation of transference—have been revered as hallmarks of dynamically oriented psychotherapy. It is clear that until fairly recently, supportive psychotherapy has occupied a background position in the literature. This is rather paradoxical given the prevalence of supportive psychotherapy and the number of patients who receive it. Nevertheless, the predominant role of interpretive psychotherapy has at times generated questions about the legitimacy of supportive psychotherapy.

As noted previously, the argument has been made that if the technique is supportive, it is not psychotherapy (Crown, 1988). Consistent with this argument is the idea that what is referred to as supportive psychotherapy is merely the absence of interpretive psychotherapy, or stated alternatively the absence of the most effective ingredients (features) of interpretive psychotherapy. Therefore, it does not qualify as a legitimate therapy. This idea fails to recognize that many features of supportive psychotherapy are not the absence of interpretive psychotherapy. A less extreme argument is that supportive psychotherapy is really just a part of interpretive psychotherapy. This appears to be based on the observation that many of the technical features of supportive psychotherapy—for example, offering praise—are useful in establishing what have been referred to as common therapeutic factors in the literature. These are therapeutic factors that are present in many, if not all, therapies. Examples include positive expectations, a sense of mastery, and a strong therapeutic alliance between the patient and the therapist, which is clearly a requirement for interpretive psychotherapy. Because many of the techniques that bring about the common factors are not unique to supportive psychotherapy, it is argued that they do not deserve recognition as part of a separate form of therapy. This argument fails to distinguish the nature of features and the nature of therapies–in other words, the fact that a given form of psychotherapy is commonly composed of a wide range of features. It also fails to recognize that features of interpretive psychotherapy also bring about common factors and that such features are not unique to interpretive psychotherapy.

Contrary to the historical attitudes and perceptions about supportive psychotherapy that have been noted in the previous paragraphs, we believe that there is good reason to recognize supportive psychotherapy as a legitimate form of therapy with identifiable features. We have highlighted many of its features in the text and in Table 3-1. We realize that the multidimensional perspective that we have proposed and the particular overall therapy objectives, session objectives, and therapist techniques that we have associated with supportive psychotherapy and interpretive psychotherapy differ in some ways from the conceptions of other authors. Our current conception also differs in important ways from our own conception of only a few years ago (Piper, 1996). Accordingly, we offer our current conception only for the present time. We expect it to change over time as a function of its limitations and further developments in the field. Nevertheless, we believe that our current conception represents a clearer perspective that avoids certain problems that other conceptions have encountered. We also believe that it is provides certain advantages for training and research applications, topics that we will take up in subsequent chapters.

II

EMPIRICAL FINDINGS

4

OPTIMAL MATCHING OF PATIENTS AND SHORT-TERM PSYCHOTHERAPIES

It has long been recognized that not all patients benefit equally from the same treatment. It makes sense that patients who differ on personality, motivation, problem severity, or other characteristics also differ in the benefit they receive from different therapeutic approaches. However, some studies in the psychotherapy field have produced counterintuitive results. By and large, research that has addressed the question of who benefits more from which therapy has been relatively rare. When conducted, it has sometimes produced inconsistent results, and it has often lacked a theoretical basis. Nevertheless, efforts toward bridging the gap between intuition and research are being made.

The goal of finding the optimal treatment for different types of patients has primarily followed two strategies. The first most commonly used research strategy involves aptitude-treatment interaction (ATI) designs. *Aptitude* is a general term. It refers to any measurable characteristic of the person or the person's environment that can affect response to treatment. It is not restricted to measures of patient ability. An aptitude can be a demographic variable (e.g., gender, age), a disorder-specific characteristic (e.g., "endogeneity" of depression, alcoholism severity), any personality state or trait, an aspect of the patient's interpersonal environment (e.g., quality of social support), or a characteristic of the patient's life style (Frank, 1979). Often, aptitudes represent either resources or deficits of the patient or the patient's environment. In ATI studies of psychotherapy, intrapersonal and interpersonal variables have received the most attention. Personality traits that are conceptually related to the presumed change mechanisms of the therapy under study have so far provided the greatest yield from ATI psychotherapy research (Shoham-Salomon & Hannah, 1991). The goal of ATI research is to develop empirically validated and practical guidelines for clinicians to use in assigning patients to different types of treatment.

The second, more recently developed strategy involves prescriptive therapy research. Prescriptive therapy is based on a set of guiding principles that directs the therapist's use of different interventions. The principles that guide selection of techniques are founded on theory and empirically based evidence of the effectiveness of different interventions for patients with certain defining characteristics. These characteristics may represent the domains of patient diagnosis, personal characteristics (expectations regarding treatment, usual coping style, personality variables such as dependency), or the environmental or situational circumstances associated with the patient's presentation (Beutler & Clarkin, 1990). Prescriptive therapy begins with an assessment of key patient characteristics that are thought to have an important impact on treatment outcome. Then the clinician, following a set of guiding principles, plans treatment around the patient's presentation of these key characteristics. Treatment planning involves adopting appropriate techniques from a variety of therapeutic approaches. This approach has been referred to as "technical eclecticism" (Beutler & Crago, 1987). It differs from ATI research in that it does not match a particular form of treatment to a particular type of patient, but rather selectively matches interventions (from different technical orientations) to certain key patient characteristics. Thus prescriptive therapy research aims to determine if treatment is optimally effective if interventions are selected on the basis of key qualities that characterize the patient. Although this research strategy is intriguing, it is difficult to carry out. Thus few researchers have attempted to use it in their work.

In each of these approaches, the objective is to provide a treatment that most effectively addresses the patient's problems. The potential clinical benefits of this work include enhanced treatment effectiveness, improved use of resources, increased cost-effectiveness, and avoidance of inappropriate interventions that may result in poor patient response or premature termination. As indicated previously, the majority of researchers in the psychotherapy field have used the ATI research strategy. This chapter will focus on a number of aspects of ATI research: (a) development of ATI research, (b) the range of aptitudes available for study, (c) methodological and design issues, and (d) evidence for patient–treatment matching from a variety of empirical studies.

DEVELOPMENT OF THE ATI RESEARCH PERSPECTIVE

The study of ATIs has emerged in psychotherapy research only during the past two decades. The development of ATI research in psychotherapy was a response to three earlier developmental stages. The first was Kiesler's (1966) recognition of the "myths" of patient and treatment uniformity.

Kiesler argued that clinicians and researchers need to recognize the important differences between patients and between different forms of treatment. Paul (1967) echoed Kiesler's recommendation in his often-quoted research question, "What treatment, by whom, is most effective [for which patient] under which set of circumstances?" (p. 111).

The second stage of development was the discovery of equivalent effectiveness in many comparative studies of psychotherapy. Results of comparative trials consistently indicated moderate improvement for psychosocial interventions over wait-list or placebo control conditions, and minimal differences between active treatments (Lambert & Bergin, 1994; Shapiro & Shapiro, 1982; M. L. Smith et al., 1980). This phenomenon came to be known as the "Dodo bird verdict" (Luborsky et al., 1975), referring to the footrace in *Alice in Wonderland* where "all have won and all must have prizes!" Findings of no differential effectiveness are commonly based on the analysis of group means. This analytical approach tends to obscure the substantial variation in outcome observed across individual cases *within* particular treatments. The variation, which has typically been ignored, suggests that unmeasured characteristics of the patient and the treatment may interact to facilitate or retard therapeutic progress (Beutler et al., 1991).

The third stage of development was the attribution of the similar effectiveness of the different therapies to commonly shared factors (Frank, 1982; Garfield, 1986). An example of a common factor that has received substantial empirical support as a predictor of outcome is the quality of the therapeutic relationship or alliance (Horvath & Symonds, 1991). Without denying the importance of the alliance and other central therapeutic techniques, the common factors perspective does not allow one to conclude that discrete therapy approaches have no differential effects. Rather, there is the possibility that specific effects may emerge with better designed research that takes patient characteristics into consideration.

Aptitude–treatment interaction research acknowledges the heterogeneity of patients and the variation of outcome with single treatments, and aims to identify patient variables that predict differential treatment responsiveness (Dance & Neufeld, 1988). ATI methodology is

> designed to take individual differences into account systematically in treatment evaluation—to assess the degree to which alternative treatments have different effects as a function of person characteristics and thus determine whether particular treatments can be chosen or adapted to fit particular persons optimally. (Snow, 1991, p. 205)

An ATI may be understood in several ways. First, an aptitude–treatment interaction indicates that there are limits to the generalizability of a treatment effect—in other words, the treatment works better with some patients or under some conditions than others (B. Smith & Sechrest, 1991).

Second, an ATI indicates that there are limits to the generalizability of an aptitude effect—the aptitude is related to better outcome with some treatments rather than others. Third, the ATI may be specific to a particular outcome measure—one therapy has a strong effect on social functioning for particular patients relative to another therapy. ATI research findings can be translated directly into differential therapeutics, thus being more informative to practitioners than traditional, comparative clinical trials.

Theory and technique are integrated components that the mental health professional brings to the therapy situation. Theoretical perspectives and clinical strategy develop in an interdependent fashion. Clinical observations lead to theory building, which systematizes the phenomena. Theory is then applied to new clinical situations and consequently undergoes further modification. The cycle continually repeats itself (Shoham-Salomon, 1991). The ATI paradigm operates in this manner. At an overt level, the ATI paradigm represents a shift in focus from differences between treatments to differences between patients. At a more fundamental level, the shift in focus is toward the combination of treatment differences and patient differences—in other words, their interaction. Theory is important in accounting for such interactions.

APTITUDES AND THEORY IN ATI RESEARCH

Certain patient characteristics affect outcomes from all types of treatment in the same manner. Motivation for change is one such *outcome predictor*. Of more interest to the ATI approach are *matching factors* (Mattson, 1994)—in other words, patient characteristics that have a distinct effect only within certain types of treatment. A strong ATI indicates that patients scoring high on an aptitude do better in one form of treatment whereas patients with low scores on the aptitude show more improvement in another form of treatment. Different theories may suggest that the therapy *compensates* for a particular patient deficit or *capitalizes* on a patient's strength (Cronbach & Snow, 1977). Theoretically derived and empirically tested interactions can therefore shed light on the change mechanisms that determine the outcome of particular therapies. For example, Shoham-Salomon, Avner, and Neeman (1989) tested theory-derived hypotheses that paradoxical interventions (e.g., directives to maintain a problematic interpersonal dynamic) would capitalize on a patient's tendency to resist demands made by others (reactance potential), whereas self-control interventions would capitalize on a patient's tendency to be compliant. The selection of aptitudes was directed by the theory to be tested; assessment of the interactions provided support for the theory.

Beutler (1979, 1991) has listed a vast number of potentially relevant characteristics of patient, treatment, and environment. Most have weak conceptual linkages to theories of change or cannot be measured reliably and validly. Variables often have been selected because of convenience or based on a post hoc search for individual differences that account for outcome variance following a finding of equivalence among treatment conditions. "In the absence of a theory that provides a compelling reason why a particular interaction should be searched for, serendipitous interactions remain exactly that, and replication of the finding is doubtful" (Shoham-Salomon & Hannah, 1991, p. 220). Others agree with Shoham-Salomon and Hannah (e.g., Beutler, 1991; B. Smith & Sechrest, 1991), and have emphasized the need for *a priori* theoretical hypotheses and corresponding assessment of construct validity in the measurement of any factor in the ATI design.

METHODOLOGICAL AND DESIGN ISSUES IN ATI RESEARCH

Comparative studies have examined different types of therapy with relatively little attention given to the differential responses of patients. Two aspects of the comparative clinical trial approach have made the identification and elaboration of relevant ATIs unlikely. These aspects are associated with the design principles of homogeneous patient samples and consistency in treatment implementation. Both principles aim at reducing "extraneous" variation and are important when testing for treatment main effects. Simultaneously, however, this reduction in patient and treatment variability acts to lower the probability of finding significant differential effects. Moreover, data from clinical trial studies are generally analyzed using the ANOVA (analysis of variance) approach, which has lower power for detecting ATIs. The conversion of continuous measures to categories (i.e., levels of an independent factor) may further reduce the sensitivity of clinical trial designs to detect ATI effects. Regression techniques, which capitalize on continuous data, may be a more sensitive data analysis alternative for the detection of ATI effects.

Interaction effects are more likely to be observed when there is systematic but theoretically relevant variability present in both the contrasting therapy approaches and in the patient characteristic under investigation. Striking a balance on the degree of variability is important. Greater heterogeneity in the patient sample may present challenges to treatment integrity because therapists may be more likely to deviate from guidelines to manage a more varied patient sample (Carroll et al., 1998). At minimum, an ATI design requires (a) explicit treatment matching hypotheses, (b) at least one group of research participants assessed on some relevant aptitude, and (c) random assignment to one of at least two forms of well-defined treatment.

The sample of participants used should reflect the entire range of possible scores on the patient variable of interest (Cronbach & Snow, 1977; Snow, 1991). The common practice of dichotomizing treatment samples has the potential to reduce the information available regarding the aptitude under investigation. Most important, the study should be designed to test for aptitude–treatment interactions that are *practically* meaningful.

As noted earlier, research on ATIs demands specific *a priori* hypotheses and attention to the construct validity of aptitude measures. The regression approach, although sensitive to interaction effects, requires large sample sizes to have reasonably sufficient power. Treatments considered should also be highly discriminable and contrasting on relevant technical dimensions; any overlap in the "active ingredients" between approaches can obscure patient–treatment matching effects. This demands that therapies be manualized and that checks be conducted to ensure therapist adherence to the guidelines of the manual (Carroll et al., 1998; B. Smith & Sechrest, 1991; Yeaton & Sechrest, 1981). Given that ATIs may be identified for specific outcomes, it is critical to assess multiple dimensions of patient change (Dance & Neufeld, 1988). Finally, the identification of a significant ATI requires that the investigator provide evidence indicating *why* the ATI occurs as it does. This evidence is usually gathered through case-by-case analysis. At its best, then, the ATI approach reflects a blending of the two essential empirical perspectives—the nomothetic and the idiographic—on treatment response. The clinical utility of the ATI research paradigm is a function of this blending. Table 4-1 presents the characteristics of methodologically sound ATI research. The table also illustrates how our recent comparative study of short-term psychotherapy, which was based on an ATI paradigm, met each of these criteria (Piper, Joyce, McCallum, & Azim, 1998). Our study will be presented in detail in chapter 6. It investigated two forms of short-term individual psychotherapy (interpretive, supportive) for psychiatric outpatients. In this study we also examined whether two personality characteristics, quality of object relations and psychological mindedness, interacted with form of therapy to maximize the effectiveness of treatment.

EVIDENCE FOR OPTIMAL PATIENT–TREATMENT MATCHING IN SHORT-TERM PSYCHOTHERAPY

Research on patient–treatment matching in short-term therapies has been varied with regard to the diagnostic groups that have been studied and the patient characteristics that have been conceptualized as important matching variables. With regard to diagnostic groups, matching in the treatment of alcoholism and other substance abuse problems has had the

Table 4-1
Methodological Requirements for ATI Research and
the Edmonton Comparative Study

ATI Research Methodological Requirement	Edmonton Comparative Study Design Feature
Selection and measurement of patient characteristics must be backed by theory or an *a priori* rationale.	Quality of object relations (QOR) and psychological mindedness (PM) are theoretical constructs relevant to psychodynamic therapy; the operationalization of each construct was based on a clinical assessment interview.
Studies require large sample sizes to permit the study of interactions.	Referrals originated from a hospital-based outpatient clinic that records 2000 new assessments per year; over a three-year period, 258 patients were referred to the project.
Treatments must be specified and distinct.	Both forms of short-term individual therapy were dynamically informed but each was developed to emphasize distinctly different therapist techniques (interpretive, supportive).
Treatment delivery needs to be true to protocol and consistent.	Each treatment approach was manualized. Therapists participated in an ongoing training seminar. Adherence checks demonstrated therapy integrity and discriminability.
Outcome measures need to be appropriate to the treatment goal and assessed in a standardized way.	Questionnaire or interview measures addressed psychiatric symptomatology, interpersonal distress and functioning, self-esteem, life satisfaction, use of defenses, and individual target objectives. Interview measures were highly reliable.
Statistical analyses should be appropriate to the problem posed and the data collected.	Data analyses employed multiple regression techniques that had sufficient power to detect interactions.
When a significant ATI is identified, the mechanism of action underlying the interaction must be understood.	Process analyses of significant patient-treatment interactions are ongoing.

Source: From Mattson (1994) and Smith and Sechrest (1991).

longest history. The culmination of work in the area was Project MATCH (1997), a major undertaking that involved the systematic testing of a number of *a priori* matching hypotheses in a clinical trial design. The study, reviewed later, has been described as "the largest, statistically most powerful, psychotherapy trial ever conducted" (p. 25, Project MATCH Research Group, 1997). Research on ATIs in the short-term therapy of other psychiatric disorders, most often for patients with major depression, has emerged more recently. The following review of ATI research findings will be organized into two sections: findings from research on (a) substance abuse problems and (b) other psychiatric disorders. A wide variety of patient variables have been studied in the two areas.

Time-Limited Therapy for Substance Abuse Problems

Studies have demonstrated that alcoholics are more likely to benefit substantially from treatment if their socioeconomic status is at least moderate and they show evidence of good work and family functioning (Finney & Moos, 1986) and less psychopathology (McLellan, 1986). For these patients, the substance abuse has not assumed a position of centrality in the individual's life—work and family remain priorities for them, as well as sources of stability. These findings, however, apply to a variety of treatments for a number of substance abuse problems. The predictors are so global that the results offer little help to the clinician seeking to match patients to an appropriate form of therapy.

Psychiatric severity has been regarded as an important matching variable for different treatments of substance abuse. McLellan (1986) developed an index of problem severity based on the psychiatric subscale of the Addiction Severity Index (McLellan, Luborsky, O'Brien, & Woody, 1980), a commonly used measure in substance abuse treatment research. Low-severity patients improved most in outpatient treatment unless there were significant family or employment problems. Moderate-severity patients or those with more severe family–employment problems did better in inpatient treatment so long as antisocial personality traits were not part of the presentation. High-severity patients did poorly in all treatments. Woody et al. (1983) followed up this work by comparing the effectiveness of psychotherapy plus drug counseling versus counseling alone in a methadone maintenance program. Compared to counseling, supportive–expressive or cognitive–behavioral therapy provided better outcome for both moderate- and high-severity patients but did not prove more helpful for low-severity patients. A subsequent study of the psychotherapy cases (Woody, McLellan, Luborsky, & O'Brien, 1985) indicated that antisocial personality patients who were comorbid for major depression did as well as patients with no additional psychiatric disorder or depression alone, but that patients with antisocial personality disorder only did very poorly. Thus, the presence of a major depression was associated with *benefit* from psychotherapy for patients with antisocial personality disorder. An important observation is that successive studies in this program of research identified progressively more specific, higher order interactions involving multiple patient and treatment variables (Finney & Moos, 1986).

In related research, a number of authors have considered the interaction between severity of the patient's problems and the structure of treatment. For example, Maude-Griffin et al. (1998) found that cocaine-abusing patients with a history of major depression had better outcomes in a 12-week, individual cognitive–behavioral therapy (greater structure) than in a 12-step facilitation therapy model (less structure). Carroll et al. (1994) found that patients with more severe cocaine abuse had better outcomes in relapse prevention therapy (greater structure) than in an interpersonal therapy approach (less structure). Kadden, Cooney, Getter, and Litt (1989) examined patients' levels of sociopathy and psychopathology as matching variables for two types of six-month, time-limited group therapy for alcoholic patients. Coping-skills training was a structured cognitive–behavioral approach; interactional group therapy was an unstructured, interpersonal approach. They found that patients high in global psychopathology and sociopathy improved more in the coping skills group condition, and patients with low levels of sociopathy improved more in the interactional group therapy. At two-year follow-up, the patient–treatment interactions observed at posttreatment were maintained (Cooney, Kadden, Litt, & Getter, 1991). In general, patients manifesting greater psychiatric severity have shown more improvement in treatments that are more structured—for example, have a focus on symptoms or aim at specific skill development. In contrast, patients manifesting less psychiatric severity have benefited more from treatments that are more unstructured—for example, focus on a broader range of functioning.

The interaction of psychiatric severity and structure of the substance abuse treatment is clearly not a simple direct relationship. Moreover, these interactions are unlikely to involve only a combination of two variables but rather higher order relationships with other patient and outcome variables. These findings imply that the direction of methodologically sound ATI research is toward more specific hypotheses regarding the interactions in question.

Other researchers have examined variables that reflect characteristics of the patient's behavior. One such variable is patient coping style. Coping style has been variously defined in the substance abuse treatment literature, leading to problems identifying convergent findings. McLachlan (1972) defined coping style in terms of conceptual level (CL), ranging from concrete cognition of low complexity to abstract reasoning of greater complexity. High CL patients did better in unstructured groups and low CL patients showed more improvement in structured groups. Nielsen, Nielsen, and Wraae (1998) reported similar results: The match between patient CL and the structure of intensive 12-month treatment resulted in a compliance rate of 63% versus a rate of 38% among mismatched patients. Annis and Davis (1989) defined coping style in terms of situational differentiation. "Differentiated" drinkers—

those recognizing more situations that prompted drinking—did better in relapse-prevention therapy than in traditional counseling, whereas undifferentiated drinkers did equally well in both treatments. Hartman, Krywonis, and Morrison (1988) related coping style to locus of control. Alcoholics with an internal locus fared better in brief nondirective treatment, whereas those with an external locus showed more improvement following intensive structured treatment. Finally, Miller, Benefield, and Tonigan (1993) defined coping style in terms of the attributions offered for drinking problems. Patients who viewed drinking as a bad habit had better outcomes with therapists who were empathetic rather than confrontational, whereas no difference was observed for patients who viewed their alcoholism as a disease.

Although much of the ATI research for substance abuse problems has focused on patient characteristics, other studies have examined characteristics of the patient's environment as important matching variables. Longabaugh, Beattie, Noel, Stout, and Mallow (1993) and Longabaugh, Wirtz, Beattie, Noel, and Stout (1995) investigated two related dimensions: the patient's *social investment* or dependence on others for reinforcement and the degree of *social support* for drinking versus abstinence in the alcoholic's network. Longabaugh et al. (1993) reported that patients who were low in social investment did better in an individual focused cognitive–behavioral treatment (CBT) than in a relationship enhancement CBT, whereas those high in social investment did equally well in both treatments. Longabaugh et al.(1995) conducted a randomized controlled trial that investigated both social investment and social support. Three treatments were contrasted: brief broad spectrum behavioral treatment (BBS), extended cognitive–behavioral therapy (ECBT), and extended relationship enhancement therapy (ERE). The ERE approach was found to be more effective in increasing abstinence among patients who were highly invested in a network supportive of drinking *or* with low investment in a network supportive of abstinence. In contrast, ERE was least effective with patients who were either uninvested in an environment supportive of drinking or were highly invested in an environment supportive of abstinence. The BBS approach was most effective with these latter patients. Patients in ECBT achieved outcomes that were relatively unaffected by pretreatment investment and environmental support. These complex findings demonstrate not only the specificity of the treatments with particular patients but also the strong likelihood that identifying meaningful ATI effects may require including higher order matching variables (Finney & Moos, 1986).

As indicated earlier, ATI research in the area of substance abuse problems culminated in a large-scale endeavor called Project MATCH. In 1989 the National Institute on Alcohol Abuse and Alcoholism initiated a multisite, randomized clinical trial titled Matching Alcoholism Treatments to Client Heterogeneity (MATCH). The study addressed the limitations of previous matching research, particularly in the area of statistical power. The project actually consisted of two clinical trials, one with outpatients ($N = 952$) and the other with patients receiving aftercare following inpatient or partial hospital treatment ($N = 774$). The project was conducted to assess the benefits of matching alcohol-dependent patients to three different treatments. At pretherapy, patients were clearly in the pathological range in terms of frequency of drinking and amount consumed. More than half the patients had a history of previous alcoholism treatment, and almost all showed effects of chronic consumption across many domains of life functioning. Patients (outpatients and aftercare patients) were randomly assigned to one of three 12-week manualized individual therapies: CBT, motivational enhancement therapy (MET), or 12-step facilitation therapy (TSF). Relative to the other two conditions, MET was substantially less intensive (one-half the number of sessions). The approach was focused on rapidly producing internally motivated change in the patient; motivational strategies were used to mobilize the individual's own coping resources toward fulfilling a structured plan for recovery. The MET condition was characterized by less therapist guidance than the other two treatments. Evaluations of treatment integrity included assessments of therapy fidelity and discriminability, treatment dose, and monitoring of therapist skillfulness and the therapeutic alliance (Carroll et al., 1998). Aftercare patients were followed over a one-year posttreatment period, and outpatients were followed for an additional two years. Sixteen planned comparisons based on theory and previous empirical findings were conducted. The study examined 10 matching variables: severity of alcohol involvement, psychiatric severity, sociopathy, conceptual level, social support for drinking versus abstinence, cognitive impairment, gender, meaning-seeking, readiness to change, and alcohol typology. The main outcome measures were percentage of days abstinent and drinks per drinking day.

Patient compliance to treatment and follow-up were each high. Substantial improvements were achieved from baseline to one-year posttreatment. There was little difference in outcome by type of treatment, despite the differences in philosophy and procedures. Patients were abstinent for more than 85% of the days during the year following treatment, and overall alcohol consumption decreased five-fold. Patients showed significant decreases in depression and use of other drugs and improvements in several areas of social functioning.

Matching as a treatment strategy was generally not found to substantially enhance outcomes. Orford (1999) pointed out, however, that Project MATCH identified two matching effects that predicted both posttreatment and long-term outcome and specified a mediational causal model for each match. One effect involved a match between the TSF treatment and alcohol dependence. The TSF treatment resulted in greater improvement for the more alcohol-dependent aftercare patients. This effect was attributed to TSF's greater emphasis on abstinence. The second effect involved the match between TSF and social support for drinking. Among the outpatients, TSF had a greater positive impact on patients who reported a social network that was supportive of drinking. This matching effect was partly attributed to the higher frequency of participation in Alcoholics Anonymous (AA) by TSF patients. That is, the AA involvement allowed the patient to overcome the pressures of his or her social network to continue drinking.

With such a large investment, the Project MATCH findings appear to represent little useful yield. Each treatment was associated with substantial and sustained improvement—in other words, there was little variation in outcome across therapies. This may have left little room for matching effects to emerge. Moreover, the intensive research-related activities (thorough assessments, contact with patients after absences, intensive follow-ups) may have provided a substantial amount of the "nonspecific" qualities of a treatment relationship, inadvertently reducing the negative effects of mismatches and thus also contributing to the relatively weak matching findings. The Longabaugh et al. (1995) findings addressed earlier suggest that the few findings may have followed from the relative generality of the hypotheses: Instead of lower order interactions, important ATIs may be represented by interactions of higher order and complexity. Finally, the selection criteria for the clinical trial may have further reduced variability among the patients. The beneficial effects of giving certain patients a particular treatment, or the harmful effects of giving others that treatment, may only be apparent toward the extreme ends of a client-aptitude continuum. Studies such as Project MATCH, designed to be strong on internal validity, may exclude just those participants whose characteristics are comparatively extreme. This may preclude the identification of those matching effects the study is actually designed to test.

TIME-LIMITED THERAPY FOR OTHER PSYCHIATRIC DISORDERS

Findings from ATI research on psychotherapy for other psychiatric conditions have been equally varied as those from the substance abuse treatment research reviewed previously. A number of patient characteristics have garnered attention as matching factors. For example, the dimensions of externalization and reactance were originally articulated by Beutler (1979) following a review of 52 comparative studies of psychotherapy, and subsequently endorsed by Beutler and his colleagues (Beutler, 1991; Beutler & Clarkin, 1990; Beutler & Crago, 1987; Beutler & Mitchell, 1981; Beutler et al., 1991). These constructs have been found to interact with type of treatment and the directiveness of therapy.

Externalization–internalization refers to the person's characteristic manner of dealing with subjective distress. A number of constructs have been proposed to capture the distinction between externalization (e.g., extroversion and impulsivity) on the one hand and internalization (e.g., self-constraint and emotional withdrawal) on the other. Externalizing patients have been shown to respond better to skills-oriented, symptom-focused treatments, whereas internalizing patients have shown more improvement in insight-oriented, relationship-focused treatments. For example, Beutler et al. (1991) reported that depressed patients who scored higher on a measure of externalization responded better to CBT than to insight-oriented therapy, whereas the reverse was true for patients who made use of internalizing activities (see also Beutler & Mitchell, 1981). In a study based on the NIMH Treatment of Depression Collaborative Study, Barber and Muenz (1996) found cognitive therapy to be more effective than interpersonal therapy among patients who used direct avoidance (externalizing), and the reverse was true among obsessional (internalizing) patients (see also Blatt, Quinlan, Pilkonis, & Shea, 1995).

Reactance refers to an individual's trait-like proclivity to resist the directives provided by others, based on a high valuation of personal freedom and initiative. Evidence suggests that high reactance is a contraindication for directive therapy approaches—for example, behavioral or gestalt treatments—but an indication for therapies that rely more on self-direction—for example, psychodynamic treatments (Beutler, 1991; Shoham-Salomon & Hannah, 1991). Beutler et al. (1991) demonstrated that a nondirective therapy was more effective than two directive approaches in eliciting change in depressive symptoms among high-reactant patients, whereas the reverse was true among low-reactant patients. This finding was further validated at a one-year follow-up of depression severity and relapse (Beutler, Machado, Engle, & Mohr, 1993). The use of paradoxical interventions has also been found to capitalize on the oppositional tendencies of highly reactant patients (Horvath & Goheen, 1990; Shoham-Salomon et al., 1989) in promoting sustained treatment benefit.

Other patient personality characteristics have been explored as matching variables. For example, Blatt and his associates have explored anaclitic and introjective personality characteristics (1992; Blatt & Felsen, 1993). Anaclitic patients are primarily preoccupied with issues of relatedness (intimacy) and primarily use avoidant defenses, such as withdrawal, denial, and repression, to cope with conflict and stress. Introjective patients are primarily concerned with establishing and maintaining a viable sense of self (autonomy) and primarily use defenses such as projection, intellectualization, and reaction formation. Blatt and Felsen (1993) reviewed findings indicating that anaclitic patients are more responsive to the quality of the therapeutic relationship, whereas introjective patients are more responsive to the interpretive activity of the therapist.

Horowitz, Marmar, Weiss, et al. (1984) explored the importance of the patient's self-concept as a potential matching variable. They defined different levels of self-concept in terms of the degree of sophistication and complexity of internal models of relationships—for example, self and object schema. Greater maturity is reflected in more fully elaborated schema and flexibility in interpersonal situations. Horowitz and his colleagues examined the interaction of the organizational level of the self-concept with the process and outcome of brief dynamic therapy for bereavement reactions. A significant direct relationship was identified between organizational level and change in the areas of work and interpersonal functioning. Interactions with therapist technique were also identified. Exploratory interventions (e.g., differentiating reality versus fantasy-based meanings of the loss) led to better outcomes with the more developmentally organized patients, whereas supportive interventions (e.g., encouraging a change in the patient's self-image to be more in accord with reality) were more helpful for those patients at the lower developmental levels. This finding is similar to the results of the Menninger Psychotherapy Project, which found that patients with greater ego strength showed better improvement in the expressive therapies, whereas those with less ego strength improved more in the supportive approaches (Kernberg et al., 1972).

Zettle, Haflich, and Reynolds (1992) and Zettle and Herring (1995) have examined the interaction of a sociotropy–autonomy dimension with different formats of CBT. Patients who scored highly on sociotropy were most concerned with social support and attachment and showed greater improvement in a group treatment format. In contrast, patients scoring high on autonomy had an individualistic problem-solving orientation and benefited more when treatment was provided in an individual format.

One of the patient variables that our research group has concentrated on as a matching variable is the patient personality characteristic quality of object relations (QOR; Piper et al., 1998). In general, low QOR patients—those with a history of nongratifying relationships and a more primitive personality structure—appear to be less suited to an interpretive therapy approach and to benefit more from the relationship with the therapist. By contrast, high QOR patients—those of greater maturity in developmental level and relationships—are readily able to collaborate with the therapist and can benefit from an interpretive approach. Detailed findings involving QOR and two approaches to therapy (interpretive, supportive) are provided in later chapters.

Researchers have also considered aspects of the patient's presenting problems as potential matching variables. One such aspect is level of impairment, which represents the degree of dysfunction associated with the patient's presentation for treatment. There is some evidence that the interaction between level of impairment and the intensity–duration of treatment is a determinant of therapy benefit. For example, Shapiro et al. (1994) have reported that patients of higher initial impairment showed greater benefit from more intensive or longer treatments. They reported that a 16-week treatment was more effective for depressed patients with the highest levels of impairment, regardless of the therapy orientation, whereas patients with low levels of impairment showed equivalent improvement after 8 or 16 weeks of therapy. In the NIMH Treatment of Depression Collaborative Study, depressed patients reporting the most severe distress benefited more from interpersonal therapy than CBT (Imber et al., 1990).

CONCLUDING COMMENT

Research on ATIs in psychotherapy is in its infancy, and its full promise has yet to be realized. Methodologically strong ATI research requires conceptual clarity, a substantial investment of resources, and the collection of data from large patient samples. A minority of investigative teams has the means and longevity necessary for rigorous ATI research. Still, the paradigm has considerable potential for identifying and illuminating the change mechanisms associated with different forms of therapy. ATI research in the treatment of substance abuse and other psychiatric disorders has identified several key patient variables. The validity of these matching variables depends on additional study and corroboration by clinicians and researchers. This corroboration should encourage a more productive dialectic between theory, practice, and research, and should ultimately result in greater benefits for clinical practice. Subsequent chapters in this book report on the findings of the ATI study conducted by our research group in Edmonton, which examined the interaction of two forms of brief dynamic therapy and two theoretically relevant dimensions of patient personality.

5

QUALITY OF OBJECT RELATIONS AND PSYCHOLOGICAL MINDEDNESS: PREDICTIVE PATIENT CHARACTERISTICS IN TIME-LIMITED THERAPIES

As indicated in the previous chapter, patient characteristics have been a central interest of clinicians and researchers who have been invested in individual and group therapies. They are believed to be determinants of important clinical events such as whether patients remain, work, and benefit from therapy. For clinicians, they represent potential selection criteria that can be used to make decisions about which patients should be offered therapy. In the case of group therapy, selection decisions not only affect the patient in question but the entire group. Because of its interdependent nature, Yalom (1975) stated that "the fate of a therapy group and its members is to a large extent determined before the first group session" (p. 219). For researchers, patient characteristics represent predictor variables that can be used to determine the probability of important clinical events. They also represent descriptive features that identify the sample that is being studied. Clinicians can then determine whether the research sample is comparable to their caseloads and researchers can decide the extent to which the findings can be generalized and what is required for attempts at replication.

There are many different types of patient characteristics. They include demographic, diagnostic, pathologic, and personality features. Their large number presents a challenge to both clinicians and researchers. Clinicians must settle for a manageable but limited number in their clinical formulations and researchers must try to control or balance the effects of many variables

---

Parts of this chapter have been taken, verbatim or adapted, from "Object Relations Theory and Short-Term Dynamic Psychotherapy: Findings From the Quality of Object Relations Scale," *Clinical Psychology Review, 19*, 669–685, 1999. Copyright 1999 by Elsevier Science. Adapted by permission of the publisher and author.

while attempting to understand the effects of a few at a time. Choosing which variables to focus on is also difficult. Ideally, the research literature should guide clinicians and researchers in their choice.

Many research reviews of patient characteristics have been published in the research literature during the past 25 years. Unfortunately, though, most reviews indicate that there are few strong studies where the investigation of patient characteristics has been a primary objective. Usually, the exploration of patient characteristics has been an afterthought in that they have been examined retrospectively. Investigators have typically focused on readily available variables such as demographic or diagnostic characteristics. They have checked for significant associations between patient characteristics and other variables in the study. It is not difficult to find reports of statistically significant associations between some patient characteristics and important clinical variables in the literature. However, the report of nonsignificant associations far outnumbers significant ones. Because of the large number of statistical tests conducted, the potential that many of the significant associations represent chance findings is high. Second, many of the associations are small in magnitude and, therefore, of questionable clinical importance. Third, there is a lack of replication of findings.

To improve, reviewers have made a number of recommendations to researchers. They have suggested that (a) researchers use a multivariate approach that explores interactions among predictors; (b) more than one type of therapy should be studied; (c) the approach should be theoretically based and should use interpersonal and behavioral measures; (d) multivariate statistical procedures should be used to maximize prediction and determine the unique contribution of individual predictors; (e) comparisons between predicted rates and base rates of improvement should be made; (f) and attempts at replication should be made. Unfortunately, few studies have come close to achieving this set of recommendations.

The initial approach of our research team in Canada to studying patient characteristics was typical. Our main interest was to study the effectiveness of various forms of time-limited individual and group psychotherapies: We were interested in conducting treatment outcome studies. In doing so, we realized that for little additional cost, we could assess patient characteristics. Demographic and diagnostic variables were readily available, and our therapists were willing to provide some simple ratings of personality variables. Thus, at the same time that our initial studies began to provide some interesting results concerning different outcomes among the treatment conditions, the studies also began providing some interesting findings concerning the personality variables. Certain variables began to emerge as the more powerful predictors—for example, the variables known as quality of object relations (QOR) and psychological mindedness (PM). We were compelled to take these variables more seriously and devise ways of measuring them more accurately and reliably. As time progressed, we became interested in how the relationship between each personality variable and outcome might differ for different forms of therapy. Thus, we began to expand the designs of our outcome studies to be able to detect interaction effects. In doing so, we were able to meet most of the methodological recommendations of reviewers.

This chapter will provide a perspective of the studies and the findings that led to our designing and completing an aptitude–treatment interaction (ATI) study. The study involved the two patient personality variables (QOR and PM) and the two forms of therapy (time-limited, interpretive individual therapy and time-limited, supportive individual therapy) that are highlighted in this book. For ease of communication, we refer to it as the *comparative study*. It will be presented in the next chapter. In this chapter, the focus is on the two patient personality variables, QOR and PM, and their relationship to important events in several different forms of psychotherapy in the clinical trials. Explanations for the findings as well as clinical and research implications will also be considered.

Between 1977 and 1998, we completed a series of six, psychotherapy clinical trials. The studies shared a number of common features concerning their objectives, design, and methodology. (a) Each investigated the efficacy of one or more forms of dynamically oriented psychotherapy. (b) Most were short-term—a time-limited period of three to six months. Some studied individual therapy, some group therapy, and some group-oriented partial hospitalization. (c) Each involved a large sample of patients, typically 150 to 250, who sought services from a university department of psychiatry. (d) Each monitored a large battery of outcome variables before and after therapy and at one or more follow-up assessments. The battery included measures of symptoms, interpersonal functioning, self-esteem, life satisfaction, and target objectives from the perspectives of the patient, therapist, and independent assessors. (e) Each trial also monitored one or more process variables during therapy—therapeutic alliance and therapist technique in the case of individual therapy, and patient work in the case of group therapy. (f) In regard to patient personality variables, each included QOR or PM or both. (g) Patients were usually matched on certain criteria and randomly assigned to conditions, which consisted of different forms of time-limited treatment or a wait-list control condition. (h) Each study usually took between three to five years to complete the data collection. Thus, each was a large-scale, randomized clinical trial of psychotherapy. First, we will consider QOR and next PM. Afterward, we discuss possible explanations for the findings, clinical implications, and research implications.

QUALITY OF OBJECT RELATIONS

Quality of object relations is defined as a person's internal enduring tendency to establish certain types of relationships that range along an overall dimension from primitive to mature (Azim et al., 1991; Piper & Duncan, 1999). It refers to a life-long pattern rather than one that characterizes only recent relationships. As the word *quality* suggests, the kinds of relations at high levels represent a more favorable and desirable set of circumstances for the person. Both relationships with recent and past significant persons and the immediate relationship with the interviewer are examined. Although for measurement purposes, we focus on external relationships, we assume that they reflect the internal object representations and conflictual components of the patient's internal world. Again, what we try to assess is the patient's life-long pattern of relationships.

We have differentiated five levels of relations. They serve as anchor points for the scale. At the *mature* level, the person enjoys equitable relationships characterized by love, tenderness, and concern for objects of both sexes. There is a capacity to mourn and tolerate unobtainable relationships. At the *triangular* level, the person is involved in real or fantasized triangular relationships. Competition for one object is inspired by victory over the other object. There is concern for the objects. At the *controlling* level, the person engages in well-meaning attempts to control and possess objects. Relationships are characterized by ambivalence. At the *searching* level, the person is driven to find substitutes for a longed for lost object. Substitutes provide a short-lived sense of optimism and self-worth, which is followed by disillusionment and the re-experience of loss. At the *primitive* level, the person reacts to perceived separation or loss of the object, or disapproval or rejection by the object, with intense anxiety and affect. There is inordinate dependence on the lost object, who provides a sense of identity for the person.

To assist us in assigning scores for each level, there are criteria for each that are organized under four areas. *Behavioral manifestations* refer to descriptions of an individual's typical relationship patterns. *Affect regulation* refers to the type of relationships the person wishes for and engages in to reduce anxiety and increase gratification. *Self-esteem regulation* refers to the relationships that enhance self-esteem and reduce mortification. *Antecedents* refer to past events or relationships that predispose a person to a given level. Because of their experience-near nature and to improve reliability of measurement, greater weight is given to behavioral manifestations.

Initially, QOR was assessed during two one-hour interviews that were conducted a week apart. However, in a current clinical trial that we are conducting, we have been assessing it in a one-hour semistructured interview. As presented in Table 5-1, 15 questions are considered to be essential. The questions fill a grid that covers three time periods (childhood, adolescence,

Table 5-1
Essential Questions for the QOR Assessment Interview

Time Periods to Be Covered	Major Levels				
	Primitive	Searching	Controlling	Triangular	Mature
Childhood (family of origin)	Do you remember much abuse or disorder in your childhood?	Was there a major event that changed the course of your childhood?	How would you describe your parents in terms of their being controlling of your thoughts, feelings, or behavior?	Was there anything special or unique about your relationship with your (opposite sex) parent that you did not share with your (same sex) parent?	In what ways did members of your family express love and concern for each other?
Adolescence: Period of transition (peers, parents)	Tell me about any incident you can recall where you felt hurt or betrayed by peers at school or socially.	Were there times as a teenager or young adult where you found yourself "falling in love"? How did those experiences turn out?	How did you engage in "rebellion" as a teenager or young adult?	Can you tell me about any incident where you and another were both vying for the attention of a third person? How did that work out?	Were there things about your high school friends that irritated you? How did it affect your relationships?
Adulthood (partners, children)	In what way would you say your intimate relationships have been stormy or hurtful?	Looking back over your relationships, have they been a bit like a rollercoaster—lots of ups and downs?	Do you find yourself taking care of your partner; sort of looking out for him/her, trying to help him/her with his/her problems?	How would you say you've been competitive with people that you are close to?	Do you have good male and female friends?

and adulthood) and the five levels of relations (primitive, searching, controlling, triangular, and mature). After the interview(s), the interviewer distributes 100 points among the five levels. Although one level usually receives the most points, it is common for a second level to also receive considerable points—for example, triangular followed closely by primitive. A bimodal pattern is consistent with our notion that levels are not discrete categories with rigid boundaries but rather sets of criteria that blend into each other. It is also consistent with the idea that a person's usual mode of relating may be at one level, whereas at other times, for example when under stress, it may be at another level. A simple arithmetic formula is used to weight the ratings for the five levels and to generate an overall score that ranges from 1 to 9.

Interviewers and raters follow an assessment manual that is available from the authors (Piper, McCallum, & Joyce, 1993). The rater reliability for the Quality of Object Relations Scale was determined in four of the clinical trials that preceded our comparative study of time-limited, interpretive and supportive individual therapies. Independent raters provided scores using audiotapes of the original interview. Intraclass correlation coefficients for the trials were .50, .68, .62, and .72. Thus, there was general improvement in reliability over the studies.

The first clinical trial, the Montreal Comparative Study (Piper et al., 1984), compared four forms of time-limited therapy: short-term individual, short-term group, long-term individual, and long-term group. The short-term therapies lasted 6 months and the long-term therapies 24 months. The best outcomes were found for short-term individual therapy and long-term group therapy. Less good outcomes were found for long-term individual therapy and short-term group therapy. Therapist ratings of three object relations variables were made before the onset of therapy. Although simple in nature, the ratings were directly related to patient ratings of the therapeutic alliance in short-term individual therapy and favorable outcome in all four forms of therapy (de Carufel & Piper, 1988; Piper, de Carufel, & Szkrumelak, 1985). This study provided encouragement to continue studying QOR as a predictor variable.

The second clinical trial was the Edmonton Controlled Study of Short-term Individual Therapy (Piper et al., 1990). It compared time-limited short-term individual therapy of five months duration to a wait-list control condition. The sample consisted of a diagnostically mixed group of outpatients who presented with difficulties related to depression, anxiety, low self-esteem, and interpersonal conflict. In regard to the general outcome findings of the study, treated patients had better outcome than control patients according to statistical and clinical criteria. The best outcome was found for treated patients with high levels of QOR, and the worst outcome for untreated patients with low levels of QOR. QOR was directly related to patient and therapist ratings of the therapeutic alliance and favorable outcome at posttherapy and follow-up (Piper, Azim, Joyce, McCallum, Nixon, et al., 1991).

The third clinical trial was the Edmonton controlled study of day treatment (Piper, Rosie, Azim, & Joyce, 1993; Piper, Rosie, Joyce, & Azim, 1996). It compared time-limited day treatment, which is an intensive, group-oriented, partial hospitalization program of four months duration to a wait-list control condition. The sample included a high proportion of patients with affective and personality disorders. This treatment is considerably different than once a week outpatient psychotherapy. Patients are expected to attend the program all day, five days a week, for 18 weeks. The average daily census is 35 patients. Each day begins with a large therapy group that includes all patients and staff. For the remainder of the day, each patient attends a set of small groups. They range in format from those that are unstructured and insight-oriented to those that are structured and skill-oriented. The treatment program is viewed as a total system that operates according to modified principles of a therapeutic community. In regard to the general outcome findings of the study, treated patients had better outcome than control patients on a variety of outcome criteria. In addition, QOR was directly related to remaining in the program and favorable outcome on two of three primary outcome factors (Piper, Joyce, Azim, & Rosie, 1994).

The fourth clinical trial was the Edmonton predictor study of evening treatment (McCallum, Piper, & O'Kelly, 1997), which studied the predictive ability of QOR in a similarly structured, group-oriented, partial hospitalization program of four months duration that met in the evenings. It included a high proportion of patients with affective and personality disorders. In regard to the general outcome findings of the study, treated patients experienced significant improvement over the course of treatment on a wide range of outcome variables. QOR, however, was not related to remaining or favorable outcome in this study.

Thus, from three of the four clinical trials, there was evidence that QOR was directly related to the alliance in individual therapy and to favorable outcome in both individual and group therapy.

PSYCHOLOGICAL MINDEDNESS

Psychological mindedness is the ability to identify intrapsychic dynamic components and relate them to a person's difficulties (McCallum & Piper, 1997). The components—wishes, fears, and defenses—are often in conflictual relationship to each other. We have differentiated nine levels of PM, and the levels represent a hierarchy. In general, the higher levels incorporate the lower levels such that each level becomes more comprehensive and

Table 5-2
The Nine Levels of Psychological Mindedness

Level	Description
9	The participant recognizes that despite the use of defenses, the patient remains disturbed by a conflict.
8	The participant recognizes that the patient uses defenses to deal with a conflict.
7	The participant identifies a causal link where tension (fear, anxiety) motivates an expression.
6	The participant identifies a causal link where a conflict generates an expression.
5	The participant identifies conflictual components of the patient's experience.
4	The participant recognizes that the motivating force is largely or totally out of the patient's awareness.
3	The participant identifies a causal link between an internal experience of the patient and its resultant expression.
2	The participant recognizes the driving force of an internal experience of the patient.
1	The participant identifies a specific internal experience of the patient.

complex in its focus. As Table 5-2 indicates, the scale ranges from level 1, where the research participant merely identifies a person's specific internal experience, to level 5, where the participant identifies conflictual components, to level 9, where the participant recognizes that despite the use of defenses, the person remains disturbed by the conflict.

To measure PM, we have developed a 15-minute interview measure that uses a videotape. It presents two simulated patient–therapist interactions (scenarios). Each begins with an actress–patient describing a recent event to her therapist. In scenario 1, the patient describes seeing her former husband from a distance in a department store. In scenario 2, the patient describes an argument with her boyfriend in a restaurant. After viewing each scenario, the person being assessed is asked, "What seems to be troubling this woman?" The person's responses are scored according to how well they met the criteria for the nine levels. The highest level achieved represents the overall PM score. To provide an impression of how the score is derived, the following example is offered. After viewing scenario 1, the patient said,

> Well, she is troubled by anxiety. She had an anxiety attack in the store. I think that's because she is angry that her marriage didn't work out. Maybe she's more disappointed than angry. She's angry and disappointed and still wants him back. That's why she is having anxiety attacks. She doesn't know what she wants. She doesn't want to admit that she still wants him back. She's angry because she can't have what she wants.

> She's in denial. She denies that she wants him. If that were true, she wouldn't be so angry.

This patient's response is full of dynamic components. Examples include "wants him back" (wish), "denial" (defense), and "angry" (affective component). Also, the patient identified the conflictual nature of her feelings (being angry and disappointed but still wanting him back). In addition, the patient conveyed an understanding that the defense of denial was only partly successful in dealing with the problem. This example received the highest rating of 9.

The interviewers and raters of PM follow a manual that is available from the authors (McCallum & Piper, 1993). The rater reliability for the measure has been determined in four of the studies. The intraclass reliability coefficients were .96, .88, .96, and .80, thus indicating high reliability. In the Montreal comparative study (Piper et al., 1984), which compared four forms of time-limited therapy, PM was directly related to therapist-rated alliance in short-term individual therapy and directly related to favorable outcome in short-term group therapy.

The second clinical trial was the Edmonton controlled study of short-term group therapy (Piper, McCallum, & Azim, 1992), which was not mentioned previously because it did not include QOR. This study compared short-term group therapy of three months duration to a wait-list control condition. Sixteen therapy groups were studied. The sample consisted of a diagnostically mixed group of outpatients, who experienced difficulties adapting to the loss of one or more persons in their lives. The groups were especially designed to deal with loss issues. In regard to the general outcome findings of the study, treated patients experienced greater improvement than control patients according to statistical and clinical criteria. Although PM was not related to outcome in the study, it was directly related to remaining in therapy. High-PM patients had a dropout rate of only 14%, and low-PM patients had a dropout rate of 53%. In addition, PM was directly related to how hard patients worked in the group therapy sessions.

The third clinical trial was the Edmonton controlled study of day treatment (Piper, Rosie, Azim, et al., 1993; Piper, Rosie, Joyce, et al., 1996). PM was directly related to favorable outcome on three primary factors. PM was also directly related to how hard patients worked in the program.

The fourth clinical trial was the Edmonton predictor study of evening treatment (McCallum, Piper, & O'Kelly, 1997). PM was directly related to the degree to which patients worked in the program, but was not related to treatment outcome.

Thus, PM consistently has been directly related to process variables such as alliance and work in both individual and group therapies. In one of the trials, it was strongly related to remaining in group therapy. In terms of outcome, the findings have been mixed. In two of the trials, PM was directly related to favorable outcome, and in two of the trials it was unrelated.

This brief review of the major findings from the various clinical trials indicates that there is evidence of direct relationships between each of the personality variables, QOR and PM, and important clinical outcomes such as whether patients remain, work, and benefit in time-limited forms of psychotherapy.

POSSIBLE EXPLANATIONS FOR THE QOR FINDINGS

Let us first consider the direct relationships between QOR and the variables of remaining, alliance, and benefiting. The strongest evidence involved interpretive short-term individual therapy and day treatment. In interpretive therapy, the therapist was active, interpretive, and transference-oriented. This created a situation that was demanding, depriving, and anxiety-arousing. The patient was expected to begin each session and assume responsibility for what followed. There was ongoing pressure for the patient to talk, and the therapist abstained from providing direct gratification or praise. The therapist encouraged the patient to explore conflicts, which often involved uncomfortable emotions. Interpretations about sensitive topics, including transference, were often made. These features were expected to create tension in the patient–therapist relationship. Whether such tension was regarded by the patient as an opportunity for learning or as mistreatment may have depended on the patient's QOR. Patients with higher QOR, who had a history of satisfactory give-and-take relationships, may have been more able to tolerate the demands of the interpersonal situation. A stronger working alliance and more favorable outcome may have followed. In contrast, patients with lower QOR may have been less able to tolerate the demands with a corresponding weaker alliance and less favorable outcome. That a life-long pattern of higher quality of relationships was related to a better working relationship and better treatment outcome is logically consistent and clinically meaningful.

The same can be said for the results of the day treatment study. The day treatment program was an intensive one that demanded that each patient establish working relationships with a large number of patients and staff members in a variety of therapy groups each day. Being able to adjust and adapt to different compositions of people in the groups was essential. We believe that the ability to establish mature, give-and-take relationships allowed patients to tolerate the daily interpersonal demands and stresses of the program and remain until treatment was completed. It also allowed them to engage in productive working relationships with others that would facilitate favorable outcome.

POSSIBLE EXPLANATIONS FOR THE PM FINDINGS

Let us begin with the most consistent finding, the direct relationship between PM and alliance or work. PM was defined and measured as the ability to identify dynamic components and relate them to a person's difficulties. It is consistent with the task of the different forms of therapy that we have studied and the definitions of alliance or work that we have used. PM is regarded as a valuable skill in interpretive therapy. The lack of such skill would likely lead to difficulty in understanding what was being emphasized in therapy. In certain cases, this might lead to frustration and premature termination. It should also be noted that the measure assesses a participant's ability to understand another person, which would be a particularly valuable skill in group therapy. With regard to outcome, direct relationships between PM and favorable outcome were sometimes, but not always, found. Single variables that are measured initially are not always significant predictors of outcome, given many other influential variables and the time between assessment and outcome.

It is also important to note that in the day treatment study, QOR and PM each made significant independent contributions to better outcome. The fact that QOR and PM have been found to be statistically independent of each other in our studies enhances their ability to make significant independent contributions to better outcome.

CLINICAL IMPLICATIONS

The findings suggest that QOR and PM might serve as useful selection criteria for forms of time-limited psychotherapy, in particular if they are used in combination. Although the probability of a patient remaining, working, and benefiting in many time-limited therapies appears to be enhanced with higher QOR or PM scores, it must be recognized that prediction is never perfect. Patients sometimes pleasantly surprise us. For that reason, clinicians may wish to take on a certain number of higher risk patients as a means of providing them with an opportunity to benefit. Some undoubtedly will benefit, and in our experience this has been the case. Thus, high QOR or high PM might be regarded as favorable but not *essential* selection criteria. Researchers can inform clinicians about risk factors, and the clinicians can make decisions about how much risk or how many high-risk patients to accept for treatment. In a therapy group, having a few high-risk patients is far different than having many.

The predictive ability of QOR and PM stands in contrast to the frequently reported lack of predictive ability of diagnostic categories, at least those that are usually assigned to psychotherapy patients. The two approaches are quite different. QOR and PM are dimensional. Each spans a number of levels. In contrast, diagnoses have been organized as categorical. Patients with a given diagnosis may have different QOR or PM scores.

As clinicians, we are accustomed to making diagnoses. For those of us who practice psychotherapy, we are also accustomed to considering the quality of the patient's previous relationships and psychological mindedness in our formulations about the patient. The evidence presented in this chapter suggests that such patient personality characteristics have clinical validity for time-limited therapies. As therapists or supervisors of therapists who provide time-limited therapies, we may wish to assess them more systematically. In the realm of private practice or the clinic, spending an hour or more to assess QOR or using a videocassette recorder to assess PM may seem daunting or impractical. That may be the case, although computer-assisted information and diagnostic systems for psychiatric patients are beginning to appear in clinical settings. The return on the financial investment of computer and video equipment may turn out to be well worth the investment. At the very least, familiarity with the criteria for QOR and PM can enable the clinician to listen for confirmation of the criteria while routinely interviewing potential candidates for psychotherapy. This we believe is definitely worth the investment. It is an example of how research findings can inform and one might say reaffirm the wisdom of the clinician.

RESEARCH IMPLICATIONS

Research implications for the study of patient characteristics as predictor variables are readily apparent from the evidence that has been presented. Previous reviewers of the research literature have done a good job of highlighting what is needed in the recommendations that they have offered. These, of course, concern such features as using a multivariate approach and exploring interaction effects. At one level, it is important that researchers do not miss opportunities to study patient predictor variables in clinical trials that investigate the effectiveness of various therapies. At another level, it is important that they conduct trials in which the investigation of patient predictor variables occupies a central place in the design and methodology of the studies. If they do so, the chances of discovering significant findings will be greatly enhanced. The challenge is for clinicians and researchers to work together toward the discovery of predictive criteria. Our focus on QOR and PM came about as a result of a continuing dialogue between our research team and the many clinicians who served as assessors and therapists in our projects. In regard to our own research team, we believed that the evidence concerning QOR and PM from the five psychotherapy clinical trials cited in this chapter was strong enough to merit their use in a new clinical trial that investigated the interaction between each of the two personality characteristics and two forms (interpretive, supportive) of time-limited individual therapy. We now turn to that study in the next chapter.

6

INTERACTION OF INTERPRETIVE AND SUPPORTIVE FORMS OF PSYCHOTHERAPY AND PATIENT PERSONALITY VARIABLES

In this chapter, we present our comparative (aptitude–treatment interactions; ATI) research project, which receives primary focus in this book. In this project we investigated the effectiveness of interpretive and supportive forms of short-term, time-limited individual psychotherapy and the interaction of each form of therapy with the patient's quality of object relations (QOR) and the patient's psychological mindedness (PM). In this chapter, we focus primarily on the clinical outcome of the patients in the project at the end of treatment and during follow-up. Chapter 8 presents findings concerning the relationships among different aspects of therapy process (e.g., the therapeutic alliance), therapist technique (e.g., transference interpretation), dropping out, and outcome. In chapters 9 and 10, we provide case examples that illustrate the main findings.

Our interest in conducting the research project was generated by a number of factors that are mentioned in previous chapters. As indicated in chapter 1, we were aware of considerable interest in dynamically oriented, short-term interpretive therapy (STI). Although there has been a general shift toward eclecticism in the mental health field in the past 20 years, recent surveys have indicated that a large proportion of therapists have maintained their allegiance to the psychodynamic model (Jensen, Bergin, & Greaves, 1990; Levensen, Speed, & Budman, 1992; Sammons & Gravitz,

---

Parts of this chapter have been taken, verbatim or adapted, from "Interpretive and Supportive Forms of Psychotherapy and Patient Personality Variables," *Journal of Consulting and Clinical Psychology*, 66, 558–567, 1998. Copyright 1998 by the American Psychological Association. Adapted by permission of the publisher and author.

Parts of this chapter have been taken, verbatim or adapted, from "Follow-Up Findings for Interpretive and Supportive Forms of Psychotherapy and Patient Personality Variables," *Journal of Consulting and Clinical Psychology*, 67, 267–273, 1999. Copyright 1999 by the American Psychological Association. Adapted by permission of the publisher and author.

1990). STI has allowed dynamically oriented therapists to retain familiar concepts, such as unconscious processes, intrapsychic conflict, resistance, transference, interpretation, and insight, while at the same time making technical innovations. The innovations include greater therapist activity, focus, and early interpretation of transference.

As indicated in chapter 2, we were also aware of the growing prevalence and recognition of the usefulness of supportive psychotherapy. However, most examples of supportive psychotherapy have involved the extremes of a few sessions of crisis intervention for traumatized patients or many sessions of long-term, continuous treatment for low-functioning patients. Missing from consideration was the use of intermediate length, supportive therapy—for example, 12 to 25 sessions—with higher functioning patients.

Clearly, there are many different forms of dynamically oriented short-term therapies. Despite their prevalence, only a small number of controlled or comparative outcome trials have been conducted. A recent meta-analytic review by Anderson and Lambert (1995) included only 26 studies. Although the number of studies was limited, the reviewers were positive about the evidence for the effectiveness of STI. The number of trials involving supportive therapy is considerably fewer than STI, and the results have been mixed. For example, Klein, Zitrin, Woerner, and Ross (1983) and Rosser et al. (1983) presented positive evidence, and Guthrie, Creed, Dawson, and Tomenson (1993) presented negative evidence. The mixed results suggest that other variables, such as patient personality characteristics, may play an important role. A limitation of review methods such as meta-analysis, which rely on extensive averaging, is that the effects of such variables as patient personality, therapist technique, and the interaction between the two are usually overlooked within individual studies. It is unfortunate that with so many different forms of dynamically oriented short-term therapy available, there is an absence of data that indicates what forms to use with whom to maximize benefit.

As indicated in the previous chapter, we have been interested in studying the role of two patient personality characteristics, QOR and PM. These personality characteristics have been cited frequently in the literature as important selection criteria for brief therapy (Lambert & Anderson, 1996). Our own findings and those from a study by M. J. Horowitz, Marmar, Weiss, et al.(1984) suggest how QOR may differentially interact with supportive and interpretive forms of therapy. Horowitz and colleagues found that therapist interpretive actions were more effective with patients who were more motivated and who had a higher level of object relations. The opposite was found for therapist-supportive actions. In the case of PM, a similar pattern of relationships can be predicted.

The different relationships that QOR or PM can be expected to have with interpretive therapy and supportive therapy are jointly determined by the nature of the personality characteristics and the nature of the therapies. In regard to QOR, we hypothesized that patients in our study who had higher levels of QOR would be better able to tolerate, work with, and benefit from the more demanding aspects of interpretive therapy. Conversely, we hypothesized that patients with lower levels of QOR would be better able to work with and benefit from the more gratifying aspects of supportive therapy. In regard to PM, we hypothesized that patients with higher levels of PM would be better able to work and benefit in interpretive therapy where internal conflicts are explored repeatedly. Conversely, we hypothesized that patients with lower levels of PM would be better able to work and benefit in supportive therapy where internal conflicts are not explored

On the basis of these rationale, our previous clinical experience, and our previous research findings, we made three predictions: (a) There will be no outcome differences between the two forms (interpretive, supportive) of therapy. Both will be effective. (b) There will be an interaction between QOR and form of therapy. Higher levels of QOR will be associated with more favorable outcome in interpretive therapy, and lower levels of QOR will be associated with more favorable outcome in supportive therapy. (c) There will be an interaction between PM and form of therapy. Higher levels of PM will be associated with more favorable outcome in interpretive therapy, and lower levels of PM will be associated with more favorable outcome in supportive therapy.

In summary, the study had two primary objectives. The first was to compare the effectiveness of two different forms (interpretive, supportive) of time-limited, short-term, dynamically oriented individual psychotherapy. The second was to investigate the interaction of each of two personality characteristics (quality of object relations, psychological mindedness) with the two forms of psychotherapy. In the service of carrying out these objectives and testing the hypotheses in a valid manner, we implemented procedures that represent state of the art methodology for psychotherapy clinical trials. We used a randomized method of patient allocation in a comparative design, a large patient sample, a comprehensive set of outcome criteria, trained and experienced therapists, therapy manuals, technical adherence checks, and follow-up assessments. We believe that these methodological features enhanced our chances of detecting significant results and enhanced the validity of the findings.

SETTING, REFERRALS, PROCEDURE, AND DESIGN

Patients were referred to the project from the Walk-in Clinic of the Department of Psychiatry, University of Alberta Hospital Site, Edmonton, Alberta, Canada. The Walk-in Clinic is part of a large, multifaceted, psychiatric outpatient service that is located within a 600-bed university hospital. Approximately 2000 initial assessments are conducted in the clinic each year by a staff of 10 from the disciplines of psychology, social work, occupational therapy, and nursing. Approximately 18% of the patients are offered some form of weekly psychodynamic therapy (individual, couple, family, group). A variety of other treatments are also offered, and some patients are referred outside the clinic. During the referral period (September 1993 to March 1996), an average of nine patients per month were referred—about 6% of all assessments and 31% of available psychodynamic psychotherapy cases. Patient preference and therapist capacity to carry simultaneous cases influenced the referral rate to the project. The patients in the project were regarded by the referrers as representative of the psychotherapy cases within the clinic.

A total of 258 patients were referred to the project. Patients read a detailed information form and provided signed consent. Each patient was scheduled for a set of pretherapy interviews and questionnaire assessments that focused on a fairly large set of predictor, demographic, diagnostic, and outcome variables. The assessors were blind to the results of each other's assessments. A research coordinator matched patients in pairs on the basis of their QOR score, PM score, use of medication, and when possible gender and age. Exact matches on the continuous QOR and PM scales were not always possible. The best possible match was achieved from the group of patients who were currently available for assignment. One patient from each pair was randomly assigned to interpretive therapy and the other to supportive therapy for a given therapist. Therapist assignments were also made randomly. The therapist contacted the patient to arrange for treatment. Soon after therapy ended, patients were reassessed on the outcome variables. Patients were also reassessed on the outcome variables 6 months and 12 months after therapy ended. The design of the project is depicted in Table 6-1. The study is a randomized clinical trial that compares different forms of psychotherapy.

PATIENTS

Of the total of 258 referred patients, 69 (26.7%) did not complete the pretherapy assessments and proceed to therapy; they were labeled *decliners*. Of the 171 patients who started therapy with one of the project therapists, 27 dropped out prematurely; they were labeled *dropouts*. An attempt was made to reassess dropouts on the outcome variables at the time they otherwise would have completed therapy. Dropouts were replaced with another matched patient. The 144 patients who finished therapy were labeled *completers*. An additional 18 patients could not be matched and assigned to a

Table 6-1
Design for Interaction of Form of Psychotherapy and
Patient Personality Variable Trial

Patient suitability	5-month period	6-month follow-up	
		Period I	Period II
Psychological mindedness (low to high) Quality of object relations (low to high)	Interpretive psychotherapy	Follow-up	Follow-up
Psychological mindedness (low to high) Quality of object relations (low to high)	Supportive psychotherapy	Follow-up	Follow-up

project therapist in a timely manner and were, therefore, treated by a nonproject therapist in the clinic.

All of the 144 treatment completers received diagnoses according to the *Diagnostic and Statistical Manual of Mental Disorders* (*DSM-III-R*; American Psychiatric Association, 1987). Axis I diagnoses were identified by the computer-administered Mini-SCID (Structured Clinical Interview for *DSM-III-R*; First, Gibbon, Williams, and Spitzer, 1990) and validated by an independent clinical diagnosis assigned jointly by the intake assessor and a rounds psychiatrist, both of whom saw the patient on the day of intake. Axis II diagnoses were determined by the computer-administered SCID-II PQ and Auto-SCID II (Structured Clinical Interview for *DSM-III-R*; First, Gibbon, Williams, & Spitzer, 1991). The computer-assisted diagnostic procedures were carried out by a team of bachelor's-degree-level research assistants. Rater reliability for the Axis II diagnoses was calculated for 10 randomly selected cases and 5 raters. A kappa was calculated for each pair of raters for each disorder. The mean kappa for all pairs and disorders was .70.

The diagnoses of the patients are summarized in Tables 6-2 and 6-3. A total of 72.9% of the patients received an Axis I diagnosis. The most frequent disorders were current major depression (48.6%) and dysthymia (26.4%), followed by anxiety disorder (7.6%), adjustment disorder (6.9%), and alcohol abuse (6.2%). A total of 60.4% of the patients received an Axis II diagnosis. The most frequent Axis II disorders were avoidant (29.2%), obsessive–compulsive (24.3%), borderline (22.2%), and paranoid (21.5%). A total of 46.5% of the patients received both Axis I and Axis II diagnoses. Patients with primary problems related to psychosis, substance abuse, or sociopathic behavior were excluded. The patients' presenting problems were consistent with the previously described diagnostic profile and representative of an outpatient psychotherapy population—namely difficulties with depression, anxiety, low self-esteem, and interpersonal conflict.

Table 6-2
Frequencies and Percentages of Patients Receiving Axis I Diagnoses According to the Computer-Administered, Ministructured Clinical Interview for DSM-III-R and Clinic Validation

Disorder	Interpretive Therapy Patients ($n = 72$)		Supportive Therapy Patients ($n = 72$)	
	f	%	f	%
Mood				
Current major depression	32	44.4	38	52.8
Past major depression	18	25.0	20	27.8
Current manic/hypomanic	0	0.0	0	0.0
Past manic/hypomanic	0	0.0	1	1.4
Current dysthymia	10	13.9	4	5.6
Past dysthymia	0	0.0	2	2.8
Depressive disorder NOS	3	4.2	1	1.4
Anxiety				
Panic	3	4.2	4	5.6
Agoraphobia	0	0.0	0	0.0
Social phobia	1	1.4	0	0.0
Simple phobia	0	0.0	0	0.0
Obsessive/compulsive	0	0.0	1	1.4
Current generalized anxiety	1	1.4	1	1.4
Past generalized anxiety	0	0.0	0	0.0
Posttraumatic stress	0	0.0	0	0.0
Substance abuse				
Alcohol	8	11.1	1	1.4
Drugs	1	1.4	0	0.0
Somatoform	0	0.0	1	1.4
Eating				
Anorexia nervosa	1	1.4	0	0.0
Bulimia	1	1.4	4	5.6
Adjustment	2	2.8	8	11.1
No	22	30.6	17	23.6

The average age of the patients was 34.3 years ($SD = 9.6$; range = 18–62 years). Sixty-one percent were women. Forty-two percent were married or living with a partner, 21% were separated or divorced, and 37% had never been married. Sixty-seven percent were educated beyond high school, and 71% were employed. The racial composition was White (94%), East Indian (2%), Native American (2%), Asian (1%), and Semitic (1%). Many (73%) reported receiving previous psychiatric treatment, but few (8%) reported a history of psychiatric hospitalization.

THERAPISTS

There were eight therapists (three psychologists, two social workers, two occupational therapists, one psychiatrist). Seven were White and one

Table 6-3
Frequencies and Percentages of Patients Receiving Axis II Diagnoses
According to the Computer-Administered, Structured Clinical Interview for
DSM-III-R Personality Questionnaire and Auto-Structured
Clinical Interview for *DSM-III-R*

Disorder	Interpretive Therapy Patients ($n = 72$)		Supportive Therapy Patients ($n = 72$)	
	f	%	f	%
Cluster A				
Paranoid	15	20.8	16	22.2
Schizoid	3	4.2	3	4.2
Schizotypal	7	9.7	4	5.6
Cluster B				
Antisocial	2	2.8	2	2.8
Borderline	21	29.2	11	15.3
Histrionic	0	0.0	4	5.6
Narcissistic	1	1.4	3	4.2
(conduct history)	4	5.5	6	8.3
Cluster C				
Avoidant	18	25.0	24	33.3
Dependent	14	19.4	11	15.3
Obsessive–Compulsive	18	25.0	17	23.6
Passive–aggressive	9	12.5	6	8.3
Other				
Self-Defeating	8	11.1	11	15.3
Not Otherwise Specified	4	5.6	6	8.3

East Indian. Five were female. The therapists' average age was 43.6 years ($SD = 6.1$; range = 37–52), and their average experience practicing individual psychotherapy was 11.8 years ($SD = 4.9$; range = 3–19). Each therapist treated nine interpretive therapy patients and nine supportive therapy patients.

THERAPIES

Each patient received a form of psychotherapy that emphasized interpretive or supportive features. They were labeled interpretive therapy and supportive therapy, respectively. Their general contractual and structural features were similar. The patient was scheduled for 20 weekly 50-minute sessions at a regular, prearranged time. Punctual attendance was emphasized, and missed sessions were not rescheduled. The therapist was paid by a third party. Apart from these similarities, the overall objectives, session objectives, and therapist technique for the two forms of therapy were quite different. As emphasized at the beginning of this chapter, in interpretive therapy, the primary objective is to enhance the patient's insight about repetitive conflicts (intrapsychic and interpersonal) and traumas that serve to underlie and sustain the patient's problems. The therapist encourages the patient to explore uncomfortable emotions and withholds direct praise and gratification. The therapist is active, interpretive, and transference-focused. In supportive therapy, the primary objective is to improve the patient's immediate adaptation to his or her life situation. The therapist attempts to minimize anxiety and regression in the session and provides praise and immediate gratification. The therapist is active, noninterpretive, and other-focused (focused on current external relationships).

Although the therapists were experienced in providing a variety of interpretive and supportive therapies in the clinic, they participated in a six-month training seminar before taking cases in the project. This included treating pilot cases and attending a weekly training session in which technical principles were covered and cases were presented. The weekly seminar continued throughout the project. The therapists followed the two technical manuals that are described in chapter 11 and are presented in appendixes I and II. The manuals describe, illustrate, and compare the technical emphases associated with the two forms of therapy.

All therapy sessions were audiotaped. Adherence to the technical manual was monitored by external observers (bachelor's-degree-level research assistants), who were blind to the treatment conditions, using two measures. First, the Interpretive and Supportive Technique Scale (ISTS), which is described in chapter 12 and is presented in appendix III, was used. The ISTS consists of 14 items (seven interpretive, seven supportive) that are rated on a 5-point, Likert-type scale ranging from "no emphasis" to "major emphasis" after the rater listens to the entire session. The psychometric properties of the scale are presented in chapter 12. The full-scale score, which is keyed in the interpretive direction, ranges from 0 to 56. The ISTS was used with nine sessions (numbers 3, 5, 7, 9, 11, 13, 15, 17, 19) of each patient's therapy. For the 72 interpretive therapies, the mean for the full-scale score was 39.1 ($SD = 3.8$). For the 72 supportive therapies, the mean for the full-scale score was 14.9 ($SD = 3.5$). A t test comparing these means was significant, $t(142) = 39.81$, $p < .001$. According to the ISTS, the two therapies were well-differentiated. The second measure of adherence was the Therapist Intervention Rating System (TIRS; Piper, Debbane, de Carufel, & Bienvenu, 1987). All therapist statements from each session are assigned to one of nine categories that range from simple utterances (e.g., "Mm hm") to complex interpretations. The five lower categories include brief expressions, reflections, clarifications, questions, and directives that do not make reference to patient dynamic components such as wishes, anxiety, and defenses. Thus, they are defined as interventions but not interpretations. The four upper categories make reference to patient dynamic components and are defined as interpretations. They differ only in the number of dynamic components referred to—one, two, three, or four. The rater reliability for the scale was assessed using one session from each of 12 randomly selected cases (six interpretive, six supportive). Three raters scored each of the 12 sessions. A kappa was calculated for each pair for each session. The mean kappa for all pairs and sessions for the nine categories was .71. The TIRS was used with six sessions (numbers 3, 7, 9, 11, 15, 19) for the first 80 completers. For the 40 interpretive therapies, the mean number of interventions, interpretations, and transference interpretations per session were 74.2, 14.4, and 3.7, respectively. For the 40 supportive therapies, the mean number of interventions, interpretations, and transference interpretations per session were 125.6, 3.3, and 0.2, respectively. Comparison by t tests revealed that in the interpretive therapies, therapists were significantly less active $[t(78) = 6.28, p < .001]$, more interpretive $[t(78) = 10.02, p < .001]$, and more transference-oriented $[t(78) = 6.26, p < .001]$. According to the TIRS, the two therapies were well-differentiated.

Third, the patient and therapist rated the therapist's technique after each session, using eight items that paralleled a subset of the ISTS items. Each item was rated on a 5-point Likert-type scale ranging from "no emphasis" to "major emphasis." The ratings for each item were averaged across the therapy sessions and then averaged across the eight items to create an overall score keyed in the interpretive direction. On the overall score, both patients, $t(140) = 11.28, p < .001$, and therapists, $t(142) = 43.98, p < .001$, perceived significant differences in the technique provided by the therapist in the two forms of therapy as intended. Thus, the evidence from the patient and therapist ratings was similar to the two external rater measures. The two forms of therapy were well-differentiated and conformed to the technical manual.

Session attendance for the two therapies was high. More than 94% of the patients attended 15 or more sessions. For interpretive therapy, the mean number of sessions attended was 18.0 ($SD = 1.8$). For supportive therapy, the mean number of sessions attended was also 18.0 ($SD = 2.1$).

MEDICATION

Medication was managed by an independent project psychiatrist, who met with each patient before and after therapy. A total of 60 (41.7%) of the 144 completers were prescribed a therapeutic dosage of a psychotropic medication. In nearly all cases (93.3%), the medication was an antidepressant (tricyclic or SSRI). For an antidepressant, a therapeutic dosage was defined as equivalent to 150 mg/day of imipramine for a minimum of six weeks. In the remaining cases (6.7%), an anxiolytic or hypnotic was prescribed.

PATIENT PERSONALITY VARIABLES

Patients were matched on the two personality variables (QOR and PM) before random assignment to one of the two therapies. The nature of the variables and the psychometric properties of the interview-based scales that were used to assess them were presented in chapter 5.

For QOR, the interviewer followed a scoring manual (Piper et al., 1993) and assigned 100 points along the five levels of the scale and an overall score that ranged from 1 to 9. In the project, two psychologists and three psychiatrists served as raters. To determine rater reliability, 24 cases were rated by all five raters, who used audiotapes of the original interviews. The Intraclass Correlation Coefficient (ICC; 2, 2) for the overall score was .68, which is comparable to reliabilities obtained in two of our completed clinical trials (McCallum et al., 1997; Piper et al., 1993). In this project, the original interviewer's overall score was used as the matching score and the average of two raters' overall scores was used as the predictor score. The correlation between the two scores was high, r (142) = .85, $p < .001$.

For PM, the interviewer followed a scoring manual (McCallum & Piper, 1993) and assigned an overall score that ranged from 1 to 9 to each of the two scenarios. One of seven bachelor's-degree-level research assistants assessed each patient. To determine interrater reliability, 20 cases were rated by all six assistants, who used audiotapes of the original interview. The ICC (2, 1) was .80 for scenario I and .71 for scenario II. These levels are lower, but similar to those obtained in three of our clinical trials (McCallum & Piper, 1997). In this project, the score for scenario I was used as the matching score, and the scores for scenario I and scenario II were used as the predictor scores. The correlation between the two scenario scores was significant but low, r (142) = .21, $p < .01$.

OUTCOME VARIABLES

Assessment of outcome included nine measures (questionnaire or interview) that covered 16 variables in the areas of interpersonal distress and functioning, psychiatric symptomatology, self-esteem, life satisfaction, and use of defenses. Severity of disturbance associated with individualized target objectives was also assessed.

The overall score from the 64-item Inventory of Interpersonal Problems (L. Horowitz, Rosenberg, Baer, Ureno, & Villasenor, 1988) was used to measure interpersonal distress. A modification of the Social Adjustment Scale interview (Weissman, Paykel, Siegal, & Klerman, 1971) was conducted by an independent assessor (bachelor's-degree-level research assistant) to measure interpersonal functioning in six areas: work, social, family of origin, sexual, partner, and parent. Rater reliability for this interview measure was assessed during the project using the ICC (2, 1) with six raters and 12 patients. The ICC's for the six areas were work (.88), social (.91), family of origin (.83), sexual (.95), partner (.94), and parent (.94). This represents a mean reliability of .91 and a range of .83 to .95.

For psychiatric symptomatology, depression was assessed by the 13-item short form (Beck & Beck, 1972) of the Beck Depression Inventory (Beck & Steer, 1987), anxiety by the 20-item Trait Anxiety Scale (Spielberger, 1983), and general symptomatic distress by the global severity index of the 90-item Symptom Distress Checklist—Revised (SCL-90-R; Derogatis, 1977). Self-esteem was measured by Rosenberg's (1979) 10-item Self-Esteem Scale. Life satisfaction was measured by a single item rated on a 7-point Likert-type scale that ranged from "completely dissatisfied" to "completely satisfied." The 40-item Defensive Style Questionnaire (Andrews, Singh, & Bond, 1993) was used to measure the patient's report of derivatives of defensive mechanisms. For this recently developed questionnaire, Andrews et al. reported moderate to high internal consistency (Cronbach's alpha ranging from .58–.80 and high test–retest reliability ranging from .75–.85) for the three subscales. In this study, a principal components analysis with orthogonal rotation of the three subscales revealed two factors, which represented use of mature defenses and maladaptive defenses. Individualized target objectives were formulated by the patient with the assistance of an independent assessor (bachelor's-degree-level research assistant). The patient's average rating and the assessor's average rating of severity of disturbance for the objectives were used as outcome scores. A rater reliability determination for the assessor's rating, using 5 raters and 15 cases, yielded an ICC (2, 1) of .99, indicating high reliability.

APPROACH TO STATISTICAL ANALYSES

First, the similarity between the patients in the two forms of therapy on the matching, demographic, diagnostic, and initial disturbance variables was examined. Second, dropouts were examined. Third, change over the course of therapy on the outcome variables for all completers and for completers in each of the two forms of therapy was investigated and compared. Fourth, the interaction of each of the two predictor variables (QOR, PM) and form of therapy on outcome over the course of therapy was examined. Fifth, a number of effects involving the 6-month and 12-month posttherapy follow-up data were examined. These primarily concerned whether the findings at posttherapy were maintained at follow-up or whether they differed.

SIMILARITY BETWEEN INTERPRETIVE AND SUPPORTIVE THERAPY SAMPLES

Before making outcome comparisons between the 72 interpretive therapy patients and the 72 supportive therapy patients, the two samples were compared on four sets of possible confounding variables. Confounding variables are those variables that create differences between the outcomes of the research conditions of a study that can be attributed mistakenly to the research conditions. First, we examined the matching variables. There were no significant ($p < .05$) differences between the two samples on the primary matching variables of QOR (original interviewer's score, average of two raters' scores), PM (scenario I score, scenario II score), and use of medication (initial use, pattern of use during treatment). Second, we examined the demographic variables. There were no significant differences for the demographic variables of age, gender, educational status, employment status, marital status, race, previous psychiatric treatment, and previous psychiatric hospitalization. Third, we examined the diagnostic variables. Similarly, there were no significant differences for the presence of the following diagnostic categories: Axis I, Axis II, Axis I and Axis II, current mood, current anxiety, adjustment. Fourth, we examined initial disturbance as represented by the initial (pretherapy) levels of the 13 outcome variables that are listed in Table 6-4. The reason why these 13 outcome variables were examined rather than all 16 is explained in the section that follows regarding change during the course of therapy. A one-way (interpretive versus supportive therapy) multivariate analysis of variance (MANOVA) on the pretherapy scores for the 13 outcome variables was significant, $F(13, 116) = 2.63$, $p < .003$. However, inspection of the means for both therapies revealed that the interpretive therapy patients were more disturbed on five of the variables and the supportive therapy patients were more disturbed on eight of the variables. Corresponding univariate, one-way ANOVAs yielded two significant differences. Supportive therapy patients were initially more disturbed in the area of social functioning, $F(1,128) = 7.64$, $p = .007$, and sexual functioning, $F(1,128) = 6.26$, $p = .014$. However, considering the entire set of matching, demographic, diagnostic, and initial disturbance variables, the two patient samples were regarded as well-balanced.

DROPOUTS

Of the 27 dropouts from treatment, 22 (81.5%) were from interpretive therapy and 5 (18.5%) were from supportive therapy. This represents 23.4% of the patients who started interpretive therapy and 6.3% of the patients who started supportive therapy. The difference in dropouts between the

Table 6-4
Means, Standard Deviations, and Effect Sizes for Outcome Variables at Pre- and Posttherapy

	Interpretive Therapy							Supportive Therapy						
	Pretherapy		Posttherapy				Effect	Pretherapy		Posttherapy				Effect
Variable	M	SD	M	SD	n		Size	M	SD	M	SD	n		Size
Interpersonal distress	1.40	0.56	1.21	0.58	69		0.34	1.51	0.54	1.13	0.63	70		0.70
Social functioning	4.3	1.3	3.9	1.3	67		0.34	4.9	1.6	4.2	1.4	70		0.47
Family functioning	4.2	1.4	3.8	1.4	67		0.34	4.3	1.1	3.8	1.2	70		0.41
Sexual functioning	4.2	2.1	3.6	2.0	67		0.26	5.1	2.1	4.6	2.3	70		0.22
Depression[a]	19.8	11.7	11.1	10.0	69		0.74	17.3	10.3	8.5	8.7	70		0.86
Anxiety	52.3	9.9	45.4	10.1	69		0.70	52.7	10.3	42.1	11.4	70		1.03
General symptomatic distress	1.14	0.59	0.72	0.55	69		0.71	1.13	0.57	0.64	0.56	70		0.86
Self-esteem	3.7	2.0	2.5	1.9	69		0.59	3.8	2.0	2.0	1.9	70		0.91
Life satisfaction[b]	3.1	1.2	4.3	1.2	67		0.96	3.2	1.1	4.6	1.3	68		1.23
Mature defenses[b]	4.8	1.2	5.3	1.2	69		0.40	4.5	1.1	5.1	1.2	69		0.47
Maladaptive defenses	4.2	0.9	4.1	1.0	69		0.14	4.4	0.8	4.0	0.9	69		0.44
Target severity (patient)	3.9	0.6	2.5	0.6	68		2.31	3.8	0.7	2.5	1.1	71		1.86
Target severity (assessor)	3.7	0.6	2.3	1.1	67		2.15	3.7	0.7	2.2	1.1	70		2.19

[a] Prorated to approximate a 21-item inventory score.
[b] High scores are favorable.

two therapies was significant, $\chi^2(1, N = 171) = 7.88, p < .006$. We wondered whether the personality variables were related to dropping out. Analyses were conducted and revealed no significant relationship between either QOR or PM and dropping out. Also, no significant interaction was found between QOR and form of therapy or between PM and form of therapy in regard to dropping out. Additional analyses (t-test, chi-square, MANOVA) were conducted to determine whether all dropouts differed from all completers on demographic and initial disturbance variables, and whether interpretive therapy dropouts differed from interpretive therapy completers on QOR, PM, demographic variables, and initial disturbance variables. None of the tests were significant. Most of the dropouts (73% in interpretive therapy, 80% in supportive therapy) left during the first third of therapy. In regard to reassessment of the dropouts on the outcome variables, compliance was unfortunately very poor, with only five dropouts providing complete data. This prevented further analyses concerning the outcome of the dropouts.

CHANGE OVER THE COURSE OF THERAPY

Change was investigated from the three perspectives of statistical significance, magnitude of effect, and clinical significance. This provided comprehensive coverage. Although the three perspectives are often directly related to each other, they can be independent.

Statistical Significance

A one-way (pretherapy versus posttherapy) MANOVA on the outcome variables for all patients was conducted. Because multivariate statistics such as MANOVA require complete data, three of the interpersonal functioning outcome variables (work, partner, and parent) that were applicable to only part of the sample were deleted to avoid analyses based on a small, unrepresentative sample. A total of 130 patients (64 interpretive therapy and 66 supportive therapy) had complete data for the remaining 13 outcome variables. The MANOVA was significant, $F(13, 117) = 29.44, p \leq .001$. All 13 corresponding univariate F-tests were also significant at $p \leq .009$. The analyses were repeated for each of the two forms of therapy. Similarly, both the one-way MANOVA for interpretive therapy patients, $F(13, 51) = 13.18, p < .001$, and the one-way MANOVA for supportive therapy patients, $F(13, 53) = 19.59, p < .001$, were significant. For interpretive therapy, 11 of the 13 corresponding univariate F-tests were significant at $p \leq .017$. Only the F-tests for sexual functioning and maladaptive defenses were nonsignificant. For supportive therapy, 12 of the 13 corresponding univariate F-tests were significant at $p \leq .005$. Only the F-test for sexual functioning was nonsignificant. All significant tests indicated favorable change.

To compare change over the course of therapy for the two therapies, a one-way (interpretive versus supportive) MANOVA on the residual gain scores (posttherapy minus pretherapy) of the 13 outcome variables was conducted. As used in this study, the residual gain scores represent change that has been adjusted for the correlation between prescores and postscores. They are regarded as a more accurate representation of change compared to raw change scores. The multivariate F-test indicated no significant difference between the two therapies. Overall, the various analyses indicated evidence of significant improvement for both therapies, which did not differ from one another.

Magnitude of Effect

The outcome results presented thus far have been expressed in terms of statistical significance, which is defined in terms of probability. In reference to the analyses conducted concerning the change over the course of therapy for each of the two forms of therapy, we wanted to determine whether the change that occurred could have occurred by chance. If the probability of obtaining the change is less than 5 in 100, which represents the conventional $p < .05$ standard, the difference is regarded as significant and not a result of chance. That, of course, is what was found. Statistical significance is an important criterion. However, like any single criterion, it does not provide all of the information that is important. For example, it does not provide information about the size of impact that a variable such as therapy has on a second variable such as outcome. It is well-known that with relatively large samples, relatively small differences can be statistically significant. In such a circumstance, evidence of statistical significance may be misunderstood to mean evidence of large impact.

In contrast to statistical significance, the criterion known as magnitude of effect directly expresses the size of impact that one variable has on another, in our case, therapy on outcome. Also in contrast to statistical significance, magnitude of effect has nothing to do with probability. A formula for calculating magnitude of effect appropriate for this project is provided by Cohen (1988). He defined *magnitude of effect* (also called effect size) as the pretherapy mean minus the posttherapy mean divided by the pretherapy standard deviation. This definition was used in this project.

Magnitude of effect was investigated by calculating an effect size for each of the 13 variables for each form of therapy. The effect sizes, which are presented in Table 6-4, all indicated favorable change. For interpretive therapy, the average effect size was .77. For supportive therapy, the average effect size was .90. These are regarded as large effect size averages in the literature. In general, the largest effect sizes were for the target objective severity variables, followed by the life satisfaction and symptomatology variables. The effect sizes for the interpersonal and defensive style variables were smaller.

Clinical Significance

A third criterion that differs from both statistical significance and magnitude of effect is clinical significance. Clinical significance refers to the clinical importance of an effect. It is possible for the results of a treatment to be both statistically significant and large in effect size yet be clinically unimportant. Central to the meaning of clinical significance is the consideration of norms. If a patient moves from a pathologic level to a normal level on a particular variable and the change exceeds that which could be attributed to measurement error, a clinically significant change has occurred. Accordingly, in this project, clinical significance was investigated using the two-part procedure (clinical cut-off criterion, reliable change index) developed by Jacobson and colleagues (Jacobson, Follette, & Revenstorf, 1984; Jacobson & Revenstorf, 1988; Jacobson & Truax, 1991) and refined by others (Christensen & Mendoza, 1986; Tingey, Lambert, Burlingame, & Hansen, 1996). According to the first part, a patient must move from a dysfunctional range to a functional range on an outcome variable. According to the second part, a patient must change by a reliable amount taking into account measurement error.

In the present study, clinical significance was investigated for each of three of the outcome variables that have considerable normative data. In regard to normative data, for the Beck Depression Inventory, Beck and Steer (1987) reported a mean of 17.5 for 99 dysthymic patients, and Nietzel, Russell, Hemmings, and Gretter (1987) reported a mean of 7.2 for a large sample of collegiate–general population research participants from 12 studies. For the Trait Anxiety Scale, Spielberger (1983) reported a mean of 48.1 for 60 "anxiety reaction" patients and a mean of 34.8 for 451 female working adults. For the SCL-90-R global severity index, Derogatis (1977) reported a mean of 1.26 for 1002 psychiatric outpatients and a mean of .31 for 974 nonpatients. In Table 6-4, the pretherapy means of the interpretive and supportive therapy patients for the three outcome variables clearly confirm the clinical nature of our sample.

Using Jacobson and Revenstorf's (1988) formula, the clinical cut-off criteria were calculated to be 12.1 for the Beck Depression Inventory, 40.1 for the Trait Anxiety Scale, and .61 for the SCL-90-R. Only patients whose pretherapy scores were above the criteria were considered. The number of such patients were similar between the two therapy conditions. For interpretive and supportive therapy, respectively, there were 52 and 45 patients for the Beck Depression Inventory, 60 and 60 patients for the Trait Anxiety Scale, and 55 and 56 patients for the SCL-90-R. In the case of interpretive therapy in this project, the percentages of patients who traversed the criteria were 53.8%, 28.3%, and 57.2%. With the exception of the percentage for anxiety, which was lower, these figures are similar to those reported in our previous controlled trial of interpretive therapy (Piper et al., 1990). In that study, the percentages were 57%, 52%, and 56%, respectively. In the case of supportive therapy in this project, the percentages of patients who traversed the criteria were 55.6%, 48.3%, and 53.6%, respectively. A chi-square analysis revealed that the number of patients who traversed the cut-off criterion for anxiety was significantly higher for supportive therapy when compared with interpretive therapy, $\chi^2 (1, N = 120) = 4.27, p < .04$.

Using the modified formula of Jacobson and Revenstorf (1988), as reported in Tingey et al. (1996), the reliable change indexes were calculated to be 8.7 for the Beck Depression Inventory, 11 for the Trait Anxiety Scale, and .55 for the SCL-90-R. In the case of interpretive therapy in this project, the percentages of patients who achieved reliable change were 53.6%, 34.8%, and 37.7%, respectively. In the case of supportive therapy in the present project, the percentages of patients who achieved reliable change were 45.7%, 38.6%, and 45.7%, respectively. There were no significant differences between the two therapies in the number of patients who achieved reliable change for these outcome variables.

Finally, the percentage of patients who both traversed the clinical cut-off criteria and achieved reliable change was calculated. In the case of interpretive therapy, the percentages were 46.2%, 20.0%, and 36.4%, respectively. In the case of supportive therapy, the percentages were 48.9%, 31.7%, and 41.1%, respectively. There were no significant differences between the two therapies in the number of patients who met both of these conditions.

QOR AND FORM OF THERAPY

To investigate the interaction of QOR and form of therapy, a multivariate analysis of covariance (MANCOVA) was conducted on the residual gain scores of the 13 outcome variables. Form of therapy (interpretive versus supportive) was the independent variable and QOR (a continuous variable) was the covariate. Using the SPSS program (Norušis, 1993), the MANCOVA determines an effect for the independent variable, an effect for the covariate, and an effect for the interaction between the independent variable and the covariate. Of the three effects, only the interaction effect was significant, $F (13, 114) = 2.18, p < .015$. Five of the corresponding univariate interaction effects were also significant. These included sexual functioning, $F (1, 126) = 7.92, p < .006$; anxiety, $F (1, 126) = 4.32, p <$

.040; self-esteem, $F(1, 126) = 5.19$, $p < .024$; life-satisfaction, $F(1, 126) = 10.27$, $p < .002$; and mature defenses, $F(1, 126) = 6.04$, $p < .015$.

The nature of the interaction effect is evident by examining the Pearson correlation coefficients between QOR and the outcome variables for the patients in each therapy and for all patients (Table 6-5). For interpretive therapy, the higher the patient's QOR score, the better the outcome in interpersonal functioning (distress, sexual), symptoms (depression, anxiety), self-esteem, life satisfaction, and defensive style. In contrast, for supportive therapy, there are no outcome variables that have better outcome with higher QOR scores. In fact, the higher the patient's QOR score, the worse the outcome in life satisfaction. Thus, the overall pattern indicates a number of direct relationships between QOR and favorable outcome in interpretive therapy and no direct relationships in supportive therapy.

There is another way of examining the nature of the interaction effect that has clearer implications for the clinical decision of choosing one form of therapy over another. The outcome of high-QOR patients in interpretive therapy is compared with the outcome of high-QOR patients in supportive therapy, and the outcome of low-QOR patients in interpretive therapy is compared with the outcome of low-QOR patients in supportive therapy. This was done for each of the five outcome variables for which there was a significant, univariate interaction effect. Patients with QOR scores of 5 or higher were defined as high and patients with QOR scores less than 5 were defined as low. Tukey's (1949) honestly significant difference test for

Table 6-5
Correlations Between Quality of Object Relations and Outcome Variables

Variable	Interpretive Therapy Patients ($n = 64$)	Supportive Therapy Patients ($n = 66$)	All Patients ($n = 130$)
Interpersonal distress	−.27[a]	.01	−.11
Social functioning	−.24	.02	−.10
Family functioning	−.03	−.14	−.09
Sexual functioning	−.40[b]	.09	−.12
Depression	−.26[a]	.07	−.08
Anxiety	−.38[c]	.00	−.17
General symptomatic distress	−.14	−.02	−.08
Self-esteem	−.39[b]	.00	−.19[a]
Life satisfaction[d]	.28[a]	.28[a]	−.02
Mature defenses[d]	.37[c]	−.04	.15
Maladaptive defenses	−.19	.07	−.05
Target severity (patient)	−.21	−.12	−.16
Target severity (assessor)	−.24	.00	−.11

[a]$p < .05$. [b]$p < .001$. [c]$p < .01$. [d]High scores are favorable.

multiple comparisons was used. The analyses indicated that high-QOR patients in interpretive therapy had better outcome in sexual functioning than high-QOR patients in supportive therapy, $Q\ (126) = 4.29$, $p = .019$. They also indicated that low-QOR patients in supportive therapy had better outcome in self-esteem than low-QOR patients in interpretive therapy, $Q\ (126) = 3.89$, $p = .043$. For this same comparison, outcome in anxiety was almost significant, $Q\ (126) = 3.29$, $p = .074$. These findings support the choice of interpretive therapy for high-QOR patients and supportive therapy for low-QOR patients.

PM AND FORM OF THERAPY

The scenario I and scenario II PM scores were analyzed separately. Again, a MANCOVA on the residual gain scores was conducted for each. For scenario I, there were no significant effects. For scenario II, only the main effect for PM was significant, $F\ (13, 115) = 1.89$, $p < .039$. Four of the corresponding, univariate, PM main effects were also significant. These included interpersonal distress, $F\ (1, 127) = 7.43$, $p < .007$; sexual functioning, $F\ (1, 127) = 5.02$, $p < .027$; general symptomatic distress, $F\ (1, 127) = 8.06$, $p < .005$; and life satisfaction, $F\ (1, 127) = 5.11$, $p < .025$. Table 6-6 presents the Pearson correlation coefficients between PM (scenario II) and the outcome variables. One significant relationship between PM and favor-

Table 6-6
Correlations Between Psychological Mindedness (Scenario II) and Outcome Variables

Variable	Interpretive Therapy Patients ($n = 64$)	Supportive Therapy Patients ($n = 66$)	All Patients ($n = 130$)
Interpersonal distress	−.16	−.33[a]	−.26[a]
Social functioning	.01	.01	.00
Family functioning	−.14	−.18	−.14
Sexual functioning	−.15	−.26[b]	−.17[b]
Depression	−.11	−.21	−.16
Anxiety	−.15	−.14	−.17[b]
General symptomatic distress	−.26[b]	−.23	−.26[a]
Self-esteem	.11	−.20	−.06
Life satisfaction[c]	.02	−.41[d]	.21[b]
Mature defenses[e]	.11	−.01	.05
Maladaptive defenses	−.09	−.24	−.17[b]
Target severity (patient)	.04	−.14	−.03
Target severity (assessor)	.05	−.24	−.08

[a] $p < .01$. [b] $p < .05$. [c] High scores are favorable. [d] $p < .001$.

able outcome was found for interpretive therapy patients, three for supportive therapy patients, and six for all patients. This pattern illustrates the overall main effect for PM.

FOLLOW-UP FINDINGS

Follow-up assessments with the outcome variable battery were conducted 6 months and 12 months after the completion of therapy. At six months, 121 (or 84%) of the patients provided follow-up data. This included 57 from interpretive therapy and 64 from supportive therapy. At 12 months, 98 (or 68%) of the patients provided data. This included 47 from interpretive therapy and 51 from supportive therapy. The difference between the two therapies in the number of patients at each assessment was not significant. Similarly, patients from the two therapies did not differ on initial disturbance (pretherapy levels of the outcome variables) or on seven of eight demographic variables. Although interpretive therapy had a higher proportion of patients with previous psychiatric treatment, this variable was not significantly related to outcome. Comparisons were also made between providers and nonproviders of follow-up data. At each follow-up assessment, providers did not differ from nonproviders on initial disturbance or on seven of eight demographic variables. Providers were a few years older, but age was not significantly related to outcome.

We also attempted to assess the degree to which patients had participated in formal therapy or counseling during the follow-up period. We defined participation as engagement in at least one-half hour of intervention per week for six weeks during the previous two months. At the six-month follow-up assessment, 15% of the interpretive patients and 15% of the supportive patients reported receiving treatment. At the 12-month assessment, the percentages were 24% and 17%, respectively. Neither of the differences was significant.

Because of the reduced sample sizes at the follow-up assessments and high correlations among many of the outcome variables, we decided to reduce the set of 13 outcome variables to a smaller set of factors by means of a principal-components analysis. The analysis used the residual change scores from pretherapy to posttherapy. Three factors with eigenvalues greater than 1 emerged. The factors, which accounted for 61% of the variance, were labeled general symptomatology and dysfunction, social–sexual maladjustment, and nonuse of mature defenses and family pathology. The outcome variables and their loadings are presented in Table 6-7.

There were four parts to a primary set of follow-up data analyses that we conducted. First, we investigated outcome change over the follow-up periods and differential change for the two therapies. We used a repeated-

Table 6-7
Outcome Factors, Variables, and Loadings

Outcome factor and variables	Loading
General symptomatology and dysfunction (42% of variance)	
Anxiety	.84
General symptomatic distress	.80
Depression	.78
Self-esteem	−.75
Interpersonal distress	.74
Life satisfaction	−.72
Target severity (assessor rated)	.63
Target severity (patient rated)	.62
Maladaptive defenses	.59
Social–sexual maladjustment (10% of variance)	
Social dysfunction	.84
Sexual dysfunction	.74
Nonuse of mature defenses and family dysfunction (9% of variance)	
Mature defenses	−.74
Family dysfunction	.47

measures ANOVA to investigate the main effect of treatment (interpretive versus supportive), the main effect of time (posttherapy versus 6-month follow-up versus 12-month follow-up), and their interaction for each of the three outcome factors for the sample of 98 patients who provided data. There were no significant effects. Thus, the outcome effects achieved at posttherapy were maintained during the follow-up assessments for both forms of therapy.

Second, we investigated whether there were differences between the two therapies in clinically significant change and reliable change for the same three outcome variables that we had used for the pretherapy to posttherapy data—in other words, depression, anxiety, and general symptomatic distress. We considered both favorable change and unfavorable change (or deterioration). We defined seven possible types of change: clinical improvement, reliable improvement, both clinical and reliable improvement, clinical deterioration, reliable deterioration, both clinical and reliable deterioration, and no clinical or reliable change. The comparison base was always the pretherapy status of the patient. The figures for these categories are presented in Table 6-8. We conducted chi-square analyses between the interpretive and supportive patients for each of the seven categories, three outcome variables, and three assessment times. Of these 63 chi-square analyses, only one was significant. Thus, there was very little difference between the two therapies in clinically significant change and reliable change.

Third, we investigated whether there was change in category status from posttherapy to 12-month follow-up. Chi-square analyses were

Table 6-8
Percentages of Clinical and Reliable Change From Pretherapy
to Posttherapy, Pretherapy to 6-Month Follow-Up, and Pretherapy
to 12-Month Follow-Up for Three Outcome Variables for
Interpretive Therapy and Supportive Therapy

Category	Posttherapy	6-month Follow-up	12-month Follow-up
Interpretive therapy: Depression as outcome variable			
Clinical improvement	60.0	50.0	63.3
Reliable improvement	53.2	47.6	46.3
Clinical and reliable improvement	51.4	36.7	50.0
Clinical deterioration	0.0	0.0	9.1
Reliable deterioration	0.0	0.0	4.9
Clinical and reliable deterioration	0.0	0.0	9.1
No change	40.4	42.9	39.0
Supportive therapy: Depression as outcome variable			
Clinical improvement	62.8	75.0	67.7
Reliable improvement	49.0	45.8	55.3
Clinical and reliable improvement	54.3	62.5	67.7
Clinical deterioration	6.3	12.5	6.3
Reliable deterioration	2.0	2.1	0.0
Clinical and reliable deterioration	6.2	6.2	0.0
No change	43.1	41.7	42.6
Interpretive therapy: Anxiety as outcome variable			
Clinical improvement	33.3	28.6	45.7
Reliable improvement	36.2	40.5	54.8
Clinical and reliable improvement	23.1	22.8	42.8
Clinical deterioration	25.0	0.0	12.5
Reliable deterioration	2.1	4.8	2.4
Clinical and reliable deterioration	12.5	0.0	12.5
No change	51.1	50.0	40.5
Supportive therapy: Anxiety as outcome variable			
Clinical improvement	46.7	50.0	48.9
Reliable improvement	43.1	47.9	51.1
Clinical and reliable improvement	33.3	45.2	46.3
Clinical deterioration	0.0	16.7	0.0
Reliable deterioration	0.0	4.2	0.0
Clinical and reliable deterioration	0.0	16.7	0.0
No change	45.1	43.8	42.6
Interpretive therapy: Distress as outcome variable			
Clinical improvement	48.6	40.0	48.4
Reliable improvement	36.2	26.2	33.3
Clinical and reliable improvement	34.3	30.0	32.2
Clinical deterioration	8.3	8.3	9.1
Reliable deterioration	2.1	2.4	2.4
Clinical and reliable deterioration	0.0	8.3	9.1
No change	48.9	64.3	52.4

continued

Table 6-8
Continued

Category	Posttherapy	6-month Follow-up	12-month Follow-up
Supportive therapy: Distress as outcome variable			
Clinical improvement	55.8	62.5	53.8
Reliable improvement	49.0	50.0	48.9
Clinical and reliable improvement	41.9	52.5	38.5
Clinical deterioration	12.5	0.0	0.0
Reliable deterioration	2.0	0.0	0.0
Clinical and reliable deterioration	12.5	0.0	0.0
No change	37.2	41.7	38.3

calculated for each category, for each outcome variable, for each of the two forms of therapy. Of the 42 chi-square analyses, none was significant. Thus, there was very little change in category status over the 12-month follow-up period.

Fourth, we investigated whether there were main effects and interaction effects for each personality variable (QOR or PM) and form of therapy. We did this for each outcome factor at each of the two follow-up assessments. We used hierarchical regression analyses. In the case of QOR, for each analysis, QOR was entered first, then treatment (interpretive versus supportive), and then the interaction product. As indicated in Tables 6-9 and 6-10, a main effect for QOR was found for general symptomatology and dysfunction at 6 months and 12 months, and nonuse of mature defenses at 12 months. The main effects indicated direct relationships between QOR and improvement. In addition, an interaction effect was found for social–sexual maladjustment at 12 months. It resembled the type of interaction effect that had been found at the end of therapy, a direct relationship between QOR and improvement in interpretive therapy, and virtually no relationship in supportive therapy. Further examination of this interaction effect using

Table 6-9
Hierarchical Regression Analysis With a Significant Main Effect at the Six-Month Follow-Up Assessment

Step	Predictor variable[a]	R	R^2	ΔR^2	dfs	Partial F
1	QOR	.21	.04	.04	1,119	5.32[b]
2	Treatment[c]	.26	.07	.03	1,118	3.28
3	Interaction	.26	.07	.00	1,117	0.00

Note. QOR = quality of object relations.
[a]Dependent variable was Factor 1: General Symptomatology and Dysfunction.
[b]$p < .05$.
[c]Interpretive versus supportive therapy.

Table 6-10
Hierarchical Regression Analyses With Significant Main and Interaction Effects at the 12-Month Follow-Up Assessment

Step	Predictor Variable	R	R^2	ΔR^2	dfs	Partial F
	Factor 1[a] as dependent variable					
1	QOR	.27	.08	.08	1,88	7.16[b]
2	Treatment[c]	.32	.10	.02	1,87	2.39
3	Interaction	.32	.10	.00	1,86	0.21
	Factor 2[d] as dependent variable					
1	QOR	.20	.04	.04	1,84	3.45
2	Treatment[c]	.20	.04	.00	1,83	0.12
3	Interaction	.30	.09	.05	1,82	4.13[e]
	Factor 3[f] as dependent variable					
1	QOR	.25	.06	.06	1,94	6.44[e]
2	Treatment[c]	.30	.09	.03	1,93	2.74
3	Interaction	.35	.12	.03	1,92	3.04

Note. QOR = quality of object relations.
[a]General symptomatology and dysfunction.
[b]$p < .01$.
[c]Interpretive versus supportive therapy.
[d]Social–sexual maladjustment.
[e]$p < .05$.
[f]Nonuse of mature defenses and family dysfunction.

Tukey's (1949) honestly significant comparison test revealed that high-QOR patients improved significantly more on social–sexual maladjustment in interpretive therapy than in supportive therapy, $Q(82) = 4.03$, $p < .05$. This finding provided additional support for the choice of interpretive therapy for high-QOR patients. For PM, we used a similar approach to investigate main and interaction effects, but found no significant effects.

CONCLUSION

Overall, the research project was carried out according to plan. Contemporary methodology for conducting psychotherapy clinical trials was followed. Similar patient samples were treated with either an interpretive or supportive form of time-limited, short-term individual therapy. The two therapies were well-differentiated as confirmed by the impressions of patients, therapists, and external observers. A comprehensive set of outcome variables was assessed at multiple times before and after therapy. Patient personality characteristics were also assessed. Because of the large number of variables and assessment times in the project, a number of different conclusions can be drawn. We will begin with those that address the treatments in general.

Then we will consider more complex conclusions that address the interaction of the treatments and patient personality characteristics.

At posttreatment, patients in each therapy experienced substantial improvement on a range of outcome variables as evidenced by criteria of statistical significance, magnitude of effect, and clinical significance. The greatest improvements involved target objectives, life satisfaction, and symptomatology. Less improvement occurred for interpersonal distress, interpersonal functioning, and defensive style. The latter variables may be more resistant to change in short-term therapy, which is consistent with the findings of our previous controlled trial of individual interpretive therapy (Piper et al., 1990).

Comparisons between the two therapies were made using the same criteria. In terms of statistical significance, patients in supportive therapy did not differ from patients in interpretive therapy on overall improvement. In terms of magnitude of effect, the mean effect size for supportive therapy was a little higher but essentially similar to the mean for interpretive therapy. In terms of clinical significance, more supportive therapy patients than interpretive therapy patients met the clinical cut-off criterion for anxiety. The emphasis in supportive therapy on minimizing anxiety during the sessions may have resulted in a report of less anxiety after therapy ended. However, supportive therapy was not superior to interpretive therapy in achieving reliable change or the combination of the clinical cut-off criterion and reliable change for anxiety. In addition, there were no substantial differences on the criteria of clinical significance, reliable change, or their combination for depression or general symptomatic distress.

Maintenance of improvement during follow-up was found for both interpretive therapy and supportive therapy at 6- and 12-month follow-up assessments according to the criteria of statistical significance, clinical significance, and reliable change. In general, the benefits associated with the two therapies at posttherapy and follow-up were similar. The results suggest that when treatment is carried out by experienced therapists who follow a treatment manual, time-limited supportive therapy can be as effective as time-limited interpretive therapy. These findings are consistent with recent claims regarding the usefulness of supportive therapy. Although the emphasis in interpretive therapy on dealing with underlying conflicts rather than achieving immediate adaptation is theoretically predictive of greater lasting effects, we did not find such effects. It is possible that the length of the therapies (20 weeks) or the length of the follow-up periods (6 and 12 months) was not long enough to allow differential effects to occur. There are other possible explanations for the absence of differential effects. The presence of therapeutic factors that were common to the two therapies may have contributed to the similar outcomes. These include such factors as the presence of a helping relationship, a convincing rationale, and feedback concerning progress, which are believed to increase morale, a sense of mastery, and positive expectations. Of course, it was also possible that differential effects would be found if other important variables, such as patient personality characteristics, were taken into consideration in the analyses. Such effects can be overlooked if one considers only averaged findings. Before considering the effects involving QOR and PM, we will consider the general findings regarding dropouts.

There were significantly fewer dropouts in supportive therapy (6.3%) than interpretive therapy (23.4%). The dropout rate for interpretive therapy was not unusually high for outpatient psychotherapy; the dropout rate for supportive therapy was unusually low. The difference in dropout rates may reflect some of the salient differences in the two therapy situations. Relative to supportive therapy, the interpretive therapy situation was more demanding, depriving, and anxiety arousing. The patient was expected to begin each session and assume responsibility for what followed. There was ongoing pressure for the patient to talk, and the therapist abstained from providing direct gratification or praise. The therapist encouraged the patient to explore conflicts, which often involved uncomfortable emotions. Interpretations about sensitive topics including transference were often made. These features of the interpretive situation may have created tension that exceeded the threshold of tolerance for dropouts, particularly at the beginning of therapy when most dropouts occurred. Less strict adherence to interpretive features by the therapist and greater provision of supportive features might have resulted in fewer dropouts in interpretive therapy. This possibility is further explored in chapter 9, where specific cases of dropouts are reviewed. Regardless of the explanation, the low dropout rate for supportive therapy is a definite advantage. Premature termination constitutes a selection failure and usually represents a waste of time and effort for both patient and therapist. It is often accompanied by negative affect for both parties. If a sense of failure concerning premature termination can be avoided, it should be.

The general outcome finding of no difference between the two therapies in combination with the dropout finding, which favors supportive therapy, suggests that perhaps all patients should be offered supportive therapy. However, this conclusion overlooks two possibilities. First, some patients and therapists prefer an interpretive approach. Preferences can have a powerful influence on the process and outcome of psychotherapy. Second, some patients benefit more from an interpretive approach. This raises the issue of the importance of patient personality characteristics in the selection of patients for interpretive or supportive therapy.

Turning to the topic of personality variables, a significant interaction effect was found between QOR and form of therapy at posttherapy for the entire set of outcome variables and specifically for several of the variables.

The general pattern indicated a direct relationship between QOR and improvement in interpretive therapy, which replicated the finding from our previous controlled trial of interpretive therapy, and almost no relationship between QOR and outcome in supportive therapy. We believe that the interaction effect that we found at posttherapy can again be understood by considering the differences between the two therapy situations.

As indicated previously, the features of the interpretive situation can be expected to create strain in the patient–therapist relationship. Whether such strain is regarded by the patient as mistreatment or as an opportunity for learning and change may depend on the patient's QOR. Patients with higher QOR, who have a history of satisfactory give-and-take relationships, may be more able to tolerate the demands of the interpersonal situation, be less fearful of losing the relationship, and be more receptive to the therapist's interventions. Patients with lower QOR may be less able to tolerate the demands, be more fearful, and be less receptive. In contrast, in the supportive therapy situation, where the level of tension and strain are comparatively low, the patient's QOR may have been less relevant, at least to improvement for most outcome variables. There was also evidence of a similar significant interaction effect between QOR and form of therapy at follow-up. The effect involved the social–sexual functioning outcome factor.

An alternate way of analyzing the interaction effects at posttherapy and follow-up provided findings with clearer clinical implications regarding treatment provision. When patients were divided into high-QOR and low-QOR groups, differential therapy effects were found for some outcome variables. At posttherapy, high-QOR patients in interpretive therapy did better than high-QOR patients in supportive therapy in the area of sexual functioning. Similarly at follow-up, high-QOR patients in interpretive therapy did better than high-QOR patients in supportive therapy in the area of social–sexual functioning. In contrast, at posttherapy, low-QOR patients in supportive therapy did better than low-QOR patients in interpretive therapy in the area of self-esteem. These findings represent reasons to provide interpretive therapy to high-QOR patients and supportive therapy to low-QOR patients. If interpretive therapy were provided, precautions would need to be taken to reduce the dropout risk. A number of strategies for doing so are discussed in chapter 8. If supportive therapy were provided, much less concern about dropouts would be warranted.

At follow-up, a direct relationship was also found between QOR and favorable outcome for two of the outcome factors (general symptomatology and dysfunction, and nonuse of mature defenses and family dysfunction). A lifelong pattern of more mature interpersonal relationships may have helped patients sustain what they had learned during the course of therapy and endure the loss of the therapist during the follow-up period. The follow-up findings provide additional support for the continuing importance of

QOR as a patient characteristic. We will now consider the characteristic of PM.

A significant direct relationship between PM and outcome was found for the combined interpretive and supportive therapy samples at posttherapy. The relationship for interpretive therapy had been predicted because of the assumed usefulness of PM to understanding and working with interpretations. The relationship for supportive therapy had not. Nevertheless, several explanations are apparent. In supportive therapy, high-PM patients may have engaged in psychodynamic work (exploration of internal conflicts) during their therapy sessions or outside of their sessions, despite the fact that their therapists did not facilitate it. Alternatively, PM may reflect a useful general ability to analyze conflicts and problem solve, whether the conflicts are internal or external. Thus, PM may be of value to a variety of individual therapies, even those of different theoretical and technical orientations—for example, cognitive–behavioral therapy.

In contrast to QOR, the main effects for PM at posttherapy were no longer present at 6 and 12 months. Active engagement in the process of therapy may be required for PM to have a significant effect. In the absence of a therapist or a therapy session to provide focus, its effects may diminish. Explanations for the differences in the posttherapy and follow-up findings in this study are admittedly speculative and open to future investigation. However, it should be noted that the follow-up part of the study was naturalistic in design. Uncontrolled events, shrinkage of the sample, and reduction in statistical power may have contributed to differences in some of the QOR effects and the absence of PM effect at follow-up.

Integrating the QOR and PM findings, success in therapy may be facilitated by two factors, a positive patient–therapist relationship and a process of psychodynamic work. Both the patient and therapist contribute to these factors. In interpretive therapy, where the therapist actively stimulates psychodynamic work through interpretations, it may be particularly beneficial if the patient brings in a strong potential (high QOR) to form a positive relationship. In addition high PM may be useful but not as important as high QOR. In supportive therapy, in which the therapist actively creates a positive relationship, it may be particularly beneficial if the patient brings in a strong potential (high PM) to engage in psychodynamic work—in other words, focusing on components of internal conflict with past, current, and immediate figures. The match between particular patient characteristics and form of therapy appears to be important. In the case of the current study, the match is between patient personality dimensions and form of therapy. This is somewhat different than the more common search in the field for different treatments for different disorders (or diagnoses).

The findings of the research project and those of previous studies suggest that clinicians may find it useful to assess patients for QOR and

PM. In regard to time, the assessment of PM is clearly more efficient, although it requires the use of video equipment. In the case of QOR, it may be possible to integrate its assessment with routine clinical procedures such as history taking. We believe that the assessments would be well worth the effort.

All research projects have limitations that should be considered. Limitations associated with this project concern a number of issues. First, two caveats concerning the design of the study are important: Because the design did not include a no-treatment or placebo control condition, the findings do not address the basic efficacy question concerning each of the two forms of therapy. Although a growing number of controlled studies have provided support for the efficacy of interpretive forms of short-term psychodynamic therapy (Anderson & Lambert, 1995), there are almost no controlled studies of supportive therapy (Piper, 1996). This is related to the fact that supportive forms of short-term psychodynamic therapy have often been regarded as control conditions in themselves. The need for controlled studies of supportive therapy is evident. Also, because the design did not include a randomized medication or combination of medication and psychotherapy condition, conclusions concerning the effects of medication are not possible. In addition, although the use of medication was balanced in the two therapy conditions, the improvement that was achieved may have been enhanced by the approximately 42% of patients in each condition who were prescribed psychotropic medication in addition to therapy.

Second, characteristics of the patients, therapists, and technique may limit the extent of generalization of the findings. The patients were fairly well-educated and primarily White. In addition, they represented a subset of all patients assessed at the outpatient clinic—in other words, those who were regarded as suitable for some form of weekly, psychodynamic psychotherapy. The therapists were experienced in providing forms of interpretive and supportive therapy. The therapies were time-limited and manual-guided. Third, the PM findings involved only scenario II. Reasons for the low correlation between scenario I and scenario II and the absence of significant findings for scenario I are not apparent. In our previous day treatment trial that involved the group treatment of somewhat lower functioning patients (Piper et al., 1994), scenario I was a stronger predictor than scenario II. Although we suspect that the higher functioning individual therapy patients in this study identified more with the patient portrayed in scenario II, this remains a speculation. Fourth, this report focuses primarily on outcome findings. It does not emphasize the assessment and analysis of process variables such as the extent of patient work, which might reveal mechanisms that underlie the outcome findings. That remains a task for future investigation. Fifth, because multiple statistical tests were conducted, particularly in the case of the follow-up analyses, the family-wise alpha exceeded .05 in some cases—for example, the QOR findings. We advocate a less stringent approach that allows a more even balance between Type I and Type II errors. This is based on the attrition in sample size and corresponding decrease in statistical power, which is a common problem in follow-up studies, the *a priori* theoretical basis of our predictions involving QOR, and the previous empirical support for QOR as an important predictor variable. Sixth, the effect sizes for many of the significant findings are modest in magnitude. This suggests that they may be limited in importance regarding their clinical or practical application.

Seventh, with regard to maintaining improvement for both therapies, it is important to recognize that the patients consisted of therapy completers. The patients who provided data for the follow-up phase of the study complied with requests for reassessment. Thus, the sample may represent the relatively more satisfied completers from each therapy. On the one hand, it is important to know that a large proportion of patients who completed interpretive or supportive therapy maintained improvement 12 months after the end of treatment. On the other hand, caution should again be exercised in generalizing from the sample in the study. Although differences between providers and nonproviders of follow-up data on demographic, diagnostic, and initial disturbance variables were not found, it is possible that they differed on one or more undetected variables, a possibility that exists for all follow-up studies that experience attrition.

The search for optimal patient–treatment matches in psychotherapy has met with mixed success in the literature as well as in the case of the present study. Optimal matches may be restricted to certain patient variables, patient problems, treatments, and time intervals. Averaging across such variables is likely to lead to a failure to detect optimal matches. We believe that the discoveries that have been reported in the research literature, the findings of the present study, and the potential importance of the topic justify the continued search for specific significant effects.

7

DETERMINING THE ROLE GENDER PLAYS AS A PATIENT APTITUDE FOR THERAPY

Personality characteristics of the patient occupy a central place in the treatment formulations of clinicians. In chapter 6, we described how two personality characteristics, quality of object relations (QOR) and psychological mindedness (PM), were related to the outcome of interpretive and supportive forms of psychotherapy. The findings were suggestive of optimal matches between patients and treatments. A third patient characteristic that we have been interested in is gender. Although gender is not a *personality* characteristic, there are norms regarding appropriate modes of behavior for men and women. Regardless of the extent to which we consciously accept or reject these norms, we often act and are often experienced by others in relation to them. This is not to deny that there is variability in the degree to which we are influenced by gender norms and variability in personality and behavior among men and women.

The effect of gender norms on the quality of the psychotherapy experience remains poorly understood, despite considerable attention in the clinical and research literature. In part, gender emerged as a theme in the psychotherapy literature in response to contemporary social issues. During the decade of the 1970s and the early part of the 1980s, when women's rights and feminist advocacy issues were strongly voiced, much attention was devoted to gender. More recently, gender in psychotherapy has received less attention.

Much of the focus on gender, particularly in earlier years, was directed at examining whether the gender of the patient or the gender of the therapist had an important effect on the outcome of therapy. Although a few studies indicated that female patients tended to derive more benefit from therapy than male patients (Jones & Zoppell, 1982; Kirshner, Genack, & Hauser, 1978), the majority of studies found that patient gender did not have a strong association with the outcome of therapy (Garfield, 1994; Sotsky et al., 1991; Thase et al., 1994; Zlotnick, Shea, Pilkonis, Elkin, & Ryan, 1996).

Similarly, there is some empirical evidence that therapist gender is related to the process and outcome of therapy, which favors female therapists (Jones, Krupnick, & Kerig, 1987; Jones & Zoppell, 1982). However, Beutler, Machado, and Neufeldt (1994) concluded that the evidence available from existing studies is weak and largely nonsignificant regarding the association between therapist gender and treatment outcome.

Others have argued that there may be interaction effects between the gender of the patient and that of the therapist, and that focusing solely on one party may not provide meaningful answers (Garfield, 1994). The idea of an optimal fit between patient gender and therapist gender has received considerable attention. A common notion in popular literature (magazines, newspapers) and clinical literature is that female patients do better in therapy with female therapists, because female therapists are more able to understand the stresses and pressures experienced by their female patients and are less likely to disempower them (Kaplan, 1985; Kirshner, 1978; Mogul, 1982). Attempts to test these claims, however, have failed to provide empirical support (Kirshner et al., 1978; Thase et al., 1994; Zlotnick, Elkin, & Shea, 1998).

Relatively absent from the psychotherapy literature on gender is the issue of whether male patients and female patients respond similarly to different forms of psychotherapy. No author has described which form of therapy may be most suitable for men or women. However, a number of writers have argued that male and female patients may *prefer* or *benefit* more from different aspects of psychotherapy. For example, Kaplan (1986) and Stiver (1986) have argued that female patients *prefer* to be listened to and understood in a way that precludes the kind of distancing that may occur in more traditional interpretive models of therapy. These authors posited that women prefer to participate in a relationship that is characterized by mutual empathy, affiliation, and affective expressiveness. These are qualities that tend to be more characteristic of the patient–therapist relationship in supportive forms of therapy (Piper, 1996).

Others (Jordan, Kaplan, & Surrey, 1983; Lemkau & Landau, 1986) have argued that female patients benefit more from an approach that considers external pressures (societal pressures for women to be both homemakers and income earners), which permits an understanding of many women's sense of inadequacy in the face of these pressures. Such consideration counters the tendency to place responsibility for their failures on themselves. Diminished self-blame can, in turn, free women for more effective problem solving (Nolen-Hoeksema, 1987). This suggests that a supportive form of therapy may be more beneficial to female patients because it focuses on external circumstances, encourages problem solving, and makes use of praise and gratification.

Relevant to male patients, Hare-Mustin and Marecek (1986), Kaplan (1987), and O'Neil (1980) noted that a man's sense of self is more characterized by independence, distinction, and separation from others. Thus, men may *prefer* a form of treatment that provides them with a relationship that allows them to maintain some emotional distance and sense of independence. Such a relationship tends to be more characteristic of interpretive forms of therapy.

Certain aspects of therapy may be more *beneficial* to male patients. Stiver (1986) has suggested that the very factors involved in rearing men for independence may lead to underdevelopment of affective awareness and expressiveness. Men typically use coping strategies that involve suppression or denial of their emotions. Thus, interventions that enable them to examine their emotions may be more beneficial in facilitating change (Allen & Gordon, 1990; Fine, 1988). Interpretive therapy, with its focus on uncomfortable emotions and intrapsychic conflicts, is more likely to provide males with new methods for dealing with their problems and new experiences of expressing and examining their emotions.

Although interesting, this set of ideas concerning what male and female patients may differentially *prefer* or *benefit* more from in psychotherapy is not based on strong empirical research but rather on the clinical experience of the various authors. Thus, they must be regarded as speculative.

Our review of the literature found only one study (Zlotnick et al., 1996) that examined the interaction between patient gender and form of treatment. The study used follow-up data provided by the NIMH Treatment of Depression Collaborative Research Program. The treatments studied were cognitive–behavioral therapy, interpersonal therapy, imipramine plus clinical management, and placebo plus clinical management. No significant gender effects were found.

The two forms of therapy in our comparative treatment study differed considerably on aspects that the literature suggests may be differentially preferred by and beneficial to men and women. Supportive therapy involves education, advice, praise, and an emphasis on strengths and talents. The supportive therapist actively directs therapy, focuses on external circumstances related to the patient's difficulties, encourages adaptive functioning, and facilitates problem solving. In contrast, interpretive therapy involves ongoing pressure on the patient to talk, exploration of uncomfortable emotions, and interpretation of internal conflicts. The therapist abstains from providing direct praise and gratification. The patient is responsible for beginning each session and deciding what follows.

Given these differences between the two therapies, the study's methodology, and the suggestions from the literature about different preferences and benefits, there was an opportunity to examine a number of questions regarding the association between gender and the process and outcome of treatment. Specifically, we investigated whether patient gender or therapist gender had a direct effect on the therapeutic alliance and treatment outcome or whether gender interacted with form of therapy to influence the alliance and outcome.

Outcome was represented by the three outcome factors that were described in chapter 6 (general symptomatology and dysfunction, social–sexual maladjustment, nonuse of mature defenses and family pathology). The alliance, defined as the working relationship between the patient and therapist, was represented by two variables: patient-rated alliance and therapist-rated alliance. These variables reflected each participant's perception of the quality of the working relationship in therapy. A more detailed description of the alliance is provided in chapter 8.

RESULTS

Before investigating gender effects in our study, we believed that it was important to determine whether there were any differences between male patients and female patients on any of the demographic (e.g., age), diagnostic (e.g., presence of an Axis II disorder), initial disturbance (e.g., initial levels of depressive symptomatology), or predictor (i.e., QOR and PM) variables that were assessed at pretherapy. There were 25 variables in total. Systematic differences on any of these variables could potentially confound subsequent findings involving interactions between gender and form of treatment. Thus, their effects would have to be accounted for in additional analyses. Of the 25 variables, significant differences between males and females were observed for only three: education, family functioning as indicated by the family subscale of the Social Adjustment Scale interview (SAS; Weissman et al., 1971), and general symptomatic distress as indicated by the Global Severity Index (GSI) of the Symptom Distress Checklist—Revised (SCL-90-R; Derogatis, 1977). There was a greater proportion of males who had been educated beyond high school. In addition, males were found to have lower levels of initial disturbance in family functioning and general symptomatic distress. We examined the association that each of these three variables had with the alliance (patient-rated, therapist-rated) and treatment outcome (posttherapy, 12-month follow-up). Those that were significantly associated with the alliance or outcome were included as covariates in the main analyses that investigated gender effects to control for possible confounding effects.

Therapeutic Alliance

Analysis of variance procedures were used to determine whether differences in the therapeutic alliance existed as a function of the gender of the patient or therapist, the form of therapy provided, or some combination of these variables. For patient-rated alliance, we conducted a three-way analysis of variance (ANOVA), and for therapist-rated alliance, we conducted a three-way analysis of covariance (ANCOVA). The three independent variables in each analysis were patient gender, therapist gender, and form of therapy. Thus, for each analysis, there were three main effects, three two-way interaction effects, and one three-way interaction effect.

We found a significant interaction effect between patient gender and form of therapy for patient-rated alliance [F (1, 134) = 4.08, p = .05]. Male patients had higher alliance scores in interpretive therapy than in supportive therapy, and female patients had higher alliance scores in supportive therapy than in interpretive therapy.

We also found a main effect of therapist gender for patient-rated alliance [F (1, 134) = 14.95, p = .00]. Patients of female therapists (M = 5.82) rated the alliance higher than patients of male therapists (M = 5.05) in both forms of therapy. No significant results were found for therapist-rated alliance.

Posttherapy Outcome: Statistically Significant Change

Analysis of variance procedures were also used to determine whether differences in treatment outcome existed as a function of the gender of the patient or therapist, the form of therapy provided, or some combination of these variables. We conducted a three-way ANCOVA for each of the three outcome factors. The three independent variables were patient gender, therapist gender, and form of therapy. Each ANCOVA tested for three main effects, three two-way interaction effects, and one three-way interaction effect. The results are presented in Table 7-1.

General Symptomatology and Dysfunction

For this outcome factor, we did not find a significant three-way interaction effect. We did, however, find a significant two-way interaction effect between patient gender and form of therapy. The findings indicated that male patients had better outcomes in interpretive therapy than in supportive therapy, and female patients had better outcomes in supportive therapy than in interpretive therapy. No main effects of gender or form of therapy were found.

Social–Sexual Maladjustment

We did not find a significant three-way interaction effect, but did find a significant two-way interaction effect between patient gender and form of therapy. Male patients had better outcomes in interpretive therapy than

Table 7-1
Prediction of Posttherapy Outcome Factors

Predictor	General Symptomatology and Dysfunction[a]		Social–Sexual Maladjustment[b]		Nonuse of Mature Defenses and Family Pathology[c]	
	F	p	F	p	F	p
Patient gender	.20	.66	.10	.75	.51	.48
Form of therapy	.78	.38	.19	.08	.79	.38
Therapist gender	.43	.51	.44	.51	4.26	.04
Patient gender × form of therapy	5.06	.03	4.18	.04	.77	.38
Patient gender × therapist gender	.11	.74	.11	.74	1.01	.31
Therapist gender × form of therapy	.54	.46	5.24	.02	1.46	.23
Patient × therapy × therapist	.00	.98	.00	.95	.07	.80

[a] df = 1, 131
[b] df = 1, 128
[c] df = 1, 131

in supportive therapy. Female patients had similar outcomes in supportive therapy and interpretive therapy.

We also found a significant two-way interaction effect between therapist gender and form of therapy. Patients of male therapists had better outcomes in interpretive therapy than in supportive therapy. Patients of female therapists, however, had similar outcomes in supportive therapy and interpretive therapy. No significant main effects were found.

Nonuse of Mature Defenses and Family Pathology

As Table 7-1 shows, we did not find a significant three-way interaction effect, nor did we find evidence of any significant two-way interaction effects. The findings did, however, reveal a significant main effect of therapist gender. Patients of female therapists ($M = -.12$) had better outcomes compared to patients of male therapists ($M = .19$).

Posttherapy Outcome: Clinically Significant Change and Reliable Change

Clinically significant change and reliable change at posttherapy were also investigated for three of the outcome variables (depression, anxiety, general symptomatic distress). *Clinically significant change* indicates whether a patient moved out of the range of dysfunctional scores into the range of functional (normal) scores. *Reliable change* indicates whether the amount of change that a patient made was statistically reliable. Depression was measured by the Beck Depression Inventory (BDI; Beck & Steer, 1987), anxiety by the Trait Anxiety Scale (TAS; Spielberger, 1983), and general symptomatic distress by the GSI of the SCL-90-R. These three variables were chosen because of their frequent use in the research literature and because of their well-established normative data. Procedures for calculating the specific criteria are described in chapter 6. A series of logistic regression analyses were conducted to determine the effect of patient gender and the interaction of patient gender and form of therapy on the achievement of clinically significant change, reliable change, and both clinical and reliable change. Logistic regression is a statistical procedure that is similar to simple regression that is used when the dependent variable is dichotomous. In our case, the dependent variables were achieved versus did not achieve clinically significant change, reliable change, or both.

Clinically Significant Change

There was a significant interaction effect between patient gender and form of therapy for the BDI [$\chi^2(1, N = 97) = 6.8, p = .01$]. A greater proportion of males made clinically significant change in depression in interpretive therapy (68%) than in supportive therapy (35%), and a greater proportion of females made clinically significant change in depression in supportive therapy (68%) than in interpretive therapy (45%).

Reliable Change

There was a significant interaction effect between patient gender and form of therapy for the GSI [χ^2 (1, N = 139) = 3.8, p = .05]. A greater proportion of males made reliable change in distress in interpretive therapy (44%) than in supportive therapy (32%), and a greater proportion of females made reliable change in distress in supportive therapy (55%) than in interpretive therapy (33%). Also, there was a nearly significant interaction effect for the BDI [χ^2 (1, N = 139) = 3.4, p = .06].

Both Clinically Significant Change and Reliable Change

There was a significant interaction effect between patient gender and form of therapy for the BDI [χ^2 (1, N = 97) = 7.3, p = .01]. A greater proportion of males made clinically significant change and reliable change in depression in interpretive therapy (63%) than in supportive therapy (29%). A greater proportion of females made clinically significant change and reliable change in depression in supportive therapy (61%) than in interpretive therapy (36%). Also, there was a nearly significant interaction effect for the GSI [χ^2 (1, N = 111) = 3.2, p = .07].

Follow-Up Outcome

The analyses performed on the posttherapy outcome factors were repeated using 12-month follow-up data. The series of ANCOVAs revealed a significant interaction between therapist gender and form of therapy for one of the outcome factors: social–sexual maladjustment [F (1, 76) = 6.32, p = .01]. Male therapists had considerably better outcomes in interpretive therapy than in supportive therapy, and for female therapists there were similar outcomes for the two therapies.

Although not statistically significant, we found some evidence for an interaction between patient gender and form of therapy for the social–sexual outcome factor as well [F(1, 76) = 3.64, p = .06]. Male patients had substantially better outcomes in interpretive therapy than in supportive therapy, whereas outcomes for female patients were similar for the two therapies.

Clinically significant change and reliable change were also examined at 12-month follow-up. A series of logistic regression analyses revealed a significant interaction between patient gender and form of therapy for reliable change on the GSI [χ^2 (1, N = 89) = 3.9, p = .05]. A greater proportion of male patients made reliable change in interpretive therapy (46%) than in supportive therapy (33%), and a greater proportion of female patients made reliable change in supportive therapy (59%) than in interpretive therapy (28%).

DISCUSSION

In this section we will initially consider the findings for patient gender and the findings for therapist gender. Then we will consider limitations of our research. This will be followed by a consideration of higher order interactions involving patient gender, quality of object relations, and form of therapy.

Patient Gender

Our investigation revealed a number of significant findings involving patient gender and the process and outcome of psychotherapy. Many were interaction effects. For patient-rated alliance, a significant interaction effect was found for patient gender and form of therapy. Male patients reported stronger alliances with their therapists in interpretive therapy than in supportive therapy. Conversely, female patients reported stronger alliances with their therapists in supportive therapy than in interpretive therapy.

For outcome at posttreatment, a similar significant interaction effect was found for patient gender and form of therapy. Male patients improved more in interpretive therapy than in supportive therapy, and female patients improved more in supportive therapy than in interpretive therapy. Improvement was indicated by statistically significant change on outcome factors of general symptoms and dysfunction, social–sexual functioning, and by clinically significant change and reliable change on the specific outcome measures of depression (BDI) and distress (GSI). For outcome at 12-month follow-up, evidence of a similar interaction effect between patient gender and form of therapy for reliable change on the GSI and a nearly significant interaction effect for the social–sexual outcome factor was found. Thus, the interaction between patient gender and form of therapy was present for both the process and outcome of treatment.

The psychotherapy field has devoted little attention to the issue of whether male patients and female patients respond similarly to different forms of therapy. Thus, there is no research evidence and only suggestive clinical reports in the literature to help explain the interaction findings that we found. Nevertheless, some of the ideas expressed in the literature concerning how males and females differentially prefer or benefit from different aspects of therapy may provide explanations for our findings.

As reviewed earlier in this chapter, some authors have suggested that female patients may prefer a more collaborative and personal relationship with the therapist and benefit more from problem solving and interventions that externalize blame for current difficulties. These are characteristics that are consistent with the supportive form of therapy that was provided in our study. For male patients, it has been suggested that a more neutral relationship between the patient and therapist may be preferred and that males may benefit more from interventions that encourage introspection and examination of uncomfortable emotions. These are qualities that are more consistent with the interpretive form of therapy in our study.

In summary, providing patient–therapist relationships that are consistent with female and male patients' preferences may facilitate trust and willingness to work. Patients may then work on difficult topics and engage in new coping strategies that otherwise would have been avoided. For female patients, this may involve a greater focus on external problem solving to counter a ruminative response style that amplifies vulnerability to depression (Nolen-Hoeksema, 1987). For male patients, this may involve introspective examination to facilitate greater affective awareness. The result of such work would likely be greater benefit from treatment.

Therapist Gender

We also found an interaction effect between therapist gender and form of therapy for the social–sexual outcome factor at posttherapy and again at 12-month follow-up. Patients of male therapists improved more in interpretive therapy than in supportive therapy. Patients of female therapists, however, appeared to benefit equally from interpretive or supportive therapy. The differential outcomes between the interpretive and supportive forms of therapy for male therapists can be understood in a similar way to that of the male patients. Male therapists also may prefer the emotional distance created by the neutral therapist stance in the interpretive therapy approach. This distance may allow the male therapist to be more objective and effective. Male therapists have been described as more demanding, less encouraging, and less active than their female counterparts (Kaplan, 1985). These qualities are more consistent with behavior expected of the therapist who provides interpretive therapy. Thus, the male therapist may feel more comfortable in his role when he is providing interpretive therapy. Females therapists may not have a preference for providing either an interpretive or supportive emphasis in therapy.

Other findings revealed a main effect of therapist gender for the small nonuse of mature defenses and family pathology outcome factor at posttherapy. The finding indicated that patients of female therapists improved more than patients of male therapists. A main effect of therapist gender was also found for patient-rated alliance, whereby patients of female therapists rated the alliance stronger than patients of male therapists. Jones and Zoppell (1982) reported that male and female patients who were seen by female therapists perceived their therapists as more accepting, attentive, and comprehensible, and in general reported forming more effective therapeutic alliances, which in turn tended to promote more successful outcome (p. 271).

Limitations

Although we found a number of significant and interesting findings, there are some limitations of our investigation that should be acknowledged. We did not use process measures that could elucidate how the therapy process evolved differently for men and women. Such measures would have proven useful in attempting to identify which patient and therapist behaviors were responsible for the different outcomes. The differences in outcome for men and women in the two forms of therapy may have been influenced by patients' preferences for a particular type of therapy. Unfortunately, such preferences were not assessed. An additional limitation of our investigation is the lack of consideration of the patients' gender-role identity. A person's behavior and the socialization process that he or she engages in is likely to reflect the gender role that he or she identifies with. Thus, preference and benefits of certain techniques in psychotherapy may differ for those who identify with either a feminine gender role or a masculine gender role. Assessing gender-role identities in future studies could help clarify this issue. Generalization is limited by the fact that the majority of the patients and therapist were White. Finally, the findings are based on only one study, and the explanations offered are admittedly speculative. However, despite their speculative nature, the ideas provide plausible explanations of the findings. Further research is needed to substantiate or refute these explanations.

Patient–Treatment Matching

This chapter and the previous one each presented findings concerning an interaction effect on treatment outcome that involved a characteristic of the patient and form of therapy. This chapter described an interaction effect between patient gender and form of therapy. Chapter 6 described the interaction between the patient personality characteristic QOR, which refers to the patient's life-long pattern of relationships, and form of therapy. We were interested in examining whether the two interaction effects were independent of each other or whether there was some higher order interaction that involved all three variables (i.e., patient gender, QOR, form of therapy).

To investigate the contribution of each of these three independent variables and their interactions in predicting treatment outcome, we performed three hierarchical regression analyses. The dependent variable in each analysis was one of the three posttherapy outcome factors. Thus, we tested for three main effects, three two-way interaction effects and one three-way interaction effect. Significant results were found for one of the three outcome factors. For the general symptoms outcome factor, we found that the two-way interaction between QOR and form of therapy [$F (1, 135) = 4.0$, $p = .05$] and the two-way interaction between patient gender and form of therapy [$F (1, 134) = 3.9$, $p = .05$] each made a significant independent contribution to the prediction of outcome. The more complex, three-way interaction effect was not significant. Consistent with what we have reported previously in this chapter and in chapter 6, the two-way interactions revealed that patients with high levels of QOR had better outcomes in interpretive therapy than patients with low levels of QOR, and male patients improved more in interpretive therapy, whereas female patients improved more in supportive therapy.

The findings suggest that each patient characteristic (gender, QOR) plays an important role in determining the patient's response to interpretive or supportive therapy. Treatment recommendations based on the consideration of one or the other of these two characteristics are relatively straightforward. Treatment recommendations based on the *combination* of these two characteristics are more complex. Some are fairly clear. For example, it seems clear that males with more mature levels of object relations (i.e., high QOR scores) are likely to receive considerable benefit from interpretive therapy. For other combinations, however, recommendations are less clear—for example, females with higher QOR scores. Additional research is required to make more definitive conclusions.

CONCLUSION

Success in psychotherapy is determined by many variables. The significant interaction effects of our comparative study have identified some of the potentially influential patient characteristics that can influence the therapeutic alliance and treatment outcome. The alliance and other process variables can also be seen as influencing subsequent events—for example, outcome of therapy. These variables represent different aspects of the therapy encounter and help elucidate the mechanisms of change in psychotherapy. The following chapter details our efforts at examining different elements of the therapy process and how these may be related to treatment outcome and to dropping out of therapy.

8

RELATIONSHIPS AMONG THERAPY PROCESS, OUTCOME, AND DROPPING OUT

Clinical studies of treatment efficacy inform us about the degree to which different forms of therapy bring about desirable outcomes. As our comparative (attitude–treatment interactions; ATI) study that was described in chapter 6 demonstrated, such studies can also inform us about optimal matches between certain patient characteristics and particular forms of therapy. Such findings have important implications for selecting patients and providing therapy. If the information derived from clinical studies were limited to only the topics of treatment outcome and optimal matching, they would still serve a very useful function. However, if they were appropriately designed and included measures of therapy process, they would be capable of being even more useful because of their added potential to identify and clarify the specific sequences and mechanisms of change in psychotherapy. Identifying these processes could allow therapists to further improve the efficiency and effectiveness of their therapies. A side benefit could also be improved training.

Unfortunately, many clinical studies stop short of realizing their potential by not adequately investigating therapy process. At times, there seems to be a climate of impatience in the field that pressures investigators to clarify the next outcome question and get on with the next outcome project soon after completing the current one. To be fair, however, conducting process research can be an uncertain, time-consuming, and expensive endeavor. Nevertheless, it has usually been our experience, and we believe

---

Parts of this chapter have been taken, verbatim or adapted, from "Transference Interpretations in Short-Term Dynamic Psychotherapy," *Journal of Nervous and Mental Disease, 187*, 572–579, 1999. Copyright 1999 by Lippincott Williams & Wilkins. Adapted by permission of the publisher and author.

Parts of this chapter have been taken, verbatim or adapted, from "Prediction of Dropping Out in Time-Limited, Interpretive Individual Psychotherapy," *Psychotherapy, 36*, 114–122, 1999. Copyright 1999 by the American Psychological Association. Adapted by permission of the publisher and author.

the experience of others, that the investment of resources in process research has been worthwhile. Our understanding of the findings has been enhanced and the future direction of our research clarified.

Our comparative study of interpretive and supportive therapies provided an opportunity to examine the relationships among process variables, therapy outcome, and dropping out of treatment. The set of process variables included both general and specific measures. We devoted primary attention to the therapeutic alliance and to therapist technique. In the sections that follow, we will present our research findings and some ideas about what they may mean.

THE THERAPEUTIC ALLIANCE

A number of definitions of the alliance exist in the literature (Gaston, 1990). Although it is sometimes divided into subtypes (Bordin, 1979), in general the *alliance* refers to the collaborative working relationship between the patient and the therapist. The alliance represents a major component of nearly all psychotherapy approaches; its importance does not lie within the specifications of one theoretical orientation. Thus, we regard it as a general or common factor. It is a well-known finding that the alliance is an important and consistent predictor of favorable therapy outcome (Horvath & Luborsky, 1993; Horvath & Symonds, 1991). Less well-known is whether patients and therapists share similar views of the alliance.

Our comparative study provided an opportunity to investigate the similarity between the patients' and therapists' ratings of the alliance. We also tested the relationship between the different perceptions of the alliance and outcome. As described in the previous chapter, the *therapeutic alliance* was defined as the working relationship between the patient and therapist. It was assessed by soliciting brief ratings by the patient and by the therapist after each therapy session. The patient and therapist each rated six 7-point Likert-type items that ranged from "very little" to "very much." The items focused on whether the patient: (a) had talked about private important material, (b) felt understood by the therapist, (c) understood and worked with what the therapist said, and (d) felt that the session enhanced understanding. The remaining two items focused on (e) whether the therapist was helpful, and (f) whether the therapist and patient worked well together (Luborsky, 1984). For each party, the ratings for the six items were averaged for each session and then averaged across sessions to arrive at an overall alliance score. Thus, two scores (patient-rated alliance and therapist-rated alliance) represented the therapeutic alliance over the entire course of therapy.

Table 8-1
Comparison of Patients' and Therapists' Alliance Ratings

	Mean Patient Rating	Mean Therapist Rating	t	df	p
Interpretive therapy	5.53	5.10	3.99	70	0.00
Supportive therapy	5.73	5.26	4.21	70	0.00

Perceptions of the Alliance

Comparisons between the levels of the patients' and the therapists' ratings of alliance scores for each form of therapy (Table 8-1) were made using paired-samples *t*-tests. For each form of therapy, the patients' ratings of the alliance were significantly higher than those of the therapists' ratings. That is, the strength of the alliance was rated as more favorable from the patients' point of view. The correlations between the patients' and the therapists' alliance ratings in interpretive therapy [r (69) = .36, p = .00] and in supportive therapy [r (69) = .25, p = .04] were significant but not high. We also compared the two forms of therapy on the patients' ratings of alliance and then on the therapists' ratings of alliance. There were no significant differences between the two forms of therapy for patients or therapists.

The finding that the patients rated the alliance as stronger compared to the therapists for each form of therapy is consistent with the findings of Bachelor (1991) and those of a previous study of interpretive therapy that we conducted (Piper, Boroto, Joyce, McCallum, & Azim, 1995). One possible reason for the higher patient ratings is that the patients were in a more novel situation in therapy and had stronger emotional reactions to the patient–therapist relationship. Their reaction to the relatively unique experience of being in therapy, being understood, and receiving help with their problems may have contributed to a stronger sense of a positive working relationship with the therapist. By comparison, the therapists had many previous and current patient–therapist relationships to use as references by which to evaluate the relationship with the patient. Accordingly, the therapists may have been more reserved or more conservative in their perceptions of the strength of the therapeutic alliance.

Relationship Between Alliance and Outcome

We also used Pearson correlations to investigate the relationships between the alliance (patient-rated, therapist-rated) and outcome for each form of therapy. We used the three outcome factors that we described in chapter 6. These were general symptomatology and dysfunction, social–sexual maladjustment, and nonuse of mature defenses and family pathology. In interpretive therapy, patient-rated alliance was significantly related to favorable outcome in the area of defensive style and family functioning [$r (66) = -.24$, $p = .05$]. In supportive therapy, patient-rated alliance was related to favorable outcome in the area of general symptoms [$r (68) = -.37$, $p = .00$]. Therapist-rated alliance was not found to be significantly associated with outcome for either form of therapy.

Thus, the relationship between the alliance and outcome differed for patients and therapists. There was a direct association between patient-rated alliance and favorable outcome in both forms of therapy. Therapist-rated alliance, however, was not found to be significantly related to outcome. These findings are consistent with those of C. R. Marmar, Gaston, Gallagher, and Thompson (1989) and those of Horvath and Symonds (1991) in a meta-analysis of the relationship of alliance and outcome that indicated that patients' reports of the alliance are more predictive of outcome than are therapists' reports. Our results, however, do not support the argument made by Krupnick et al. (1994) that the predictive capacity of different rater perspectives vary with different treatment approaches. Rather, our findings indicated that the patient's perspective of the alliance was a better predictor of outcome across the two different forms of psychotherapy in our study. Different explanations for the positive effect of the alliance on outcome are provided in the literature. Explanations often refer to beneficial common factors such as being involved in a helping relationship, hearing a convincing rationale, and receiving positive feedback concerning progress, which are believed to increase morale, a sense of mastery, and positive expectations. Another explanation is that the patient's report of the alliance reflects the patient's perception of his or her progress in therapy. That is, the more the patient feels that therapy is helping, the stronger he or she perceives the working relationship with the therapist to be. In addition, it is also true that many of the outcome variables in our study were provided by patient self-report. Thus, the influence of common measurement methods also cannot be ruled out.

THERAPIST TECHNIQUE

In contrast to the therapeutic alliance, which is a general factor that is present in all therapies, therapist technique is a specific factor that refers to the strategies and behavioral interventions made by the therapist for particular forms of therapy. A specific type of intervention that has been of interest to our research team and many other investigators in the field is known as transference interpretation. Historically, transference interpretation has been one of the distinguishing features of insight-oriented dynamic psychotherapy. Although various definitions have been proposed, transference interpretation is commonly understood to refer to the therapist making reference to the patient's reaction to him or her, which is to some extent determined by the patient's previous relationships. There is consensus that the exploration of the patient's transferential reaction to the therapist is a unique opportunity for insight and psychic change. However, questions have been raised concerning the effective use of transference interpretations in brief therapy. As indicated in chapter 1, both conservative and radical positions have been taken.

One of the technical innovations of brief therapies is greater therapist activity. Limited time creates pressure on the therapist to make transference interpretations earlier and more frequently. Although advocates of transference interpretations in psychoanalysis and psychotherapy have warned therapists about their overuse (Gill, 1982; Strachey, 1934), champions of short-term psychodynamic psychotherapies have, nevertheless, recommended providing early and frequent transference interpretations (Davanloo, 1978; Mann, 1973; Sifneos, 1972). Initial efforts to provide empirical support for this position indicated a direct relationship between transference interpretations and favorable outcome (Malan, 1976b; Marziali & Sullivan, 1980). However, these studies suffered from a number of methodological shortcomings, thus weakening the validity of their findings. More recent and methodologically stronger studies have provided little additional support for a link between transference interpretations and favorable outcome (Marziali, 1984; Piper, Debbane, Bienvenu, & Garant, 1986).

In addition to examining the general effects of transference interpretations in short-term therapies, it is also important to identify relevant patient characteristics that interact with such use of technique. For example, Luborsky (1984) has suggested that patients vary in how much supportive or expressive (interpretive) technique they require. He argued that interpretive features (including transference interpretations) should receive greater emphasis for patients with "adequate ego strength and anxiety tolerance, along with the capacity for reflection about their interpersonal relationships" (p. 90). There is, in fact, previous evidence that patient characteristics interact with technical variables in affecting therapy process and outcome. In an earlier study of transference interpretations (Piper, Azim, Joyce, & McCallum, 1991), we found that the patient's quality of object relations (QOR) was associated with the patient's response to the concentration of transference interpretations. *Concentration* is defined as the proportion of a particular type of intervention relative to all types of interventions. We found evidence of an *inverse* relationship between the concentration of transference interpretations and the therapeutic alliance and an *inverse* relationship between the concentration of transference interpretations and outcome for high-QOR patients in short-term interpretive psychotherapy. Similar findings were reported by Hoglend (1993), who found that the frequency of transference interpretations was inversely related to favorable outcome and dynamic change for high-QOR patients. In contrast, Connolly and her associates (1999) found that the patient's level of current interpersonal functioning was associated with the patient's response to the concentration of transference interpretations provided early in therapy (up to session 3). They found that patients with a low level of current interpersonal functioning showed less favorable improvement in depressive symptomatology with greater concentrations of transference interpretations.

One noticeable difference in the findings of the three studies reviewed is that our study and that of Hoglend found that the negative effect of transference interpretations was more pronounced for those patients who had a history of high level of interpersonal functioning, whereas Connolly et al. found that the negative effect of transference interpretations was more pronounced for those with a low level of interpersonal functioning. This contrast in findings may be partly the result of differences in how the patient's interpersonal functioning was characterized. Piper et al. and Hoglend regarded the patient's level of interpersonal functioning as a personality characteristic and evaluated the patient's life-long history of interpersonal relationships. Connolly et al. evaluated only the patient's current level of interpersonal functioning. The contrast in findings may also be the result of differences in the overall amount of transference interpretations provided to patients in the three studies; the amount was lower in the Connolly et al. study. This explanation will be elaborated on later in this chapter. Despite their differences, each study highlighted the importance of the patient's level of interpersonal functioning when providing transference interpretations in short-term dynamic therapies.

In our comparative clinical study of interpretive and supportive forms of short-term individual psychotherapy, we repeatedly assessed the therapist's technique (including transference interpretation) from audiotapes of the sessions. Thus, the study provided a new opportunity to examine the relationship between transference interpretations, the therapeutic alliance, and treatment outcome in the context of patient QOR. We were interested in discovering whether significant associations would again be found, and whether the strength of the associations would be more pronounced among patients with high or low QOR scores.

Therapist technique was rated by external observers (bachelor's-degree-level research assistants) using the Therapist Intervention Rating System (TIRS; Piper et al., 1987). All therapist statements from each session were assigned to one of nine categories that range from simple utterances (e.g., "Mm hmm") to complex interpretations. An intervention was defined as an interpretation if it contained a reference to one or more dynamic components. A dynamic component is one part of a patient's conflict that exerts an internal force on some other part of the patient—for example, a wish, anxiety, or defense. The TIRS also assesses the type of object (person) included in the intervention. A transference interpretation is operationally defined as an interpretation that includes a reference to the therapist. Qualitatively, it addresses a dynamic conflict involving the therapist. Because of the considerable time required to provide ratings (rating time varies from two to six hours per session), the TIRS was used for only the first 40 completers of interpretive therapy. The TIRS was applied to six sessions (numbers 3, 7, 9, 11, 15, and 19) for each of the 40 cases. The mean numbers of interventions, interpretations, and transference interpretations per session were 74.2, 14.4, and 3.7, respectively. The rater reliability of the scale, based on the kappa coefficient, was .71, which indicated moderate reliability. The TIRS allowed us to calculate scores for both the frequency and concentration of transference interpretations (FTI and CTI, respectively). Consistent with previous definitions, *frequency* referred to the number of transference interpretations, and *concentration* referred to the proportion of transference interpretations relative to all types of interventions.

Transference Interpretations and the Therapeutic Alliance

The relationship between each of the two transference interpretation variables (frequency, concentration) and each of the two therapeutic alliance factors (patient-rated, therapist-rated) was examined using Pearson correlation coefficients. As Table 8-2 indicates, a significant inverse relationship was found between FTI and patient-rated alliance for the low-QOR patients. In addition, a significant direct relationship between FTI and therapist-rated

Table 8-2
Correlations Between Transference Interpretations and Therapeutic Alliance

Patient Sample	Patient-Rated Alliance		Therapist-Rated Alliance	
	r	p	r	p
FTI[a]				
All cases ($N = 40$)	−.18	.26	.21	.20
Low-QOR ($n = 30$)	−.41	.03	.11	.58
High-QOR ($n = 10$)	.43	.22	.66	.04
CTI[b]				
All cases ($N = 40$)	−.01	.96	.06	.74
Low-QOR ($n = 30$)	−.17	.37	−.07	.70
High-QOR ($n = 10$)	.52	.12	.45	.20

[a]FTI = Frequency of transference interpretation.
[b]CTI = Concentration of transference interpretation.

Table 8-3
Significant Interaction Effects for Patient-Rated and
Therapist-Rated Alliance

	Step	R^2	df	Partial F	p
Patient-rated alliance					
	QOR[a] × FTI[b]	.238	1, 36	4.83	.034
	QOR × CTI[c]	.193	1, 36	4.89	.033
Therapist-rated alliance					
	QOR × FTI	.296	1, 36	12.19	.001
	QOR × CTI	.148	1, 36	5.20	.029

[a]QOR = Quality of object relations.
[b]FTI = Frequency of transference interpretation.
[c]CTI = Concentration of transference interpretation.

alliance was found for the high-QOR patients. There were no significant relationships found when all patients were combined.

The correlations presented in Table 8-2 suggested that the association between technique and alliance differs for the two levels of QOR. That is, it appeared that QOR moderated the relationship between transference interpretation and outcome. To test for a significant moderating effect of QOR, four hierarchical regression analyses were performed. For each, the three independent variables were QOR, FTI (or CTI), and the interactive product of QOR and FTI (or CTI). The dependent variable was one of the two alliance factors. As expected, none of the main effects for QOR and FTI (or CTI) were significant. In contrast, the interactive products were significant in all four analyses, as shown in Table 8-3. This was strong evidence of the moderating effect of QOR. The interaction effects indicated that the relationship that FTI or CTI each had with patient-rated alliance or therapist-rated alliance was dependent on the patient's level of QOR. For high-QOR patients, there were sizeable direct relationships between FTI or CTI and both patient-rated and therapist-rated alliance. That is, greater frequency or concentration of transference interpretations was associated with a stronger alliance from the perspective of the patient and the therapist. For low-QOR patients, there was a significant inverse relationship between FTI and patient-rated alliance. A greater frequency of transference interpretations was associated with a weaker alliance from the patient's perspective.

Transference Interpretations and Treatment Outcome

The relationship between transference interpretations (FTI, CTI) and the three outcome factors was also examined using Pearson correlation coefficients. For all patients, a significant inverse correlation was found between FTI and favorable outcome in the area of defensive style and family functioning [r (38) = .40, p = .01]. However, the relationship was the result of a substantial significant relationship for low-QOR patients [r (28) = .43, p = .02] and a small, nonsignificant relationship for high-QOR patients [r (8) = .10, p = .78]. For low-QOR patients, greater concentration of transference interpretations was associated with less favorable outcome. A similar relationship was found between CTI and outcome in the area of defensive style and family functioning for low-QOR patients, although this relationship did not quite reach the conventional (p = .05) level of statistical significance [r (28) = .35, p = .06].

Summary of the Transference Interpretation Findings

Similar to the findings by Connolly et al., we found a negative association between the frequency of transference interpretations and both patient-rated alliance and favorable outcome among low-QOR patients but not high-QOR patients. In regard to the alliance, high-QOR patients appeared to have benefited from the dosages of transference interpretations provided. The findings join a small but growing body of evidence that indicate that there may be limitations in the use of transference interpretations with certain types of patients.

Our findings are consistent with recommendations from Luborsky (1984) and Gabbard and colleagues (1994), who suggested that transference interpretations should be reserved for patients who have the capacity to reflect on their interpersonal relationships (e.g., high-QOR patients). Conceptually, transference interpretations serve the purpose of helping patients understand their interpersonal difficulties as they are currently enacted within the therapeutic relationship. Thus, it is likely that patients with poor interpersonal functioning outside of therapy would have difficulty making use of the therapeutic relationship as a means of understanding their problems. The findings from the current study may reflect the negative effect of providing transference interpretations to these patients.

Alternatively, the findings may reflect the therapist's transference interpretation response to a weak alliance, resistance, negative transference, or some other indicator of potential poor outcome among low-QOR patients. Therapists may be especially prone to focus on the transference with patients who do not progress well through therapy. In other words, the therapist could be reacting to the patient's lack of progress with an increased examination of the transference as a way to resolve the impasse and facilitate improvement. Such increased examination could make the situation worse.

Frequency of transference interpretations was found to be directly related to therapist-rated alliance for high-QOR patients. One possible explanation for this positive association is that a strong alliance stimulated the therapist's use of transference interpretations. Clinical experience suggests that a strong alliance is essential for the effective use of transference interpretations. With high-QOR patients, it is possible that the therapist waited for a strong alliance to develop before exploring the transference. Alternatively, transference interpretations may facilitate a positive alliance. The therapist may feel that high-QOR patients may be in a better position to work with transferential issues and may actually be stimulated by such work. The therapist may thus perceive the alliance to strengthen with greater focus on the transference.

The findings from our comparative study are clearly different from those of our earlier 1991 investigation, which found an inverse relationship between transference interpretations and both alliance and favorable outcome for high-QOR patients but not low-QOR patients. Despite their different conclusions, the two studies may actually complement each other. Although in our previous study we highlighted significant inverse relationships between CTI, alliance, and favorable outcome for high-QOR patients, a number of similar but statistically nonsignificant associations were found for the low-QOR patients in that study. This was particularly true for the relationship between transference interpretations and alliance. In our earlier investigation, transference interpretations were inversely associated with alliance and, to some extent, with outcome for all patients. The relationships were more pronounced for the high-QOR patients.

It is also important to consider the activity level of the therapists in our two studies when comparing their findings. Interpretive therapists in the current comparative study were considerably more active yet focused significantly less on the transference. Approximately 6% of the therapist interventions in the comparative study were transference interpretations, whereas there were 12% in our 1991 investigation. As Connolly et al. (1999) suggested, low-QOR and high-QOR patients may respond differently to different levels of transference interpretations. In our earlier investigation, moderate to high levels of transference interpretations were provided. Low-QOR patients showed less improvement than the high-QOR patients throughout this moderate to high range. With limited variation in outcome scores for the different levels of transference interpretations for the low-QOR patients, no significant associations were found. High-QOR patients benefited from moderate levels of transference interpretations but experienced difficulty with high levels, thus producing the inverse relationship for this group of patients. In contrast, our more current study examined comparatively low to moderate levels of transference interpretations. High-QOR patients benefited from these levels of transference interpretations. Low-QOR patients benefited from treatment at low levels of transference interpretations but had less favorable outcome at moderate levels. In summary, the findings of our more current study and our earlier investigation suggest that high-QOR patients may benefit from low to moderate levels of transference interpretations and only have difficulty with high levels, and low-QOR patients may benefit only from low levels. Thus, the relationship between transference interpretations, alliance, and outcome might be a function of the patient's QOR and the level of transference interpretations provided.

DROPPING OUT OF INTERPRETATIVE THERAPY

Dropping out of psychotherapy generally refers to the situation in which a patient has made a unilateral decision to stop coming to therapy, which is contrary to initial expectations, a contract, or the recommendation of the therapist. It usually represents a negative state of affairs. The patient often experiences dissatisfaction with therapy or the therapist, which may include lack of improvement or worsening of problems. In addition, both parties may experience a sense of failure, wasted effort, and demoralization. The therapist or clinic may lose income and, if therapy is part of a study, researchers may experience a compromised design. For all of these reasons, dropping out is generally an event to be avoided.

In general, the search for pretherapy predictors of dropping out has been disappointing. In their review, Wierzbicki and Pekarik (1993) reflected the conclusions of other reviewers who point out that there are many inconsistencies and replication failures, and that statistically significant associations between predictors and dropping out are often small in magnitude. An example is the frequently cited association between low social class and dropping out. They suggest that it may be time to abandon the search for simple demographic predictors in favor of more complex variables such as mutual expectations and interactions between patient and therapist. In addition to identifying stronger associations, investigating such variables may provide greater understanding of the mechanisms that underlie dropping out of psychotherapy.

One variable that has been investigated in a number of dropout studies and that provides insight into the nature of the patient–therapist relationship is the therapeutic alliance, which generally reflects how well the two parties are working together. The literature is suggestive of a relationship between a weak therapeutic alliance and dropping out. Although this relationship is important to document, it remains descriptive and does not provide an understanding of the patient's and therapist's interactional contributions to the weak alliance and the dropout process.

Studies that have investigated the relationship between therapy session interactions of the patient and therapist and dropping out are quite rare. One example is a study by Najavits and Strupp (1994) that focused on the therapist's contribution to effective treatment, which was defined in terms of a composite of outcome variables and patient length of stay. They reported that effective therapists displayed more positive behaviors and fewer negative behaviors, and that most of the significant associations involved relationship-oriented behaviors. The Vanderbilt group (Strupp, Schacht, Henry, & Binder, 1992) also published a case study of a patient who dropped out of treatment that detailed many therapist technical errors that appeared to contribute to the premature termination.

In chapter 6 we reported the dropout rates for the two forms of therapy in our comparative study. The dropout rate for interpretive therapy (23%) was significantly higher than the rate for supportive therapy (6%). As indicated by reviews of the dropout literature, the rate for interpretive therapy in the clinical trial was not particularly high, the rate for supportive therapy was unusually low. Nevertheless, losing nearly one quarter of one's patients is undesirable, which motivated our interest in identifying predictors of dropping out. Our initial effort to identify pretherapy patient characteristics was unsuccessful. A number of demographic, personality, and initial disturbance-outcome variables, as well as interactions between certain personality variables and form of therapy, failed to differentiate all dropouts from all completers or interpretive therapy dropouts from interpretive therapy completers.

Nevertheless, we continued the search for predictor variables, specifically how the patient and therapist interacted with each other during therapy sessions. Among a set of process variables, we investigated the therapeutic alliance, patient work, patient exploration, and focus on the transference (patient–therapist relationship). Ratings of the process variables were provided by multiple sources (patient, therapist, external observer) for multiple sessions. We focused on interpretive therapy, which produced most (82%) of the dropouts in the study. The study provided the opportunity to compare the therapy process of 22 interpretive therapy dropouts with the therapy process of 22 interpretive completers—in other words, patients who completed therapy. An additional strength of the study involved the variables that were controlled in making the comparison. The dropouts and completers were matched on personality, demographic, and use of medication variables. In addition, they were matched on therapist, which controlled for such aspects as the therapist's personal characteristics (personality, psychological adjustment, demographic attributes) and professional characteristics (training, experience, theoretical orientation). We believed that control of these variables would enhance our chances of identifying patient–therapist interaction differences between dropouts and completers.

Three measures of the therapy process were used. The first was our measure of the therapeutic alliance, which was described earlier in this chapter and in the previous chapter. The second was the Vanderbilt Psychotherapy Process Scale (VPPS). This is a "general purpose instrument designed to assess both positive and negative aspects of the patient's and therapist's behavior and attitudes that are expected to facilitate or impede progress in therapy" (Suh, Strupp, & O'Malley, 1986, p. 287). Ratings are provided by external observers, who use a 5-point Likert-type scale with each item. In our study, a team of seven raters was trained to listen to audiotapes of the therapy sessions and provide ratings. The five variables and their respective intraclass correlation coefficient, ICC (2, 2), reliabilities were patient hostility (.68), patient exploration (.79), patient focus on transference (.77), therapist exploration (.66), and therapist focus on transference (.76). The third process measure used was an instrument that our research team developed that assessed the extent to which the patient engaged in dynamic work. *Dynamic work* is defined as the degree to which the patient identifies, elaborates, and causally links dynamic factors (e.g., wishes, fears, defenses) related to the patient's problem. It, too, was rated by external observers, who used a 5-point Likert-type scale. The ICC (2, 2) reliability for dynamic work was .51.

Our primary focus was on the last session attended by each dropout and the comparable numerical session of the matched completer—for example, session number 6 for each. We believed that the last session might be particularly charged and important to examine given that the dropout never returned. VPPS and work-variable ratings were obtained from the audiotape of the last session. Although therapist-rated therapeutic alliance ratings were also obtained, too few dropouts provided patient alliance ratings after their last session to allow a meaningful comparison with completers. We also focused on an early session in therapy, usually session number 3 or 4. VPPS and work ratings were obtained from the audiotape of the early session. Again, although therapist-rated therapeutic alliance ratings were also obtained, there were many missing alliance ratings for the patients. Therefore, we instead used the average of the available patient ratings for session numbers 1 through 3. Comparisons were made between dropouts and completers using independent t tests.

Last Session Quantitative Findings

For therapist-rated therapeutic alliance, dropouts were lower than completers, [$t(42) = 3.18$, $p = .003$]. For VPPS variables, dropouts were lower on patient exploration, [$t(41) = 2.33$, $p = .025$], and higher on patient focus on transference, [$t(41) = 2.23$, $p = .031$]. They were also higher on therapist focus on transference, [$t(41) = 1.99$, $p = .054$]. There were no significant differences for patient hostility and therapist exploration. Similarly, there was no significant difference for dynamic work.

Last Session Qualitative Findings

To achieve a better clinical understanding of the patient–therapist interactions during the last session, we listened to the audiotapes of each of the last sessions of the dropouts. We were particularly interested in the sessions of those patients who had the highest ratings for patient and therapist focus on transference. In the present study, these process variables significantly differentiated dropouts from completers; and in our previous study of interpretive therapy, a high focus on transference was associated with difficulties in the patient–therapist relationship (Piper, Azim, Joyce, & McCallum, 1991). For the dropouts in this study who had the highest focus on transference, the pattern that we observed over the course of the last session was consistent and striking. The pattern is represented by a sequence of nine features. For the seven dropouts with the highest transference focus (top third), the features were nearly unanimously present. For the middle third, the features were present for many of the patients, and for the bottom third, only some of the features were present for a few of the patients. The nine features follow.

1. The patient made his or her thoughts about dropping out clear, usually early in the session.
2. The patient expressed frustration about the therapy sessions. This often involved expectations that were not met and the therapist's repeated focus on painful feelings.
3. The therapist quickly addressed the difficulty by focusing on the patient–therapist relationship and the transference. Links were made to other relationships.
4. The patient resisted the focus on transference and engaged in little dynamic exploration (work). Resistance was often active—for example, verbal disagreement—and sometimes passive—for example, silence.
5. The therapist persisted with transference interpretations.
6. The patient and therapist argued with each other. They seemed to be engaged in a power struggle. At times the therapist was drawn into being sharp, blunt, sarcastic, insistent, impatient, or condescending.
7. Although most of the interpretations were plausible, the patient responded to the persistence of the therapist with continued resistance.
8. The session ended with encouragement by the therapist to continue with therapy and a seemingly forced agreement by the patient to do so.
9. The patient never returned.

Early Sessions Quantitative Findings

For patient-rated therapeutic alliance, dropouts were lower than completers, $[t\ (26) = 2.25, p = .003]$. Similarly, for dynamic work, dropouts had lower scores than completers, $[t\ (41) = 2.05, p = .047]$. There were no significant differences for therapist-rated therapeutic alliance and the VPPS variables.

Summary of Findings

This investigation provided additional information about predictors of dropping out in time-limited, interpretive individual therapy. Following our initial report of a significantly higher dropout rate for interpretive-therapy patients relative to supportive-therapy patients in our comparative clinical study, we compared the interpretive dropouts with a matched group of interpretive therapy completers on additional pretherapy variables and on process variables. We found no significant differences on pretherapy predictors, which is similar to the findings of many previous investigators. However, when we turned to process variables that reflected patient–therapist interactions, a number of significant differences emerged.

A weaker therapeutic alliance was reported by patients early in therapy and by therapists at the last session of therapy for the dropouts. These findings are consistent with most previous studies that have examined the therapeutic alliance of dropouts and completers. We also found evidence indicating that dropouts engaged in less dynamic work early in therapy. Taken together, these findings suggest that it may be possible to identify potential dropouts early in therapy. This could be achieved through indirect observations or direct inquiries by the therapist during therapy sessions, or through written feedback (brief rating forms) provided by the patient immediately following therapy sessions. This could allow the therapist time to address and remedy the problems before they result in dropping out. Suggested interventions such as clarifying the patient's and the therapist's roles in interpretive therapy, facilitating positive transference, and providing support early in therapy have been made in the literature. Although such interventions are recommended and may strengthen a weak alliance and facilitate work, they, of course, do not always do so. Unfortunately, the early difficulties may indicate that the patient lacks the capacity to engage in interpretive therapy, which, despite the therapist's best efforts, may persist and eventually lead to dropping out.

At the last session, we found that dropouts engaged less in exploration of their problems. They also focused more on transference, as did their therapists. Clinical observations of the last session revealed a consistent pattern for many of the dropouts, in particular those with the greatest focus on transference. The patient–therapist pattern that was observed is consistent with findings from our previous controlled study of interpretive therapy and our comparative (ATI) study in which higher use of transference interpretations were found to be associated with a weaker alliance and less favorable outcome. Examination of the therapy process in the earlier study also revealed that experienced therapists at times got caught up in a negative cycle involving patient resistance and transference interpretation. This tendency may be heightened in a situation in which the therapist is faced with the threat of premature termination. Once reasonable efforts have been made to address evident problems through the use of transference interpretation or other types of noninterpretive interventions and those efforts have not been successful, the therapist may be best advised to refrain from making additional transference interpretations. It may be preferable to allow the patient to save face and end therapy under more amicable conditions.

It is worth noting that patients and therapists who are engaged in therapies of very different theoretical and technical orientations sometimes get caught up in similar types of negative cycles. Castonguay, Goldfried, Wiser, Raue, and Hayes (1996) reported a similar process among a number of depressed patients who were receiving cognitive therapy. Qualitative analysis revealed that therapists sometimes increased their adherence to cognitive rationales and techniques to correct problems in the therapeutic alliance. Unfortunately, the increased focus seemed to weaken the alliance and interfere with therapeutic change.

Limitations in our knowledge in the current study should prevent us from unequivocally attributing primary responsibility for the dropout phenomenon to the therapists. We do not know whether a different technical or stylistic approach could have prevented the dropping out or whether, given the particular patients, dropping out was inevitable. We also do not know whether there were sessions in which the completers also threatened to dropout but were dealt with differently and successfully. What we do know is that the approach taken by the therapists in the case of the dropouts was not successful in resolving the problem despite the fact that it met criteria for technical adherence regarding transference interpretation, which is a hallmark of insight-oriented dynamic therapy.

In addition to suggesting potential technical pitfalls in providing interpretive therapy, our study also endorses the investigation of process variables that focus on patient–therapist interactions. A small but conceptually meaningful number of interactional, therapy-process variables differentiated the two groups. In contrast, of the many pretherapy variables examined, none significantly differentiated dropouts from completers. Although it will continue to be important to discover significant pretherapy predictors of dropping out, our study indicates that researchers should not limit themselves to studying such variables.

CONCLUSION

Identifying events or behaviors that have an impact on the overall outcome of treatment is obviously important. The findings reviewed in this chapter provide evidence for the importance of two particular process factors in predicting treatment outcome. The patient's view of the working relationship with the therapist—the therapeutic alliance—was found to be directly related to favorable outcome for both forms of therapy involved in the comparative study. The consistency of this finding across numerous studies of various forms of treatment attests to the importance of developing a positive relationship with the patient. Most therapists would agree that if a poor relationship develops between therapist and patient, the most likely outcome is premature termination from therapy or very little, if any, positive change.

We also found that the therapist's use of transference interpretation has a significant impact on the outcome of treatment. The findings underscored the potentially negative effects of transference interpretations for low-QOR patients. The findings also illustrated that low to moderate levels of transference interpretations, provided in a context of greater noninterpretive therapist activity, may be helpful to high-QOR patients. Thus, therapists should not only consider the patient's level of interpersonal maturity, but also the amount of transference interpretations being provided to the patient.

The findings concerning the importance of the alliance and technique for facilitating positive treatment outcome suggests that these variables may also be important in preventing therapy dropouts. Indeed, in our investigation of the therapeutic processes of the interpretive therapy dropouts, we found that those patients who terminated therapy prematurely perceived their relationship with their therapists as considerably less positive than did patients who completed therapy. In addition, we identified a pattern of a persistent, but ineffective, use of transference interpretations in the last session for those patients who dropped out.

Taken together, the findings presented in this chapter suggest that establishing and maintaining a positive working relationship with the patient early on is likely to help keep patients in therapy and facilitate positive change. We recommend actively monitoring the patient's impression of the therapeutic alliance. With regard to technique, when transference interpretations are used, they should be used judiciously, with due consideration of the patient's capacity to tolerate such interventions. As well, focusing on the transference appears to be an ineffective strategy for resolving impasses in therapy and engaging the patient when the patient is threatening to drop out.

Despite the progress made by these and previous findings, there remains a task for clinicians and researchers to identify other significant predictors of who will remain in therapy and how to maximize benefit for those who do. The field will only benefit from future discoveries that link the processes of therapy to the outcome of therapy. In the next chapter, we further explore the findings reported in this chapter by focusing on two case illustrations, an interpretive therapy dropout and an interpretive therapy completer.

III

CASE STUDIES: MATCHING PATIENTS AND THERAPIES

9

CLINICAL ILLUSTRATIONS OF DROPPING OUT FROM INTERPRETIVE PSYCHOTHERAPY: THE IMPORTANCE OF FLEXIBILITY

As presented in chapter 6, the two therapy approaches (interpretive, supportive) had a differential effect on dropping out. Of the 27 patients studied who dropped out of treatment, 22 were from interpretive therapy and only 5 were from supportive therapy. When the 22 interpretive dropouts were compared with a sample of 22 matched completers, the two groups did not differ on pretherapy variables such as demographics, diagnoses, or initial disturbances. Similarly, our two patient predictor variables, psychological mindedness (PM) and quality of object relations (QOR), did not differentiate dropouts from completers. Therefore, our patient predictor variables were not sufficient to ensure a good match with the appropriate form of therapy. In contrast, several of the therapy-process variables, including the therapeutic alliance, work, patient exploration, and focus on transference, significantly differentiated the interpretive dropouts from completers. Specifically, for dropouts there was a weaker alliance, less work, less exploration, and greater focus on transference. The differential process between dropouts and completers underscores the importance of a flexible therapeutic approach whereby the interpretive form of therapy is adapted to the particular needs of the patient through the integration of supportive features.

In this chapter we attempt to clinically illustrate these empirical findings. We present the case of Ian, who dropped out of interpretive therapy after the sixth session. We also present the case of Cameron, who completed interpretive therapy. The two patients were very (or exactly) similar in terms of gender, age, level of PM, and QOR. Each therapy was conducted by a male therapist, and each therapy featured difficulties with a weakened alliance. By examining differences between the therapists' approaches to the alliance in these cases, we hope to elucidate how Cameron's therapist was able to neutralize the impending power struggle, strengthen the weakened alliance, and retain the patient in therapy.

THE CASE OF IAN: A DROPOUT FROM INTERPRETIVE THERAPY

Ian, a 53-year-old man, was referred to the Walk-in Clinic by his general practitioner for complaints of "work stress." Over the past five years, Ian had steadily lost interest in his job as an instructor at a local college. He found the work less challenging and rewarding. Simultaneously, because of the institution's financial constraints, he worked longer hours and had bigger classes. For the previous six months, he felt chronically stressed and unmotivated, with complaints of impaired concentration and an inability to focus. He had also missed quite a few days from work. His common-law wife of eight years, who had accompanied him to intake, added that Ian had become increasingly irritable.

During the intake assessment, Ian revealed he was also upset over an incident that had recently occurred in the household. Two of his four children from his first marriage had been living with him for the past year. Two months before the initial assessment, Ian awoke to an argument between his two teenaged daughters. Furious that his sleep was interrupted, he stormed into their bedroom, joining and escalating the argument. The conflict culminated in Ian slapping both girls across the face. His daughters returned to their mother's home the next day. Ian felt distraught and guilty about the entire incident.

Ian was also upset by a letter he had received just before the incident with his daughters. His father, who lived in Europe, had been diagnosed with cancer five years previously. In the letter Ian received, his father was bidding him goodbye. Ian was ambivalent about returning to Europe to see his father before he died. When Ian had emigrated 30 years ago he had been on poor terms with his father. There had been little contact between them over the years. Ian also had guilty ruminations about this estranged relationship. To understand the significance of these events, the intake therapist explored the history of his family and romantic relationships.

Relationship History

Ian was born into a large family with seven brothers and two sisters. Both his parents were teachers. He described his father as a cold, detached man, who never encouraged Ian or showed any interest in his activities. Although distant from his father, Ian was his mother's favorite. Ian believed his father verbally abused his mother. Although his mother did not protest her husband's tirades, Ian often intervened to protect her. Being mother's favorite, Ian was somewhat ostracized by his siblings and did not consider himself close to any of them. At the age of 23, he left to seek his fortune in Canada. His mother died the following year.

Ian reported three, long-term romantic relationships. At the age of 18, he had his first romantic relationship with a 28-year-old woman. It was primarily a physical relationship. Ian was tortured by guilt regarding this relationship because he had apparently deceived her about the depth of his love and devotion. On arriving in Canada five years later, he met a woman whom he quickly married. He soon wondered if he had married too hastily to counter the loneliness of being a new immigrant. He began to doubt that he loved her and soon felt trapped in the marriage. They tried to save the marriage by having four children. The relationship continued to be conflictual and unhappy. After 15 years of marriage, Ian had an affair and moved out for 6 months. He could not commit to the new woman and returned to his marriage. Six years later, he left the marriage permanently. The following year, Ian moved in with his current common-law wife, the woman he had been dating while still with his wife. He reported being very happy in this eight-year relationship. However, he continued to feel guilty for not emotionally supporting his wife during their 21-year marriage. He also felt guilty for not being closer to his children.

Formulation and Treatment Plan

Ian met the criteria for major depression. He was prescribed the antidepressant Serzone (Nefazadone). However, Ian became alarmed when he could not find the medication listed in his *Compendium of Pharmaceuticals and Specialties*. Hence, he had not begun the medication when he returned for his follow-up appointment one week after intake. After being reassured and informed again about the antidepressant, Ian agreed to take it. Two weeks later, he stopped the medication, stating that he felt better now that the school term was over.

The intake therapist believed that although Ian's problems manifested themselves at work, the underlying issues were associated with loss. The therapist hypothesized that Ian was grieving the loss of his father, whose diagnosis five years before coincided with the beginning of Ian's disinterest in work. The letter of goodbye from his father had exacerbated Ian's chronic sense of loss that dated back (at least) to his departure from Europe some 30 years before. The letter had also coincided with and perhaps even triggered Ian's loss of temper with his daughters, precipitating their return to their mother's house. Their departure was another loss that re-activated Ian's grief and guilt about the break-up of the family nine years before, when he separated from his wife. To address these issues of loss and survivor guilt, Ian agreed to a referral to the study. Ian was very cooperative with the research personnel, promptly attending his appointments and returning his questionnaires. He scored high (8) on the PM assessment procedure and in the midrange (4.7) on the QOR scale. (See chapter 5 to review these measures.) Ian was randomly assigned to a male therapist.

Course of Interpretive Therapy

The therapy began and continued as a battle of wills, interspersed with some productive work. The therapist began the first session by asking Ian to tell him about himself. Ian complained about his time was being wasted by repeating the same information to the therapist that he had told the research team. The therapist explained the different roles served by himself and the research team. Ian was not mollified. He plaintively stated his wish that the procedures were more coordinated so as not to waste his time. The following is a transcript of a segment of that first session.

Therapist: Help me understand more of that feeling, that sense that you have that people waste your time. Maybe that when you have a need it doesn't get met. Help me understand 'cause that's a good example of what therapy is all about; what we'll be working on together.

Ian: No, don't read too much into that. I'm just wondering why some of the stuff isn't coordinated.

Therapist: Well, here's a good chance to talk about our roles here. 'Cause you said don't read too much into it but that's part of how therapy works. I take you seriously, take your feelings seriously. And they're important, they mean something. So my job is to read things into your feelings. That's what you want me to do. That's what I'm trained to do. Your job is to talk about your feelings. My job is to understand them. We work together.

Ian: See, I've met all kinds of people, answered a bunch of questions but I haven't got anything back, y'know. So, I'm feeling like unless there's a big climax soon, I haven't gotten anything out of it except for the sessions I had with Dr. S (the QOR assessor).

Therapist: So you want something and you haven't gotten it. So, frustrating all around.

Ian: No chance for me to get feedback.

Therapist: Maybe what's frustrating is that when you have needs, others don't seem that interested in meeting your needs, only their needs, like getting their research questions answered and you're left not feeling helped or taken care of.

Ian: Well, I wouldn't put it that way. I don't think I need a lot of help in that respect. I just expected some feedback.

Therapist:	This need for immediate feedback, my feeling is that if we pursue it, it may lead us to other areas of your life, in the past, that have felt similarly frustrating. I mean, can you tell me about yourself? Have people tended to meet your needs or have you been left on your own?
Ian:	I didn't need much as a child. But see, I've been through all this with Dr. S. 'Cause I'm just reluctant, I'm just repeating myself over and over again.
Therapist:	Well, let's hear about your reluctance. What are you afraid is going to happen here?
Ian:	Just a waste of time, just a ritual, a routine. And I have to be a player in that ritual.
Therapist:	That's what you hate; having to be a player in someone else's agenda and your needs being left out. Is this a new feeling or is this a frustration that's been part of your life?
Ian:	Just in this context really.
Therapist:	This is the only time it's ever come up in your whole life?!
Ian:	Yes, generally, I'm in control of what I do.
Therapist:	See, now we're getting down to it. This is a place where you don't feel in control. You don't know me, you feel I have some kind of agenda and you want to know what it is, otherwise you're feeling quite reluctant to carry on.
Ian:	I'm an instructor, have been for 25 years. I'm in control of my agenda, what I do in class and so on and things happen very logically to me, while in this context I'm repeating myself and it doesn't make sense to me.
Therapist:	Let's stick to the feeling part, of not feeling in control.
Ian:	Rather than feeling not in control, I fail to see the reason for these things that have happened.
Therapist:	Part of the way you work at dealing with not being in control is to understand.
Ian:	Right!
Therapist:	Here's a situation where you don't understand and you want me to explain the logic of it so you'll feel ok, feel back in control.
Ian:	Well, when you said "can you tell me about yourself?", unless you have specific questions I have said enough about myself on tape that you—I don't mean to criticize you but—if you had bothered to listen to the tapes that Dr. S. made, y'know.
Therapist:	Here we get down to it, the feelings, more clearly. You say you don't mean to criticize me but you're feeling upset that I haven't done my homework from your point of view.
Ian:	Exactly!

Therapist: So, I should have got myself up to speed, not wasted your time, you're more crushed.
Ian: Exactly!
Therapist: This is what our work together will be about. About your feelings, not about me giving you answers. This is a great example of what your feelings are and that's fair game to talk about in psychotherapy. So tell me about your family and I'll be listening with an ear to understanding what your frustration is all about.
Ian: So, basically, we're starting fresh again? You know nothing about me?
Therapist: Right.
Ian: So, what I've answered before won't be used here?
Therapist: I have nothing to do with the research assessments. I do the therapy and your feelings about the research are part of therapy.
Ian: The least I expect of you is to listen to those tapes of Dr. S, two hours of tapes, very painful things on those tapes.
Therapist: I understand what you're saying.

At this point, Ian relented and began to matter-of-factly report his family history. It appeared that the therapist had won the battle of wills for the time being. However, Ian often returned to his complaint that he was wasting his time. The therapist seemed to be feeling pressured to deliver an interpretive approach from the first session onward. Although the therapist's interventions appear to have been quite valid, they were also somewhat premature for this patient, especially at this stage of therapy. In addition, the therapist's annoyance was betrayed in his somewhat sarcastic question: "This is the only time it's [the patient's frustration] ever come up in your whole life?!" Ian's agenda was to express his frustration with the research protocol. The research assessments *are* somewhat frustrating for patients. There are numerous questionnaires to complete in addition to interviews by three research personnel. Some of the assessments require the patient to repeat information disclosed to the intake therapist. Ian stated that only the QOR interview with Dr. S. was helpful, albeit painful. It is possible that Ian would have preferred to continue therapy with Dr. S. Given the nature of the QOR assessment, the assessors are often experienced by patients as kind and empathic clinicians. In contrast, the interpretive therapists are often experienced as somewhat cold and aloof. It is interesting to speculate whether the power struggle of the first session could have been curtailed if the therapist had simply agreed that the research protocol was frustrating and repetitive and that perhaps Ian regretted the loss of Dr. S. Not surprisingly, out of a possible score of 7, the alliance for this session was rated only 1.8 by Ian and 2.7 by the therapist.

Nevertheless, Ian returned the following week. His alliance scores increased to the midrange of the scale, where they remained for sessions 3 and 4. The theme of sessions 2 through 4 concerned the anger he felt toward his father and his grief over his impending death. Inevitably, his anger was followed by heart-wrenching guilt. At session 5, the therapist attempted to interpret how Ian's anger at his father was reenacted in the transference. Specifically, Ian perceived the therapist as having high expectations like his father, against whom Ian felt compelled to rebel. Ian was unable to work with these interpretations. He also failed to complete the alliance ratings after the session. Conversely, the therapist rated the alliance a healthy 4.8. About an hour after the session, Ian telephoned the project coordinator requesting a change of therapist. The coordinator suggested that Ian discuss this with his therapist at the next session, and also informed the therapist of the request. The following section presents the beginning segment from Ian's sixth and final session. Atypically, the therapist was the first to speak.

Therapist: So, you were upset after last week.
Ian: Uh, huh, how do you know?
Therapist: Well, they spoke to me.
Ian: Oh, did they?
Therapist: Yeah, you wanted to fire me.
Ian: Oh, I don't want to fire you. No, I can't fire you. It's that I thought it was a waste of time totally, y'know.
Therapist: You were upset with me 'though.
Ian: Yeah, for a couple of reasons. I thought we had a good relationship and we were on our way and it obviously doesn't seem that way.
Therapist: Well, what was going on? What made you think that? 'Cause [the coordinator] was saying to me that you were asking to be switched to a new therapist.
Ian: Yes, if I was going to continue—
Therapist: [interrupting] So you *were* wanting to fire me! I just want to get that straight. You were upset enough to want to fire me.
Ian: I wouldn't use that word. I wanted to fire myself from you. Because I thought, y'know, it was really, I have to trust you and respect you so I'll be able to peel away all the emotional veneer and all the insulation that I have. And I can't do that unless I trust you.
Therapist: What's making it hard to trust me?
Ian: Well, I don't know, a couple of things you said. For one thing, you told me that I wasn't supposed to bring food and drink in and I had no idea I wasn't supposed to and then on top of that you told me that it had to do with my father, as a defiance to

	the rules. You implied that, correct me if I'm wrong, you said I was doing that because I wanted to defy the rules or something. It couldn't be further from the truth. You know, I had no idea that that was a rule. So I checked with [the coordinator] on that, I said is there a rule about not bringing in food or drink. First thing I did when I went home is I checked the instructions. I couldn't find anything like that so I telephoned [the coordinator] and asked if I had all the instructions, 'cause I don't like losing anything. And she said I had everything. So I wondered why you said that. If it's a personal choice, you should have told me that you don't like people bringing in food and drink to the session. So, that started a whole cycle going in my head. Why did you say that?
Therapist:	You were mad at me, let's put it straight.
Ian:	No! Not mad at you.
Therapist:	No?!
Ian:	No! I'm really puzzled, y'know.
Therapist:	Let's stick to the feelings 'cause this is what we need to keep working on. Wanting to fire yourself from me or fire me is about being angry.
Ian:	Not so much angry as not wanting to waste my time.
Therapist:	It's about being angry 'though, with me, we need to be clear.
Ian:	I admit, angry at first, maybe but more disappointed that—
Therapist:	It's about feelings, let's say that. Let's be clear too that I was saying last week that the fear you have is that I would be like your father.
Ian:	No, no, not at all! If I have to work with you, you're a human being first—but I don't see that, maybe that's one of your techniques, you don't want to show me your human side but I can't operate like that. I need to know you're a human being first.
Therapist:	What are you feeling right now?
Ian:	Oh, so you come back to that (sigh).

The session continued in much the same vein. Finally, Ian announced he wanted to terminate therapy. The therapist continued to insist that Ian was angry with him and that this was a reenactment of his relationship with his father. Conversely, Ian talked about not trusting the therapist. Eventually, he became quite subdued, no longer initiating any disclosures. Ian's final statement was: "I'll do some hard thinking about it." He did not return.

The experience with Ian is representative of the dropouts from interpretive therapy. As presented in chapter 8, the dropouts manifested a weaker alliance, less work, less exploration, and greater focus on transference than the completers. Ian's final session is also representative of the final session of the dropouts. There was a nonproductive pattern characterized by resistance and transference interpretation. This final session seems to depict an overzealous focus on the patient's anger as being a reenactment of his relationship with father. As a matter of interest, there were no "instructions" regarding eating or drinking during the session. Those guidelines were for a previous research project. Therefore, the interpretation appears to have been erroneous: Ian was not necessarily defying his father's rules in the transference by bringing coffee into the session. It is likely that Ian "resisted" the interpretation because it was inaccurate. Nevertheless, one could conclude that there was a reenactment of Ian's relationship with his father in that the therapist did not seem able to respond to Ian's yearning for closeness with him, and Ian's disappointment that his therapist "did not show his human side." Given Ian's torment with his feelings of guilt whenever he felt anger toward his father, it is perhaps not surprising that he resisted owning his anger toward the therapist. Clearly, Ian was more in touch with his sadness and disappointment regarding his father than his anger. It was those former feelings that may have been reenacted in the transference. Perhaps if the therapist had felt freer to incorporate more supportive aspects with his interpretive technique, Ian would have felt satisfied that the therapist was human after all and continued in therapy.

The next section presents Cameron, a case that was very similar to Ian's. Unlike Ian's therapist, however, Cameron's therapist did incorporate more supportive aspects into his interpretive technique when the alliance showed signs of weakness.

THE CASE OF CAMERON: STRENGTHENING A WEAKENED ALLIANCE

Cameron, a 33-year-old man, presented at the Walk-In Clinic at the suggestion of a friend to address feeling "not happy." He stated that he had felt unhappy for 10 years. His dysphoria interfered with his motivation for playing sports or socializing. He identified no precipitant or concomitant to his dysphoria. Professionally, he reported doing well in his role as an engineer. He noted a current increase in demands at work, which required him to work on weekends. He later acknowledged, however, that he may be working more than required to avoid feelings of loneliness. In addition to feeling unhappy and lonely, Cameron acknowledged that he also felt anxious. To understand the etiology of Cameron's dysphoria, the intake therapist explored the history of his family and romantic relationships.

Relationship History

Cameron was the third of four boys born to a farming family on the Canadian prairies. Hard work was a priority for the entire family. He described his mother as domineering and restrictive. His father was quiet. He experienced both as emotionally depriving. Feeling unloved and neglected, Cameron ultimately withdrew becoming a lonely and solitary adolescent.

Cameron had two previous long-term romantic relationships with women he described as "serious types." He initially saw both women as damsels in distress, in need of rescuing. He described a pattern of initial optimism whereby he felt special, followed by eventual disillusionment when they became "domineering." Both women eventually broke off the relationships. Cameron used sex to fill the emptiness of being alone and to displace the anger at these women who left him. In his current common-law relationship, the initial exultation had given way to pessimism. Cameron was aloof and moody. His partner responded with advice, against which Cameron rebelled. At the time of his presentation, Cameron's common-law wife was threatening to leave him.

Formulation and Treatment Plan

Cameron met the criteria for a "double depression"—major depression juxtaposed on a chronic dysthymia. Obsessive–compulsive and dependent traits were noted on Axis II, but no personality disorder was diagnosed. He was prescribed Paxil (Paroxetine) and Rivotril (Clonazepam). Complaining of side-effects, Cameron stopped taking the medications by his follow-up appointment one week after intake. On query he acknowledged that he was uncomfortable with the idea of taking medications, fearing that he would become dependent.

Cameron's history suggested that he also feared becoming dependent on women. This fear seemed to block what Cameron desired most: intimacy. He experienced women as either casual lovers whom he exploited or as "serious types" who were domineering like his mother. In addition to feeling controlled by women, he also displayed a need to control them. This need seemed to have evolved in childhood as a way to defend himself against his aggressively intrusive mother. To address these conflicts concerning control, intimacy, and dependency, Cameron was referred to the study. His scores on the personality variables were very similar to those of Ian (described earlier). Cameron scored high (8) on the PM assessment procedure and in the midrange (4.2) on the QOR scale. Cameron was randomly assigned to a male therapist for interpretive therapy.

Course of Interpretive Therapy

Perhaps consistent with Cameron's fear of dependency, his therapy had an inauspicious beginning: He arrived 10 minutes late. In addition, he rated the alliance for that first session at a weak 2.2 (out of a possible 7). Conversely, the therapist rated the alliance a strong 5.5 and charted the session as a typical first session of history taking. In fact, the session was exceedingly unremarkable. Yet we know that such weak early alliance ratings by patients often portend dropping out.

First Session

The therapist did not initially comment on Cameron's tardiness. Instead, he began the session with, "I'm aware you've told your story before and that, but I think just so we can get a better understanding, maybe you can let me know what brought you in here for help at the beginning." Cameron proceeded to recount the history of his presenting complaint. He freely disclosed areas of disappointment in his past and present life. The therapist empathically reflected Cameron's feelings and clarified details of his story. In terms of transference, the therapist prepared the patient by pointing out that Cameron's tendency to "hold back" in all areas of his life might be replayed in the therapy. He added encouragingly that if indeed this became the case, it would be a very important issue to explore.

With 10 minutes remaining in the shortened session, the therapist addressed Cameron's lateness.

Therapist: So, I noticed you cut yourself shaving this morning.
Cameron: Yeah. Oh, I still have salve on there!
Therapist: Is that like you?
Cameron: That's from going too fast.
Therapist: What was that about?
Cameron: I was late. I just lay in bed; didn't want to get up.
Therapist: So, was there a bit of you reluctant about coming here?
Cameron: No! Well, I was getting scared in the last couple of days.
Therapist: What was that about?
Cameron: It wasn't facing the fact I have problems. It's the fact, more, that we're going to start finding things out.
Therapist: So if you're kinda late, you get five or ten minutes less, maybe you won't find out as much?
Cameron: No, I wanted to be here for eight o'clock. I should have got up with the alarm. Then I wouldn't have cut myself or been late.
Therapist: There's lots of ways of cutting your own throat.

Cameron returned to an earlier theme about his tendency to sabotage himself. The therapist ended the session on time.

Cameron: Time's up?
Therapist: Yes, the session is 50 minutes; it's now ten to. I'll see you next week. Just come down to my waiting room; no need to check in at the front desk. I'll come and get you.

Clearly there were significant differences between Cameron's and Ian's approach to therapy. Although both appeared to be ambivalent, Cameron was able to openly disclose and work with some of his central conflicts throughout the first session. However, we believe that differences between the two therapists may have facilitated Cameron's ability to work despite his obvious discomfort with therapy. Cameron's therapist began by acknowledging that the first session would be repetitive for Cameron. He implied that he was not aware of Cameron's history and that it would be helpful to hear it from him. This statement of the obvious may have been enough to validate Cameron's feelings such that they did not impede his disclosures.

Despite Cameron's tardiness, his therapist restrained himself from prematurely focusing on its transferential implications. Instead, he engaged Cameron in therapy. Finally, with 10 minutes remaining in the session, the therapist explored whether the shaving cut was a significant reflection of Cameron's frame of mind that morning. He did not assume that the cut and the lateness were necessarily indicative of Cameron's anxiety about therapy. Rather, he explored their possible significance for his first therapy session. Cameron seemed surprised that the session ended after 40 minutes. The therapist clarified that the session ended at "10 to" regardless of when Cameron arrived. There was no punitive tone in his explanation. Indeed, the therapist was quite caring in explaining to Cameron where to come the following week, closing the session with the reassuring, almost fatherly statement, "I'll come and get you."

Cameron returned for his second session and rated the alliance a neutral 4. At session 3, he rated the alliance a very strong 6.7. Both patient-rated and therapist-rated alliance scores remained strong with the pair working steadily. Session 13 was a particularly intense working session. After session 14, Cameron's alliance rating plunged to 3.5. Perhaps frightened by the intimacy or depth of the previous session, Cameron was highly resistant to work. He refused to consider his own contribution to problems or to acknowledge his defensiveness in the session. The therapist was confrontational in response to Cameron's resistance. His tactic only seemed to entrench Cameron's stance. At times, the interaction resembled a power struggle. One could sense the therapist's struggle to remain tolerant and patient. Cameron returned for session 15, which is summarized below.

Cameron:	Didn't feel like coming here again. I'm very tired and making excuses not to come here, like it's inconvenient. Sometimes I don't feel like I have a lot to say. And you keep saying that I'm the only one I hurt by not opening up. Like Chantal [his common-law wife] asked me today, "Do you cry with [the therapist]?" Not very often. I said, "I cry more with you than I do with him." I told her, "you're the only therapy I need."
Therapist:	What did you mean by that?
Cameron:	Well, I just need some emotional support. Just be there. That's all I need to boost my confidence, make me feel okay, no anxiety. I look forward to seeing her.
Therapist:	Maybe that in itself is you opening up to her.
Cameron:	I think so. [He begins describing a situation at work with which he is dissatisfied.]

As this segment depicts, Cameron began session 15 in the typical way that dropouts began their final session. He described his ambivalence about continuing therapy. He suggested that Chantal had replaced his therapist's role. It is possible that the intimacy he felt with his therapist frightened him and that he needed to reassure himself of the intimacy he felt with Chantal, a more sexually appropriate confidante. Although consciously speaking about Chantal, Cameron seemed to be hinting at needing some "emotional support" from his therapist. Rather than interpreting the transferential wish for support or the fear of intimacy, Cameron's therapist fulfilled the wish by praising Cameron's progress: "Maybe that in itself is you opening up to her."

Cameron changed the topic and began discussing in a very rational and superficial manner various concerns he was facing at work. He was demonstrating his ambivalence about delving into anything deeply. Finally, Cameron gave the therapist an opening.

Cameron:	I'm just not a part of the group.
Therapist:	How much did you feel a part of your family?
Cameron:	I said, this is the way it is. I wanted my family to be different. It wasn't. So I guess I felt empty. I missed something that I never had. So then, I really didn't miss it. It was maybe something that I wanted but how can you miss something that you never had?
Therapist:	You certainly can.
Cameron:	Well, I don't know if you can. It's like driving a Corvette. Until you drive it, you can't miss it.
Therapist:	So what is it you feel you didn't get?
Cameron:	Well, the love. But I accept it. They were who they were and you have to accept that and go on and not dwell on the fact

	you may have wanted something that you think about now but you weren't aware of then. I was being childish wanting that now that I'm an adult and know what I didn't get. But as a child I never saw all this. So, I didn't know any better. So there was not a problem; nothing to worry about.
Therapist:	But you're saying it was something you craved after.
Cameron:	I craved it because I was alone. But now I've got Chantal.
Therapist:	But this is something you didn't have growing up.
Cameron:	(Heatedly) Look! I wanted it so I blamed my parents. It was childish. Get over it. Don't complain. So that's it!
Therapist:	You look like you've got tears in your eyes.
Cameron:	No. It's very hard for me to cry.
Therapist:	(Gently) But do you have tears in your eyes?
Cameron:	No! Well, I'm emotional. Yes.
Therapist:	So, what's the emotion?
Cameron:	Well, let's move on. I mean, 'cause I'm sad that it's over. I don't have to think about this. I don't have to analyze it. I just have to go with it.
Therapist:	Part of going with it is allowing yourself to feel that sadness.
Cameron:	Yeah, to feel but not to look at it all the time!
Therapist:	Can you say what the sadness is about just now?
Cameron:	Yeah, it's over. I'm happy. (Silence)
Cameron:	Now I feel it's off my shoulders.
Therapist:	Something's lifted off your shoulders?
Cameron:	I've accomplished a lot but we're not finished.
Therapist:	Yet you seem to be talking about finishing.
Cameron:	Yeah, I told Chantal this morning that I didn't want to come. . . . I have nothing more to say. You can't beat a dead horse. Well, you can but you won't get a response. . . . Just to go over the same things over and over again. It's repetitive.
Therapist:	But letting your tears come out is new for you.
Cameron:	Doesn't happen often that I cry. . . . But life is too short to dwell on this. Don't analyze the future. Worrying about money. That's my parents, always penny-pinching. Can't buy myself anything.
Therapist:	You said you weren't going to analyze this. Now you're busy analyzing.
Cameron:	Well, it bugs me that I can't just go out and buy myself things. . . .

This second segment illustrates the therapist's fine balancing act between nurturing a weakened alliance while not capitulating to Cameron's rationalizations and jejune arguments. Reviewing the session, one gets the sense that Cameron was trying to bait his therapist into an argument. The therapist avoided the power struggle. He did not debate whether you can miss something you never had. In contrast to Ian's therapist, Cameron's therapist did not attempt to convince Cameron to "analyze the future." Rather, he waited until Cameron began to analyze his insecurity about the future and then he pointed out the contradiction: "You said you weren't going to analyze this. Now you're busy analyzing." Similarly, the therapist was not detoured by Cameron's all-or-nothing argument about feelings: "Yeah, to feel but not to look at it all the time!" Finally, and perhaps most important, the therapist focused on the sadness that lay beneath Cameron's anger. He disregarded the content and focused on the here-and-now process, simply inquiring, "Can you say what the sadness is about just now?"

After this impasse was successfully resolved, another working phase of the session evolved. The theme involved Cameron's wish to be able to count on something or someone. He talked about feeling insecure in his job, with his therapist, with Chantal. Cameron recounted, for the first time, when Chantal broke off the relationship several years before.

Therapist: How did you feel?
Cameron: I didn't understand it.
Therapist: Well, you didn't understand it. But how did you feel?
Cameron: I felt sad. I was hurt. And maybe it was because enough was going so good.
Therapist: So you think maybe that's why you've been holding back then, so, cagey?
Cameron: Yeah, maybe. I think there's something you're going to do to me that—[interrupting himself]—that's not right! Cagey? Makes me sound like a fox.
Therapist: You know what the word means, don't you?
Cameron: Well, evasive, cagey.
Therapist: Not necessarily. It means kind of not willing to commit, being very careful.
Cameron: Cat and mouse; careful—that's not it! Cagey means like a wolf.
Therapist: A wolf?
Cameron: A fox! (Voice rising) Cagey's like a criminal's cagey!
Therapist: That certainly wasn't the way I meant it.
Cameron: (Laughs) Okay—"careful," let's just use "careful." Yes, I guess I'm careful. But not too careful 'cause I say things and other people pick up on it. I mean you.
Therapist: So you've been careful here too.
Cameron: Well, careful, sure, yes, I guess I have.

Therapist: And of course, inevitably here will end.
Cameron: Yeah. But if I'm at a point where I feel successful here, then I'm a success. Not all problems, I mean. You still have to work at them. I'm more open with Chantal. I'm really happy about that. Sooner or later this will have to end so maybe I'm ending it before it even happens. I'm looking forward to it too, 'though.
Therapist: Are you saying you're not opening up completely 'cause it's inevitably going to end?
Cameron: I've never sat in a room, except with Chantal, and told people my feelings to this extent. Inevitably, yes, it will end but I've accomplished more here than I have in my lifetime about my feelings. So, yes it will happen. And am I holding back? No. And am I happy with my progress? The answer is yes. I know I have five sessions left and well, am I holding back? I guess I'll have to go back to that. I know we don't have a lot of time left, so I guess I should be getting out most of what I have for feelings. I'm at a level that I'm comfortable and nothing more needs to be said but I guess that's wrong. I'm sabotaging it. But I know I'm going to walk out this door today and feel better even 'though I didn't want to come this morning. See, I put excuses in my head which tires me out subconsciously.
Therapist: You do that about other situations?
Cameron: Yes [goes on to elaborate how this defense manifests itself at work].

This segment depicts a return to the theme raised in the first therapy session: the patient's tendencies to "hold back" and self-sabotage. These tendencies were being replayed in the transference. Ultimately, Cameron's reticence was related to the impending termination. The segment demonstrates the therapist's skill in repairing a ruptured alliance while continuing to probe its meaning. Most notable in this latest segment was the therapist's deftness in avoiding a debate over the pejorative meaning of the word "cagey." With the transferential fear acknowledged, the therapist explored other areas of Cameron's life that were similarly affected.

In summary, during session 15, the therapist deftly avoided power struggles and arguments with Cameron. He acknowledged and praised the patient's steps toward new behavior, used more gentle inquiry than direct confrontation, and made a greater use of reflection and clarification than interpretation. The session was therefore notable for its emphasis on empathy more than interpretation. Nevertheless, the therapist was not held hostage by Cameron's anger or other defensive posturing. In particular, he pressed Cameron to experience and explore his sadness. Cameron returned for the remaining five sessions. He rated each of these sessions a strong 6 on the alliance measure.

COMPARING THE THERAPIES OF IAN AND CAMERON

There were significant similarities between Ian and Cameron. Both patients took themselves off their medications within a week of intake. This cessation of medications suggested a mistrust of authority in both cases. Both patients had an inauspicious beginning to their therapy. Their initial ratings of the alliance were very low. Nevertheless, both returned for their second session, and the alliance recovered. Both patients baited their therapists into arguments. Both therapists struggled to avoid an escalating power struggle.

The therapists' response to the power struggle was very different. Ian's therapist seemed to succumb to the struggle. Cameron's therapist avoided such an escalation. The former therapist appeared autocratic, and the interaction could be characterized as adversarial. Conversely, the latter therapist appeared genuinely curious, and the interaction could be characterized as invitingly exploratory. Ian's alliance soon experienced renewed difficulties that were not successfully resolved. Ian dropped out. Cameron's alliance experienced renewed difficulties much later in therapy, at session 14. Once again, the alliance was strengthened. Cameron completed therapy.

We believe that differences in the therapists' techniques influenced the different course of the two therapies. From the very first session, Ian's therapist used a strictly interpretive approach. Conversely, throughout the therapy and particularly when the alliance was threatened, Cameron's therapist used supportive techniques without abandoning the interpretive approach. With a weakened alliance, we have come to recommend a modified interpretive approach. The therapist's flexible use of supportive techniques may help prepare the patient for interpretations, especially transference interpretations. Such a modified interpretive therapy capitalizes on the strengths of both treatment approaches.

As presented in chapter 8, in the comparative trial we empirically explored the relationships among therapist technique, alliance, and outcome. Our results indicated that for the patient, both interpretive and supportive techniques were important to the development of the alliance, with interpretive techniques having the greater impact. For the therapist, interpretive techniques appeared essential to maintaining the alliance, whereas supportive techniques became important when the alliance was perceived as faltering. With the aim of minimizing disruptions in the therapy process, we have subsequently modified our model of brief interpretive therapy to encourage therapists to flexibly use supportive techniques when strains in the alliance require attention.

THE FLEXIBLE INTEGRATION OF SUPPORTIVE TECHNIQUES IN INTERPRETIVE THERAPY

The therapist's intention in using supportive interventions is to remove particular obstacles to progress at different stages during interpretive therapy. In this section, we present four specific situations in which supportive techniques can prove particularly useful. We present customary problems associated with each of these situations and provide guidelines for how the interpretive therapist can address them by means of a flexible integration of supportive techniques.

Situation 1: Weak Alliance Early in Therapy

1. Patient is frightened or intimidated by the process.
2. Patient is overly sensitive to criticism.
3. Patient avoids affect.
4. Patient externalizes responsibility for problems.

Corrective Supportive Techniques

1. Inquire about current concerns rather than historical determinants of conflict. Encourage catharsis.
2. Clarify and reflect, but avoid being overly reassuring, which conveys that the patient needs rescuing.
3. Empathically acknowledge emotional concomitant of content, slow the pace, track the patient's immediate affective state.
4. Convey curiosity and interest in the patient's subjective experience. Emphasize the patient's painful shame.

Situation 2: Strains in the Alliance Later in Therapy

1. Therapist enters into a power struggle with the patient.

Corrective Supportive Techniques

1. Convey an attitude of curiosity, acceptance, and interest in understanding the patient *without additional interpretive comments*. Use reflection, restatement, and clarification. Provide educative comments about the nature of therapeutic process.

Emphasize the collaborative nature of the process—for example, use "we" statements.

Situation 3: Resistance to Transference Exploration

1. Patient is frightened of reexperiencing earlier abuse. Patient is frightened by the suggestion that earlier abusive or depriving relationships are being reenacted with the therapist.
2. Patient is frightened of his or her anger, equating it with the abuse he or she experienced.

Corrective Supportive Techniques

1. Acknowledge the patient's resilience in surviving earlier abuse and deprivation. Point out how his or her coping mechanism no longer works or that the price associated with it is too high. Reassure patient that change is possible.
2. Reassure the patient that the experience of anger is separate from the expression of anger, which is separate from being abusive. Normalize the experience of emotional reactions to the therapist; inquire about feelings that followed the previous session.

Situation 4: Resistance to Termination

1. Patient is afraid the termination is premature; the gains are illusory; any future need for therapy is not permitted or means failure.

Corrective Supportive Techniques

1. Provide education about the termination process, acknowledge gains made by the patient, provide reassurance about subsequent therapy should the need arise.

We believe that these types of supportive modifications of interpretive technique will serve to decrease the likelihood that patients will drop out of interpretive therapy.

10

RELATIONSHIPS BETWEEN PATIENT PERSONALITY VARIABLES AND THE PROCESS OF PSYCHOTHERAPY: CLINICAL ILLUSTRATIONS OF SUCCESSFUL AND UNSUCCESSFUL CASES

In this chapter, we present clinical illustrations of good and poor patient matches with the two approaches (interpretive, supportive) to therapy. By a *good match*, we mean those patients who did particularly well in each approach to therapy. By a *poor match*, we mean those patients who did relatively less well than others in each approach to therapy. We do not mean patients who deteriorated in therapy. Very few patients failed to achieve *some* benefit from therapy, and even fewer patients actually deteriorated on certain outcome variables as a result of therapy. Regarding quality of object relations (QOR) as a suitability criterion, our findings (see chapter 6) indicated that QOR was positively related to improvement in interpretive therapy but not in supportive therapy. Therefore, patients with high QOR would be considered a good match with interpretive therapy, whereas patients with low QOR would be considered a poor match with interpretive therapy. Regarding psychological mindedness (PM), our findings indicated that PM was positively related to improvement in both interpretive and supportive therapy. Therefore, patients with high PM would be considered a good match with supportive or interpretive therapy, whereas patients with low PM would be considered a poor match with either therapy approach.

In this chapter, we first present Robin, a patient who scored high on both QOR and PM. According to these criteria, Robin would be considered particularly suitable for interpretive therapy. Then we will present Patricia, a patient who scored low on both QOR and PM. She would be considered to be relatively unsuitable for interpretive therapy.

Switching to supportive therapy, we will present Corey, a patient who scored high on PM. He would be considered suitable for supportive therapy.

Finally, we will present Bryan, a patient who scored low on PM. He would be considered to be relatively unsuitable for supportive therapy. These four patients achieved outcomes that were consistent with the suitability criteria.

THE CASE OF ROBIN: A GOOD MATCH FOR INTERPRETIVE THERAPY

Robin, a 33-year-old man, was referred to the Walk-in Clinic by an inpatient psychiatrist after being hospitalized overnight for suicidal ideation with the potentially lethal plan of shooting himself. The suicidal ideation was triggered a few days earlier. His live-in girlfriend and his former wife had decided to sever their relationships with him on exactly the same day. He felt overwhelmed by the loss of both relationships.

Four years before, after nine years of marriage, three children, and numerous affairs, Robin and his wife separated. Robin immediately moved in with his girlfriend, and a year later he had another child with his girlfriend. Shortly after his daughter's birth and unknown to his girlfriend, he resumed a sexual relationship with his wife, who seemed to prefer the role of mistress. Now his girlfriend had ended the relationship and his wife had ended their postseparation affair. Robin reported feeling sad, guilty, hurt, afraid, and unable to let go.

Robin was diagnosed with adjustment disorder with mixed emotional features. Medications were not considered to be immediately warranted, but the need would be monitored. Robin was accepted as a patient for the study.

The Research Protocol

In this section of each case illustration, we present only those aspects of the research protocol that pertain to the issue of suitability. Specifically, we describe the QOR and PM assessments. To begin, we summarize the family and relationship history, which served as the bases for the QOR assessor's rating.

Relationship History

Robin was the eldest of five children, with two brothers and two sisters. His father was a very successful businessperson whom Robin described as "alcoholic" and "rough." By rough he meant that there were daily spankings, but they were never what Robin considered to be abusive. His mother was described as "pretty neat," although "a little overprotective." Being the target of his father's punishments left Robin feeling more important than his siblings. It also meant that he received more attention from his mother, who would try unsuccessfully to stop father's spankings but who would comfort her son afterward. Robin coped with the dysfunction in his family by attempting to make things better for everyone. Although he was primarily protective of his mother and siblings, he also defended and explained his father's behavior to his mother. When his parents' separated, Robin was 12 years old. He feels guilty about their divorce, believing he "had something to do with it" and because he "love[s his] parents a lot."

After the divorce, both parents quickly remarried. Robin feels close to his step-father, whom he described as "ideal." The step-father has three children from a previous marriage. Robin's relationship with his biological father and step-mother was distant. Both his parents' second marriages ended in divorce when Robin was 24. Again, both quickly remarried. His mother's third husband is just two years older than Robin.

Robin continued his role of protector with his wife, such that their marriage of nine years was a loving one in many ways. However, he resented having to share his wife with his children, becoming competitive with them for her attention. He had numerous affairs. When his wife eventually told him to leave, he moved in with his girlfriend. When their child was born, he felt resentful of having to share his girlfriend with his daughter. He started having an affair with his wife. Although guilt-ridden, Robin believes he would have continued to live with his girlfriend while having an affair with his wife. However, both women announced that they were "dumping" him because each had found another man. The synchronized timing of their announcements appeared on the surface to be completely coincidental.

Quality of Object Relations Assessment

The QOR assessor gave Robin a rating of 5.1. Although this is the midpoint of the scale, it reflects a relatively high level of QOR for the patient sample. For patients with a relatively unimodal QOR, a score of 5.1 corresponds with the scale's conceptual midpoint, the controlling level. However, in Robin's case, his score reflects an averaging of the various patterns of his object relations.

Consistent with triangular themes, the family history reflects an "Oedipal victory," whereby his mother showed a preference for Robin over her husband. She protected and comforted Robin rather than taking her husband's side in the disputes. Being the eldest male, perhaps Robin perceived, correctly or incorrectly, that his father saw him as a threat, a rival. Compounding the Oedipal victory, Robin became the protector of the family, thereby usurping his father's role. At age 12, his father was finally driven away, and to this day, Robin continues to feel implicated and guilty. His victory was temporary, however, given that his mother quickly remarried, thereby bringing another competitor into the household.

Perhaps because of his Oedipal guilt, his developing maturity, the abandonment by his biological father after the divorce, or merely the nature of his step-father, Robin's relationship with his step-father was very different from the one with his father. He established a cooperative relationship with him, characterized by mutual caring and concern. Robin seemed to have identified with this benign father figure and contentedly handed over responsibility for his mother to him. In short, Robin seemed to have successfully resolved his Oedipal conflict. Liberated from his responsibilities to his family, Robin married at age 20. The marriage was initially characterized by mutual love and concern, reflecting mature object relations. However, within a few years, Robin became unhappy in the marriage and began to act out sexually.

The numerous extramarital affairs suggest a pattern more reflective of the searching level of object relations. By revisiting the family history as reported by Robin, we can easily imagine antecedents more consistent with low than high object relations. For example, it is unclear how abusive the biological father really was. Perhaps he was "rougher" than Robin acknowledged. The abandonment by the biological father when Robin was 12 years old is representative of antecedents of a searching pattern of QOR. In addition, there is some question of a somewhat idealized recounting of the relationship with his step-father. For example, not only was there no acknowledgement of competitive feelings with him, there was no acknowledgement of sibling rivalry with his step-father's children. When this marriage also ended in divorce, Robin had lost another father. One wonders about the extent to which Robin unconsciously blamed himself for the failure of this second marriage. With his mother's third marriage, Robin had to share his mother with a more potent competitor given his comparable age. However, by this time there were other competitors with whom Robin had to contend.

Robin believed he had "lost [his wife] to the children." He began engaging in numerous affairs. The affairs were characterized by an initial period of excitement and optimism only to be followed by disappointment and pessimism. It was as if Robin was retrieving the yearned for relationships that he initially experienced with his mother. He repeatedly enjoyed then lost an exclusive and special relationship. This pattern is consistent with searching QOR. The pattern is complicated by his having lost his father and step-father as well as his mother. It is unclear the extent to which Robin is trying to retrieve the mother he lost to her second and third husbands versus the extent to which Robin is trying to retrieve the lost fathers. The pattern is complicated by triangular aspects as well.

The fact that many of Robin's affairs were with married women reflects a continuation of the triangular pattern of relationships. Although the spouses of these women were presumed to be unaware of the rivalry, Robin entered into a rivalrous relationship with them. However, we emphasize the searching aspect of his affairs. Specifically, this type of triad has been called a "split-object triangle" whereby the protagonist splits his attention between two objects (Person, 1988). Hence, two objects compete for the attention of the protagonist (Robin). This is different from a reenactment of the Oedipal rivalrous triangle whereby the protagonist competes with another for the preferential treatment by a third person.

Furthermore, we believe that Robin's pattern reflected a special case of the split-object triangle called the "reverse triangle" (Person, 1988). The reverse triangle is seen as an equal and opposite reaction to an Oedipal loss or betrayal. Rather than competing with another for the favours of a third person, the protagonist is now the one who bestows favors on the winner of the competition for him. For Robin, the original Oedipal betrayal was by his mother. After winning his mother fair and square, she quickly remarried. Again, Robin vanquished the step-father as a competitor by identifying with him. Yet again, his victory was short-lived; mother quickly remarried.

The Oedipal struggle was replayed in his marriage, wherein he lost his wife to the children. When he began his first extramarital affair, Robin was no longer in competition with a rival but was the object of a rivalry. Rather than fighting to win back his wife from his children, Robin presented his wife with the challenge of winning him back from the other woman. He always "confessed" about the affairs. Similarly, each mistress was presented with the challenge of winning him away from his wife. The affairs were meant to protect Robin from fears of abandonment or humiliation, but were unsuccessful. His decision to begin the postseparation affair with his wife is again consistent with a searching pattern.

In circumstances reminiscent of the retributive justice one usually finds in Greek mythology, both of Robin's women chose other men over him. This double Oedipal betrayal, on the very same day, triggered suicidal ideation in Robin. Such a catastrophic response to loss is consistent with primitive QOR. In general, however, Robin's QOR score primarily reflected relationships consistent with triangular and searching patterns.

Psychological Mindedness Assessment

Robin obtained the highest possible score (9) on the PMAP. As reviewed in chapter 5, the first scenario of the Psychological Mindedness Assessment Procedure (PMAP) depicts a female patient recounting a chance sighting of her ex-husband in a department store. Robin's response follows.

> She's still concerned about what he thinks of her. She seems to have a desire to want to be with him. She has conflicting feelings; wanting him and not wanting him. She goes from wanting him and being happy about it and not wanting him and being angry about what he's done in the past. She's having trouble letting go of her ex-husband. She referred to him as a husband and then changed it to ex-husband. Her anger might be her way of dealing with the pain of rejection.

This response warranted a score of 9. He correctly identified the woman's wish to be with her husband again. Furthermore, he identified the conflictual nature of her wish; wanting and not wanting him, and the ensuing conflictual emotions they created. Finally, he identified the defensive maneuver of using her anger to deal with the pain of rejection.

Course of Interpretive Therapy

Robin was randomly assigned to interpretive therapy with a female therapist. In a rather inauspicious beginning, Robin failed to keep his initial therapy appointment. Robin began his therapy with his female therapist by focusing on the deprivation and humiliation he suffered as a child. This focus was in contrast to the consistent theme of Oedipal victory that Robin gave the male intake therapist and the male QOR assessor. Specifically, Robin focused on his alcoholic, demeaning father. He spoke of how at age 6 he worried about his family's needs, especially those of his mother and siblings. He drew a parallel between his father and his wife as both neglectful of his needs. The therapist confronted him about his sexual acting out. He stated contentedly that the affairs helped him make up for his lost childhood.

Robin was 20 minutes late for his next session. He attributed his lateness to parenting duties. Robin had custody of his four children and took his responsibilities for them very seriously. The theme evolved into a discussion of his lifelong pattern of short-changing himself to take care of other people's needs. He denied any resentment about this. He denied any link between his extramarital affairs and resentment toward his wife and between his coming late to the session and resentment over the therapist's confrontation during the previous session. He failed to show for his next session.

When Robin returned for session 5, and for the next few sessions, the therapist persisted in her interpretation of how he protected everyone, including the therapist, from his feelings of resentment for fear of rejection and abandonment. He was equally persistent in denying this interpretation until session 10, the midpoint of therapy. He began by expressing frustration with an error his bank had made that had resulted in many bounced checks. He was debating how to address the situation.

Therapist: So what's the fear?
Robin: It's the fear of standing in front of people and not knowing what to say; being in public in your underwear.
Therapist: So that's what you're avoiding—
Robin: (Interrupting) That's what I ask when I get like this. Why do I want all this chaos? I don't. But it keeps happening so there

	must be something. So what am I avoiding? I need to find it out myself. I need a method of parting the chaos and the underlying fear. There must be something upsetting or maybe it's the fear that there is nothing there; that it isn't anything. (Long silence) The chaos is the lack of control. And if I have control then I'm responsible? (Long silence) The biggest thing bugging me is finances; that I can articulate a feeling to. (Long silence) I want to trust that institutions know what they're doing.
Therapist:	Mum's always right; dad's always right. And it is dangerous to confront them with your feelings as a little kid?
Robin:	Yes, it was dangerous to confront dad with my feelings. I was thinking about that. Sara (wife) always was direct with her feelings. Why do I hold it in? I couldn't vent my feelings with my mum either and that wasn't about danger. And venting to an institution still means venting to a person and doesn't feel right.
Therapist:	What would have happened when you were a little kid?
Robin:	(very quietly) Didn't matter if I were right or wrong. "Don't talk back."
Therapist:	So you'd be punished in some way; then and now.
Robin:	Yes there's a bit of a puritan inside me. (Long silence) Y'know what it is? I'm still looking for ways to express myself. That's from not wanting to be like my dad. Ways of expressing myself that are; I don't want to attack someone like I was attacked 'cause that hurts and feels wrong. But I haven't learned other ways to express my feelings without feeling I'm attacking somebody. I'm just going with what's in my head about this bank thing and I can do something about it and I can be successful about it. It's not about attacking someone. (Heatedly) It's about customer service, good customer service and that's a different approach than yelling and screaming at someone and calling them a jerk—that's not fair.
Therapist:	Which is what your dad would have done.
Robin:	Yeah. And my dad always resorted to force and that's what makes it so hopeless; cause I won't do that and maybe I won't do it right the first time but I can do this.

In the next few sessions, Robin began to express his mixed feelings toward all his parents. Each parent was experienced as a complex mix of positive and negative qualities that he had positive and negative feelings toward. Hence, his mixed feelings translated into ambivalence and his tolerance of the same.

As the therapy moved toward termination, the therapist focused on the theme of loss and goodbye. Conversely, Robin reintroduced themes reflecting triangular QOR. For example, he spoke of his wish to be special and explored the bases of his competitiveness in athletics. In addition, he playfully teased his therapist, at times openly flirting with her. One could argue that he reintroduced these "sexy" themes in an attempt to extend therapy and therefore avoid termination. However, because he had originally presented to the intake therapist and the QOR assessor with these themes, perhaps he was just more comfortable discussing them, finding them less threatening than the more searching theme of loss. The searching themes of his earlier sessions intertwined with the triangular themes of his later sessions during the termination session—for which he was on time.

Robin: I had a memory come back to me. It didn't upset me much. It was more that I just thought that's too bad.
(Silence)

Therapist: What kind of memory came back?

Robin: Sara (his wife) had an affair with our next door neighbor after I left. I guess that's not really an affair. But that reminded me of when we were first married and I'd be away and she'd be at parties, and stuff, with her ex-boyfriend. I never had any concrete proof in that no-one saw anything and she never told me. But she spent the night alone with her boyfriend in a bedroom—cause my sister was at the same party. And then she lied to me about being there. But anyway, I suspected that she had had an affair right after we'd just got married and it really hurt me and bothered me.

Therapist: You always had to share your women; your mother and all her husbands and your wife with her affairs. And I guess all your hurt and resentment got played out in your own affairs.

Robin: I never understood why I was jealous—even before the affairs. Then her affair with [the neighbor] started after we were split up anyway; so why was I jealous?

Therapist: It felt like a betrayal.

Robin: It's more of a sad feeling. No longer a panic. I was hiding from the pain, the fear of the pain. Now I'm thinking about it without getting caught up in a panic. Ironic that it comes full circle. When my mother got married I was the last one to accept my step-father and then when they broke up I was the last to accept that—with all the rumors and I said just wait; you don't know. That really is a focal point of my life; so many things branching

off like feeling guilty about sex when I was younger. (Silence) I understand now why I felt the need to own my wife; all my girlfriends. But I don't understand why I felt the need to own my mum.
(Long Silence)

Therapist: Well, she was the only stabilizing force growing up; fathers blew hot and cold; fathers came and went. Always someone else like husbands, brothers, and sisters. It's like you never got enough from her and kept trying to.

Summary

Robin's outcome scores were among the most favorable in the study. We believe his benefit is related to his high PM and QOR. The transcripts reproduced in this chapter testify to Robin's diligence in working toward understanding his neediness, emptiness, self-sabotage, and primitive and Oedipal guilt. Although his tardiness mirrored the chaos and self-sabotaging of his life, it lessened as therapy progressed. Regarding the role of his high PM, as demonstrated by his responses to the PMAP, Robin appreciated the concepts of intrapsychic conflict, ambivalence toward a lost object, and defense mechanisms. In his therapy, he almost immediately struggled to understand his fears, defenses, and conflicts. However, it took until session 10 before he was able to appreciate his own ambivalent feelings toward the major figures in his life. Once this concept was applied to his own life, he continued to explore and understand his issues.

It is interesting to note that the issues he presented to his therapist were more reflective of themes associated with searching QOR. It was very late in therapy when the triangular themes reemerged. Perhaps it was his shame over the Oedipal loss that prevented him from first telling the intake therapist that both his mistresses had left him for other men. This same shame prevented him until the very last session from telling the therapist that his wife had had an affair early in the marriage and that his sense of betrayal was what had triggered and justified his string of affairs. It is challenging to explain why a high QOR score positively influenced the outcome of a therapy that focused on low QOR themes. We believe the searching themes were more difficult and threatening for Robin to address, because they were fraught with shame and humiliation. His high QOR, as reflected in triangular relationship patterns, may arguably have provided Robin the resourcefulness to tolerate such an exploration in a short-term therapy. In other words, his more primitive qualities were redressed in the therapy because his more mature qualities permitted such an exploration.

THE CASE OF PATRICIA: A POOR MATCH FOR INTERPRETIVE THERAPY

Patricia, a 44-year-old woman, was self-referred to the Walk-in Clinic. She reported feeling a loss of control over her life and "being in trouble emotionally." She initially focused on her occupational concerns. Six months earlier she had lost her job. Although frightened by this sudden loss of security, she managed to cope quite well. She quickly entered a secretarial upgrading program offered by Canada Manpower and was now approaching graduation. She had a choice of job offers, but stated the choice made her anxious and worried about making the right decision. On query, Patricia acknowledged that two weeks previously, her relationship of six weeks had ended somewhat abruptly. Apparently, her boyfriend told her that he did not want a serious relationship. Patricia acknowledged that the break-up was the precipitant to feeling anxious, out of control, tearful, and lethargic, as well experiencing insomnia. As a consequence, she was having trouble coping with all aspects of her life, including the decision about which job to accept. Patricia was diagnosed with a major depressive episode and prescribed the antidepressant Serzone (Nefazadone). She did not receive an Axis II diagnosis, but dependent traits were identified. Patricia was referred and accepted into the study.

The Research Protocol

We will present the patient's relationship history and QOR and PM assessment findings in this section before considering her course of therapy.

Relationship History

Patricia was the product of her mother's affair with a married man. Her biological father abandoned her mother during the pregnancy. Patricia only met her father once, when as an infant she and her mother accidentally encountered him in a store. Patricia has no memory of this encounter. In her teens, her mother apparently told her that her father denied paternity, stating that Patricia was "too ugly to be my kid." When Patricia was 3 years old, her mother married a man described as domineering, controlling, and critical. He was also an alcoholic who was verbally and physically abusive to Patricia and her mother. Patricia's mother began drinking with him, and soon developed an alcohol problem herself. Nevertheless, her mother had five children with him. In this new family context, Patricia described feeling unloved and afraid. She felt abandoned by her mother with whom she had enjoyed an intensely close relationship. She tried to maintain this closeness to her mother by becoming her mother's confidante and by parenting her five half-siblings. As a teenager, she challenged her step-father in an attempt to protect herself, her mother, and her half-siblings. Her mother chose to remain with her husband, and Patricia was exiled from the home. She has since had little contact with her family.

Patricia had five long-term romantic relationships and numerous casual relationships. All her relationships with men followed the same pattern. She was attracted to emotionally unavailable men. Patricia accommodated them to maintain the relationship. She tended to lose herself in the relationship, acquiring each man's point of view, adopting his interests, and abandoning her women friends. Whenever she saw differences between herself and her partner, she felt disconnected. Despite her fear of abandonment, she unwittingly contributed to the break-up of the relationships by withdrawing from her partner because she inevitably found the differences between them to be intolerable. As each relationship ended, Patricia felt devastated and lost. She then quickly began another relationship, in an attempt to replace the lost object and avoid grieving.

Quality of Object Relations Assessment

The QOR assessor gave Patricia a rating of 3.2. For patients with a relatively unimodal QOR, a score of 3.0 corresponds with the scale's searching level. As is usually the case, Patricia's score reflects a combination of various patterns of object relations, primarily searching and primitive.

Patricia's relationship with her parents was rated as primarily primitive given the physical abuse by her step-father and the rejection by all three parental figures. Her biological father disowned her and her mother made the rejection worse by recounting the remark, "too ugly to be my kid." Given the alcohol abuse by her mother and step-father, Patricia experienced neglect during her childhood and adolescence. When she challenged her step-father in an attempt to protect the rest of the family, she quickly found herself exiled from the home, yet another experience of rejection.

Her relationships with men received equivalent points on the searching and primitive levels. She received points on the searching level because she repeatedly reenacted her relationship with her mother with men. She sought a substitute for the lost intense attachment with mother. On establishing a relationship with these emotionally remote men, she initially felt optimistic and whole. Soon her heightened sensitivity to abandonment interfered with the relationship. She interpreted any difference between her and her partner as a threat to the wished-for enmeshed relationship. She would then attempt to detach from the relationship by withdrawing, unwittingly contributing to the man's abandonment of her. She responded to the abandonment with a feeling of devastation, emptiness, and longing. She quickly replaced the lost mother substitute by entering another relationship.

She received points on the primitive level because of the function served by her relationships with men. The relationships provided Patricia with an identity: theirs. It was as if she melded with each man, adopting his personality as her own. This inordinate attachment left Patricia vulnerable to any threats of abandonment. With the loss of the relationship came Patricia's loss of identity and the experience of inconsolable anguish. With the exception of one, the relationships were not physically abusive. However, given the emotional unavailability of these men, Patricia often felt neglected. She experienced the relationships as hurtful and destructive, a primary criterion of the primitive level of object relations.

Psychological Mindedness Assessment

Patricia obtained a low score on the PMAP. The following section reproduces Patricia's response to the first scenario.

> Very unhappy with life. Jumps from one emotion to another. She doesn't finish how she feels. She switches to another feeling. She's out of touch with how she feels. I guess it all stems from her loneliness.

Patricia identified one internal experience of the patient–actress on the PMAP, her loneliness. She also implied that this internal experience was causing the woman's problems. For this response, Patricia received a score of 2 out of a possible 9 points. She did not obtain additional points because she did not identify a causal sequence involving this emotion, the resultant effect. Similarly, she failed to identify a motivating wish, an inhibiting fear, or a defensive process. Furthermore, Patricia's response failed to reflect an appreciation of ambivalent or conflictual feelings. She stated that the actress "jumps" and "switches" between emotions. Patricia did not seem to realize that the actress felt a variety of emotions simultaneously. Given her score, one would predict that in therapy Patricia would be unable to appreciate her own motivations, conflictual emotions, fears, or defensive maneuvers.

Course of Interpretive Therapy

Patricia was randomly assigned to interpretive therapy with a female therapist. A major theme of the therapy was Patricia's history of abandonment and rejection. Throughout the therapy Patricia lamented the many losses in her life and agonized over her inability to find a man to love and take care of her. Between sessions 14 and 15, her therapist had planned a five-week interruption. Patricia "forgot" to attend sessions 11 and 13. She was 25 minutes late for the (prehiatus) 14th session. Given the importance of abandonment in Patricia's life, and the suspected acting out in reaction to the therapist's imminent departure, her therapist attempted to explore Patricia's feelings with respect to the break. The following section presents a segment of session 14. Patricia spent the first 10 minutes of the shortened session talking about her fear of losing a close woman friend who was becoming serious with a man. She had picked a fight with her friend.

Patricia: So maybe I'm sabotaging the friendship because I'm losing it.
Therapist: Well, interesting choice of words "sabotaging because I'm losing it." Because of course, I'm going to be away for five weeks and is it again a coincidence that you short-changed yourself today by being about half-an-hour late?
Patricia: Yeah.
Therapist: Well, maybe there are some feelings about this relationship ending.
Patricia: I don't know. I'm angry with myself again for doing this to myself today and I don't understand why.
Therapist: What about some feelings about *me*?
Patricia: About you?
Therapist: About me or about this situation.
Patricia: Again, I don't feel anything negative. I feel I have a lot more work to do in developing the relationship. I don't know, there's still a certain amount of it that feels forced. Like I'm supposed to feel all these things and sometimes I'm at a loss. Well what do I say? And yes, insecurity or being unsure. But it's not enough for me to be aware of. . . . I tend to forget because I get involved—once I'm involved in a project my memory just goes. I seem to have problems with my memory right now. I attribute it to doing too many things.
Therapist: So maybe there's a feeling of relief that you'll have one less thing to do. You won't have to come and feel like you're on the spot having to give to me what you think I might want.
Patricia: Maybe 1%—but for the most part I know I'm here to help me; not to please you and not to feel uncomfortable. Because basically, why should I be uncomfortable with myself when I'm talking about me? I don't know. I just know I was really upset again 'cause I looked up at the clock and it was 4:05. So I threw everything in my desk and ran out and then I got stuck in traffic longer than I anticipated. My only conscious feeling was one of remorse.
Therapist: And remorse because I might punish you? Or because you short-changed yourself?—And you really wanted to talk about stuff. Remorse that I might think differently of you? What do you think the remorse is about?
Patricia: Mostly the remorse is short-changing myself. That's what I would think it is. Because I'm not seeing you for a few weeks

	and I know you're going to be away. And again to me subconsciously, this is important to me and it's out of character for me to forget like this but. . . .
Therapist:	Well maybe there's also a part of you that doesn't want to open yourself up to the pain and the anger knowing that we can't continue it.
Patricia:	I don't know. I could explore it on my own.
Therapist:	Well, maybe the feelings become overwhelming.
Patricia:	Well, definitely the anger is so far down there still and I know it has to come up. I know that because it seems like—well, everyone negates my anger so why talk about it? I'd like to call [my friend] and tell her how I feel.
Therapist:	What would you say?
Patricia:	That I feel really wronged. . . .

In this segment, the therapist explored whether Patricia was harboring any feelings regarding the five-week hiatus. Patricia's insight that she may be sabotaging her friendship because she was losing it may have emboldened the therapist that the time was right for this exploration. Although Patricia acknowledged that forgetting appointments was out of character for her, she could not explain her forgetfulness. The therapist offered several hypotheses. She wondered if Patricia was relieved about the break. She also wondered if there was some reluctance to open up the painful feelings right before the break because there may not be any closure for several weeks. The therapist also explored many possible reasons for the remorse that Patricia acknowledged feeling. Despite the seemingly nonthreatening threads of exploration offered by the therapist, Patricia could only admit that "1%" of her was anything but remorseful that she had short-changed herself of her therapy time. She returned to the safer target of her friend and her anger with her. The therapist relented and allowed the patient to move on.

This segment depicted Patricia's low PM. She was unable to work with the therapist's interventions. According to this criterion, Patricia was a poor match for interpretive therapy. In addition, we believe that her low QOR also interfered with her ability to benefit from the interpretive approach. In the previous segment, the therapist was exploring the transference. She was inviting Patricia to see her as yet another person who abandoned her. Patricia resisted this association. Initially, she had difficulty with the idea that she might have any feelings about the therapist, asking, "About you?" Then she stated that the whole idea "seemed forced." It is possible that Patricia needed to see the therapist as a benign figure toward whom she had no feelings, or at least only positive ones. The interpretive approach is by design more depriving and frustrating for patients than the supportive one. However, for Patricia, who had experienced neglect, deprivation, and abandonment throughout her life, this interpretive therapist may have been experienced as rather nurturing in comparison. Perhaps the therapist had become the idealized lost mother listening attentively and noncritically to her. As a consequence, it may have been the relationship that was sustaining Patricia rather than the therapist's (verbal) interventions. The question remained, therefore, about what would happen to Patricia when therapy came to an end rather than just to an interruption. The following section presents the beginning segment from session 20.

Patricia: I feel sad, and a little anxious 'cause I know I still have lots of things to work on. But I think I've made a decision to join ACOA [Adult Children of Alcoholics] 'cause I think that might help me. . . . I've thought about it a lot and I think that a lot of this anger that's inside has been here since I was little and that maybe going to ACOA will help me deal with it.

Therapist: And that was a realization that you were very reluctant to look at. And maybe it's no surprise that it came up at session 19; that there may be some mixed feelings about having to address the alcoholism that was part of your life growing up.

Patricia: Yes I just swept it under the carpet. Again I protected my parents—made excuses and I didn't have to deal with my pain either that way. So I feel kind of good making that decision 'cause I think I'm not leaving myself hanging. Because if I just walked out of here and didn't have any other plan in place I think my anxiety would be greater. I do believe that I have a long way to go in many aspects of healing. And unless I do that I'm going to deteriorate to a certain extent in that my motivation will continue to be a problem. And I also realize that a lot of my depression stems from not taking any kind of action. I spent a lot of the weekend alone and I was really lonely. But I think it was because I spent a lot of time thinking and feeling about this coming to an end. I mean these sessions with you. And where have I got with it and doing some reflection. Plus accepting that I'm not prepared to go out on my own. I'm more open to looking at it as an ongoing therapy.

Therapist: And 'though theoretically there are no problems with continuing on, and you're saying ACOA seems to be what you need next, is this also, though, a way of limiting the impact of this goodbye, given the difficulty you have with goodbyes? So does it make it easier to leave me and protect me from the feelings of, perhaps, feelings of abandonment or anger? So you have perhaps a safety net there?

Patricia: Possibly. Very true. When it comes to saying goodbye it is hard (cries). Especially when I feel that it went so fast and just touched the tip of the iceberg—looking out at the deep sea of issues and I'm scared. Last week I was very optimistic looking at what I had accomplished. And I was taking away the feelings of the unknown and my feelings of feeling dysfunctional. I have to be honest with myself. I have made some steps but there's still a battle to remain positive. I still have a lot of negativity and its destroying me. And it's really hard to accept that I still need help. And to admit that weakness within me is really hard. And I get angry 'cause why can't I just do what needs to be done instead of letting others control me?

Therapist: Yes, the fear of taking responsibility for yourself. . . .

SUMMARY

Patricia's reaction to the termination of therapy was to choose to join ACOA. Her choice was a repetition of her tendency to replace the lost object rather than grieving its loss. The therapist addressed the defensive aspect of her choice—"a way of limiting the impact of this goodbye." However, the therapist may have been in somewhat of a dilemma. Clinically, it was preferable for Patricia to grieve the loss of the therapist rather than replacing her with ACOA. The research protocol recommended that patients avoid subsequent therapy during the follow-up period. Given Patricia's low QOR, it seems likely that the therapist believed that Patricia was grieving her loss as much as she was able to. Also, given Patricia's early history, it seems equally likely that the therapist agreed that Patricia could benefit from further therapy. It may be that Patricia's decision to seek further help actually reflected her increasing mental health. She was acting in her own best interests rather than conforming to the wishes of the authority figures of her therapist and the researchers. Indeed, the theme evolved into Patricia's fear yet determination to take care of herself. In any case, the therapist did not persist in dissuading Patricia from joining ACOA.

The previous segment is perhaps most notable and impressive for the type of work engaged in by Patricia. She identified her own defensive processes when she spoke of protecting her parents as a way of protecting herself from the pain of growing up with their alcoholism. She also acknowledged that by deciding to join ACOA, she was perhaps limiting her anxiety about the termination. Over the course of the therapy, Patricia seems to have developed a way of working with the interpretive approach. If she had begun the therapy with this ability, she may have engaged in a more productive therapy process and benefited more from therapy. It is important to remind the reader that although Patricia's case was chosen to depict a poor match with interpretive therapy, her outcome was only *relatively* poorer than other patients. She did benefit somewhat from treatment. Perhaps it would be more accurate to say that Patricia was a poor candidate for *short-term* interpretive therapy. As the therapy terminated, she certainly appeared to be suitable for longer term interpretive therapy. Patricia herself stated that the short-term therapy had "just touched the tip of the iceberg—[and that she was] looking out at the deep sea of issues" she still had to address.

In terms of the role of her low QOR, we believe that it prevented Patricia from tolerating explorations of negative transference reactions and therefore prevented her from completely using the interpretive approach. She needed to preserve the relationship to the therapist as the idealized lost early object relation to her mother. It is worth noting, however, that despite her low QOR, she was able to form and maintain a positive transference that at least partially served her throughout and hopefully beyond treatment. She was able to internalize the positive object of the therapist rather than resorting to devalue or destroy the relationship, especially as termination approached. As such, the therapy seemed to help her begin to let go of the early destructive object relations, thus paving the way for healthier ones. However, given that Patricia's outcome was among the least impressive of patients treated with interpretive therapy, we must conclude that her treatment represented only a partially successful therapy. In the next part of the chapter, we will illustrate a good and poor match with supportive therapy.

THE CASE OF COREY: A GOOD MATCH FOR SUPPORTIVE THERAPY

Corey, a 31-year-old man, was self-referred to the Walk-in Clinic complaining of "depression," which had manifested itself as a sense of overwhelming doom for six months. His dysphoria was triggered by the (expected) closing of the theater production in which he was acting. Shortly thereafter, he and his boyfriend, a fellow actor in the same troupe, ended their brief relationship. Feeling depressed, Corey did not seek employment in the theater or otherwise. After six months of living off his savings, he began to experience financial problems. An additional stressor was a dramatic change in his relationship with his parents. Shortly before the break-up with his boyfriend, he had told his parents of his homosexuality and was now dealing with their reaction. In addition to feeling doomed, Corey felt sad, hopeless, worthless, and anxious, and described himself as shy. He acknowledged that these latter symptoms were chronic in that he did not remember a time when he did not feel them. He did not complain of any other symptoms of depression.

Corey was diagnosed with dysthymia and a dependent personality disorder. The rounds psychiatrist prescribed the antidepressant Paxil (Paroxetine). Corey was referred and accepted into the study.

The Research Protocol

Next we will consider the patient's relationship history, QOR assessment findings, and PM assessment findings before considering his course of therapy.

Relationship History

Corey was the only son of a dominant father and a rather submissive mother. Corey was close to his mother, whom he described as "sweet," "naive," "generous," and "emotional." His father was an evangelical minister who took an unyielding approach to morality. He had high standards and expectations and was a strict disciplinarian, yet never abusive. Corey described his father as a man who never displayed emotion nor conveyed an understanding of his son. Time spent together involved Corey participating in activities that interested only his father, such as hunting and fishing. Corey felt alienated from his father and his father's interests. He believed that his father viewed his son's interests as foreign and somehow "sinful," conveying an embarrassment and disapproval. Corey felt shamed, intimidated, and devalued by his father and withdrew from him. Inexplicably, he simultaneously withdrew from his mother.

Despite withdrawing from his parents, Corey believed that they always wanted what was best for him. He could appreciate their concern that an acting career was precarious at best. He also appreciated that despite their reservations, they never forbade him from participating in drama, and they came faithfully to all his productions.

Corey's tendency to lead a secretive life generalized outside of the family. At school, he isolated himself following his Grade 6 year, where he was mercilessly bullied for being an uncommonly sensitive youth in his rural community. He became involved in drama in high school, and credited it with literally saving his life. He had many acquaintances in his acting life, but never experienced a close relationship with anyone. Whenever he felt himself becoming close to someone who shared his interests, Corey inevitably drifted away. He explained that he anticipated rejection, and so feared the evolving closeness and the expectation of more openness. He feared rejection by his heterosexual acquaintances should they discover his sexual orientation. He also feared other homosexual men's interest in him. Hence he told no one of his sexual preference and denied himself friendship, love, and intimacy.

At the age of 30, he joined an acting troupe, where much to his unexpected joy he felt validated, loved, and respected. He met an attractive actor in the troupe who pursued Corey sexually. For the first time in his life, Corey allowed himself to explore his own sexuality. Buoyed by the support of the troupe and the love affair with his boyfriend, Corey disclosed his homosexuality to his parents, who did not take the news well.

After the play had run its course, the troupe disbanded. Corey felt lost and admitted that he began to cling to his boyfriend. Corey sensed that his lover was distancing himself and later announced that he had taken a job in another province. He did not invite Corey to accompany him. Corey felt "devastated," and withdrew from everything and everyone.

Quality of Object Relations Assessment

As indicated previously, QOR was not found to be significantly associated with benefit from supportive therapy. Nevertheless, we believe that consideration of the assessment sheds some light on Corey's character. The QOR assessor gave Corey a rating of 3. This reflects a relatively low level of QOR. For patients with a relatively unimodal QOR, a score of 3 corresponds with the scale's searching level. However, in Corey's case, his score reflects a condensation of the various patterns of his object relations. Most patterns of relationships reflected low QOR, although there were some relatively mature aspects to his relationship with his parents.

Consistent with patterns reflecting a primitive QOR was Corey's tendency to be guarded and aloof in his relationships. He reported no close relationships during the first 30 years of his life. Furthermore, when he did establish his first close relationships with the acting troupe members and his lover, they seemed to provide a sense of identity for him. He was open and honest with them and with his parents. With the dissolution of the troupe, Corey felt "devastated" and in essence ceased functioning for six months.

The relationships with the acting troupe members and his lover were experienced as joyful, unconditional, intense, and passionate. Corey was filled with an optimism that quickly turned to pessimism and despair once these relationships ended. These relationships appear to reflect a searching pattern of object relations. Corey's experience of these relationships seems to be overvalued and perhaps even idealized, given their brevity. It was as if he retrieved a lost relationship that was indulgent and intense, recapitulating his relationship with his mother. It is interesting to speculate whether more triangular themes would have dominated his relationships if he had managed to maintain a close relationship with his mother.

Another characteristic of his relationships that is consistent with the searching level of QOR was his heightened fear of loss, which led to various distancing maneuvers throughout his life. Whenever he was becoming close to someone, he would inevitably drift away. In this respect, it is unclear whether Corey attempted to move with his lover to the new province or whether he withdrew, anticipating imminent abandonment.

Corey's relationship with his father has elements reflecting primitive and controlling QOR. Consistent with the primitive level are Corey's perceptions that his father devalued and rejected him because he was ashamed of his son. Moreover, he felt his father did not exhibit adequate empathy, not understanding Corey or his interests. Finally, Corey felt that his father failed to distinguish between his son as a person and his behavior conveying disapproval of his interests as foreign and sinful. Nevertheless, there are aspects of this relationship that are consistent with the controlling level and, therefore, relatively more mature QOR. Despite feeling his father's disapproval, expectations, and attempts to control him, Corey felt that his parents had his best interests at heart, never forbade him from pursuing his acting career, and came faithfully to every play. Moreover, Corey did not rebel in a particularly self-damaging manner. Beginning in his teens, he withdrew into a secretive, guarded, private life while flamboyantly depicting a host of characters on stage. Regardless of the complex relationship Corey had with his parents, the QOR assessment places a higher scoring priority on behavioral manifestations of relationships and less on the antecedents of those relationships. As a consequence, Corey scored in the low range of the scale because his relationships were generally consistent with primitive and searching patterns.

Psychological Mindedness Assessment

Corey obtained the highest possible score on the PMAP. The following section reproduces Corey's response to the first scenario.

> She's angry; she's blaming herself for everything. "It's me I don't know how I feel," etc. Seems to be another defense about her not accepting or knowing how to handle or express herself or let go of things. She's idealizing the past; filtering images to come up with the idealistic situation. A lot of deluded thinking; she's got herself trapped into this fantasy world that she wants to believe in and not face the reality of the situation. For example, seeing her husband in the store and jumping to insane conclusions about what he's doing there; presumptions; she goes into her little dream about how nice it would be if he was back—living in a fantasy; not grounded in reality. Oh she thinks she wants him back, but on some level she knows she doesn't, 'cause it was all built on sand anyway.

This response warranted a score of 9. Most notable were Corey's focus and emphases on her defense mechanisms of denial and fantasy. He stated several times how she is "living in a fantasy" and "not grounded in reality." He also identified that these defenses reflect her inability to let go of the relationship. Finally, he identified her wish to believe in the fantasy world that she is creating of her husband versus the conflicting knowledge "on some level" that she does not want him.

Course of Supportive Therapy

Corey was randomly assigned to supportive therapy with a female therapist. Two major themes dominated Corey's therapy. The first was his financial difficulties. Initially, this theme involved his procrastination in looking for any type of gainful employment. Later, this theme involved his trying to balance working as an actor and being able to support himself between plays. The second theme concerned his current romantic relationship with a man called Scott. The following section presents a segment of session 6, where he explored the issue of gainful employment.

Corey: The job search is really not going well at all. I don't even know why I'm not doing it. I tend to think: Well I've put in these applications, let's wait to hear about them first. Then I'll do something else instead of sending in a whole pile of applications. And, y'see, this is the way my mind works; I think: What if I put in all these applications and I get five or six offers from it and then I'll have to turn people down which—I know—it's ridiculous but that's kind of where I'm operating from still.

Therapist: No doubt about it; job seeking is a very stressful endeavor.

Corey: I think too that I don't know how to go about doing it properly other than looking in the paper and then I don't know where to go from there. I could go down to Canada Manpower but I'd have to get a resume together and I don't know how to do a resume. Ach, I keep coming up with these excuses!

Therapist: Well have you been down to the Alberta Career Centre?

Corey: No, I don't know what that is.

Therapist: It is a government agency which will guide you toward a job or at least give you some things to think about. Now about the resume, can you think of how you can get yourself prepared?

Corey: Well, I'd have to sit down and put down all the previous jobs. And then take it to my sister to help organize it into formal presentation.

Therapist: Exactly! And then you can pull out from all your jobs the skills that are transferable to all jobs; to really give yourself credit for all that you did on the different jobs without being too boastful.

Corey: Yes, right.

Therapist: Are there any friends that might be able to give you some job leads—that would be kind to actors?

Corey: Well my parents gave me a lead and I haven't done anything. I guess 'cause it's not what I want to be doing and I guess I think I shouldn't have to be doing that kind of stuff. Oh, I really am pathetic! Y'see, in the back of my head I feel if I take the job, I'm admitting to my parents that they're right about acting. It's a pride thing; after I've told them I have to live my own life.

Therapist: Well, the career you've chosen is pretty discouraging and demoralizing at times. But you gotta eat! That's the sad reality for every actor and you need a job. It is hard 'cause the jobs you get are pretty mind numbing.

Corey: And theatre is the priority. I don't want a job that will interfere with getting acting jobs. I have a 10-week contract acting but that won't start until July [three months away].

This segment demonstrates the supportive therapy technique. The therapist used several supportive elements, including empathic mirroring, problem solving, praise, and advice giving. The segment also demonstrated the manner in which the supportive therapist works with transference. A parental transference seemed to have developed. Corey invited guidance and direction by depicting himself as helpless and clueless in the job search. As with the case of Robin, such insecurity often results from overprotective, overcontrolling parenting. The dilemma for the therapist is that Corey rebels against his parents' advice. For example, he has not followed up on their suggested job lead. Rather than interpreting the transference—that is, pointing out how he was setting up the therapist as another authority figure against whom he can rebel—the supportive therapist gratified the transference wish. She provided Corey information regarding the Alberta Career Centre. Rather than directly telling him how to do a resume, she invited him to problem-solve with her about creating his resume. The therapist also offered him encouragement by reminding him that there were many skills he could record on his resume. At the same time as she addressed the pragmatics of the job search, she empathized with the stress of seeking employment. She also empathized with the occasionally discouraging nature of his chosen career without judging or criticizing it. Conversely, Corey's parents, as with many overprotective parents, were commonly judgmental and critical of Corey's choices. Finally, the therapist absolved him of his shame regarding taking a "mind-numbing" job by reminding him that all actors, including him, "gotta eat!"

Although the therapist provided a consistently supportive approach, Corey was engaging in the type of therapy behaviors valued in psychodynamic therapy. He identified his own defenses regarding the job search. For example, he became exasperated with himself: "Ach, I keep coming up with these excuses!" When the therapist defused Corey's defensiveness by addressing the pragmatics of the job search, it became clear that his difficulties with the job search were a bit of a red herring. It seemed likely that he could easily procure employment if he followed up on his parents' lead. He identified his internalized debate with his parents as the psychological reason for his procrastination regarding a job. Hence, it is possible that Corey benefited from supportive therapy because he engaged in both supportive and interpretive processes. The former was provided by the therapist and the latter was provided by his own highly psychologically minded thinking.

Corey's relationship with Scott, a more recent boyfriend, was the other predominant theme addressed. Corey described Scott as being remarkably similar to his father: controlling, demanding, judgmental, critical, and unemotional. Corey was never particularly content with Scott, but continued to date him hoping the relationship would improve. During the course of therapy Corey broke up with Scott three times, only to quickly reconcile a few days later. Whenever Corey tried to end the relationship, Scott stalked him and threatened violence. The following section demonstrates how the therapist addressed Corey's attempts to end the relationship.

Corey: I don't know what else I can do to bring closure to this. I've as much as said, "I don't want you around." Maybe what I have to do is have a formal meeting with him.

Therapist: I would suggest that that would be inappropriate. Any time you give him the slightest bit of time it only reinforces that you are maybe hookable.

Corey: What I'd absolutely do is I'd make sure we'd meet at the middle table of a restaurant; a very public place.

Therapist: I think that would only feed the hopes that you can be wooed back. In your own mind, have you been very clear about saying that it's over?

Corey: I've said, "I have no interest in having a relationship with you; I don't want you in my life; you're not welcome around my place."

Therapist: Well, those are pretty clear statements, I would agree. But just to follow up on something you said earlier; you said something about you going past his place to see if his car is there. What's that about?

Corey: Well, if I see his car there, it's to pinpoint here and know where's he's at. I feel safer knowing where he's at and so he's not going to sneak up on me somewhere, unexpected.

Therapist: The only thing I was thinking was that if he sees your car cruising by, that might fuel false hopes; what kind of meaning might he give it?

Corey: Well, I think there's little chance of that 'cause of where his apartment is vis-a-vis the parking lot.

Therapist: Well it gives you a feeling of safety and this is pretty unnerving for you.

Corey: And the lawyer says that now that I've been in touch with the police, they'll talk to him and that might be more of a deterrent.

Therapist: Yes, to get the message across that action has been taken, and further action will be taken, and you'll not be held hostage. Now, you may want to consider changing your phone number, and proceeding with the peace bond [restraining order].

This segment demonstrates the supportive therapy technique, advising. The therapist attempted to dissuade Corey from meeting with Scott, and reinforced the idea of proceeding with the peace bond. She also challenged Corey regarding the clarity of his message to Scott regarding ending the relationship and giving Scott false hope by driving by his residence. However, given that this latter activity provided Corey with a sense of safety, the therapist did not undermine his own problem-solving strategy by persisting with the idea that he was counter-stalking Scott. Instead, she empathized with how unnerving the situation was.

Corey's repeated reconciliations with the unsatisfactory and potentially dangerous Scott suggested the contribution of an unconscious dynamic conflict. The next segment demonstrates how Corey again explored the unconscious reasons for his difficulties in ending this relationship.

Corey: I wanted to have sex and he didn't. So he just lay there like a corpse—except a corpse would have been warmer. So I just threw up my hands and walked away; so disappointed. But there it is; a reflection of the whole relationship. I don't know what it is but he's pretty tired, lethargic, uninterested in being alive.

Therapist: So, lots of hurt feelings.

Corey: Yes, hurt. But not painful, more frustrated. I don't get it. I try and change the person; it's useless. I find myself waiting around, waiting for something to happen; waiting for him to get untired. Like maybe I just want to talk. It's so peculiar; I find him so much like my dad—or maybe more to the point—how I perceived my dad, especially in my teen years—as him being very uncommu-

	nicative. Things like I'll ask some kind of question and either won't get an answer or get just a grunt for an answer. I've very little patience for that. It's—well, it's rude really. To pull a conversation out of him is like pulling teeth. I don't understand it.
Therapist:	So what keeps you in this relationship?
Corey:	Maybe I'm looking for it—more than what really is there. Or waiting for it to come and what if it is there.
Therapist:	Any joy in the relationship?
Corey:	Very little. And I find it puzzling that I've ended up in one like this too. That's what's odd for me. Is this something I've attracted to myself or did he attract me to him?
Therapist:	Well you're interested in this relationship and said, Yes I'll accept your offer.
Corey:	Yes I did. But he needs it more that I do and that's a new thought. So I'm wondering why I stick around and indulge him.
Therapist:	Hm, yes, so he doesn't touch you. Well, if the two of you started talking, who knows what you might discover.

Summary

This segment demonstrates the effective use of supportive technique. The therapist clarified the nature of the relationship without judgement or criticism. For example, she pointed out that Corey had accepted the relationship and his continued attachment to Scott. In this regard, she hinted at one unconscious reason: "so he doesn't touch you." The breakup of his previous relationship precipitated a total withdrawal from the world. Hence, it is very possible that Scott represented a safer relationship psychologically in that Corey was not that attached to him. Corey engaged in an alternative explanation of his unconscious bond to Scott. He explored the similarity between Scott and his father. If his therapy had been an interpretive approach, the therapist may very well have pointed out that he chose a man like his father to succeed with his lover where he had failed with father. The therapist may also have pointed out that he was searching for the wished-for father. Instead, consistent with the supportive technique, the therapist focused on his life's current problems. Nevertheless, this highly psychologically minded patient revisited his relationship with his father and its impact on his relationships with men. Hence, Corey benefited from both supportive and interpretive elements in this supportive therapy. We suspect that this combination proved very helpful. The next case presents another supportive therapy of a man whose issues are remarkably similar to Corey's. However, the outcome is quite different.

THE CASE OF BRYAN: A POOR MATCH FOR SUPPORTIVE THERAPY

Bryan, a 37-year-old man, was referred to the Walk-in Clinic by his girlfriend one month after she had terminated their relationship. He reported feeling devastated by the break-up, explaining that this was the "first girl I really loved." Bryan felt the break-up was his fault because his girlfriend, Nancy, was frustrated with his inability to sustain gainful employment. During their two-year relationship, Nancy, who worked for a staffing agency, provided Bryan with leads on several employment opportunities. Given his bachelor's-level education, he was consistently successful in obtaining these positions. However, after a few days, he would quit, glibly stating to her, "I can't do that kind of work." He explained to the intake therapist that he would feel "stuck," "trapped," and "worthless" on the job.

Simultaneously, Bryan toyed with numerous ideas for starting his own business, but never implemented any of them. His employment difficulties had persisted since age 24, before which he had worked in his father's business.

According to Bryan, Nancy was also frustrated with his inability to commit to living with her. She wanted him to live permanently with her and her two children. Conversely, he would alternate between living at her house and his father's luxurious "cabin" in the Rocky Mountains.

Bryan began to feel particularly bleak about his employment prospects. He also stopped socializing and communicating with Nancy. After six months in this state, Nancy insisted he seek professional help. Instead, Bryan moved permanently to his father's cabin. Nancy ended the relationship. Bryan presented at the Walk-in Clinic, where he was diagnosed with a major depressive episode and prescribed the antidepressant Serzone (Nefazadone). He also received Axis II diagnoses of narcissistic and passive–aggressive personality disorders. Bryan was referred and accepted into the study.

The Research Protocol

Similar to the previous case presentations, we will present the patient's relationship history, QOR assessment findings, and PM assessment findings in this section.

Relationship History

Bryan was an only child. His mother was experienced as self-centered, depriving, and critical. Bryan's father was more emotionally and physically available to him. Despite spending a lot of time together, Bryan did not consider their relationship as having been close. His father was described as a very intelligent man who became a self-made millionaire. He was also experienced as very controlling with little tolerance for anyone doing things other than his way. Bryan tried to win his father's approval by accommodating to his desires and interests.

When Bryan was 12, his mother discovered that his father was having an affair with his secretary. The secretary was pregnant. Bryan's parents immediately separated, and his father married the secretary. At the time, Bryan angrily blamed his father and refused to have much contact with him. After the divorce, his mother became very bitter. She displaced her anger from his father onto Bryan. She took his father to court for child maintenance and alimony. Bryan stayed with his mother until age 22. At that time, his mother started a common-law relation with a man. Bryan reconciled with his father and started working in his father's business.

At age 24, his father stymied Bryan's ambitions to assume more responsibilities in the business. Although his father cited Bryan's lack of experience, Bryan interpreted this decision as reflecting his father's competitiveness with him and his inability to tolerate anyone else's success. Seeing no future there, Bryan left his father's business. He has had no steady work in the 13 years since then. He feels his father continues to sabotage plans for his own business. Bryan reported that his father is initially supportive of his various business ideas but when Bryan is about to proceed, his father "shoots it down." Bryan experiences his father, therefore, as controlling, critical, depreciating, and undermining. Conversely, his father apparently insists that he just wants Bryan to benefit from his experience.

Regarding his relationships with women, Bryan dated casually but had no serious relationship until he met Nancy. Although he felt she was the first woman he had loved, he had difficulty committing to her. The relationship was characterized by Nancy's attempts to encourage, cajole, and coerce Bryan into obtaining and sustaining gainful employment as well as assuming the roles of husband to her and father to her two children. In response, Bryan would withdraw, complaining of feeling pressured, judged, and unaccepted.

Quality of Object Relations Assessment

As with Corey, we believe that consideration of the QOR assessment conveys Bryan's character. The QOR assessor gave Bryan a rating of 5. This rating reflects a relatively high level of QOR. For patients with a relatively unimodal QOR, a score of 5 corresponds with the scale's controlling level. In Bryan's case, his score reflects a condensation of the various patterns of object relations, specifically, triangular, controlling, and searching.

Bryan's experience of his relationship with his father was rated as primarily controlling. His father held high expectations for his son. He had little tolerance for Bryan's attempts at autonomy and independence and demanded compliance to his way of doing things. The effect on Bryan was that he felt he could never please his father. Bryan felt inadequate and lost confidence in himself. He seems to have internalized these aspects of his relationship with his father.

At the same time, his father was emotionally invested in his son. When Bryan was a child, they were constant companions. As an adult, his father repeatedly bailed him out financially and allowed him free access to his cabin. The meta-communication of his father's benevolence was the infantalization of Bryan, further underscoring his sense of inadequacy. Unfortunately, a self-fulfilling prophecy evolved. As a result of being treated as someone who could not be trusted to make competent decisions in life, Bryan had developed into that very man who could not be trusted to make competent decisions for himself.

Rather than interpreting his father's benevolence as the actions of a loving, invested father, Bryan experienced his father as competitive, undermining, and sabotaging. Bryan's perception that his father's motives were competitive rather than supportive suggests that Bryan may have projected onto his father his own competitiveness. Bryan's yearning for success was reflected in his desire for more responsibilities in his father's business and the numerous business ventures he tried. Because neither track garnered his father's unequivocal enthusiasm, Bryan abandoned both his father's business and his own business plans. His disappointment and anger never translated into a rebellious, oppositional, "I'll show you!" attitude. Instead, he withdrew, underachieved and decompensated by failing, particularly at work. He became stagnate in his life. He continued to dream of success yet he also continued to seek his father's advice, knowing by now that he would only end up feeling undermined and sabotaged. Therefore, he was sabotaging himself.

For his father, who continuously encouraged his son, Bryan's lack of success was a major frustration. Therefore, Bryan's anger with his father appeared to be expressed in a passive–aggressive, self-sabotaging manner. The triangular features reflected the hypothesis that Bryan was defending against Oedipal strivings. Although feeling intensely competitive with his father, he would not openly compete by implementing one of his own business plans. It was as if he avoided success to avoid vanquishing his father. Furthermore, in his stagnation, he could neither separate from father nor identify with him.

The searching features reflected the hypothesis that Bryan's relationship with his father had been reenacted with Nancy. Although they were loving toward each other in many ways, a power struggle developed between them. Nancy wanted Bryan to sustain gainful employment and contribute to the household financially. She also wanted him to marry her and assume the role of father to her two children. In short, Nancy wanted Bryan "to be a man." In her attempts to help him, she unwittingly undermined him. In an attempt not to pressure him financially, she allowed him to move in with her and her children but demanded very little financial contribution from him. In an attempt to help him find employment, she used her position with a staffing agency to obtain numerous employment opportunities for him. All of these opportunities Bryan squandered. Her attempts to help Bryan only served to infantalize him, thereby underscoring yet again his incompetency and inadequacy to take control of his life. Although her objective was that Bryan become a "man," the meta-communication of her actions toward him were incompatible with that outcome. In summary, the QOR assessor scored Bryan's relationships as reflecting a complex blend of searching, controlling, and triangular patterns of object relations.

Psychological Mindedness Assessment

Bryan obtained a low score on the PMAP. The following section reproduces Bryan's response to the first scenario.

> Looks like obviously she's depressed. She's got low self-esteem. She just doesn't know what to do. She doesn't know why she's feeling the way she is. She's wanting help. Maybe she's mad with herself too. She gets angry because maybe she feels guilty. It's natural, I guess to feel guilty when you feel resentment. Making that decision to pull the plug has affected her.

Bryan identified a causal relationship between the emotions of resentment and guilt, and between anger and guilt. For this identification, Bryan received a score of 3 out of a possible 9 points. He did not obtain further points because he failed to convey the defensive aspect of the anger or of the guilt. Similarly, he failed to identify a motivating wish or indeed any components of conflict whatsoever. Given his score, one would predict that in therapy, Bryan would be able to identify causal sequences between his own affects, behaviors, and cognitions. He would not, however, be expected to comprehend his own motivations or defensive maneuvers.

Course of Supportive Therapy

Bryan was randomly assigned to supportive therapy with a male therapist. The therapy had an inauspicious beginning: Bryan missed his first session. After attending his second session, he promptly decided against continuing with treatment. Shortly thereafter, Bryan recontacted his therapist stating his commitment to therapy. He was accepted back into treatment.

The following section presents a segment of his second (attended) session.

Bryan: My dad had promised me he was going to take care of the rent for six months or for however long it took me to get back on my feet again, right?

Therapist: Hm-hm

Bryan: And then November 1st came and he said, "No, no more money"; no more nothing.

Therapist: So, he just cut you off?

Bryan: Yeah. . . . He pulls it all out just beneath me after he told me, "Don't worry about getting a job" and all that. So, of course, I wasn't worrying about money and so hence I was feeling better, and then when that happened it was a major stress all of a sudden. I phoned him November 1st and he said, "No, no, I don't mind helping somebody who wants to help himself but you just don't want to work."

Therapist: This is your father saying this?

Bryan: Yes. So I get this job at a sandwich shop. But people were yelling at me 'cause I was slow. I just hated the job anyway. So I thanked him for the two days work and left. So I phoned my dad and said, "I need to borrow some money and then I won't bother you anymore." And he makes a big deal out of it.

Therapist: So you were hoping he'd give you some money just to get over the hump?

Bryan: Yeah. Made me feel like an idiot—grovel some more, y'know? I asked for $1500 and he decided to give me $900 on three conditions: if I stay away from the cabin, get a job, and forget about my business ideas; just get a job and shut up. I didn't care what the conditions were; I said ok.

Therapist: That must have felt quite hurtful.

Bryan: Yeah. So I get a job at a sporting goods shop and I was really anxious.

Therapist: What did the job entail?

Bryan: Just receiving goods, selling inventory; simple stuff. I started getting really nervous, anxious.

Therapist: What do you think the anxiety's about?

Bryan: It's just so hard for me but I knew I had to get some money. But anyway, there was this box of sweatshirts and you had to match the code with what was on the sheet.

Therapist: You're checking to see you get the right amount of stuff?

Bryan: Yeah, the right stuff. So I'm doing this, slowly, and he starts yelling "C'mon!" So I start to screw up, wondering why I can't do such a simple thing.

Therapist:	Well, I guess it's hard with someone standing over you; watching over your shoulder. Is that how it seemed?
Bryan:	Yeah, losing confidence. . . .

This segment depicts the one theme that dominated Bryan's therapy: his sense of incompetence regarding earning a living. In this session, his therapist focused on Bryan's current problems of keeping a job and earning enough money to live on. The therapist accepted and empathized with Bryan's experience of his predicament. He did not confront or contradict him. Bryan was fluent, and recounted events easily. When the therapist attempted to investigate any emotion that may have been (consciously) associated with these events (e.g., hurt, anxiety), Bryan was not receptive. He returned to the details of the events.

This nonreceptivity to exploring conscious emotions was an obstacle to the supportive approach. Bryan was equally nonreceptive to other aspects of supportive therapy. Throughout the therapy, Bryan was resistant to every suggestion from the therapist regarding how he could assume more control over his life, especially the financial–occupational aspects. Nevertheless, he faithfully attended the next 17 consecutive therapy sessions. Reciprocally, the therapist persistently encouraged Bryan to assume responsibility for his life by being more independent of his father. However, throughout the therapy, Bryan blocked any attempt to develop strategies for how he might change.

Bryan cancelled his 19th session and failed to appear for his termination session. The following section presents a segment of session 18, the last session Bryan attended. The section graphically depicts how the therapy deteriorated into a reenactment of Bryan's relationship with both his father and his former girlfriend, Nancy.

Bryan:	I'm tired.
Therapist:	Are you getting enough sleep?
Bryan:	I guess so. Sometimes I wake up in the middle of the night. (Silence)
Therapist:	Do you find yourself thinking about things?
Bryan:	I try not to. (Silence)
Therapist:	Sometimes it just happens—like what kind of things do you find yourself thinking about?
Bryan:	All negative things. (Silence)
Therapist:	Such as?
Bryan:	Whole bunch of things. (Silence)
Therapist:	Yes well, I think it would be helpful to break down just what all these things are so we can focus on them a bit more. (Silence)

Therapist:	Hm?
	(Silence)
Therapist:	What comes to mind?
Bryan:	I don't know. I can't remember anything. I can't plan anything.
Therapist:	You sound frustrated.
Bryan:	Yes.
Therapist:	Maybe to sound off would help.
Bryan:	I don't know. I don't know what the hell to do, where to go, or how to do it.
Therapist:	Well, one of the things we talked about last week was that maybe you need to get up and start doing things rather than kind of sitting down fretting and worrying.
Bryan:	I don't feel good about doing anything anyway.
Therapist:	Well, maybe by getting up and doing things you'll start to feel a bit better. Like priming a pump; sometimes you've got to put some water in to get some out.
	(Silence)
Therapist:	So we talked about getting up and doing some volunteer work—that might at least get you going; get you active, get you out meeting people again.
	(Silence)
Therapist:	Hm?
	(Silence)
Bryan:	Well, y'know, I don't even like talking about it.
Therapist:	Well, what's the alternative, Bryan?
Bryan:	I don't know.
Therapist:	You can't just sit in the corner and waste away. . . . The longer you sit in this the more difficult it's going to get. I imagine when you wake up in the middle of the night you think, "What happened to me? Am I going to get a job?" Is that what it's like?
Bryan:	Hm.
Therapist:	Inactivity contributes to depression.
	(Silence)
Therapist:	What I'm suggesting is that if you get up into some volunteer work it'll get you back on your feet; meeting people, back with some sort of routine, get you feeling a bit better about yourself.
	(Silence)

SUMMARY

In contrast to the earlier session, this final session was slow and plodding, with several long silences often interrupted by the therapist. Also in contrast to the earlier session was the therapist's activity. He responded to Bryan's sense of helplessness and apathy by suggesting that he get involved in some volunteer work. Although the suggestion was perfectly valid, the meta-communication may have only served to underscore to Bryan that he was indeed incompetent and incapable of finding his own solutions to his life's dilemmas. In this way, his pathological relationship with his father was being reenacted in the transference. His faithful attendance suggested Bryan was sincere about seeking help. Yet he consistently resisted all attempts to be helped. It is possible, therefore, that the meta-communication of the supportive approach facilitated this reenactment. It is also possible that if the therapist had felt freer to incorporate more interpretive techniques into his therapy, he might have addressed Bryan's conflictual feelings toward his father and how they were being reenacted in the help-seeking–help-rejecting transference.

COMPARISON OF THE THERAPIES OF COREY AND BRYAN

It is worth noting the similarities and differences between the therapies of Corey and Bryan. A major theme of both therapies was the fruitless search for work. Because both therapies were supportive, neither therapist explored or interpreted the underlying conflicts that interfered with the patients' success at securing satisfying employment. However, on his own, Corey explored his feelings and conflicts regarding the job search. Bryan did not. We believe that this difference regarding the patients' spontaneous activity was consistent with their level of PM. Corey scored very high on PM. Bryan scored in the low range. According to this criterion, Bryan was a poor match for supportive therapy, as he would have also been with interpretive therapy. He was incapable of using the support from the therapist, and his low PM prevented him from exploring what this inability was all about. Therefore, it is possible that Bryan did not experience the therapist as being supportive any more than he experienced his father or Nancy as being supportive. He could not, therefore, engage in a productive therapy process, which consequently precluded a more positive outcome.

CONCLUSION

In this chapter we presented clinical illustrations of good and poor patient matches with the two approaches to therapy. According to our criteria, a patient scoring high on both QOR and PM was considered a good match with interpretive therapy. Robin was such a patient. Conversely, Patricia scored low on both our patient predictor variables. She was considered a poor match for interpretive therapy. Regarding supportive therapy, the patients' level of PM was considered an important criterion for successful outcome. Corey, a patient who scored high on PM, was depicted as a good match for supportive therapy, whereas Bryan, who scored low on this variable, was depicted as a poor match.

IV

MANUALS AND MONITORING SCALES

11

THERAPY MANUALS FOR INTERPRETIVE AND SUPPORTIVE FORMS OF PSYCHOTHERAPY

Because forms of therapy such as interpretive psychotherapy and supportive psychotherapy are complex and differ on multiple dimensions, treatment manuals have been written to guide their use. Manuals provide explicit guidelines regarding strategies and techniques for therapists to follow. Some also provide case examples that illustrate use of the strategies and techniques, as well as difficulties typically encountered and suggestions for how to deal with them.

Some manuals are relatively brief—15 to 20 pages–and others are book-length. For example, some of the books cited in chapter 3 have been regarded as treatment manuals. Manuals also vary in terms of how much therapists are instructed to be compliant versus flexible in providing the technique. This varies with theoretical orientation.

Manuals indicating how to conduct therapy began to appear in the 1960s (Wolpe, 1969), mainly for behavioral therapies, such as systematic desensitization. Because these approaches involved specific sequences of behaviors on the part of the therapist and the patient, they were quite amenable to manualization. Since then, manuals for cognitive–behavioral (Beck & Emery, 1986), interpersonal (Klerman, Weissman, Rounsaville, & Chevron, 1984), psychodynamic (Davanloo, 1980; Strupp & Binder, 1984), and other nonbehavioral therapies (L. S. Greenberg & Goldman, 1988) have been written and used.

Treatment manuals are a relatively recent innovation, yet their use is widespread. There has been considerable pressure from funding agencies, scientific journals, third-party reimbursers, and policy makers for the use of treatment manuals. Although manuals serve useful objectives in the areas

---

Parts of this chapter have been taken, verbatim or adapted, from "Therapy Manuals and the Dilemma of Dynamically-Oriented Therapists and Researchers," *American Journal of Psychotherapy*, 53, 467–482, 1999. Copyright 1999 by the Association for the Advancement of Psychotherapy. Adapted by permission of the publisher and author.

of research, training, and practice, it has been their use in research that has most stimulated their development. Almost all current outcome studies use treatment manuals. Manuals have met a demand from the research community to address the issue of verification in psychotherapy studies. Stated simply, manuals are intended to provide a specific description of the treatment variable and control therapist effects so that researchers can be more certain that their results are a product of the treatment variable. If successful, the therapy can be said to have adhered to the treatment manual and to have been carried out competently. The need to train therapists who participate in research studies to skillfully use the therapies being studied and the need to monitor and supervise their delivery of the technique have highlighted the use of manuals for training and supervision purposes. In addition these uses have been found to be valuable in clinical and training settings, where research is not being conducted.

Despite the valuable uses of treatment manuals that have been described, potential negative effects have also been cited. Some critics (Silverman, 1996) have argued that manuals may have the negative effect of reducing therapy to a type of paint-by-numbers exercise. Others (Garfield, 1996; Strupp & Anderson, 1997) have argued that psychotherapy comprises subtle and complex change processes that are compromised by reducing it to a mechanical set of rules. They suggest that pressure to adhere to treatment manuals undermines the therapist's competence. These concerns are related to a central conflict between research and practice that dynamically oriented clinicians and researchers face when using treatment manuals. This dilemma is between the goal of controlling the technique of therapy for research purposes and the goal of not controlling the process of therapy for clinical purposes. Some clinicians have expressed doubt about whether the techniques that are carried out in psychotherapy studies are representative of techniques used in their practices. Research therapy has been seen as artificial and overly controlled. The conflict has at times contributed to a gulf between dynamically oriented clinicians and researchers that unfortunately has inhibited their collaboration and the advancement of knowledge. An alternative way to conceptualize the conflict experienced by dynamically oriented clinicians and researchers is in terms of one between adherence and competence, concepts that are becoming well-known in the psychotherapy research literature. In the immediate sections that follow, these two concepts will be defined and their role in the conflict will be described and illustrated.

ADHERENCE AND COMPETENCE

In general, the terms *adherence* and *competence* refer to whether therapists carry out certain techniques (adherence) and how well they carry them out (competence). More specifically, *adherence* is usually defined as the degree to which a therapist follows a particular set of techniques according to a therapy manual (Hill, O'Grady, & Elkin, 1992). Some would add that it also refers to the degree to which the therapist avoids certain techniques (Waltz, Addis, Koerner, & Jacobson, 1993). Central to the concept of adherence is the notion of conforming to technique as specified in a manual. In contrast, *competence* is usually defined as the skillful application of technique—how well it is provided (Shaw & Dobson, 1988). It takes into consideration the context in which the technique is provided—for example, the stage of therapy. It, too, involves a standard, in this case a standard of skillful application. So far, however, most manuals have not specified criteria for judging competence. Thus, it is quite possible for a therapist to be high in adherence but low in competence (Butler, Henry, & Strupp, 1995). Also, a therapist who attends too much to adherence may actually diminish his or her level of competence, or engage in detrimental behaviors (Henry et al., 1993).

The conflict between adherence and competence is evident in a number of areas that treatment manuals are used. These include research and training issues (Luborsky & Barber, 1993). Manuals are important in research for a number of reasons, among them (a) enhancing the internal validity of comparative outcome studies, (b) helping discover the active ingredients of therapy, (c) facilitating the replication of studies, (d) generating rating scales for adherence, and (e) generating rating scales for competence. With regard to training, manuals provide a method for training and supervising therapists. As well, they can speed up the process of training.

TREATMENT MANUALS, ADHERENCE, COMPETENCE, AND RESEARCH

In any research project, *internal validity* may be defined as the degree to which the investigator can determine that the independent variable made a difference (Campbell & Stanley, 1963). The investigator attempts to accomplish this by careful manipulation of the independent variable and control of other variables. Some are controlled by design and some by measurement and statistical adjustment. In the case of psychotherapy research, a manual is used to carefully manipulate the therapy technique, which represents the independent variable. Certain defining characteristics of the technique are permitted, and other characteristics are not permitted. If care is taken, when the effects of the therapy technique are compared to the effects of a control condition or the effects of another type of therapy, the difference may be attributed to the defining characteristics of the therapy technique: the independent variable. In subsequent studies, investigators can attempt to replicate the findings or further isolate the essential defining characteristics that make the difference. Manualization promotes specification of variables, standardization of variables, and the overall internal validity of research. Thus, its potential value is clear and without question.

Although the use of a manual can increase the chances that the defining characteristics of a therapy technique have been implemented, it does not guarantee it. There are two additional issues and corresponding questions that must be considered.

1. Did the technique that was actually provided represent the technique indicated by the manual? This, of course, is a check on the independent variable. If there was slippage between the manual and the treatment, an adherence assessment will indicate that.
2. Is the technique that is defined by the manual representative of the therapy that is practiced in clinics and private offices? This issue concerns the concept of external validity (Campbell & Stanley, 1963), which may be defined as the degree to which the findings of a study may be generalized to other situations, in this case the work of clinicians. A competence assessment can tell us if it generalizes to the work of competent clinicians. If there is slippage between the manual and skillful application, a competence assessment will indicate that.

Problems with adherence or competence can create difficulty for the researcher. If the researcher has compared two types of therapy and has found that therapy A is better than therapy B, the difference may be a result of the superiority of the defining characteristics of therapy A or the poor adherence or competence with which therapy B was applied. The situation would also be ambiguous if the researcher had found no differences.

Two clinical examples indicate how this might occur. Both involve a discrepancy between adherence and competence: Adherence was high and competence was low. The first example is provided in an article by Butler and Strupp (1993). The type of therapy was time-limited dynamic psychotherapy (TLDP; Strupp & Binder, 1984).

> A female patient disclosed concerns about her ability to remain sexually faithful in significant heterosexual relationships. Rather than exploring the patient's fears further, the male therapist immediately began probing to determine whether there was a "pattern" in her selection of men. In the midst of the patient's anxious confusion about this question, the therapist abruptly raised the issue of her feelings for him. Though she

denied any feelings for the therapist, he continued to force the issue. After a while the patient said, "I don't feel I've really opened up much yet," and switched the conversation away from her sexual concerns toward her panic symptoms. Although the therapist was attempting to adhere to TLDP by detecting an interpersonal pattern and then relating it to the therapeutic relationship, his effort was concrete and mechanical, and too vague, insensitive, and ill-timed to foster any security in self-exploration on the part of the patient. (p. 203)

It was as if the therapist was responding to the perceived dictates of the therapy model rather than the material provided by the patient. A slower, gentler approach by the therapist would likely have been more productive. This could have involved a careful exploration of what the patient meant by her concerns about remaining faithful. Her concerns could have been about betrayal, discovery, loss of an important relationship, or other potential difficulties. Once this became clear and defined in the patient's own terms, the therapist could begin inquiring about when it occurred in previous relationships. This would allow evidence to accumulate that might represent a repetitive pattern in her selection of men. If a pattern emerged as a result of this more gradual process, the patient would feel more a part of discovering it. Once established as an hypothesis, the question of whether it was occurring in the patient–therapist relationship could be explored. In this way the objectives of TLDP could more effectively be achieved.

The second example is from an article by Waltz et al. (1993). The type of therapy was cognitive–behavioral.

A cognitive therapy supervisor might consider it incompetent for a therapist to explore underlying assumptions or core schemata during the first few sessions of treatment. The same technique might be judged highly competent during later sessions when the therapist has sufficiently explored the client's automatic thoughts and when depressive symptoms have been alleviated. Similarly, at that later point, a therapist's failure to challenge the client's underlying assumptions might be judged incompetent. (p. 623)

In their article, Waltz and colleagues emphasized the notion of taking the context into consideration in determining the competence of therapy technique. Their example concerns the contextual factor of timing in regard to stage of therapy. They consider a number of other contextual factors including the patient's degree of impairment, the patient's cooperativeness, current life satisfaction and life stress. The two clinical examples illustrate how therapy can be unsuccessful, not because of the absence of the defining characteristics of the therapy, or failure to adhere to a manual, but because of incompetent adherence to the models.

TREATMENT MANUALS, ADHERENCE, COMPETENCE, AND THERAPIST TRAINING

In addition to the use of manuals, two more traditional procedures are believed to contribute to technical adherence: training and supervision. Unfortunately, however, as Binder (1993) has argued, there is still relatively little data about the efficacy of psychotherapy training, and investigations of the procedures used by psychotherapy supervisors and their efficacy are practically nonexistent. The model used by most training institutions comprises didactic courses, supervision of ongoing cases, and experiential training made up of personal therapy or group learning experiences. The effectiveness of this "apprenticeship" model depends very much on the skill and personality of the supervisor and the degree to which he or she is up to date with current forms of practice, which in this case involves short-term forms of therapy. The supervisor–supervisee relationship is, of course, another important determinant of effectiveness. Well-written manuals of such forms of therapy, which make up the bulk of research investigations, could prove to be exceedingly valuable to clinical supervisors. In addition, carrying out a study usually involves training therapists to adhere to therapy manuals. If the therapists are not accustomed to providing the therapy being studied, then the training task is more demanding and time-consuming. In one way or another, manuals and training are closely associated.

A large-scale study that investigated the impact of training therapists to provide manual-guided TLDP was conducted by Strupp and his colleagues at Vanderbilt University and is known as the Vanderbilt II study (Strupp, 1993; Henry et al., 1993). Sixteen experienced therapists (8 psychologists and 8 psychiatrists) were trained in TLDP for one year. The training involved 50 weekly, two-hour sessions with four trainees and a supervisor. The sessions included didactic presentations accompanied by the TLDP manual and audio–visual material and supervision of cases treated by the trainees. Each trainee treated one case during the training year. The average number of sessions was 21. Each trainee also treated two cases before training and two cases after training. To determine the impact of training, the process and outcome of the pretraining cases were compared with the posttraining cases.

Adherence was assessed with the 21-item Vanderbilt Therapeutic Strategies Scale (VTSS), which was divided into 12 general behaviors that reflected desirable therapist behavior at a general level—for example, the therapist encourages the patient to experience/express affect in session—and 9 specific behaviors that had been emphasized in the training—for example, the therapist specifically addresses transactions in the patient–therapist relationship. Independent assessors provided ratings for the 3rd and 16th sessions of the therapies. Significant change from before to after training in the direction of greater adherence was found for the specific behaviors subscale and for most of the specific items. A few of the general behavior items also changed.

In addition to assessing adherence to the manual, two other process assessments of patient–therapist interaction were conducted using the Structural Analysis of Social Behavior (SASB) and the 80-item Vanderbilt Psychotherapy Process Scale (VPPS). The SASB revealed that the therapists were nearly twice as active after training and delivered more "complex communications," which usually contain criticism and are regarded as countertherapeutic. There was also an increase in hostile messages. An item analysis of the VPPS indicated that after training, the therapists were less warm, less friendly, and more expressive of negative attitudes. These findings were surprising and obviously disturbing to the investigators.

In attempting to reconcile the adherence and interpersonal–interaction findings, the authors stated, "We are forced to hypothesize that although the 'treatment was delivered,' the *therapy* (at least as envisioned) did not always occur" (p. 438).

> One of the apparent paradoxical results of training was that at the same time therapists were becoming more intellectually sensitized to the importance of in-session dyadic process, they were actually delivering a higher "toxic dose" of dissafiliative and complex communications. (p. 439)

The authors reported that the therapists' posttraining interventions seemed somewhat mechanical or ill-timed. The findings are consistent with informal reports that "research therapists often report feeling that their spontaneity and intuition are curtailed, whereas patients sometimes feel 'subjected' to a treatment in a manner that overlooks their individual needs" (p. 438).

In addition to identifying evidence of negative side-effects of the training, the Vanderbilt II study provided almost no evidence of better therapy outcome for patients treated after training. According to Binder (1993), this finding is consistent with other reports. There is little evidence to suggest that training improves therapy outcome or that the degree of adherence is directly related to favorable outcome (Ogrodniczuk & Piper, 1999). Two quite different ideas and implications follow from such findings. The first idea is that too much importance has been given to training therapists and assessing their adherence. The attention back-fired by producing overly regimented, self-conscious therapists who perform in a mechanical and, at times, hostile manner. The implication is that less emphasis should be placed on training therapists to follow specific procedures. The second idea is that too little importance has been given to training therapists and assessing their competence. That is, adherence does not go far enough. The implication is that more emphasis should be placed on training therapists to be more sensitive to contextual cues when providing interventions. The difference in approach can be viewed as an attempt to exercise less control over specific patient–therapist contingencies versus an attempt to exercise greater control. The possibility of high adherence but low competence is a potential problem for any type of therapy. However, the conflict is particularly acute for the dynamically oriented psychotherapist.

THE DILEMMA

A basic tenet of dynamically oriented therapy is that the patient provides material and the therapist responds. According to the model, the therapist assumes a receptive role rather than a directive one. The therapist may be active, but it is action in response to what the patient provides or does not provide. In essence, the process is patient-driven. For example, the patient learns that he or she is responsible for beginning each session. As a consequence, both the patient and the therapist experience some uncertainty regarding how the session will begin and what will follow. Neither the content nor the process is predetermined. Unpredictability is part of the intended process. Such a climate is assumed to facilitate the emergence of unconscious material and processes involving transference reactions and maladaptive interpersonal patterns. If the form of therapy is interpretive, these events can be examined. If the form of therapy is supportive, they can be taken into account to determine the most appropriate supportive interventions. In contrast to this receptive stance, if the therapist determines the content of the session, or provides "standard" responses, the process is no longer a psychodynamic one. In accord with this viewpoint, we believe that therapists who provide dynamically oriented therapy in research projects should not be overly regimented. Certain guidelines and boundaries need to be defined that allow the therapist to comply with (i.e., adhere to) a standard model and at the same time preserve the essence of the dynamic process—in other words, not compromise the therapist's competence.

A POSSIBLE SOLUTION

During the past 15 years, we have completed five, large-scale clinical trials of dynamically oriented interpretive forms of therapy (McCallum et al., 1997; Piper et al., 1990; Piper et al., 1992; Piper, Rosie, et al., 1993; Piper et al., 1998). The most recent trial also included a supportive form of therapy. The trials were carried out in an active clinic and research setting, an outpatient service of the department of psychiatry of a large university hospital. In carrying out the therapies (some of them group, some of them individual), we used treatment manuals that emphasized general guidelines rather than detailed technical behaviors. In the two studies that focused on time-limited, dynamically oriented individual psychotherapy (Piper et al., 1990; Piper et al., 1998), the manuals emphasized the importance of the therapist facilitating a psychodynamic process in the sessions while providing an interpretive (or supportive) form of therapy. Within certain limits, the therapists were encouraged to use their judgment regarding the number and timing of interventions that they provided during each session.

The complete manuals, which are relatively brief, are presented in Appendixes I and II at the end of the book. Each manual emphasizes five basic guidelines. For interpretive therapy, they include (a) therapeutic alliance, (b) passive–receptive approach, (c) interpretive approach, (d) therapist and other transferential reactions, and (e) problem focus. For supportive therapy, they include (a) problem focus, (b) therapist and other transferential reactions, (c) resistances, (d) ego-strength, and (e) ego gratification. Each guideline is only one paragraph in length. For easy reference to an example, the first guideline for interpretive therapy (therapeutic alliance) is presented in the next paragraph. Although additional clinical illustrations and material are provided in the manual, this example is the actual guideline that the therapists were asked to follow. Its language and length convey the broad level of generality that was intended.

> *Therapeutic Alliance.* Work in psychodynamic psychotherapy is a collaborative activity. Both parties must possess the ability and willingness to pursue a particular kind of work, even when that is difficult. The patient must be willing to self-disclose, to experience unpleasant feelings, to think about interpretations that are partly experienced as puzzling and frightening, to learn even when it is painful and unflattering, to tolerate certain deprivations on the therapist's part, and to be patient. The therapist must be willing to tolerate tension and uncertainty, to withhold support and other immediately gratifying offerings (advice, instruction, compliments), to experience negative transference, to examine and contain personal countertransferential reactions, to continuously devote energy to understanding the patient and to providing useful interventions, and to be patient. Engaging in such work requires a trust in the intentions of the other party, and an optimism that in time the process will be useful. The presence of such trust, optimism, and willingness to engage in a particular kind of work is usually what is meant by the therapeutic alliance.

The five guidelines for both forms of therapy (interpretive, supportive) were followed within a particular structural framework. The patient and therapist agreed to work together 20 weeks. Fifty-minute sessions were held once a week at regular, prearranged times. The patient was encouraged to punctually attend all scheduled sessions, and responsibility for doing so was left to him or her. Each session was ended by the therapist after the allotted time. The therapist was paid by a third party. All sessions were tape-recorded. The patient was asked to talk freely about whatever occurred to him or her during each session. The therapist agreed to assist the patient in understanding and resolving conflicts that were presumed to underlie the patient's problems.

ADHERENCE IN THE STUDIES

In our 1990 study, which studied only interpretive therapy, adherence to the treatment manual was enhanced by initial therapist training, ongoing supervision, and a weekly group seminar where taped session material was played and cases discussed. Adherence was assessed with a measure called the Therapist Intervention Rating System (TIRS). The TIRS assigns each therapist intervention to 1 of 10 categories that range from simple facilitative remarks to complex constructions about the patient's internal conflicts. An intervention is defined as an interpretation if it contains a reference to one or more dynamic components. A *dynamic component* is one part of a patient's conflict that exerts an internal force on some other part of the patient—for example, a wish, anxiety, or defense. The TIRS also assesses the type of object (person) included in the intervention. A *transference interpretation* is operationally defined as an interpretation that includes a reference to the therapist. Qualitatively, it addresses a dynamic conflict involving the therapist. We used the TIRS to rate all of the therapists' interventions for 8 of the 20 sessions for 64 patients in the project, a total of more than 22,000 interventions. For each session there was an average of 44 interventions. Of these, 11 were interpretations; and of these, 4 were transference interpretations. Thus, the TIRS analysis indicated that the therapists were active, interpretive, and transference-oriented, which is what had been intended. Nevertheless, it can be argued that our measure of adherence was limited in scope.

In our 1998 study, which studied both interpretive and supportive forms of therapy, we were more comprehensive in assessing adherence. We again used the TIRS to determine adherence. It indicated that the two forms of therapy were well-differentiated as intended. In addition, we used a 14-item adherence-rating scale that focused on additional technical characteristics (Ogrodniczuk & Piper, 1999). Half of the items are interpretive in content, and half are supportive. After listening to the entire session, the assessor rated each item on a 5-point scale that ranged from "no emphasis" to "major emphasis." The rationale, development, and psychometric properties of the scale are presented in chapter 12. The adherence scale also indicated that the two forms of therapy were well-differentiated as intended. We believe that using manuals that emphasize general guidelines rather than detailed technical behaviors allowed us to achieve technical adherence and at the same time preserve the process of dynamic psychotherapy.

COMPETENCE IN THE STUDIES

Although using the adherence scale in our recently completed project resulted in more comprehensive monitoring of technique, it did not attempt to measure competence as defined by Waltz et al. (1993) and others. The ratings did not take into account the context of the treatment situation—in other words, timing in reference to the stage of therapy. They also did not consider the optimal emphasis of the item characteristics. More of a particular characteristic is not necessarily better, and in some instances it can be worse. Decisions about when to intervene and how much emphasis to put on certain characteristics were largely left to the judgment of the therapist. Although the therapists were experienced clinicians in the area of brief dynamic therapy, we know that experienced therapists are also capable of making mistakes. We attempted to strike a middle ground. To deal with the competence issue adequately, we would have had to use a more detailed manual and a more detailed rating scale. From our perspective, the more the operational criteria for competence become explicit, the more detailed the manual becomes, and the more the concept of competence becomes indistinguishable from the concept of adherence. To move in this direction would be to exercise greater control over the therapist's technique, which represents a methodological benefit. However, it might also have had negative clinical repercussions.

Our reluctance to further control the behavior of our therapists, through the provision of more specific and detailed contingencies in manuals and adherence–competence scales, stems from our desire to preserve a genuine psychodynamic process in therapy with its inherent uncertainties, and to preserve a sense of freedom among therapists that will help them avoid mechanistic and countertherapeutic behavior. In the case of our research projects, we have chosen procedures that attempt to balance methodological and clinical considerations.

Our concern about further standardizing and specifying the technique of dynamically oriented therapists is shared by other research teams. In a recent article, Strupp and Anderson (1997) have expressed similar reservations.

> Psychotherapy in general, and the therapeutic relationship in particular, represents a very broad and multifaceted social influence. . . . The threat

is very real (perhaps it has already become reality!) that the skillful, theoretically sophisticated therapist is being replaced by technicians with very limited training and expertise.... We propose that manuals can only minimize variability at the expense of other essential therapeutic phenomena. (pp. 77, 78)

In regard to training, they added,

Further emphasis on the standardization of "techniques" and manualized control of the "therapist factor" may impede, rather than further the advancement of productive models for therapist training. (p. 81)

Other researchers have attempted to develop measures of adherence and competence. Although they have experienced difficulties in reliably measuring competence, they have provided some evidence that competence may be related to therapy benefit (Barber, Crits-Christoph, & Luborsky, 1996). In general, however, the research literature indicates that demonstration of a direct relationship between competence and benefit has met with mixed success (Svartberg & Stiles, 1992). Nevertheless, it is an important area for future research.

Thus far, our clinical research team has been able to use manuals that emphasize general guidelines rather than detailed technical behaviors. In time, we may be driven further toward including detailed competence instructions and rating procedures in our studies. In addition to academic and clinical reasons, pressure from research-funding agencies and publication sources regarding what is desirable methodologically has an important impact. Obviously, we have not resolved our conflict and dilemma in any final sense. But that is what makes psychotherapy research interesting and alive: the opportunity for evolution and change.

12

USE OF THE INTERPRETIVE AND SUPPORTIVE TECHNIQUE SCALE

Despite the increasing use of treatment manuals and the growing awareness of the need for adherence checks in psychotherapy training and research, including such measurements is not standard practice in most clinical situations (Waltz et al., 1993). The challenge is to develop reliable measures of techniques that can be used to empirically verify the treatments that are provided in training or psychotherapy studies.

Many instruments for measuring therapist adherence have been developed (Barber & Crits-Christoph, 1996; Hill et al., 1992; Hollon, Evans, Elkin, & Lowery, 1984; Koenigsberg et al., 1985), but no widely accepted methodology exists. Thus, it is likely that different adherence measures assess different constructs. In addition, a common practice has been to use measures of technique frequency as measures of adherence. Although equating the two may be accurate in some circumstances, it is questionable in others. Treatment manuals generally do not instruct therapists to provide prescribed techniques as frequently as possible. Doing so may have undesirable effects. For example, although a treatment manual for interpretive therapy would likely instruct a therapist to emphasize transference interpretation, it would not instruct a therapist to provide transference interpretations as frequently as possible. Thus, it would be erroneous to equate increased frequency of this technique with increased adherence to the manual's guidelines. Clinical experience suggests that balance between different techniques that are part of a therapy approach—for example, interpretation and reflection—is more likely to be beneficial. Thus, measures of the two constructs (frequency, adherence) need to be differentiated.

Although a number of important measures of therapy technique exist, the practical utility of some scales is limited by their excessive length, weak

---

Parts of this chapter have been taken, verbatim or adapted, from "Measuring Therapist Technique in Psychodynamic Psychotherapies: Development and Use of a New Scale," *Journal of Psychotherapy Practice and Research*, 8, 142–154, 1999. Copyright 1999 by the American Psychiatric Press, Inc. Adapted by permission of the publisher and author.

psychometric properties, or representation of very specific therapy models. Examples include scales that consist of nearly 100 items (Shapiro & Startup, 1992), scales that require many (e.g., eight) raters to achieve reliable ratings (Hill et al., 1992), and scales that are designed for a very specific treatment approach (e.g., supportive–expressive dynamic therapy for cocaine dependence; Barber, Krakauer, Calvo, Badgio, & Faude, 1997). This chapter describes the development of a new rating scale, the Interpretive and Supportive Technique Scale (ISTS), which was created initially for use in our comparative treatment study that investigated the effectiveness of interpretive and supportive forms of individual psychotherapy. The ISTS is intended to be brief, reliable, and easily applicable to different forms of dynamic therapy. It is not our intention to present the ISTS as a replacement for existing measures of technique but to offer it as a reliable alternative that has general applicability. The scale is designed to measure amount of emphasis on different treatment features and adherence for a range of interpretive and supportive forms of psychodynamic psychotherapy. Thus, it has the potential to facilitate comparisons among different therapies.

THE INTERPRETIVE AND SUPPORTIVE TECHNIQUE SCALE

The 14-item ITST (see Table 12-1) was developed to quantify the degree of therapist adherence to the intended strategies and techniques of the interpretive and supportive psychotherapies of our comparative study, which were described in chapter 3. The 14 items represent a mixture of session objectives and technical interventions (we refer to these generally as *features*) that characterize differences among dynamic psychotherapies. Initial item generation was based on the treatment features described in the interpretive and supportive treatment manual. Additional items were generated from a review of relevant theoretical and clinical literature (Piper, 1996), and the clinical experience of the authors. It was our intention to develop a scale that could be used by nonclinician raters. Thus, efforts were made to make all items as clear and concrete as possible, requiring a relatively low level of inference and allowing judgments that could be provided solely on the basis of observations of audiotaped sessions. We applied an initial version of the scale to audiotaped sessions of interpretive therapy and supportive therapy. Following this, we revised or eliminated redundant, unclear, or ambiguous items. As well, we clarified the rating instructions. We developed a manual for the scale, which provided definitions of the items and illustrative clinical examples. The final version of the ISTS consists of the 14 items presented in Table 12-1. The scale does not focus on theoretical concepts of any one particular author. Rather, the scale focuses on general session goals and techniques (i.e., features) that are common to a number

Table 12-1
The Interpretive and Supportive Technique Scale

0	1	2	3	4
No Emphasis	Minor Emphasis	Moderate Emphasis	Considerable Emphasis	Major Emphasis

The therapist attempted to:
1. Gratify the patient—that is, make the patient feel good rather than anxious in the session.
2. Maintain pressure on the patient to talk—for example, by at times remaining passive, by not breaking pauses, by not answering questions.
3. Make noninterpretive interventions—for example, reflections, questions, provisions of information, clarifications, and confrontations.
4. Encourage the patient to explore uncomfortable emotions.
5. Provide guidance similar to the role of the family doctor—for example, advise a course of action more appropriate to healthy functioning regarding self-care, life skills, or interpersonal behavior.
6. Make interpretations.
7. Engage in problem solving strategies with the patient—that is, generating and evaluating alternative solutions to external life problems.
8. Direct attention to the patient's subjective impression of the therapist.
9. Offer explanations that locate the responsibility for the patient's difficulties outside him- or herself—for example, in the patient's environment, as a function of interpersonal transactions, or in the patient's body chemistry or physiology.
10. Make links between the patient's relationship with the therapist and the patient's relationship with others.
11. Praise the patient.
12. Focus on the patient and therapist in the treatment situation rather than the patient and significant others outside the treatment situation.
13. Display personal information, opinions, and values.
14. Direct attention to the patient's subjective impression of others outside the treatment situation.

of forms of psychodynamic therapy. The seven odd-numbered items of the scale describe supportive features and the seven even-numbered items describe interpretive features. Nonparticipant observers rate each item on a 5-point Likert-type scale (0 = no emphasis, 4 = major emphasis). Conceptually, each item represents a continuum. The rater is not indicating the presence or absence of interpretive or supportive technique but the degree of emphasis of an interpretive or supportive feature.

Two subscale scores (interpretive, supportive) are derived from the ISTS. Each subscale score is calculated by adding the scores of the seven items that correspond to each form of therapy. The subscale scores represent the quantity—amount of emphasis on interpretive and supportive features. The range of scores is 0 to 28, with higher scores representing greater amount.

The two subscale scores are used to calculate a full-scale score, which is the measure of adherence that we used. This operationalization of adherence reflects two important conceptual aspects: (a) characterization of each of the two psychotherapies using a set of continua, and (b) characterization of each psychotherapy as providing a *relative* emphasis on interpretive or supportive features. To create a meaningful index of adherence that satisfied these two criteria—multiple continua and a single continuum representing relative emphasis—we devised the following formula for the full-scale score:

$$(\text{interpretive subscore} - \text{supportive subscore}) + 28.$$

Thus, full-scale scores, indicating relative emphasis, fall on a continuum that ranges from 0 to 56. Zero to 27 represents the supportive range of the continuum, with lower scores indicating greater supportive emphasis. Twenty-nine to 56 represents the interpretive range of the continuum, with higher scores indicating greater interpretive emphasis. A score of 28 represents a therapy with equal supportive and interpretive emphases. Use of the ISTS requires approximately one hour per 50-minute session to generate the various scores.

PSYCHOMETRIC PROPERTIES OF THE ISTS

The psychometric properties of the ISTS were determined in two studies. The first study determined the rater reliability and internal consistency of the scale. The second study provided an opportunity to cross-validate the findings of the first study and examine the factor structure of the scale.

Study 1

Study 1 examined the rater reliability and internal consistency of the ISTS. Most often, researchers wish to demonstrate that their rating scale can be used effectively by a variety of raters. For this purpose, the appropriate *rater reliability* index is Shrout and Fleiss's (1979) intraclass correlation coefficient (ICC) model 2, a random effects model. ICC (2, 1) provides an estimate of the reliability of a rating that might be obtained by an independent rater, and represents the generalizability of the rating. To determine the ICC (2, 1), a random sample of raters is selected from a larger population, and each rater independently rates each target. The reliability coefficient indicates the degree to which any single rater can be used to represent the score. *Internal consistency* generally refers to how highly the items of a scale are related to each other. One of the most commonly used indexes of internal consistency is Cronbach's alpha (Cronbach, 1951), which is based on the average correlation of items within a scale.

In Study 1, two independent raters provided ratings for one session from each of 50 randomly selected psychotherapy cases. Thirty-six of these cases were available from our comparative treatment study. Of these 36 cases, 6 completed therapy as pilot cases and 13 completed therapy with additional nonproject therapists. Four completed therapy but had missed more than 6 sessions, and 13 were dropouts whose average attendance was only about 6.5 sessions. To achieve our sample of 50 cases for Study 1, we randomly selected the remaining 14 cases from a sample of 86 patients who completed therapy in our previous controlled trial of interpretive therapy (Piper et al., 1990). Ratings were made of audiorecordings of whole, 50-minute therapy sessions. The treatments were equally represented (25 interpretive cases, 25 supportive cases).

The two raters were randomly chosen from a larger pool of 10 trained, bachelor's-degree-level raters. As part of the training process, raters were provided with a didactic overview of psychodynamic theory and a copy of the treatment manual. The raters were then introduced to the rating scale. Group discussions of the conceptual background of the ISTS were held so that each rater could gain an adequate understanding of the material. Training also involved rating a number of practice sessions before applying the scale to therapy cases in the research project.

Eighteen staff therapists who had considerable experience practicing both interpretive and supportive forms of dynamic therapy provided treatment for the 50 cases of Study 1. They came from the disciplines of psychiatry, psychology, social work, and nursing. The therapists' average age was 42.6 years ($SD = 7.7$, range = 34–65), and their average experience practicing individual psychotherapy was 11.6 years ($SD = 7.01$, range = 3–35). Therapists were trained to carry out treatment according to a manual. To facilitate understanding and use of the manual, they participated in six-month training programs before taking patients in the clinical trials from which the 50 cases were selected. This included weekly, one-hour supervision sessions and weekly, one-hour group seminars in which session material was presented and technical principles were discussed. These seminars continued throughout the trials. In addition, each therapist treated two pilot cases of 20 weekly, 50-minute sessions. In total, therapists received approximately four hours of training per week for the two forms of treatment provided.

Rater Reliability

Rater reliability was assessed for the full-scale, subscales, and individual items of the ISTS. The ICC (2, 1) coefficient of .95 for the full-scale was high, as were the coefficients for the two subscales (.93 for the supportive subscale and .88 for the interpretive subscale). As shown in Table 12-2, the ICC (2, 1) coefficients for the individual supportive and interpretive items were in the moderate to high range, with the exception of one interpretive item (item 14, impression of others), which was low. The average ICC (2, 1) coefficient for all 14 items was .74.

Table 12-2
Rater Reliability for the ISTS Items, Subscales, and Full Scale

Item	Study 1	Study 2
1. Gratify	.81	.58
2. Pressure	.75	.41
3. Noninterpretive interventions	.80	.46
4. Uncomfortable emotions	.71	.47
5. Guidance	.84	.71
6. Interpretations	.90	.77
7. Problem solving	.81	.43
8. Impression of therapist	.87	.87
9. Explanations	.76	.44
10. Linking	.74	.53
11. Praise	.87	.43
12. Patient–therapist relationship	.70	.72
13. Personal information	.61	.28
14. Impression of others	.25	.50
Supportive subscale	.93	.69
Interpretive subscale	.88	.84
Full scale	.95	.95

Note: Rater reliability estimated using ICC (2, 1); *K* = 2 raters.

Internal Consistency

Internal consistency generally refers to how highly the items of a scale are correlated with each other. Cronbach alphas were calculated to determine the internal consistency of the full scale and the two subscales (supportive, interpretive). The full scale refers to the entire set of 14 items. The seven supportive items were reverse-scored for this part of the analysis so that all 14 items were keyed in the same direction. The ratings of each of the two raters were examined separately. The alpha coefficients were .92 and .95 for the full-scale; .92 and .94 for the supportive subscale; and .86 and .88 for the interpretive subscale, which indicated high internal consistency.

Study 2

Study 2 provided an opportunity to replicate the findings from Study 1 and also examine the factor structure of the ISTS. Examining the *factor structure* of a scale refers to identifying the general factors or dimensions that the scale purports to assess. The procedures of Study 2 varied according to the research question being addressed (i.e., confirmation of the rater reliability and internal consistency findings from Study 1 or examination of the scale's factor structure). To check the replicability of the findings of Study 1, two independent raters provided ratings for one session from each of 50 psychotherapy cases. The 50 cases were randomly selected from the sample of 144 treatment completers in our comparative treatment study, which is described in chapter 6. The 50 cases were independent of the 50 cases used in Study 1. The treatments for these cases were equally represented (25 interpretive cases, 25 supportive cases). The raters were chosen from the larger pool of 10 trained, bachelor's-degree-level raters. To prevent rater bias, neither rater had participated in Study 1. Rater reliability estimates were based on the collection of ratings from the two new raters. Also, as in Study 1, internal consistency was determined for the ratings of each of the two raters.

In regard to investigating the factor structure of the ISTS, all 10 trained raters were used to assess therapist adherence for all 144 completer cases in the comparative clinical trial. Each rater was randomly assigned to cases as the investigation progressed. The rating of the 144 cases took place over a period of three years. Nine sessions of each therapy case were rated in a fixed order, starting with the third session and proceeding with every other subsequent session (sessions 3, 5, 7, 9, 11, 13, 15, 17, 19). Whenever a tape was unavailable or inaudible, the audiotape from the previous or following session was used. A total of 1296 sessions were rated by the 10 raters; this amounted to 648 interpretive therapy sessions and 648 supportive therapy sessions.

Eight therapists provided therapy for the cases used in Study 2. They came from the disciplines of psychiatry, psychology, social work, and occupational therapy. The therapists' average age was 42.63 years (SD = 6.86, range = 35–52). The average number of years practicing individual psychotherapy was 10.88 (SD = 4.82, range = 3–19). Although the therapists were experienced in providing a variety of interpretive and supportive forms of therapy, they participated in a six-month training program before taking cases in the comparative trial. This included following a technical manual, treating two pilot cases, and attending a weekly, one-hour supervision session and a weekly, one-hour group seminar that continued for the duration of the comparative trial. Overall, therapists received approximately four hours of training per week for the two forms of therapy.

Rater Reliability

In Study 2, the ICC (2, 1) coefficient of .95 for the full scale was high and similar to the coefficient in Study 1. The coefficient for the supportive subscale (.69) was moderate, and the coefficient for the interpretive subscale (.84) was high. The ICC (2, 1) coefficients (see Table 12-2) for the individual supportive items were in the moderate range, with the exception of one item (item 13, therapist disclosure), which was low. The coefficients for the individual interpretive items were in the moderate to high range. The average ICC (2, 1) coefficient for all 14 items was .54.

In addition to the examination of rater reliability in Study 2, rater reliabilities were calculated on three occasions in the comparative trial. For each of the three reliability checks, each available rater independently rated one session from each of eight cases. ICC (2, 1) coefficients were calculated for the full-scale, the two subscales, and each of the 14 items of the ISTS. Rater reliabilities for the full-scale and two subscales were consistently high. The average ICC (2, 1) coefficients across the three periods were full-scale = .92, supportive subscale = .87, and interpretive subscale = .88. The rater reliabilities for the individual items of the ISTS varied over the three periods, yet most remained in the moderate to high range. The mean ICC (2, 1) coefficients, along with the range of coefficients, were .63 (range = .11–.84), .68 (range = .07–.94), and .63 (range = .51–.83), respectively.

Only item 13 and item 14 suffered from low rater reliability. However, the reliability for each was not consistently low at each assessment time. Should additional research using the ISTS reveal consistently low reliability estimates for either item, consideration will be given to either modifying the item or omitting it from the scale. Including the items at this time increases the comprehensiveness of the domain of technical features that are assessed by the scale. In addition, their low reliability does not substantially affect the reliability of either of the subscale scores or the full scale score. Furthermore, the high levels of internal consistency for the subscales and full scale compare favorably to that of other measures of technique reported in the literature (Hill et al., 1992).

Internal Consistency

For each of the two raters, the alpha coefficients for the full scale were .92 and .86; for the supportive subscale, .81 and .87; and for the interpretive subscale, .92 and .81.

Factor Structure

The 14 items of the ISTS were subjected to a factor analysis to identify the underlying dimensions of the scale—to identify a set of more general factors that explain the correlations among the ISTS items. On the basis of this goal and the recommendations of Floyd and Widaman (1995), a principal-axis (common factors) factor extraction method was chosen. The analysis was performed on a data set of the 144 therapy completers. The item ratings averaged across the nine rated sessions for each case were used.

One factor emerged from the analysis, which accounted for 64.9% of the variance. The eigenvalue for this factor is 9.1. The factor loadings for this factor are shown in Table 12-3. It can be seen from this table that all of the supportive items have considerable positive loadings (.69 or greater) on the factor. The interpretive items have high negative loadings (−.51 or

Table 12-3
Factor Solution for the ISTS

Items	Factor Loading
Supportive	
1. Gratify	.95
3. Noninterpretive interventions	.83
5. Guidance	.87
7. Problem solving	.77
9. Explanations	.79
11. Praise	.85
13. Personal information	.69
Interpretive	
2. Pressure	−.73
4. Uncomfortable emotions	−.79
6. Interpretations	−.93
8. Impression of therapist	−.80
10. Linking	−.79
12. Patient–therapist relationship	−.89
14. Impression of others	−.51

greater) on the same factor. It seems clear, therefore, that this bipolar factor represents the set of interpretive–supportive continua on which the ISTS was based.

DISCUSSION

This chapter has presented the development of a measure of therapist technique for different forms of dynamically oriented psychotherapy. Despite considerable interest in the role of technique in psychotherapy, only a handful of reliable, valid, and cost-efficient measures have been developed.

Rater reliability for the full scale and subscales of the ISTS was high across the two studies, among the highest reported in the literature. This is particularly promising given that bachelor's-degree-level raters were used. It is possible that their naivete—freedom from clinical or theoretical biases—assisted them in achieving reliable ratings of psychodynamic constructs. Experienced clinicians often encounter difficulty. It is also possible that assessing observable features of technique is straightforward and relatively devoid of inference compared to assessing more latent psychodynamic constructs. This might enable both clinically experienced and inexperienced raters to achieve high reliability.

Factor analysis of the ISTS yielded a meaningful factor structure underlying observed differences between SUP and STI therapy sessions. One factor, representing both supportive features and interpretive features, emerged. This bipolar factor supports our conceptualization of the full-scale as a supportive–interpretive continuum. As well, each set of interpretive items and supportive items loaded highly together, thus providing support for the rationally developed subscales. One may question, however, whether a unidimensional, bipolar factor can adequately represent a therapy session that emphasizes both interpretive and supportive features. We believe that the answer is yes. Our interpretation of this factor is that it represents the continuum on which our full-scale is based. The more a session gravitates to one end of the continuum, the more features of one form of therapy are present, and the fewer of the other form are present. Likewise, the more a session gravitates to the middle of the continuum, the more equal are the technical emphases from each form of therapy. They may be both low or both high. Although the full-scale score does not specify how much of each therapy is present, the two subscales provide this information. Overall, the findings provided evidence that the ISTS is a reliable measure of therapist technique and addressed the features of the two forms of dynamic psychotherapy as intended.

FUNCTIONS OF THE ISTS IN THE COMPARATIVE TRIAL

The ISTS performed three functions for our comparative study. The first was to inform the research team about the degree of implementation of the techniques associated with the two forms of treatment. For the 144 completed cases, the subscale and full-scale scores indicated strong differentiation of technique according to the intended designation. The second was to inform each therapist, every other week, about the technique that was provided to each patient for a particular session. The feedback included a copy of the ISTS rating form and a brief note from the research team. There were very few instances in which there was a discrepancy between the therapy designation and a session adherence rating—for example, an interpretive session conducted with a supportive therapy case. In those instances the discrepancy was discussed with the therapist, reasons for the discrepancy were explored, and the therapist agreed to attempt to shift the technique toward the therapy that was designated. However, the general understanding with the therapists was that clinical considerations have priority—in other words, a shift toward greater adherence should only be attempted if it is not perceived as detrimental to the patient. If a discrepancy were to continue with a particular case, that case would be removed from the research project. That never actually happened. The third function was to inform the entire group of therapists and some members of the research team who attended a weekly, one-hour project seminar about specific cases that were presented and discussed. The procedures involving the ISTS worked very smoothly, including providing feedback to the therapists. To our pleasant surprise, the therapists were not threatened by the feedback, and reported that they actually looked forward to receiving it. We believe that using manuals that emphasized general guidelines rather than detailed technical behaviors allowed us to achieve technical adherence and at the same time preserve the process of dynamic psychotherapy.

IMPLICATIONS FOR RESEARCH, TRAINING, AND PRACTICE

We have developed a reliable measure of adherence that has been shown to have strong psychometric properties. Inferences about how adherence and related constructs affect the process and outcome of psychotherapy cannot be made with certainty without additional empirical study. Nevertheless, some implications can be entertained if they are regarded as tentative and subject to future validation.

The ISTS has the capacity to reliably measure and differentiate interpretive and supportive forms of psychotherapy on a number of features. Historically, there has been much theoretical and research interest in interpretive therapy. Recently, considerable interest has been shown for supportive therapy. Both can be expected to be the focus of continuing research. The ISTS provides an efficient means of treatment verification.

The ISTS can be applied in several contexts. The most immediate and likely application of the scale is in a research context. The ISTS has been shown to provide reliable information about treatment integrity, which is an expected methodological requirement in psychotherapy research. Researchers studying dynamic forms of therapy could use the scale to empirically verify the treatments used in their investigations. The ISTS has several practical advantages for researchers who wish to use the scale in their studies. First, the scale is brief. Rating time requires approximately one hour per 50-minute therapy session. Second, only one rater is required for reliable ratings. Thus, staff power need not be compromised by the use of multiple raters. Third, clinically inexperienced raters can be used to achieve reliable ratings. The ratings of the therapist behaviors do not require a high level of inference. Fourth, raters can be trained in a group situation in a reasonable period of time. All four of these advantages indicate that the ISTS can be used in a cost-effective manner.

A second area in which the ISTS may be used is in training programs for therapists. A precise delineation of a trainee's technical behavior is essential to determine whether the therapy being provided is the therapy being taught. Fledgling therapists need reliable feedback about what they are actually doing in therapy. In training programs that teach dynamic forms of psychotherapy, the ISTS could be used to provide trainees and trainers with information about the trainee's technical behavior. This information could highlight areas in which the therapist is having difficulty as well as areas that are performed satisfactorily. The scale could also be used to monitor the consistency of the trainee's technique during the training period.

A related application of the ISTS could be in the clinical setting of practicing therapists. Therapists who participated in our comparative clinical trial welcomed the feedback provided by the scale. Perhaps therapists in other settings would also appreciate feedback about their technical behavior. In clinical settings not associated with teaching or research, there is often little opportunity for feedback regarding whether a therapist's technical behavior is consistent with the treatment that he or she intended to provide. It is inevitable that there will be some occasions in which a therapist will stray from the intended therapy. The ISTS could be used intermittently to supplement ongoing supervision or occasional consultation and provide therapists with information regarding his or her technique—for example, frequency, type, and consistency of interventions. In this way, therapists could learn more precisely about what they are providing in therapy and perhaps adjust their technique in response to this information.

CONCLUSION

The ISTS appears to be a potentially useful tool for assessing features of different forms of dynamically oriented psychotherapy. Future work to further substantiate the reliability of the ISTS and establish its validity should involve a wider range of modalities and different applications of the scale in research focused on therapist technique.

V
CONCLUSION

13

THEMES AND FUTURE DIRECTIONS

Throughout the previous chapters of this book, a number of themes have emerged. They are associated with historical, theoretical, clinical, and research developments in the field of short-term therapy in general, and in the areas of interpretive and supportive therapies in particular. Some of the themes have provided ways to organize the many therapies, and others have focused on patient characteristics that are associated with success in one or more of the therapies. In regard to research, the themes concern the previous work of other investigators, the previous work of the authors, and the recent work of the authors on the central research project presented in this book. In this chapter, we will attempt to clarify and highlight the most important themes, which are listed in Table 13-1. In doing so, we hope to provide an integration of some of the themes. Finally, we will consider future directions in the development of principles for the optimal matching of patients and therapies.

THEMES

In the material that follows, we will introduce and discuss each of the 15 themes. Then we will address future directions in the development of principles for optimal matching.

1. During the second half of the twentieth century, short-term therapies emerged as the predominant structure for providing psychosocial treatment to outpatients with psychological problems.

A number of factors were instrumental in bringing about this development. Strong social forces (the psychological needs of World War II veterans, the community mental health movement, and the current health care reform movement) created high demands for treatment that could only be met by short-term therapies. In addition, clinicians were interested in reducing the considerable time required of traditional psychotherapy—for example,

Table 13-1
General Themes

1. During the second half of the 20th century, short-term therapies emerged as the predominant structure for providing psychosocial treatment to outpatients with psychosocial problems.
2. Dynamically oriented therapists responded to the high demand for services and associated changes in the field by developing a variety of short-term therapies.
3. Toward the end of the 20th century, supportive forms of therapy became recognized as useful and prevalent treatments for many disorders.
4. To conceptually describe the differences among the many forms of dynamically oriented short-term therapies that have emerged, a set of supportive and interpretive dimensions has been defined.
5. Methodological requirements of contemporary psychotherapy research (e.g., therapists using treatment manuals and researchers monitoring therapist adherence to manuals) have created a dilemma for dynamically oriented therapist
6. Aptitude-treatment interaction (ATI) research, which informally is referred to as matching research, has the potential to provide practical guidelines to clinicians for assigning patients to therapies.
7. Certain patient characteristics are promising aptitudes to use in ATI research and matching with short-term therapies.
8. From the central research project presented in this book, there is evidence for an interaction between QOR and form of short-term therapy (interpretive and supportive) on therapy outcome.
9. There is evidence that the dropout rate is lower for supportive therapy than interpretive therapy.
10. There is evidence in interpretive therapy for an interaction between the use of transference interpretations and the level of QOR on the therapeutic alliance and on therapy outcome.
11. There is evidence that the average outcome of patients who receive supportive therapy is similar to the average outcome of patients who receive interpretive therapy.
12. There is evidence for an interaction between patient gender and form of short-term therapy (interpretive and supportive) on the therapeutic alliance and on therapy outcome.
13. There is evidence for a direct relationship between psychological mindedness (PM) and favorable outcome for both interpretive and supportive therapy.
14. Quality of object relations, psychological mindedness, and gender are independent patient characteristics that each contribute to the prediction of important clinical events.
15. Flexibility is required in providing the various features (dimensions) of interpretive and supportive therapies to patients.

dynamically oriented, long-term psychotherapy and psychoanalysis. Therapists were also interested in capitalizing on the therapeutic advantages associated with short-term therapies (e.g., encouragement of patient independence, pressure to work efficiently, focus on existential issues such as separation and loss). Finally, researchers and reviewers provided convincing evidence of the efficacy of short-term therapies.

2. Dynamically oriented therapists responded to the high demand for services and associated changes in the field by developing a variety of short-term therapies.

Most of the developments were insight-oriented, interpretive (expressive) forms of therapy. In developing such therapies, therapists were able to use familiar dynamic concepts, retain some of the objectives of long-term therapy, and make innovative procedural and technical modifications. Because of the limited amount of time to work in short-term therapy, such modifications included an emphasis on selecting suitable patients, formulating a circumscribed problem focus, assuming an active role, and using powerful techniques (e.g., transference interpretation) early in the course of therapy.

3. Toward the end of the twentieth century, supportive forms of therapy became recognized as useful and prevalent treatments for many disorders.

In general, supportive therapies involve teaching, problem solving, and providing guidance in the context of a supportive relationship. Most approaches have involved either only a few sessions of crisis intervention for acutely disturbed patients or many sessions of support for chronically disturbed patients. However, more recently, supportive therapies of intermediate length (e.g., 12 to 40 sessions), which is comparable to the duration of short-term interpretive therapies, have emerged.

4. To conceptually describe the differences among the many forms of dynamically oriented short-term therapies that have emerged, a set of supportive and interpretive dimensions has been defined.

What is required is a relatively complex and efficient system to conceptually differentiate the therapies. Previously, some investigators have taken a relatively concise approach by attempting to locate each form of therapy on a single supportive–expressive dimension. This has tended to result in oversimplification. Other investigators have taken a relatively comprehensive approach by attempting to list all of the features that may be present in a particular form of therapy, such as interpretive or supportive. This has tended to result in overinclusion. Between these two extremes, there is the possibility of using a moderate number of dimensions to represent features that differentiate the various forms of therapy. Accordingly, each feature represents a separate supportive–interpretive dimension. To accommodate this requirement, our research team developed a descriptive system that includes 14 dimensions (7 interpretive features, 7 supportive features) that can be used to describe any form of dynamically oriented, short-term therapy.

The features refer to treatment objectives and therapist techniques. The greater the therapist's emphases on interpretive or supportive dimensions (features), the more therapy is regarded as interpretive or supportive. To measure the 14 dimensions, we also developed the Interpretive-Supportive Technique Scale (ISTS), which has proven to be a reliable and practical rating instrument.

5. Methodological requirements of contemporary psychotherapy research (e.g., therapists using treatment manuals and researchers monitoring therapist adherence to manuals) have created a dilemma for dynamically oriented therapists.

On the one hand, manuals and adherence checks can serve very useful purposes in standardizing the therapies that are offered and providing verification of what actually transpired. They can be useful to the work of supervisors, trainees, and researchers. On the other hand, manuals and adherence checks can create problems. Therapists can adhere too rigidly to the instructions of manuals without sufficiently and skillfully considering the context (e.g., the stage of the session or the state of the patient). Techniques that are regarded as appropriate in one situation may be regarded as inappropriate in another. Also, for most forms of dynamically oriented therapy, neither the content nor the process of therapy is intended to be predetermined. A degree of unpredictability is part of the design and should be expected by both the therapist and the patient. A possible solution to the dilemma is the creation and use of manuals with general rather than detailed guidelines.

This was the strategy taken with the manuals that guided the two forms of therapy (interpretive, supportive) that were provided in the central research project presented in this book. Therapists were provided with adherence feedback from the ISTS for every other session. We were pleased to observe that rather than experiencing this continual feedback as an intrusion, the therapists came to expect and welcome it. We believe that part of the reason that the feedback succeeded was the fact that the therapists were reassured that in the case of any conflict between the dictates of the manual and the clinical needs of the patient, the clinical needs should take precedence. The therapist was to use his or her best judgment to protect the interests of the patient. We also believe that the use of manuals with general guidelines and corresponding adherence procedures resulted in treatments that resembled those that are provided in actual clinical practice. At the same time, adherence checks revealed that the therapies were well-differentiated and conformed to the guidelines of the manuals. The manuals and the ISTS are presented as appendixes at the back of this book for the use of clinicians and researchers.

6. Aptitude–Treatment Interaction (ATI) research, which informally is referred to as matching research, has the potential to provide practical guidelines to clinicians for assigning patients to therapies.

ATI research follows several assumptions. It assumes that differences among patients and differences among therapies are important determinants of treatment outcome. It assumes that there are optimal matches between patients and therapists. In addition, in the context of short-term therapies, it is assumed that patients differ in their ability to work and benefit from the specific demands of different forms of therapy. Both theory and previous empirical findings are viewed as important sources of information to guide researchers in their predictions of optimal matches and to guide clinicians in their decisions about optimal suitability for therapy for their patients. Although ATI research in the field of psychotherapy has considerable potential, it is still in its infancy. There is a promising although limited ATI literature in the area of therapies for patients whose presenting problems include depression. One of the impediments to ATI research is the considerable amount of resources that are required to conduct studies that are methodologically strong. This has greatly restricted the number of prospective studies.

7. Certain patient characteristics are promising aptitudes to use in ATI research and matching with short-term therapies.

In previous research, certain patient characteristics have proven to be significant predictors of therapy process and outcome. At times, they have demonstrated interaction effects, which have been theoretically meaningful. These characteristics include an externalization–internalization dimension, reactance, an anaclitic–introjective dimension, a sociotropy–autonomy dimension, and the two characteristics (dimensions) that were chosen for study in the central research project of this book, quality of object relations (QOR) and psychological mindedness (PM).

These latter two characteristics have been cited as promising predictors in reviews of the psychotherapy literature. Also, before conducting the central project of this book, they had emerged as predictors of important clinical events such as remaining, working, and benefiting in a series of large-scale, psychotherapy clinical studies of both individual and group short-term therapies that had been conducted by the authors. Sometimes one of the characteristics and sometimes both of the characteristics had been included in each of the studies. In four of the studies, QOR was directly related to the therapeutic alliance in individual therapy and favorable outcome in both individual and group therapy. In four of the studies, PM was directly related to the alliance and work in both individual and group therapies, and to remaining and favorable outcome in group therapies. In regard to theoretical explanations, a high level of QOR is believed to assist patients in tolerating the interpersonal demands of interpretive therapy, and a high level of PM is believed to provide the ability to work productively in examining intrapsychic conflicts in interpretive therapy. Conversely, patients with low levels of QOR are viewed as having needs and tendencies that are more conducive to the tasks and techniques of supportive therapy. Although theoretically, patients with low levels of PM can be viewed as having abilities that are also more conducive to the tasks and techniques of supportive therapy, research support for this possibility is, thus far, lacking. Manuals for conducting and scoring the interview measures of QOR and PM are available from the authors.

8. From the central research project presented in this book, there is evidence for an interaction between QOR and form of short-term therapy (interpretive and supportive) on therapy outcome.

The interaction effect was present at both posttherapy and 12-month follow up. From one perspective, the evidence strongly indicated that the higher the level of QOR, the better the outcome in interpretive therapy. From another perspective, one that is more directly applicable to clinical decisions regarding choice of therapy for patients, there was evidence at posttherapy and follow-up that patients with high levels of QOR benefited more in interpretive therapy than supportive therapy. These findings suggest that interpretive therapy may be preferable to supportive therapy for high-QOR patients and that clinicians should consider referring high-QOR patients to interpretive therapy. This is particularly the case if the patient indicated a preference for interpretive therapy—in other words, for an insight-oriented treatment. However, caution should be exercised, given the higher dropout rate associated with interpretive therapy compared to supportive therapy. As elaborated below under theme 9, the therapist in interpretive therapy should pay particular attention to the patient's impression of the alliance, the patient's tendency to work dynamically during the first few sessions of therapy, the impact of transference interpretations on the alliance, and the patient's capacity to work therapeutically.

There was also some evidence at posttherapy that patients with low levels of QOR benefited more in supportive therapy than interpretive therapy. Although this evidence was less strong than the evidence for high-QOR patients, it suggests that for certain outcomes (e.g., enhanced self-esteem), therapists should consider referring low-QOR patients to supportive therapy.

9. There is evidence that the dropout rate is lower for supportive therapy than interpretive therapy.

The dropout rate for interpretive therapy (23%) was not particularly high, and the dropout rare for supportive therapy (6%) was unusually low. Nevertheless, dropping out prematurely is usually a negative event that should be avoided, even if it involves a small number of patients. Therapists need to be aware of early risk factors such as a weak alliance and low levels of dynamic work. Therapist efforts to clarify patient and therapist roles, facilitate positive transference, and provide support early in therapy are well-advised. In addition, the evidence indicates that therapist attempts to prevent dropping out of interpretive therapy by an intensification of transference interpretation is ill-advised.

10. There is evidence in interpretive therapy for an interaction between the use of transference interpretations and the level of QOR on the therapeutic alliance and on therapy outcome.

For high-QOR patients, the greater the use of transference interpretations, the stronger the therapeutic alliance. For low-QOR patients, the greater the use of transference interpretations, the weaker the therapeutic alliance. There is also some evidence for low-QOR patients that the greater the use of transference interpretations, the poorer the outcome. These findings serve as another signal for therapists to be cautious in their use of transference interpretations with certain types of patients. The combination of the findings from the current trial and those of our previous controlled trial of interpretive therapy suggest that the effects of transference interpretation on low-QOR and high-QOR patients may also depend on the relative level of transference interpretations provided. In the current study, the level of transference interpretations ranged from low to moderate. In the previous study, where the level of transference interpretation ranged from moderate to high, inverse relationships between transference interpretations and both alliance and outcome were found for high-QOR patients but not low-QOR patients.

11. There is evidence that the average outcome for patients who receive supportive therapy is similar to the average outcome for patients who receive interpretive therapy.

The findings suggest that when treatment is carried out by experienced therapists who follow a treatment manual, time-limited, short-term supportive therapy can be as effective as time-limited, short-term interpretive therapy. The findings should serve to further reduce resistance to accepting supportive therapy as an effective treatment.

12. There is evidence for an interaction between patient gender and form of short-term therapy (interpretive and supportive) on the therapeutic alliance and on therapy outcome.

Because a large number of male and female patients participated in the research project, there was an opportunity to investigate gender effects on the process and outcome of therapy. Evidence for an interaction between patient gender and form of therapy emerged. We found that men reported stronger alliances with their therapists in interpretive therapy, and women reported stronger alliances with their therapists in supportive therapy. For outcome at posttherapy, a similar type of interaction was present. Men improved more in interpretive therapy than in supportive therapy, and women improved more in supportive therapy than in interpretive therapy. For outcome at follow-up, the findings were similar but less strong.

Explanations for these findings rely on clinical and theoretical literature rather than research literature. Thus, they remain speculative. Nevertheless, it can be argued that interpretive therapy better met the preferences and needs of men, and that supportive therapy better met the preferences and needs of women. Men may prefer a more distant (affectively neutral) relationship with their therapists and need a therapy that focuses more on affective awareness. Women may prefer a more close (affectively expressive) relationship with their therapists and need a therapy that focuses more on external pressures and problem solving. If so, the nature of interpretive therapy as provided in the research project would be more suitable for men, and supportive therapy as provided in the research project would be more suitable for women. Accordingly, therapists may wish to consider referring men to therapies that emphasize interpretive features and women to therapies that emphasize supportive features.

13. There is evidence for a direct relationship between psychological mindedness (PM) and favorable outcome for both interpretive and supportive therapy.

Contrary to initial expectations, an interaction effect between PM and form of therapy was not found. Instead, PM appeared to be valuable to both therapies. In regard to explanations, it is possible that high-PM patients engage in dynamic work (e.g., exploration of internal conflicts) either covertly or overtly, whether or not the therapist facilitates such work in the therapy sessions. Alternatively, PM may reflect a useful ability to analyze conflicts and problem solve, whether the conflicts are internal or external in nature. Thus, PM may be an important patient characteristic for many different therapies. If so, therapists of different theoretical and technical orientations may wish to incorporate the measurement of PM into their initial assessments of patients.

14. Quality of object relations, psychological mindedness, and gender are independent patient characteristics that each contribute to the prediction of important clinical events.

In previous studies and in this research project, correlations among QOR, PM, and gender have been low and nonsignificant, indicating the independence of these patient characteristics. In addition, when examined together each has been found to contribute significantly to the prediction of therapy outcome. In the case of PM, this has involved a main effect. In the case of QOR or gender, this has involved two-way interaction effects. Higher order interactions (e.g., QOR by PM by form of therapy or QOR by gender by form of therapy) have not been found. Nevertheless, the independent contributions to prediction indicate that they should be carefully considered by clinicians regarding their decisions to refer patients to psychotherapy in general or to a particular form of psychotherapy.

15. Flexibility is required in providing the various features (dimensions) of interpretive and supportive therapies to patients.

There are a number of reasons why a flexible approach to technique is required.

As emphasized in chapter 5, prediction for the individual patient is never perfect. Although in our research project, statistically significant associations were found between the primary patient characteristics and important clinical events for each of the treated samples (interpretive, supportive), prediction for the individual patient is limited by two factors. First, the associations were only moderate in size. Thus, important variation was not accounted for. Second, the associations are applicable to the treated samples taken as a group. Thus, for each individual patient, the associations are applicable only to a lesser or a greater degree—in other words, on average. The other determinants of treated samples' responses or the individual patient's response are unknown and remain to be discovered in future studies.

Patients consist of complex mixtures of characteristics and therapies represent complex mixtures of features. Pure types do not exist. Rather than viewing either an individual patient or therapy as a type (e.g., high-QOR patient or interpretive therapy), in this book we have advocated that it is more accurate to conceptualize a particular patient or therapy as occupying places on multiple continua (characteristics or features). As a consequence, sometimes a patient's scores on multiple characteristics appear to suggest different forms of therapy. For example, there is evidence from the current research project to suggest that a female patient with a high level of QOR should be referred to interpretive therapy (based on her level of QOR), and there is evidence to suggest that the same patient should be referred to supportive therapy (based on her gender). Such circumstances make it difficult to recommend a patient–therapy match.

Sometimes the location of a patient on a particular characteristic such as QOR is neither high nor low. Similarly, sometimes the location of a therapy on a particular feature such as transference interpretation is neither high nor low. The presence of moderate scores also makes it difficult to recommend a patient–therapy match.

There are obstacles to progress at different stages of therapy and responses of the patient that call for modifications in the predominant technique. For example, in a primarily interpretive therapy, it is important the therapist be supportive enough to establish a strong therapeutic alliance early in therapy. Sometimes there is a genuine threat that the patient will drop out of treatment prematurely. The therapist may need to shift emphasis to retain the patient and resume interpretive work. As interpretive therapy progresses, resistance to work on sensitive topics and weakening of the alliance are familiar events. Examining the patient's transference is a particularly sensitive process. Again, the patient's response may call for a temporary shift in emphasis to a more supportive approach. Finally, termination is a time when a shift in emphasis toward a more supportive approach may be helpful in consolidating what has been accomplished and avoiding a traumatic termination. The general principle, which is illustrated with clinical examples in chapters 9 and 10, is that supportive emphasis is sometimes required in interpretive therapy to permit the interpretive process to occur.

Regardless of the complexity of the matching decision, the therapist has to make an initial choice about the form of therapy or type of emphasis that will be provided and then be prepared to modify the technique as required. Patients often surprise us, sometimes pleasantly and sometimes unpleasantly. Although we believe that providing therapies that are primarily interpretive or primarily supportive can be very effective, we also believe that at times therapists have to be prepared to shift their approach (e.g., shift their emphasis on one or more of the interpretive and supportive dimensions to bring about an effective therapy experience). In this context, the findings of the current research project and those of other matching studies provide guidelines that represent approximations about what to offer patients or what type of emphasis seems to be the most appropriate. Over time, as a result of being informed by future studies, the approximations will become more accurate. In the meantime, the best strategy to follow is to keep informed about current research developments and be prepared to be flexible.

FUTURE DIRECTIONS

Some of the future directions concerning the optimal matching of therapies and patients with psychological problems appear to be clear. For example, it is all but certain that there will continue to be a strong demand for short-term therapies, many of which will be time-limited. The social and economic forces that gave rise to the development and acceptance of short-term therapies remain in effect. Many clinicians believe that worthwhile gains can be made for many patients in short-term therapies and that a model that allows for repeated treatments with short-term therapies over the patient's life span, if needed, is preferable to a model that routinely advocates long-term continuous treatment for most outpatients. This is not to deny that many of the very same clinicians believe that long-term or intensive treatment is needed to make significant changes in some patients—those with personality disorders, for example. The advantages associated with short-term therapies, such as the avoidance of overdependency, appear to be well-recognized. In addition, the entire health care field, including mental health, continues to experience reform. Growing increases in health care costs continue to provide strong motivation to develop less costly systems of health care. Often the total funds provided for the treatment of a particular disorder are limited for a given year. Such arrangements are conducive to time-limited and short-term treatments. During the past decade there has been much turmoil and instability regarding health care reform in countries such as the United States, which favor privately operated managed care systems. There has also been much unrest regarding health care reform in countries such as Canada, which favor publicly funded systems. However, despite considerable uncertainty concerning the eventual form of health care systems, treatments that conserve resources will be favored.

Given the emphasis on providing cost-effective treatments, there will be a continuing need for valid information concerning the optimal matching of patients and treatments. Failing to comply with, complete, and benefit from a given treatment only leads to expressed dissatisfaction and subsequent demands for services. Providing the right treatment to the patient in the first place avoids many problems for both privately and publicly funded systems. Acquiring valid information concerning the optimal matching of patients and therapies is not an easy task, as the research presented in this book has demonstrated. Conceptually, it requires abandoning simpler models that advocate that certain treatments are useful for all patients with a particular disorder or that all treatments are equally effective because they provide the same common ingredients. Methodologically, it requires resource-intensive projects that typically take several years or longer to complete. In the meantime, clinicians are forced to rely on the findings of a small number of studies and clinical experience.

If clinicians are expected to use information from research projects, they must be provided with clear and appealing therapy manuals. If the manuals are overly detailed or dogmatic, the clinician is less likely to use them. If they do, they run the risk of providing technique that is seemingly correct but in reality is rigid and ineffective. If manuals are overly general and schematic, it is unlikely that the treatment that is offered resembles the treatment that was studied in the research project. It has been our experience that a relatively brief manual that presents general guidelines and examples of application is well-received by clinicians and serves to preserve the integrity of the treatment that is intended.

If clinicians are expected to use information from research projects, they must also be provided with reliable and practical measures of the relevant patient characteristics. Measures that are difficult or time-consuming to administer and score will simply not be used. The procedures required for assessing the two primary patient characteristics that were used in the central research project of this book (QOR, PM) are moderate in their demands. We have successfully moved from a two-hour to a one-hour semistructured interview measure of QOR, and in doing so have improved its reliability considerably. Much of the information that is acquired is similar to the information that a clinician obtains in taking a routine history of the patient's developmental events and significant relationships. Thus, only a moderate amount of additional time is required. For PM, the interview measure can be conducted and scored in approximately 20 minutes. The major difference from traditional clinical interviews is the need for a video monitor. As we indicated in chapter 5, computer-assisted information and diagnostic systems for psychiatric patients are beginning to appear in many clinical settings. The cost is modest and we believe that the return is well worth the investment. Also worth the investment is simple familiarity with the criteria for scoring PM or QOR, which can serve to focus the clinician's attention to information that is predictive of important clinical events.

In continuing work on the matching objective, there is a need to develop multivariate models of prediction that cumulatively account for substantial amounts of variance of the criterion variables (e.g., remaining, working, and benefiting). In simple terms, this means that the strength of the prediction must be considerable to be useful and that this is more likely with multiple predictors. Taken separately, the predictive power of each of the predictors highlighted in this book is significant but modest. Taken together, they begin to account for a substantial amount of variance of the criterion variables. Although clinicians and researchers alike would prefer to discover single powerful predictors, the reality is that we must be willing to tolerate the complexity and assessment time that is required of a multivariate model of prediction. In the future, following the matching paradigm means working with profiles of predictor scores. As indicated in chapter 4, this is likely to involve progress in prescriptive therapy research, where the assessment of a set of predictor scores is followed by the selection of techniques from different orientations to constitute optimal treatment for the patient.

What is needed in the way of research to make significant progress in the optimal matching of patients and therapies is relatively clear. However, whether the resources that are required to make progress will be made available is less clear. As indicated, well-designed research projects involving psychotherapy and other psychosocial interventions are expensive and time-consuming. In recent years, funding bodies have invested far greater sums into biologically based treatments, including psychotropic medication, which is heavily used for psychological problems. In reality, of course, the comparison or combination of medication and psychosocial interventions in matching studies involving patient characteristics would be worthwhile. Somewhat surprising, such studies have also remained rare. We believe that the evidence presented in this book justifies the continued search for information concerning optimal patient–therapy matching. More important, we hope that it will contribute to inspire researchers and funding bodies to invest in such research in the future.

APPENDIX I
MANUAL FOR TIME-LIMITED, SHORT-TERM, INTERPRETIVE INDIVIDUAL THERAPY

A. *The Theoretical Approach.* The following five concepts are emphasized in the theoretical orientation of short-term interpretive therapy.

1. *Therapeutic Alliance.* Work in psychoanalytic psychotherapy is very much a collaborative activity. Both parties (patient and therapist) must possess certain abilities and a willingness to pursue a particular kind of work, even when that is difficult. The patient must be willing to self-disclose, to experience unpleasant feelings, to think about interpretations that are partly experienced as puzzling and frightening, to learn even when it is painful and unflattering, to tolerate certain deprivations on the therapist's part, and to be patient. The therapist must be willing to tolerate tension and uncertainty, to withhold support and other immediately gratifying offerings (advice, instruction, compliments), to experience negative transference, to examine and contain personal countertransferential reactions, to continuously devote energy to understanding the patient and to providing useful interventions, and to be patient. Engaging in such work requires a trust in the intentions of the other party and an optimism that in time the process will be useful. The presence of such trust, optimism, and willingness to engage in a particular kind of work is usually what is meant by a therapeutic alliance (helping alliance, working relationship).

2. *Passive–Receptive Approach.* Given the short-term and time-limited modality, the therapist is active relative to longer term therapies. However, the nature of the therapist's activity is passive rather than directive and receptive rather than intrusive. This approach allows the therapist to listen, to empathize, to think—to make associations, integrate material, formulate ideas, construct interpretations, and consider the appropriateness of their delivery. The patient does the majority of the talking. The process involves a talker and a listener who welcomes and encourages the provision of private material and who eventually offers clarifications and interpretations. The process should not resemble a two-way conversation or a question and answer dialogue. Questions and other noninterpretive interventions should not be used to sustain the patient's speech. Pressuring the patient to accept ideas by means of therapist activity is antithetical to this approach. Interventions should be brief and to the point, in most cases not exceeding a sentence or two. The passive–receptive approach creates a steady pressure on the patient to provide material. This pressure may serve to heighten anxiety and regressive reactions, which provide further material for interpretation.

3. *Interpretive Approach.* This approach emphasizes interpretive rather than supportive interventions. The approach does not exclude all supportive interventions, which are necessary to facilitate and maintain a working alliance as noted later. However, supportive interventions are regarded as serving interpretive work. *Interpretations* are defined as constructions that focus on the components of internal conflicts and the dynamic relationships among the components. This involves one or more wish–anxiety–defense–expression sequences. Elucidation of the objects that are associated with the components is also regarded as important. Topographically, interpretations are assumed to increase the patient's awareness of unconscious and preconscious material. Usually interpretations deal with only part of a conflict (or sequence). Integrative interpretations–in other words, those that deal with multiple components of a conflict (or sequence)—almost always follow interpretive work that is partial, that is repetitive, and that is applied to different objects and periods of time. In this context, linking similar patient relationships with different objects is viewed as important. The interpretive approach similarly tends to heighten anxiety and precipitate regressive reactions. It also serves to stimulate a progressive process of understanding and change.

4. *Therapist and Other Transferential Reactions.* The patient's transferential relationship with the therapist is viewed as a central axis for interpretive work. The immediacy and intensity of this relationship make it uniquely advantageous as a vehicle for exploring and understanding the patient's conflicts and difficulties. However, exclusive focus on therapist transferential reactions is not advocated. Examination of transferential reactions to other objects is important, particularly when they can be related to transferential

reactions involving the therapist. Because of tensions experienced by both the patient and the therapist and the obvious importance of other relationships in the patient's life, it is often easy for the therapist to neglect interpretive work involving the therapist as a transference object. Such neglect should be avoided.

5. *Problem Focus.* Because of the structure of short-term individual therapy—for example, once-a-week sessions for 20 weeks—it is important to define and maintain a focus that limits the problems that become the primary target of interpretive work. This has been designated in the literature as the patient's focal conflict or core conflictual relationship theme. It usually refers to a repetitive conflict with maladaptive outcomes with a similar set of objects. It is assumed that relative to a superficial exploration of a number of conflict areas, a more thorough exploration and understanding of a singular focal–conflict area will be more beneficial to the patient. Maintaining a focus is often difficult because of concerns that treatment will only be partial and tensions that arise when a focal conflict is examined in some depth. Given the potential range of conflict areas with different objects that could be explored for each patient, the therapist should remember that short-term individual therapy is inevitably a partial treatment. Despite its partial nature it has the potential to serve as an important model for understanding and problem solving that in the future can be applied to other areas of the patient's life (either by the patient or by the patient and a therapist) if the need arises.

B. *The Contractual Agreement.* The patient and therapist agree to work together for a fixed duration of time—for example, 20 weeks. Fifty-minute sessions are held once weekly at regular, prearranged times. The patient is encouraged to punctually attend all scheduled sessions, and responsibility for doing so is left to him or her. Each session is ended by the therapist after the allotted time. The therapist is paid by a third party. All sessions are tape-recorded. The patient is asked to talk freely about whatever occurs to him or her during each session. The therapist agrees to assist the patient in understanding and resolving conflicts that are presumed to underlie problems that have brought the patient to therapy.

C. *Implications of Theoretical Concepts for the Therapist's Activity.* The aforementioned theoretical concepts that are emphasized when conducting short-term interpretive therapy have implications for therapist activity.

A1. *Therapeutic Alliance.* Establishing a strong therapeutic alliance usually requires an initial therapist role that is relatively active, educative, and supportive. Initial attention to such topics as what can be expected of the therapist, what will be required of the patient, what can be expected about outcome, what can be expected regarding the structural features of therapy, and so forth, is often very helpful in establishing a working alliance. Maintaining a therapeutic alliance is a function of many factors. However, it is believed that a consistent provision of the passive–receptive approach (being a sensitive, empathic, inquisitive, and concerned listener) and the interpretive approach (being a provider of thoughtful clarifications and interpretations that are largely based on clinical material rather than just theory or personal reactions) will serve to maintain and even strengthen the therapeutic alliance.

Example 1:

Patient: So what should I talk about?
Therapist: You can talk about whatever goes through your mind, no matter how irrational it sounds in your own ears. The idea is to try not to censor what you say.

Example 2:

Patient: Do you have kids, too?
Therapist: I usually do not answer questions about myself because I believe that we can find out more about you and what is creating your concerns if we look at what is behind your question. For example, in asking if I have children, you might be really wanting to know if I can appreciate how challenging your children can be for you.

A2. *The Passive–Receptive Approach.* The kind of activity that is unique to the interpretive therapist is evidenced through his or her receptivity to everything that emanates from the patient. The therapist attempts to allow him- or herself to be permeated by the flow of what the patient produced (verbal, nonverbal) with as little preconception as possible. The therapist also tries to be aware of his or her own feeling reactions and his or her own flow of thinking and imagery. This free-floating and eventually focusing attention is the most constant form of activity of the therapist. The focus is on the conflictual constellation of the patient.

The following examples illustrate the manner in which the therapist responds to the patient's direct or indirect requests for intervention.

Example 3: The patient is silent. The therapist accepts this silence as reflecting introspection and reflection. He or she does not disrupt this process by intruding with questions, prompts, or cues. If the therapist believes that a protracted silence is counterproductive, he or she suggests what it conveys:

Therapist: I think that your silence today may be a way of asking me to help you decide what to talk about.

Therapist: I wonder if your silence today is a way of telling me that you feel uncomfortable or frightened to talk about what is going through your mind.

Therapist: I think that your silence may be a way of avoiding delving into some painful thoughts or feelings.

Example 4:

Patient: I do not know what to talk about.

The therapist receives this statement with acceptance; the therapist awaits the patient's decision about what to talk about. In the early phase of therapy, the therapist may reiterate that the patient is to talk about whatever goes through his or her mind:

Therapist: I guess it's hard for you to believe that you really can talk about what ever comes into your mind.

At a later phase of therapy, the therapist may suggest what the statement conveys:

Therapist: I think you might be hoping that I will tell you what to talk about, as if I knew better than you what was the "right" thing to talk about.

Therapist: I wonder if your difficulty talking today is related to what you were talking about last week: your fear that I secretly judge you.

Therapist: I think that you are perhaps trying to convince yourself and me that you are not capable of deciding for yourself what to talk about.

A3. *Interpretive Approach.* Although consistent with the passive–receptive approach, these examples illustrate the third concept that is emphasized in short-term interpretive therapy. At some point the therapist feels a certain pressure to formulate an interpretation. That point occurs when the therapist has evolved a unit of meaning that he or she believes is valid and when the therapist believes that the patient is receptive. *Receptivity* refers to whether the patient will understand the interpretation and will be able to relate to it. Before making an interpretation the therapist at times makes other interventions—for example, facilitative remarks, questions, and clarifying statements. However, the purpose of the therapist's attention and preliminary interventions is to provide interpretations.

An *interpretation* is defined as a construction that links (or associates) different components of a conflict. One or more dynamic components must be included. *Dynamic* refers to the quality of internal force. It means that the component is assumed to be exerting an internal force on some part of the patient. There are four kinds of dynamic components: impulses (drives, motives, wishes); anxiety (fear of impulse expression); defensive processes (avoiding, resisting, minimizing); and dynamic expressions. Dynamic expressions are patient affects, cognitions, and behaviors that are presented as having a dynamic influence on the patient. There are two kinds of nondynamic components: objects and resultant expressions. *Objects* are persons other than the patient. *Resultant expressions* are patient affects, cognitions, and behaviors that are presented as end states, that is as not having a dynamic influence on the patient.

An interpretation thus involves one or more dynamic components and may additionally make reference to nondynamic components. Conceptually the therapist has in mind a particular impulse to expression sequence consisting of an impulse (or wish) that is perceived unconsciously to be dangerous and in need of repression; anxiety; and various defensive processes that are used to protect the patient from high levels of anxiety. Sometimes the reverse occurs. What is consistently attempted, however, is a statement about the association between anxiety and defenses before a statement about the impulse (or wish). Reference to related dynamic expressions may occur at various points as long as the basic, anxiety–defense to impulse, interpretive sequence is preserved.

In these examples, the therapist's interventions were actually addressing the various dynamic components of the patient's conflict.

Example 1:

Therapist: You can talk about whatever goes through your mind, no matter how irrational they sound in your own ears. The idea is to *try not to censor what you say.*

In this intervention, the therapist is encouraging the patient not to be defensive or guarded.

Example 2:

Therapist: I usually do not answer questions about myself because I believe that we can find out more about you and what is creating your concerns if we look at what is behind your question. For example, in asking if I have children, *you might be really wanting to know if I can appreciate* how challenging your children can be for *you.*

In this example, the therapist is addressing the patient's wish to be understood and accepted by the therapist.

Example 3:

Therapist: I think that your silence today may be a way of *asking me to help you* decide what to talk about.

Therapist: I wonder if your silence today is a way of telling me that *you feel uncomfortable or frightened* to talk about what is going through your mind.

Therapist: I think that your silence may be a way of *avoiding delving into some painful thoughts or feelings*.

These three responses to the silent patient represent the therapist's interpretations of the dynamics hypothesized to be reflected in the silence. The first intervention addresses the patient's wish to procure direction. The second addresses the patient's anxiety or discomfort. The third addresses the patient's resistance to the introspective process.

Example 4:

Therapist: I think you might be *hoping that I will tell you what to talk about*, as if I knew better than you what was the "right" thing to talk about.

Therapist: I wonder if your difficulty talking today is related to what you were talking about last week: *your fear that I secretly judge you*.

Therapist: I think that you are perhaps *trying to convince yourself and me that you are not capable* of deciding for yourself what to talk about.

These three possible therapist responses to the patient's statement that she does not know what to talk about address her wish for direction, her fear of judgment, and her avoidance of initiative and mastery in the session, respectively.

A4. *Therapist and Other Transferential Reactions.* A second type of interpretive sequence, this time involving objects, is also attempted. In this case, an interpretation about current objects (significant others in the patient's life) is made before a related interpretation about the transference object (the therapist) or a related interpretation about historically important objects (parents and parent-like figures). Over time, and with the patient's assistance, the therapist attempts to explore the patient's conflicts as traced through his/her current relationships outside of therapy, his/her immediate relationship with the therapist, and the patient's past (early, parental) relationships.

If we reconsider Example 4, the therapist could respond in the following way such that the interpretation evolves into version 4b:

Example 4b:

Therapist: I think that you are afraid that if you decide what you want to talk about, that it will be the "wrong" thing. It is as if your father is in your mind ready to criticize your decisions just as he did when you were a child. You seem to be trying to convince yourself, and me, that your father was right; that you are incapable of deciding. You try to keep your father alive if only in your mind by remaining his little girl, his incompetent little girl. And now you would like me to be your father and make your decisions for you, or judge you; to keep your father alive by creating him in me.

In this example, the therapist links the patient's fear of being judged with her relationship with a critical father. The father is interpreted as being both an external object of her childhood and an internal or introjected object of the present. The therapist also interprets the patient's defense against letting go of her father by identifying with him such that she undermines herself, and also by projecting onto the therapist those controlling, judgmental qualities of her father. The wish for guidance is also interpreted. Hence, the therapist identifies the pathological nature of the patient's relationship with her father and links this to her relationship with the therapist. In the literature such interpretations are called parent–therapist links.

A5. *Problem Focus.* In short-term individual therapy, the therapist highlights in his or her mind a constellation of related conflicts around which his or her attention is focused. The conflicts are conceptually related to the therapist's estimate of the developmental level of the patient's most important object relations. Typical focus is around triangular-level, controlling- level, or searching-level relationships. In this way the therapist's interpretations are more focalized (or circumscribed) than would be the case in long-term therapy.

In Example 4b, the therapist is guided by this problem focus. The patient described a background wherein her father was a very controlling man. He was impatient with the patient, not allowing her to find her own way. For example, the patient wanted to take a year off after high school before pursuing university. She planned to travel through Europe with some friends during her year off. Her father disagreed with this plan, cautioning her that she would probably end up raped if not murdered. The patient succumbed to her father's pressure and entered university immediately after high school, studying education. She failed her first year and dropped out. She has never visited Europe, and has never returned to university. She works as a clerk, where she feels unappreciated, underpaid, and overqualified.

Themes related to rebelling against her father versus complying with his authority are believed to be particularly central to this woman's difficulties. Material produced by the patient is filtered through this problem focus by the therapist. Material relevant to the identified focus receives particular emphasis by the therapist. This history, therefore, guides the therapist's focus for intervention.

Whatever a patient says (and does) following an interpretation is viewed by the therapist as an association to the interpretation. The flow of subsequent material is understood in terms of the patient working on the interpretation in the way that he or she might have understood it. The material usually suggests confirmation or rejection of the interpretation. An impression of confirmation or rejection is never based on conscious statements of the patient, but rather on the overall understanding of the meaning of the flow of subsequent material. Although the patient might express disagreement, what he or she says and how the interpretation is engaged may provide evidence of confirmation of a particular part of the interpretation. The patient's response to the interpretation may highlight certain aspects of it or open up new areas in need of further exploration and clarification. This process of working on the interpretation or some part of its components is viewed as one type of working through. It of course may trigger further interpretations.

The patient in our example, may have responded to the interpretation in the following way:

Patient: My father always thought he knew what was best for me. And maybe he did. But what I wanted was never important, never valid. He never gave me any credit; he never was interested in what was important to me. He always thought I was a loser, and now look at me, I am a loser; I've never amounted to anything.

The therapist has thus been provided with more information that expands his understanding of the patient, clarifies the problem focus, and forms the basis for further interpretations:

Therapist: Yes, I think that's what you always wanted: to feel important to your father, to be taken seriously, to feel that you mattered. But the only relationship you had with him was based on you being incompetent; you needing him. So, in some ways you sabotage yourself to prove to your father that he was right, that you still need him. You maintain your attachment to your father at the cost of your own success and happiness.

B. *The Contractual Agreement.* In addition to necessitating the formulation of a problem focus, the time limit has implications for therapist activity in another way. As therapy progresses toward its prearranged, termination time, the patient's reactions to ending his/her relationship with the therapist must be carefully considered and interpreted. Interpretations are made in light of how the patient experienced and reacted to the endings of previous relationships. Termination provides a natural and realistic opportunity to examine and understand how the patient currently deals with a difficult but repetitive aspect of his/her life.

Example 4b can evolve into version 4c to appropriately address the termination issue.

Example 4c:

Therapist: Your difficulty deciding what to talk about has increased as we approach termination. I think you are trying to convince me that you still need me in a way that is similar to how you try to convince your father that you still need him. I think it is frightening for you to let go of me in the same way that you are frightened to let go of your father, or at least the type of relationship you have with your father.

General Principles that Guide the Therapist's Behavior

1. There should be an absence of narcissistic gratification of the patient. Accordingly, the therapist does not welcome the patient at each session, but merely greets him or her. He does not encourage personal familiarity. Thus, he does not attempt to display emotions or make personal disclosures. The therapist does not suggest a topic at the onset of the session nor does he or she try to establish a predetermined agenda. The therapist is not compelled to answer questions unless it is viewed as fulfilling a therapeutic purpose. The therapist does not attempt to prevent or rescue the patient from experiencing uncomfortable emotions during the sessions.

2. There should be a working alliance with the patient. The therapist attempts to ally him- or herself with the healthy, adaptive part of the patient toward the task of understanding the conflictual aspects of the patient's life. The therapist is attentive, warm, and empathic. He or she is present and receptive. He or she demonstrates interest through the attention he or she pays to the productions of the patient.

APPENDIX II
MANUAL FOR TIME-LIMITED, SHORT-TERM SUPPORTIVE INDIVIDUAL THERAPY

A. *The Contractual Agreement.* The patient and therapist agree to work together for a fixed duration of time—for example, 20 weeks. Fifty-minute sessions are held once weekly at regular, prearranged times. The patient is encouraged to punctually attend all scheduled sessions and responsibility for doing so is left to him or her. Each session is ended by the therapist after the allotted time. The therapist is paid by a third party. All sessions are tape-recorded. The patient is asked to talk freely about whatever occurs to him or her during each session. The therapist agrees to assist the patient in improving his or her adaptation to the problematic situation that brought the patient to therapy.

B. *Theoretical Approach.* The theoretical orientation of short-term supportive therapy emphasizes concepts that are characteristic of the psychodynamic orientation. The major difference between supportive therapy and interpretive therapy concerns the manner in which the therapist translates psychodynamic principles into therapeutic interventions; the difference between the two therapies relates to differences in the therapist's technique. In general, the SUP therapist responds in terms of current realities, including the realistic aspects of the transference and resistance when applicable. Transference distortion and regression are discouraged. The SUP therapist's techniques include supportive, advisory, informative, clarifying, and confronting interventions. The attention of the therapist must be on the technique as it is experienced by the patient. Although all therapies use these interventions, the SUP therapist emphasizes them in his or her therapeutic technique relative to the interpretive interventions.

C. *Theoretical Concepts and Their Implications for Therapist Technique.*
    1. *Problem Focus.* Based on the patient's history, the therapist highlights in his or her mind a constellation of related psychodynamic conflicts around which his or her attention is focused. The conflicts are conceptually related to the therapist's estimate of the developmental level of the patient's most important object relations. Typical focus is around Oedipal-level, obsessional-level, or depressive-level relationships. In this way the therapist's

interventions are more focalized (or circumscribed) than would be the case in long-term therapy. This history guides the focus of the therapist's interventions. However, the SUP therapist focuses on conscious and preconscious elements in the patient's productions; unconscious aspects of the patient's material are ignored or discouraged. The SUP therapist encourages logical and rational thought processes.

Example 1. The patient described a background wherein her father was a very controlling man. He was impatient with the patient, not allowing her to find her own way. For example, the patient wanted to take a year off after high school before pursuing university. She planned to travel through Europe with some friends during her year off. Her father disagreed with this plan, cautioning her that she would probably end up raped if not murdered. The patient succumbed to her father's pressure and entered university immediately after high school, studying education. She failed her first year and dropped out. She has never visited Europe, and has never returned to university. She works as a clerk, where she feels unappreciated, underpaid, and overqualified.

Themes related to rebelling against her father versus complying with his authority are believed to be particularly central to this woman's difficulties. Material produced by the patient is filtered through this problem focus by the therapist. Material relevant to the identified focus receives particular emphasis by the therapist:

Patient: I do not know what to talk about.
Therapist: Yes, sometimes it is difficult to know where to begin. Maybe you could begin by telling me how your week went and I am sure that will lead us into some important material.

In this example, the therapist succumbs to the patient's indirect request to be told what to talk about. However, the therapist avoids acting like her father by being general in his suggestion and by reassuring her that she is capable of leading them to important material.

2. Therapist and Other Transferential Reactions. Based on the type of pathological relationships that the patient has tended to create, the therapist is sensitive to attempts to recreate this pattern with him or her. Transference distortions involving the therapist are not encouraged. Rather, the therapist's "realness" is emphasized. The therapist promotes a feeling of security in the therapeutic relationship by communicating his or her interest in, liking for, or understanding of the patient. Negative transferences are dissipated immediately. The therapist's responses to the patient's statements focus on the reality aspects of the communication. The emphasis is to explore interpersonal relationships outside the treatment situation. Hence, the patient is, first, confronted with the reality of the treatment relationship; second, the transferences are directed out of therapy as the therapist points out parallels in similar feelings toward significant others in the patient's life.

The aim in SUP is to maintain a mildly positive transference, which is not commented on. This is encouraged by the therapist's being more real and somewhat gratifying of the patient. Distorted, excessively positive transferences (e.g., idealizing or erotic) do not need to be responded to, though the therapist may indicate skepticism of the patient's idealization. The therapist's responses will sometimes address specific defensive operations or distortions, and at other times consist of guidance more appropriate to the family doctor role. Because the therapist's interventions include the latter, there is a danger that the therapist will attempt to overly influence the patient–in other words, "do as I do." The therapist should guard against such countertransference stringently.

Example 2.

Patient: I guess it is frustrating for you to work with someone who does not get any better.
Therapist: Oh but I feel that we are making progress. But changing is long and hard work. And that might become pretty frustrating for you, especially if you are a chip off the old block. Your father, he would get frustrated with you pretty fast, wouldn't he?

3. *Resistances.* Based on the conceptualization of the patient's usual defense mechanisms, the therapist identifies adaptive defenses that should be supported, encouraged, and strengthened and maladaptive defenses that can safely be clarified, confronted, undermined, and actively discouraged without seriously compromising the patient's ability to function. Hence, defenses are evaluated according to their adaptational and homeostatic value. When defense mechanisms are reflected in the patient's resistance in the therapy situation, the therapist's response is consistent with the goal of strengthening adaptive defenses and weakening maladaptive defenses. Often, the patient's behaviors have conflicting adaptational value and the therapist must make a clinical judgement about strengthening, undermining, or ignoring the behaviors, resistances, or defenses.

Example 3.

Patient: (Silence.)
Therapist: You seem to feel a bit uncomfortable today. I guess sometimes it is hard to know where to begin. But there really is no right or wrong thing to talk about. Once the ball gets rolling, you will feel comfortable again. So tell me, what has been going through your mind since I saw you last?

4. *Ego-Strength*. SUP aims to strengthen the patient's ego functions. Hence, the therapist seeks solutions to problems in the patient's current living situation by focusing on behavior and not the meaning of behavior. Generating solutions to problematic situations involves helping the patient map out more effective coping strategies or improving his or her adaptation. An important aspect of building ego-strength is conveying to the patient that his or her feelings and predicaments are accurately understood.

Example 4.

Patient: I would just like to punch him.
Therapist: Well it sounds like you have many mixed feelings. When you say you want to punch him, I guess that means you feel pretty angry. So the question becomes: What are you going to do with all this anger? Because I know that you will not really punch him.

5. *Ego-Gratification*. Consistent with building ego-strength, the patient's direct or indirect attempts to elicit praise and encouragement from the therapist are gratified. In response to the patient's efforts to improve his or her adaptation, the therapist spontaneously offers praise and encouragement. He or she attempts to minimize anxiety and regression in the therapy sessions. Thus, the patient experiences sessions as less frustrating.

Example 5.

Patient: So I said to him, "You know dad, it makes me feel that you do not believe in me when you keep telling me what to do." And he looked so surprised and said "No, dear, I know you can sort it out, I just thought it would save you the hassle if you went to my garage."
Therapist: Well, that is excellent. It took a lot of courage to tell your dad how you feel, and it sounds like it worked out very well. So what do you make of your dad's response?

D. *Categories of Therapist's Interventions.*

The therapist's interventions can be categorized into the following types of interventions.

I. *Supportive Interventions.*

1. *Collaboration.* The therapist encourages the working alliance by conveying that therapy is a joint effort. This task is aided by frequent use of the word "we"; by showing respect for the patient; by recognizing the patient's growing ability to employ the basic tools of treatment; by referring to experiences that the patient and therapist have been through together; and by engaging in a joint effort for adaptation.

Example 6.

Patient: So what should I talk about?
Therapist: Well, we were talking last week about your difficulty in just jumping in, trusting yourself to know what is best for you. Can you describe to me any events that left you second guessing yourself during this past week?

2. *Morale.* The giving of reassurance and hope must be based on an adequate understanding of the patient. Reassurance is effective when related to the patient's goals and past successes. Reassurance based on the therapist's expert knowledge can also be given.

Example 7.

Patient: Do you have kids too?
Therapist: It certainly is challenging to raise kids these days. Of course every parent experiences different types of stressors and has different types of strengths and weaknesses. Last week you were saying that you make a point of reading to your children before bedtime, and that that is rewarding for both you and the kids. I agree that it is important for kids to feel they are a significant part of their parents' lives and for parents to show that learning can be fun. So that is one of your strengths as a parent. Now, this other part you were describing, that you find it hard to know what the right thing is when disciplining your daughter. Tell me more about what the right thing means to you.

3. *Permission.* The SUP therapist accepts the patient's abreaction without interpretation. Active responses may include tracking (indicating that the therapist is following the patient), universalizing (clarifying that many people have similar feelings, wishes, or problems), or decatastrophizing (minimizing issues or problems the patient has exaggerated).

Example 8.

Patient: I feel like I'm a big softie; my kids do not respect me. They do exactly what they want. They are out of control. They are going to have no respect for the law and will probably end up dropping out of school and landing up in jail.
Therapist: Well, I think you might be getting ahead of yourself there. They seem to respect their teachers and have not gotten into trouble with either their teachers or the law. In terms of them not respecting you, I think this is something you recognize and are working toward changing. And your kids are young enough that you will be able to exert a strong influence on them. Now this softie business, you were saying you feel guilty and sort of

mean when you have to be firm with them. Tell me more about being mean and being firm.

4. *Approval.* Encouragement and praise are supportive of the patient's self-esteem, but valuable only when given for what the patient holds as praiseworthy. A task of SUP is to make the patient's assets sources of praise; however, praise is used moderately and ideally in the context of a good psychodynamic understanding of the patient, a basic level of trust, and a positive transference.

Example 9.

Patient: So I said to my daughter, you can go to the birthday party, but you are to take a taxi home. You are not to get in a car with someone who has been drinking. That's my deal, take it or leave it.

Therapist: So you are reassuring yourself that her safety is protected but at the same time you are not controlling her the way your father used to control you. I think this is important that you can find a middle ground between being a softie and being too controlling like your father.

5. *Competence.* The therapist places emphasis on the patient's realistic strengths and talents and encourages sublimations congruent with the patient's character style.

Example 10.

Patient: I have been thinking of applying for the supervisor's position.
Therapist: Well, you are obviously very competent at your job, and in some ways overqualified. I am wondering, though, whether you would enjoy supervising other people. You say you do not like feeling like the "bad guy" with your kids. It might be hard for you to, say, discipline someone. What about that other job you were telling me about last week?

II. *Advising Interventions*

1. *Suggestions and advice.* The therapist at times makes direct suggestions urging certain behaviors. The rationale for the advice is made explicit. Requests for advice are best handled by helping the patient consider alternatives.

Example 11.

Patient: I have been thinking of quitting my job and taking out a student loan to go back to university. Maybe I will take English; I have always loved literature.

Therapist: Well, there is no doubt that you would probably do very well in school. I guess I am thinking that you are a very practical type of person. I am wondering what your plans are about finances. It would take a lot of careful planning to go back to school. And again, if you do go back to school, I am wondering if you would not be happier taking something more practical as a major, and maybe taking an English literature course just for fun?

2. *Environmental Interventions.* Interventions directly concerning the patient's functioning in his or her environment make it clear the therapist believes the patient can operate at a healthier level. Although important as a direct reality intervention, such comments also demonstrate the therapist's values and can influence the patient's ego and superego identifications.

Example 12.

Patient: If I moved in with Dave, it would be much easier financially. But I do not know, he is a bit of a bully. That might be good for the kids, though, you know, to have a father figure.

Therapist: Well, maybe you mean authority figure. It would be easier to let Dave do the disciplining for you but I think you want to learn how to do this yourself. How would you feel if Dave started running the show?

3. *Management.* The therapist directly influences the patient's negative behaviors by making prohibitions and setting limits. Management interventions are again used sparingly and based on understanding, trust, and positive transference.

Example 13.

Patient: I really lost my temper with my daughter. We came back late from the party. There she was with her boyfriend at two in the morning watching television. Now I feel so guilty and she thinks I do not trust her. I do trust her. I do not know what came over me.

Therapist: Well I guess we have talked about this before. You and alcohol just do not mix. Not even once in a while.

III. *Informing Interventions*

1. *Education.* Educative comments help the patient in handling problems more effectively and also relieve anxiety by focusing attention on cognitive elements and away from unconscious conflict.

Example 14.

Patient: I do not know how to talk to my son about the fact that he is adopted. What do you say?

Therapist: Well, you could just tell him the truth. You might tell just what you told me last week: That you wanted him, that you love him, and that if he wants to find his birth mother you would help him. I believe there is an agency now that will bring children and birth mothers together if both register with them and state their desire for reunion.

2. *Modeling.* The therapist's modeling of coping skills and values provides knowledge to be introjected and eventually identified with by the patient.

Example 15.

Patient: I do not suppose you would come down to my office and tell my colleague for me that I do not want to date him!

Therapist: I appreciate your invitation and I am flattered by your confidence in me but I do not think that would be proper given our professional relationship.

Patient: Say that again, I think I will use that line, that sounded good.

3. *"Benign delusions."* The therapist offers explanations that locate the responsibility for the patient's difficulties either outside him- or herself, in other people, or in body chemistry or physiology. These constructions diminish the patient's anxiety by relieving him or her of responsibility and by focusing attention away from the pathogenic unconscious conflict.

Example 16.

Patient: I am just such a loser.

Therapist: Well, I think you have been told that all your life. After a while you start to believe it. You live up or down to the expectations that were set for you. In your case your father thought you could do nothing right, and it will take a while to erase that tape.

IV. *Clarifying Interventions.*

The therapist clarifies by asking for more information, by pointing out connections the patient has not made but could know, by restating more directly what the patient has said, or by reframing a more objective and less distorted view about the patient's life situation. Clarification has the goal of limited insight into conscious and preconscious material and connections.

Example 17.

Patient: I just always feel so guilty whenever I try to discipline her. I just do not understand it. I was a kid once, I know what it is like to want to spread your wings. I also know that it is a dangerous world out there.

Therapist: Well I think that might be part of the problem. You know what it is like to be a teenager. So you can empathize with her wish to have fun and kick up her heels. As a parent you also know what dangers lurk out there for her. You want to protect her from the dangers but you have to clip her wings a bit to do that. You also remember what it feels like to have your wings clipped. Like when your father forbade you to go to Europe when you were the same age as your daughter. So your problem is that there is still a part of you that is a teenager like your daughter and now there is part of you that is a parent like your father.

V. *Confronting Intervention.*

Confrontation refers to the therapist's forcefully directing the patient's attention to something in the treatment, particularly when behavioral incongruities indicate that conflict or defensive operations are marked.

Example 18.

Patient: I made up my mind that I just have to trust her and that is that.
Therapist: Well, I am not so sure that trust is the issue. I think it might be more that you have real difficulty setting limits with your daughter because you feel guilty, you feel like "the bad guy." What do you think?

APPENDIX III
RATER MANUAL FOR THE INTERPRETIVE AND SUPPORTIVE TECHNIQUE SCALE

This manual has been prepared to facilitate use of the Interpretive and Supportive Technique Scale (ISTS) for supportive and interpretive forms of time-limited, short-term, individual psychodynamic psychotherapy. The ISTS is used to rate the amount of therapist emphasis on particular features of each form of therapy, which are prescribed in corresponding treatment manuals. From the ratings, scores are derived that represent the amount of emphasis on each form of therapy and the relative emphasis on the two.

Supportive psychotherapy and interpretive psychotherapy have often been referred to as distinct entities. Some investigators have suggested that it is preferable to think in terms of a supportive–interpretive continuum, with particular forms of therapy ordered along it. Even more accurate, however, is the concept of multiple supportive–interpretive continua, each representing a different feature. The features concern overall objectives, session objectives, and technique. Each form of therapy can be located on each continuum. This is the concept on which the ISTS was constructed. In regard to overall objectives, at the supportive end of the continuum, there are primary attempts to improve the patient's immediate adaptation to his or her life situation. There is a crisis-intervention orientation. A secondary objective is to teach the patient problem-solving skills. At the interpretive end of the continuum, there is a primary attempt to enhance the patient's insight about repetitive conflicts and trauma that underlie problems and to initiate a continuing process of understanding and control. A secondary objective is to alleviate the presenting problems. Thus, both short-term and long-term objectives characterize each end of the continuum. What is primary to one tends to be secondary to the other. No therapy is exclusively at one end of the continua throughout treatment. Rather, there are degrees of emphasis. Central to the construct of adherence as measured by this scale is the notion that adherence is the degree of emphasis on the features of a particular approach to therapy, relative to emphasis on the features of another approach to therapy.

CHARACTERISTICS OF THE ISTS

A. The ISTS consists of 14 items (seven supportive features and seven interpretive features). Each item is prescribed in the treatment manual for one of the two forms of therapy.

B. The ISTS is intended for use by nonparticipant raters at the bachelor's-degree-level or higher. An effort has been made to create items that permit ratings of therapist interventions as they are heard on audiotape. An intervention is defined as any therapist statement (speaking turn). Therapist interventions range from simple facilitative remarks such as "Mm-hm" to complex statements about the patient's internal conflicts.

C. The ISTS is intended to be descriptive (i.e., what is being done), rather than evaluative (i.e., how well is it being done). Items have been made as specific as possible so that ratings require a relatively low level of inference. For each therapist intervention, the rater's task is to listen for evidence that a particular feature has occurred. If so, a mark is tallied under that feature (item). More than one mark may be tallied under a feature for a single intervention if it is lengthy or detailed. Furthermore, a single intervention may generate marks for multiple features. Thus, it is acceptable to tally marks under more than one item for a single intervention.

D. After all marks have been made, each item of the scale receives an overall rating on a 5-point Likert-type scale ranging from 0 (no emphasis) to 4 (major emphasis). Half-point ratings are *not* used. The approximate number of marks corresponding to each scale point are included below.

E. Two subscale scores and one full-scale score are derived from the item ratings. The two subscale scores are calculated by adding the scores of the seven items that correspond to each of the two treatment forms. The range of scores is 0 to 28. The subscale scores represent the quantity (amount) of technique of each form of therapy.

The full-scale score is a measure of the relative emphasis on the two therapies—in other words, adherence—and is represented as a continuum. It is keyed in the interpretive direction. It is calculated by adding 28 to the remainder of the interpretive subscore minus the supportive subscore. The range of scores is 0 to 56. Zero to 27 represents the supportive end of the continuum. Twenty-nine to 56 represents the interpretive end of the continuum. A score of 28 represents a therapy with an equal supportive and interpretive emphasis.

CONVERSION SCALE(S)

An approximate conversion scale for deriving an overall item rating from the number of marks is indicated as follows:

No. of Marks	Overall Item Score
0–1	0
2–4	1
5–7	2
8–10	3
11+	4

This conversion scale was developed after a group of raters used the ISTS with a large number of therapy sessions. We estimated the approximate number of marks associated with each scale point for each feature (item). There are three items whose scoring takes exception to the above conversion scale:

Item 3 Make *noninterpretive interventions*—for example, reflections, questions, provisions of information, clarifications, and confrontations.

No. of Marks	Overall Item Score
0–19	0
20–49	1
50–79	2
80–109	3
110+	4

Item 6 Make *interpretations*.

No. of Marks	Overall Item Score
0–3	0
4–7	1
8–13	2
14–18	3
19+	4

Item 10 Make *links* between the patient's relationship with the therapist and the patient's relationships with others.

No. of Marks	Overall Item Score
0–1	0
2–3	1
4–5	2
6–7	3
8+	4

Although scoring items is primarily determined by the frequency of marks, it is not the only criterion. Other factors that may convey the degree of emphasis include the number of marks given to a feature relative to other features, repetition, timing, and therapist's tone of voice.

ITEM DESCRIPTIONS

The following item descriptions are intended as guides in making reliable distinctions between therapist interventions. When possible, rules have been specified to assist in making the rating. The nature of ratings on the ISTS requires that the rater use his or her judgment based on the guidelines provided.

1. Gratify the patient—in other words, make the patient feel good rather than anxious in the session.

   This item focuses on the therapist's attempt to relieve the patient's tension and create a warm, positive atmosphere in the session. This may include empathic validation, encouragement, a warm friendly greeting, or laughter. Examples of such include,

   Therapist: It is good to hear that it is working out for you.
   Therapist: So how are you doing today?
   Patient: I'm okay.
   Therapist: Good.

2. Maintain pressure on the patient to talk—for example, by at times remaining passive, by not breaking pauses, by not answering questions.

   This is the only item on the ISTS that primarily focuses on what the therapist does *not* say rather than what the therapist does say. This item covers therapist silences, although brief silences are not rated. Marks are tallied if the therapist does not answer a question posed to him or her, the therapist does not respond to greetings, the therapist does not break long pauses between patient statements, or there are long pauses between therapist statements or between the two. Typically, a long pause is 30 seconds or more. Brief interventions can also receive a mark for maintaining pressure. For example,

Therapist: Continue.
Therapist: Go on.
Therapist: Can you tell me more?

3. Make noninterpretive interventions—for example, reflections, questions, provisions of information, clarification, and confrontations.

This item rates all therapist interventions that are not interpretations (see item 6). These include formal, information-providing, information-requesting interventions; questions; reflections; clarifications; confrontations; and simple facilitative remarks. This item is often a direct indicator of therapist activity during the session. Examples include,

Therapist: Last week you said that you were feeling pretty anxious.
Therapist: How is your job hunting going?
Therapist: It's been found that when a person doesn't exercise very often, he often feels fatigued.
Therapist: So you are saying that you enjoy your solitude.
Therapist: But how can you blame your coworkers for that when you are the one who was responsible for that duty?
Therapist: Mm-hm.

4. Encourage the patient to explore uncomfortable emotions.

This item deals with the therapist inquiring about the patient's affective state and encouraging the patient to explore his or her feelings. Examples include,

Therapist: Tell me about your anger.
Therapist: What are the tears for?

Reflective statements do not receive a mark. Reflective statements make reference to what the patient has said, indicating that the patient's experience is understood by the therapist. For example,

Therapist: Yes, you do seem sad.

5. Provide guidance similar to the role of family doctor—for example, advise a course of action more appropriate to healthy functioning regarding self-care, life skills, or interpersonal behavior.

This item rates interventions that offer suggestions (i.e., guidance) to the patient about appropriate actions to take. These interventions are direct, advice-giving statements and not attempts to draw the patient into a discussion of the pros and cons of alternative solutions to life problems. Examples include,

Therapist: I would suggest that you get that checked out by your doctor.
Therapist: Perhaps you should take some time for yourself and away from your girlfriend.
Therapist: I think you should go to the employment center and they could teach you about job interviews.
Therapist: Have you considered hiring a babysitter?

6. Make *interpretations*.

An intervention is defined as an interpretation if it makes reference to one or more dynamic components. A dynamic component is one part of a patient's conflict that exerts an internal force on some other part of the patient. There are four types of dynamic components: wish (impulses, drives, motives), anxiety (fear), defense, and dynamic expression.

When the intervention refers to basic sexual or aggressive impulses of the patient, a wish is rated.

Therapist: I think your success in the business world is indirectly tied to your basic aggressive drive.

To score a wish the intervention must be about the presence of a wish.

Therapist: You're hoping that I will tell you what to talk about.

Anxiety is rated when there is evidence that it is part of an internal conflict. The fear may be acting as a causal agent for an expression or may be presented as being in opposition to a wish. In general, anxiety is scored when it is attributed to the patient.

Therapist: You felt anxious and that made you pick a fight with your brother.
Therapist: You want to leave your husband but you're scared to, so in fact you stay with a man you don't love.
Therapist: You feel scared.

To score a defense, the essential idea that must be communicated in the intervention is the quality of avoiding, resisting, minimizing, distorting, being reluctant, and so forth. The idea of defensiveness must be communicated to the patient. It is not enough that the rater recognizes the identified behavior as reflecting a defensive process. What is being defended against must be internal to the patient. How the defense manifests itself is not an essential quality for rating a defense.

Therapist: You are avoiding that area.
Therapist: I think your silence may be a way of avoiding delving into some painful thoughts or feelings.

A dynamic expression refers to a therapist intervention in which two patient expressions are presented in a causal sequence. One expression (the dynamic expression) is presented as motivating or giving rise to a second expression (the resultant expression). The dynamic expression represents a part of an internal conflict. The causal connection must be clear to rate a dynamic expression. It is not rated if the two expressions can be conceived of as occurring simultaneously and not solely as sequentially.

Therapist: You felt guilty, so you bought your wife an expensive gift.
Therapist: In some ways you sabotage yourself to prove it to your father that he was right.

7. Engage in problem-solving strategies with the patient—in other words, generating and evaluating alternative solutions to external life problems.

When a therapist intervention attempts to involve the patient in generating and appraising alternative solutions to life problems, it is scored as problem solving. The patient need not respond for such an intervention to be rated as long as the intervention *attempted* to engage the patient in problem solving.

Therapist: What are some things you could do to get some experience?
Therapist: Yes, that may be fine for the short-term, but what happens when you run out of money? Is there something else that you could do that could offer more stability?

If the intervention is merely instructional rather than requesting the patient's input in the problem-solving process, then it is not rated as problem solving. For example,

Therapist: You should be out looking for a job rather than sitting at home waiting for the phone to ring.

8. Direct attention to the patient's subjective impression of the therapist.

This item rates the extent to which the therapist attempts to explore the patient's feelings, thoughts, and fantasies about the therapist. This item is not rated if the intervention is in reference to events in the room or of therapy in general. The intervention must be aimed at understanding the patient's experience of the therapist.

Therapist: How do you feel about me when I say that to you?
Therapist: Do you get angry with me when I won't tell you what to do?

Therapist: I'm a woman, does that mean you distrust and hate me too?

An example of a statement that would not be rated is,

Therapist: You seem to drift off if I don't keep talking.

9. Offer *explanations* that locate the responsibility for the patient's difficulties outside *him- or herself*—for example, in the patient's environment, as a function of interpersonal transactions, or in the patient's body chemistry or physiology.

This item rates interventions that attempt to support the patient's defensive operations. Interventions that offer explanations for patient difficulties that are external to the patient are rated here. Interventions that suggest patient control or responsibility for difficulties are not scored.

Therapist: It's hard to get out and do the things you like when you're financially strapped.
Therapist: Yes, it's sure not easy to approach females after your last two girlfriends did that to you.
Therapist: When you have low metabolism, it is difficult to be active and keep those pounds off.

The following statement would not be rated:

Therapist: It's tough to run a good business when you have poor employees, but you are the boss and can hire and fire should you need to.

10. Make *links* between the patient's relationship with the therapist and the patient's relationship with others.

This item rates interventions that link the patient's patterns of interpersonal conflict with significant others in his or her life to transactions between the patient and the therapist. It is important to note that both processes must include the patient. The directionality of the link is irrelevant, as long as one relationship includes the patient and therapist and the other includes the patient and someone outside of therapy.

Therapist: Your disappointment with me resembles your disappointment with your father.
Therapist: You get upset with me when I don't give you answers, the same way you got angry with you mother when she wouldn't help you out.

11. *Praise* the patient.

When therapist interventions include praise, commendation, or admiration of the patient, it is rated as praise. The statement does not have to be explicit, as long as the intent of the therapist is to applaud the patient.

Therapist: That's great that you were able to get the job.
Therapist: Well done.
Therapist: Good for you.

12. Focus on the *patient and therapist in the treatment situation* rather than the patient and significant others outside the treatment situation.

This item rates interventions that focus on the patient–therapist relationship. This does not include interventions that mention the treatment situation without regard to the relationship between the patient and therapist.

Therapist: It seems like you're just waiting for me to give you the answers, like I know what is best for you.
Therapist: Well, how about when you are here with me?

An example of a statement that would not be rated is,

Therapist: Therapy seems to bring out a lot of hurtful memories for you.

13. Display *personal information,* opinions, or values.

Interventions that include something of the therapist's own personal opinion or information are scored. Not all "I" statements are scored. The rater must decide if the therapist's statement involves something of his or her own experience, opinion, and so forth.

Therapist: I know how you feel, I went through the same thing with my ex-wife.
Therapist: I just hate those skate-boarders out in front of the entrance way.
Therapist: My experience with children has been similar.
Therapist: You might consider a day care arrangement; it has worked for me.
Patient: I'm thinking about going on holidays next month.
Therapist: I hear Arizona is nice at this time of year.

The following would not be rated as personal information, opinion, or value:

Therapist: I think you should stick to talking about your feelings.

14. Direct attention to the patient's *subjective impression of others* outside the treatment situation.

This item rates interventions that focus on the patient's projection. Interventions that attempt to elicit the patient's thoughts, feelings, and experiences of others outside the treatment situation are scored.

Therapist: How do you think your mother feels when you do something like that?
Therapist: How do you feel about your father when he puts you down?

RECOMMENDATIONS REGARDING TRAINING FOR USE OF THE ISTS

The ISTS is a measure of therapist technical emphasis in supportive and interpretive forms of time-limited, short-term, individual psychodynamic psychotherapy. The scale is intended to be descriptive, and not evaluative, of therapist behavior. Therefore, it requires little clinical expertise or experience and a relatively low level of inference. It is recommended that training be conducted with a group of trainees to facilitate achieving acceptable rater reliability.

Training raters in the use of the ISTS consists of four primary steps:

1. Reading relevant literature,
2. Participating in training sessions,
3. Providing independent ratings,
4. Conducting reliability determinations.

Reading materials that provide an orientation to the concepts, principles, and procedures associated with the ISTS include,

A. The Supportive and Interpretive Therapy Manuals,
B. The ISTS Manual.

Following careful reading of these materials, the trainer discusses the purpose of the ISTS (what the scale intends to measure) and reviews each of the 14 items of the scale with the trainees. Training sessions begin with the trainer demonstrating the rating process with one session for each form of therapy while the trainee group observes. Each of the two sessions should clearly illustrate features of supportive and interpretive therapies. The trainer discusses each therapist intervention with the trainees regarding the relevant features (items) of the scale. A question period at the end of each session's rating allows for clarification of any uncertainties that were not addressed during the rating process. Following this stage, the trainer chooses two new sessions (one primarily supportive, one primarily interpretive). They are rated by him- or herself and the group of trainees, simultaneously. The trainer stops periodically during the rating procedure to discuss any questions or concerns. As well, trainees may interrupt during the rating to ask questions. Again, at the end of each session's rating, time is provided to discuss any concerns or inconsistencies in the ratings.

The third step in the training procedure is to have each of the trainees rate the same supportive and interpretive sessions independently. This session material is new (i.e., the sessions were not used in the previous step). Following completion of the ratings by all trainees, any inconsistencies or questions about the ratings will be addressed by the trainer and the group.

Once the trainer believes that all trainees have a competent understanding of the ISTS and the principles underlying the rating scheme, he or she proceeds with the final step of the training process, which involves a reliability determination. For this step, eight new therapy sessions that cover a range of supportive and interpretive emphasis are used. Each session is rated independently by each trainee. The intraclass correlation coefficient (ICC; Shrout & Fleiss, 1979) is used to assess rater reliability. It is suggested that the intraclass correlations be calculated on the data averaged across sessions when raters are considered to be random effects. The random model provides an estimate, ICC $(2, k)$, of the reliability of the mean rating that might be obtained under replication with an independent sample of raters and represents the generalizability of the mean rating. Once acceptable reliability has been achieved, the raters are ready to rate independent sessions.

REFERENCES

Abraham, K. (1926). Psychoanalytical notes on Coue's method of self mastery. *International Journal of Psycho-Analysis, 7,* 190–213.

Alexander, F. (1961). *The scope of psychoanalysis.* New York: Basic Books.

Alexander, F., & French, T. M. (1946). *Psychoanalytic therapy: Principles and application.* New York: Ronald Press.

Allen, J. A., & Gordon, S. (1990). Creating a framework for change. In R. L. Meth & R. S. Pasick (Eds.), *Men in therapy: The challenge of change* (pp. 131–151). New York: Guilford Press.

American Psychiatric Association. (1984). *The psychiatric therapies.* Washington, DC: Author.

American Psychiatric Association. (1987). *Diagnostic and statistical manual of mental disorders* (3rd ed. rev.). Washington, DC: Author.

Anderson, E. M., & Lambert, M. J. (1995). Short-term dynamically oriented psychotherapy: A review and meta-analysis. *Clinical Psychology Review, 15,* 503–514.

Andrews, G., Singh, M., & Bond, M. (1993). The defense style questionnaire. *Journal of Nervous and Mental Disease, 181,* 246–256.

Annis, H. M., & Davis, C. S. (1989). Relapse prevention. In R. K. Hester & W. R. Miller (Eds.), *Handbook of alcoholism treatment approaches* (pp. 170–182). New York: Pergamon Press.

Appelbaum, A. (1989). Supportive therapy: A developmental view. In L. H. Rockland, *Supportive therapy* (pp. 40–57). New York: Basic Books.

Azim, H. F. A., Piper, W. E., Segal, P. M., Nixon, G. W. H., & Duncan, S. (1991). The quality of object relations scale. *Bulletin of the Menninger Clinic, 55,* 323–343.

Bachelor, A. (1991). Comparison and relationship to outcome of diverse dimensions of the helping alliance as seen by client and therapist. *Psychotherapy, 28,* 534–549.

Balint, M., Ornstein, P. H., & Balint, E. (1972). *Focal psychotherapy.* Philadelphia: J. B. Lippincott.

Barber, J. P., & Crits-Christoph, P. (1991). Comparison of the brief dynamic therapies. In P. Crits-Christoph & J. P. Barber (Eds.), *Handbook of short-term dynamic psychotherapy* (pp. 323–355). New York: Basic Books.

Barber, J. P., & Crits-Christoph, P. (1996). Development of a therapist adherence/ competence rating scale for supportive-expressive dynamic psychotherapy: A preliminary report. *Psychotherapy Research, 6,* 81–94.

Barber, J. P., Crits-Christoph, P., & Luborsky, L. (1996). Effects of therapist adherence and competence on patient outcome in brief dynamic therapy. *Journal of Consulting and Clinical Psychology, 64,* 619–622.

Barber, J. P., Krakauer, I., Calvo, N., Badgio, P. C., & Faude, J. (1997). Measuring adherence and competence of dynamic therapists in the treatment of cocaine dependence. *Journal of Psychotherapy Practice and Research, 6,* 12–24.

Barber, J. P., & Muenz, L. R. (1996). The role of avoidance and obsessiveness in matching patients to cognitive and interpersonal psychotherapy: Empirical findings from the TDCRP. *Journal of Consulting and Clinical Psychology, 64,* 951–958.

Beck, A. T., & Beck, R. W. (1972). Screening depressed patients in family practice: A rapid technic. *Postgraduate Medicine, 52,* 81–85.

Beck, A. T., & Emery, G. (1986). *Anxiety disorders and phobias: A cognitive perspective.* New York: Basic Books.

Beck, A. T., & Steer, R. A. (1987). *Beck depression inventory manual.* New York: Harcourt Brace Jovanovich.

Bellak, L., & Small, L. (1965). *Emergency psychotherapy and brief psychotherapy.* New York: Grune & Stratton.

Benjamin, L. S. (1982). Use of Structural Analysis of Social Behavior (SASB) to guide intervention in psychotherapy. In J. C. Anchin & D. J. Kiesler (Eds.), *Handbook of interpersonal psychotherapy* (pp. 190–212). New York: Pergamon Press.

Beutler, L. E. (1979). Toward specific psychological therapies for specific conditions. *Journal of Consulting and Clinical Psychology, 47,* 882–897.

Beutler, L. E. (1991). Have all won and must all have prizes? Revisiting Luborsky et al.'s verdict. *Journal of Consulting and Clinical Psychology, 59,* 226–232.

Beutler, L. E., & Clarkin, J. F. (1990). *Systematic treatment selection: Toward targeted therapeutic interventions.* New York: Brunner/Mazel.

Beutler, L. E., & Crago, M. (1987). Strategies and techniques of prescriptive psychotherapeutic intervention. In R. E. Hales & A. J. Frances (Eds.), *American Psychiatric Association: Annual Review* (Vol. 6, pp. 378–397). Washington, DC: American Psychiatric Association.

Beutler, L. E., Engle, D., Mohr, D., Daldrup, R. J., Bergan, J., Meredith, K., & Merry, W. (1991). Predictors of differential response to cognitive, experiential and self-directed psychotherapeutic procedures. *Journal of Consulting and Clinical Psychology, 59,* 333–340.

Beutler, L. E., Machado, P. P. P., Engle, D., & Mohr, D. (1993). Differential patient x treatment maintenance of treatment effects among cognitive, experiential, and SCIF-directed psychotherapies. *Journal of Psychotherapy Integration, 3,* 15–31.

Beutler, L. E., Machado, P. P. P., & Neufeldt, S. A. (1994). Therapist variables. In A. E. Bergin & S. L. Garfield (Eds.), *Handbook of psychotherapy and behavior change* (4th ed., pp. 229–269). New York: Wiley.

Beutler, L. E., & Mitchell, R. (1981). Differential psychotherapy outcome in depressed and impulsive patients as a function of analytic and experiential treatment procedures. *Psychiatry, 44,* 297–306.

Bibring, E. (1954). Psychoanalysis and the dynamic psychotherapies. *Journal of the American Psychoanalytic Association, 2,* 745–770.

Binder, J. L. (1993). Is it time to improve psychotherapy training? *Clinical Psychology Review, 13,* 301–308.

Blatt, S. J. (1992). The differential effect of psychotherapy and psychoanalysis with anaclitic and introjective patients: The Menninger Psychotherapy Research Project revisited. *Journal of the American Psychoanalytic Association, 40,* 691–724.

Blatt, S. J., & Felsen, I. (1993). Different kinds of folks may need different kinds of strokes: The effect of patients' characteristics on therapeutic process and outcome. *Psychotherapy Research, 3,* 245–259.

Blatt, S. J., Quinlan, D. M., Pilkonis, P. A., & Shea, M. T. (1995). Impact of perfectionism and need for approval on the brief treatment of depression: The NIMH TDCRP revisited. *Journal of Consulting and Clinical Psychology, 63,* 125–32.

Bloch, S. (1977). Supportive psychotherapy. *British Journal of Hospital Medicine, 18,* 63–67.

Bordin, E. S. (1979). The generalizability of the psychoanalytic concept of the working alliance. *Psychotherapy, 16,* 252–260.

Buckley, P. (1986). A neglected treatment. *Psychiatric Annals, 16,* 515–521.

Burke, J. D., White, H. S., & Havens, L. L. (1979). Which short-term therapy? Matching patient and method. *Archives of General Psychiatry, 36,* 177–186.

Butler, S. F., Henry, W. P., & Strupp, H. H. (1995). Measuring adherence in time-limited dynamic psychotherapy. *Psychotherapy, 32,* 629–638.

Butler, S. F., & Strupp, H. H. (1993). Effects of training experienced dynamic therapists to use a psychotherapy manual. In N. E. Miller, L. Luborsky, J. P. Barber, & J. P. Docherty (Eds.), *Handbook of dynamic psychotherapy research and practice* (pp. 191–210). New York: Basic Books.

Campbell, D. T., & Stanley, J. C. (1963). *Experimental and quasi-experimental designs for research.* Chicago: Rand-McNally.

Carpenter, W. T. (1984). A perspective on the psychotherapy of schizophrenia project. *Schizophrenia Bulletin, 10*, 599–603.

Carroll, K. M., Connors, G. J., Cooney, N. L., DiClemente, C. C., Donovan, D. M., Kadden, R. R., Longabaugh, R. L., Rounsaville, B. J., Wirtz, P. W., & Zweben, A. (1998). Internal validity of project MATCH treatments: Discriminability and integrity. *Journal of Consulting and Clinical Psychology, 66*, 290–303.

Carroll, K. M., Rounsaville, B. J., Gordon, L. T., Nich, C., Jatlow, P., Bisighini, R. M., & Gawin, F. H. (1994). Psychotherapy and pharmacotherapy for ambulatory cocaine abusers. *Archives of General Psychiatry, 51*, 177–187.

Castonguay, L. G., Goldfried, M. R., Wiser, S., Raue, P. J., & Hayes, A. M. (1996). Predicting the effect of cognitive therapy for depression: A study of unique and common factors. *Journal of Consulting and Clinical Psychology, 64*, 497–504.

Christensen, L., & Mendoza, J. L. (1986). A method of assessing change in a single subject: An alteration of the RC index. *Behavior Therapy, 17*, 305–308.

Cohen, J. (1988). *Statistical power analysis for the behavioral sciences* (2nd ed.). Hillsdale, NJ: Erlbaum.

Connolly, M. B., Crits-Christoph, P., Shappell, S., Barber, J. P., Luborsky, L., & Shaffer, C. (1999). Relation of transference interpretations to outcome in the early sessions of brief supportive-expressive psychotherapy. *Psychotherapy Research, 9*, 485–495.

Cooney, N. L., Kadden, R. M., Litt, M. D., & Getter, H. (1991). Matching alcoholics to coping skills or interactional therapies: Two-year follow-up results. *Journal of Consulting and Clinical Psychology, 59*, 598–601.

Crits-Christoph, P. (1992). The efficacy of brief dynamic psychotherapy: A meta-analysis. *American Journal of Psychiatry, 149*, 151–158.

Crits-Christoph, P., Barber, J. P., & Kurcias, J. S. (1993). The accuracy of therapists' interpretations and the development of the therapeutic alliance. *Psychotherapy Research, 3*, 25–35.

Crits-Christoph, P., Cooper, A., & Luborsky, L. (1988). The accuracy of therapists' interpretations and the outcome of dynamic psychotherapy. *Journal of Consulting and Clinical Psychology, 56*, 490–495.

Cronbach, L. J. (1951). Coefficient alpha and the internal structure of tests. *Psychometrika, 16*, 297–334.

Cronbach, L. J. (1957). The two disciplines of scientific psychology. *American Psychologist, 12*, 671–684.

Cronbach, L. J., & Snow, R. E. (1977). *Aptitudes and instructional methods: A handbook for research on interactions.* New York: Irvington.

Cross, D. G., Sheehan, P. W., & Khan, J. A. (1982). Short- and long-term follow-up of clients receiving insight-oriented and behavior therapy. *Journal of Consulting and Clinical Psychology, 50*, 103–112.

Crown, S. (1988). Supportive psychotherapy: A contradiction in terms? *British Journal of Psychiatry, 152*, 266–269.

Dance, K. A., & Neufeld, R. W. (1988). Aptitude-treatment interaction research in the clinical setting: A review of attempts to dispel the "patient uniformity" myth. *Psychological Bulletin, 104*, 192–213.

Davanloo, H. (1978). *Basic principles and techniques in short-term dynamic psychotherapy*. New York: Spectrum.

Davanloo, H. (1979). Techniques of short-term dynamic psychotherapy. *Psychiatric Clinics of North America, 2*, 11–21.

Davanloo, H. (Ed.). (1980). *Short-term dynamic psychotherapy*. New York: Jason Aronson.

de Carufel, F. L., & Piper, W. E. (1988). Group psychotherapy or individual psychotherapy. Patient characteristics as predictive factors. *International Journal of Group Psychotherapy, 38*, 169–188.

Derogatis, L. R. (1977). *SCL-90: Administration, scoring, and procedures manual-I for the revised version*. Baltimore: Clinical Psychometrics Research.

Dewald, P. A. (1969). *Psychotherapy: A dynamic approach*. Oxford: Blackwell Scientific.

Dewald, P. A. (1994). Principles of supportive psychotherapy. *American Journal of Psychotherapy, 48*, 505–518.

Diguer, L., Luborsky, L., Singer, B., Luborsky, E., Dickter, D., & Schmidt, K. A. (1993, June). *The efficacy of dynamic psychotherapy versus other psychotherapies: A meta-analysis*. Paper presented at the 24th meeting of the Society for Psychotherapy Research, Pittsburgh, PA.

Eisenstein, S. (1986). Franz Alexander and short-term dynamic psychotherapy. *International Journal of Short-Term Psychotherapy, 1*, 179–191.

Ferenczi, S. (1916). Introjection and transference. In S. Ferenczi, *Contributions to psychoanalysis* (pp. 30–79). Boston: Richard A. Badger.

Ferenczi, S. (1980). The further development of an active therapy in psychoanalysis. In J. Richman (Ed.), *Further contributions to the theory and technique of psychoanalysis* (pp. 189–197). London: Karnac Books. (Original work published 1920)

Ferenczi, S., & Rank, O. (1986). *The development of psychoanalysis*. Madison, CT: International Universities Press. (Original work published 1925)

Fine, R. (1988). *Troubled men*. San Francisco: Jossey-Bass.

Finney, J. W., & Moos, R. H. (1986). Matching patients with treatments: Conceptual and methodological issues. *Journal of Studies on Alcohol, 47*, 122–134.

First, M. B., Gibbon, M., Williams, J. B. W., & Spitzer, R. L. (1990). *Mini-SCID*. Toronto, Ontario: Multi-Health Systems.

First, M. B., Gibbon, M., Williams, J. B. W., & Spitzer, R. L. (1991). *SCID-II PQ and AutoSCID II*. Toronto, Ontario: Multi-Health Systems.

Flegenheimer, W. V. (1982). *Techniques of brief psychotherapy*. New York: Jason Aronson.

Floyd, F. J., & Widaman, K. F. (1995). Factor analysis in the development and refinement of clinical assessment instruments. *Psychological Assessment, 7*, 286–299.

Frank, J. D. (1979). What is psychotherapy? In S. Bloch (Ed.), *An introduction to the psychotherapies* (pp. 1–22). New York: Oxford University Press.

Frank, J. D. (1982). Therapeutic components shared by all psychotherapies. In J. H. Harvey & M. M. Parks (Eds.), *The Master Lecture series: Vol. 1. Psychotherapy research and behavior change* (pp. 73–122). Washington, DC: American Psychological Association.

French, T. M. (1958). *The integration of behavior* (Vol. 3). Chicago: University of Chicago Press.

Freud, S. (1962). Analysis, terminable and interminable. In J. Strachey (Ed.), *Complete psychological works of Sigmund Freud, Standard Edition, Vol. 23* (pp. 209–216). London: Hogarth Press. (Original work published 1937).

Freyberger, H. (1977). Supportive psychotherapeutic techniques in primary and secondary alexithymia. *Psychotherapy and Psychosomatics, 28*, 337–342.

Freyberger, H., Küsebeck, H.-W., Lempa, W., Wellmann, W., & Avenarius, H.-J. (1985). Psychotherapeutic interventions in alexithymic patients: With special regard to ulcerative colitis and Crohn patients. *Psychotherapy and Psychosomatics, 44*, 72–81.

Gabbard, G. O., Horowitz, L., Allen, J. G., Frieswyk, S., Newsom, G., Colson, D. B., & Coyne, L. (1994). Transference interpretation in the psychotherapy of borderline patients: A high-risk, high-gain phenomenon. *Harvard Review of Psychiatry, 2*, 59–69.

Garfield, S. L. (1986). Research on client variables in psychotherapy. In S. L. Garfield & A. E. Bergin (Eds.), *Handbook of psychotherapy and behavior change* (3rd ed., pp. 213–256). New York: Wiley.

Garfield, S. L. (1996). Some problems associated with "validated" forms of psychotherapy. *Clinical Psychology: Science and Practice, 3*, 218–229.

Gaston, L. (1990). The concept of the alliance and its role in psychotherapy: Theoretical and empirical considerations. *Psychotherapy, 27*, 143–153.

Gill, M. (1951). Ego psychology and psychotherapy. *Psychoanalytic Quarterly, 20*, 62–71.

Gill, M. M. (1982). *Analysis of transference: Volume I: Theory and technique*. New York: International Universities Press.

Glover, E. (1931). The therapeutic effect of inexact interpretations: A contribution to the theory of suggestion. *International Journal of Psycho-Analysis, 12*, 397–411.

Goldman, G. S. (1956). Reparative psychotherapy. In S. Rado & G. Daniels (Eds.), *Changing concepts of psychoanalytic medicine* (pp. 101–113). New York: Grune & Stratton.

Greenberg, J. R., & Mitchell, S. A. (1983). *Object relations in psychoanalytic theory*. Cambridge, MA: Harvard University Press.

Greenberg, L. S., & Goldman, R. L. (1988). Training in experiential therapy. *Journal of Consulting and Clinical Psychology, 56*, 696–702.

Grinker, R. R., & Spiegel, J. P. (1944). Brief psychotherapy in war neuroses. *Psychosomatic Medicine, 6,* 123–131.

Gunderson, J. G., Frank, A. F., Katz, H. M., Vannicelli, M. L., Frosch, J. P., & Knapp, P. H. (1984). Effects of psychotherapy in schizophrenia: II. Comparative outcome of two forms of treatment. *Schizophrenia Bulletin, 10,* 564–596.

Guthrie, E., Creed, F., Dawson, D., & Tomenson, B. (1993). A randomized controlled trial of psychotherapy in patients with refractory irritable bowel syndrome. *British Journal of Psychiatry, 163,* 316–321.

Hare-Mustin, R. T., & Marecek, J. (1986). Autonomy and gender: Some questions for therapists. *Psychotherapy, 23,* 205–212.

Harris, M. R., Kalis, B. L., & Freeman, E. H. (1963). Precipitating stress: An approach to brief therapy. *American Journal of Psychotherapy, 17,* 465–471.

Harris, M. R., Kalis, B. L., & Freeman, E. H. (1964). An approach to short-term psychotherapy. *Mind, 2,* 198–206.

Hartman, L., Krywonis, M., & Morrison, E. (1988). Psychological factors and health-related behavior change: Preliminary findings from a controlled study. *Canadian Family Physician, 34,* 1045–1050.

Hellerstein, D. J., Pinsker, H., Rosenthal, R. N., & Klee, S. (1994). Supportive therapy as the treatment model of choice. *The Journal of Psychotherapy Practice and Research, 3,* 300–306.

Henry, W. P., Strupp, H. H., Butler, S. F., Schact, T. E., & Binder, J. L. (1993). Effects of training in time-limited dynamic psychotherapy: Changes in therapist behavior. *Journal of Consulting and Clinical Psychology, 61,* 434–440.

Hill, C. E., O'Grady, K. E., & Elkin, I. (1992). Applying the Collaborative Study Psychotherapy Scale to rate therapist adherence in cognitive-behavior therapy, interpersonal therapy, and clinical management. *Journal of Consulting and Clinical Psychology, 60,* 73–79.

Hoglend, P. (1993). Transference interpretations and long-term change after dynamic psychotherapy of brief to moderate length. *American Journal of Psychotherapy, 47,* 494–507.

Hollis, F. (1964). *Casework: A psychosocial therapy.* New York: Random House.

Hollon, S. D., Evans, M. D., Elkin, I., & Lowery, H. A. (1984). *System for rating therapies for depression.* Paper presented at the 1984 annual meeting of the American Psychiatric Association, Los Angeles.

Holmes, J. (1988). Supportive analytical psychotherapy: An account of two cases. *British Journal of Psychiatry, 152,* 824–829.

Horowitz, L., Rosenberg, S. E., Baer, B. A., Ureno, G., & Villasenor, V. S. (1988). Inventory of Interpersonal Problems: Psychometric properties and clinical applications. *Journal of Consulting and Clinical Psychology, 56,* 885–892.

Horowitz, M. J. (1986). *Stress response syndromes* (2nd ed.). Northvale, NJ: Jason Aronson.

Horowitz, M. J. (1991). Short-term dynamic therapy of stress response syndromes. In P. Crits-Christoph & J. P. Barber (Eds.), *Handbook of short-term dynamic psychotherapy* (pp. 166–198). New York: Basic Books.

Horowitz, M. J. (1994). Configurational analysis and the use of role-relationship models to understand transference. *Psychotherapy Research, 3*, 184–196.

Horowitz, M. J., Krupnick, J., Kaltreider, N., Wilner, N., Leong, A., & Marmar, C. (1981). Initial psychological response to parental death. *Archives of General Psychiatry, 38*, 316–323.

Horowitz, M. J., Marmar, C., Krupnick, J., Kaltreider, N., Wallerstein, R., & Wilner, N. (1984). *Personality styles and brief psychotherapy*. New York: Basic Books.

Horowitz, M. J., Marmar, C., Weiss, D. S., Dewitt, K. N., & Rosenbaum, R. (1984). Brief psychotherapy of bereavement reactions: The relation of process to outcome. *Archives of General Psychiatry, 41*, 438–448.

Horvath, A. O., & Goheen, M. D. (1990). Factors mediating the success of defiance- and compliance-based interventions. *Journal of Counseling Psychology, 37*, 363–371.

Horvath, A. O., & Luborsky, L. (1993). The role of the therapeutic alliance in psychotherapy. *Journal of Consulting and Clinical Psychology, 61*, 561–573.

Horvath, A. O., & Symonds, B. D. (1991). Relation between working alliance and outcome in psychotherapy: A meta-analysis. *Journal of Counseling Psychology, 38*, 139–149.

Howard, K. I., Krause, M. S., Saunders, S. M., & Kopta, S. M. (1997). Trials and tribulations in the meta-analysis of treatment differences: Comment on Wampold et al. (1997). *Psychological Bulletin, 122*, 221–225.

Imber, S. D., Pilkonis, P. A., Sotsky, S. M., Elkin, I., Watkins, J. T., Collins, J. F., Shea, M. T., Leber, W. R., & Glass, D. R. (1990). Mode-specific effects among three treatments for depression. *Journal of Consulting and Clinical Psychology, 58*, 352–359.

Jacobson, N. S., Follette, W. C., & Revenstorf, D. (1984). Psychotherapy outcome research: Methods for reporting variability and evaluating clinical significance. *Behavior Therapy, 15*, 336–352.

Jacobson, N. S., & Revenstorf, D. (1988). Statistics for assessing the clinical significance of psychotherapy techniques: Issues, problems, and new developments. *Behavioral Assessment, 10*, 133–145.

Jacobson, N. S., & Truax, P. (1991). Clinical significance: A statistical approach to defining meaningful change in psychotherapy research. *Journal of Consulting and Clinical Psychology, 59*, 12–19.

Jensen, J. P., Bergin, A. E., & Greaves, D. W. (1990). The meaning of eclecticism: New survey and analysis of components. *Professional Psychology: Research and Practice, 21*, 124–130.

Joint Commission on Mental Illness and Health. (1961). *Action for mental health*. New York: Basic Books.

Jones, E. (1913). The action of suggestion in psychotherapy. In E. Jones, *Papers on psycho-analysis* (pp. 241–282). New York: William Wood.

Jones, E. (1957). *The life and work of Sigmund Freud.* New York: Basic Books.

Jones, E. E., Krupnick, J. L., & Kerig, P. A. (1987). Some gender effects in a brief psychotherapy. *Psychotherapy, 24,* 337–352.

Jones, E. E., & Zoppell, C. L. (1982). Impact of client and therapist gender on psychotherapy process and outcome. *Journal of Consulting and Clinical Psychology, 50,* 259–272.

Jordan, J. V., Kaplan, A. G., & Surrey, J. L. (1983). *Women and empathy—Implications for psychological development and psychotherapy.* Work in Progress, No. 82-02, Wellesley College.

Joyce, A. S., & Piper, W. E. (1990). An examination of Mann's model of time-limited psychotherapy. *Canadian Journal of Psychiatry, 35,* 41–49.

Kadden, R. M., Cooney, N. L., Getter, H., & Litt, M. D. (1989). Matching alcoholics to coping skills or interactional therapies: Posttreatment results. *Journal of Consulting and Clinical Psychology, 57,* 698–704.

Kaplan, A. G. (1985). Female or male therapists for women patients: New formulations. *Psychiatry, 48,* 111–121.

Kaplan, A. G. (1986). The "self-in-relation": Implications for depression in women. *Psychotherapy, 23,* 234–242.

Kaplan, A. G. (1987). Reflections on gender and psychotherapy. *Women & Therapy, 6,* 11–24.

Karasu, T. B. (1986). Psychosomatic medicine and psychotherapy. *Psychiatric Annals, 16,* 522–525.

Kaufman, E. (1989). The psychotherapy of dually diagnosed patients. *Journal of Substance Abuse Treatment, 6,* 9–18.

Kernberg, O. F. (1986). Supportive psychotherapy. In O. F. Kernberg, *Severe personality disorders* (pp. 147–164). New Haven, CT: Yale University Press.

Kernberg, O., Berstein, E., Coyne, L., Applebaum, A., Horowitz, L., & Voth, H. (1972). Psychotherapy and psychoanalysis: Final report of the Menninger Foundation's psychotherapy research project. *Bulletin of the Menninger Clinic, 36,* 1–278.

Kiesler, D. J. (1966). Some myths of psychotherapy research and the search for a paradigm. *Psychological Bulletin, 65,* 110–136.

Kirshner, L. A. (1978). Effects of gender on psychotherapy. *Comprehensive Psychiatry, 19,* 79–82.

Kirshner, L. A., Genack, A., & Hauser, S. T. (1978). Effects of gender on short-term psychotherapy. *Psychotherapy, 15,* 158–167.

Klein, D. F., Zitrin, C. M., Woerner, M. G., & Ross, D. C. (1983). Treatment of phobias. II. Behavior therapy and supportive psychotherapy: Are there any specific ingredients? *Archives of General Psychiatry, 40,* 139–145.

Klerman, G., Weissman, M. M., Rounsaville, B., & Chevron, E. (1984). *Interpersonal psychotherapy for depression.* New York: Basic Books.

Knight, R. P. (1954). Management and psychotherapy of the borderline schizophrenic patient. In R. P. Knight & C. R. Friedman (Eds.), *Psychoanalytic psychiatry and psychology* (pp. 110–122). New York: International Universities Press.

Koenigsberg, H. W., Kernberg, O. F., Haas, G., Lotterman, A., Rockland, L., & Selzer, M. (1985). Development of a scale for measuring techniques in the psychotherapy of borderline patients. *Journal of Nervous and Mental Disease, 173*, 424–431.

Koss, M. P., & Butcher, J. N. (1986). Research on brief psychotherapy. In S. L. Garfield & E. Bergin (Eds.), *Handbook of psychotherapy and behavior change* (3rd ed., pp. 627–670). New York: Wiley.

Koss, M. P., & Shiang, J. (1994). Research on brief psychotherapy. In A. E. Bergin & S. L. Garfield (Eds.), *Handbook of psychotherapy and behavior change* (4th ed., pp. 664–700). New York: Wiley.

Krupnick, J. L., Elkin, I., Collins, J., Simmens, S., Sotsky, S. M., Pilkonis, P. A., & Watkins, J. T. (1994). Therapeutic alliance and clinical outcome in the NIMH Treatment of Depression Collaborative Research Program: Preliminary findings. *Psychotherapy, 31*, 28–35.

Lambert, M. J., & Anderson, E. M. (1996). Assessment for the time-limited psychotherapies. In L. J. Dickstein, J. Oldham, & M. B. Riba (Vol. Eds.), & K. R. MacKenzie (Section Ed.), *American Psychiatric Press Review of Psychiatry, Vol. 15* (pp. 23–42). Washington, DC: American Psychiatric Press.

Lambert, M. J., & Bergin, A. E. (1994). The effectiveness of psychotherapy. In A. E. Bergin & S. L. Garfield (Eds.), *Handbook of psychotherapy and behavior change* (4th ed., pp. 143–189). New York: Wiley.

Lemkau, J. P., & Landau, C. (1986). The "selfless syndrome": Assessment and treatment considerations. *Psychotherapy, 23*, 227–233.

Levenson, H., & Butler, S. F. (1999). Brief dynamic individual psychotherapy. In R. E. Hales, S. C. Yudofsky, & J. A. Talbott (Eds.), *The American Psychiatric Press textbook of psychiatry* (3rd ed.; pp. 1133–1156). American Psychiatric Association: Washington, DC.

Levenson, H., Speed, J. L., & Budman, S. H. (1992, June). *Therapists' training and skill in brief therapy: A survey of Massachusetts and California psychologists*. Paper presented to the Society for Psychotherapy Research, Berkeley, CA.

Levine, M. (1945). *Psychotherapy in medical practice*. New York: Macmillan.

Lindemann, E. (1944). Symptomatology and management of acute grief. *American Journal of Psychiatry, 101*, 141–148.

Longabaugh, R., Beattie, M., Noel, N., Stout, R., & Malloy, P. (1993). The effect of social investment on treatment outcome. *Journal of Studies on Alcohol, 54*, 465–478.

Longabaugh, R., Wirtz, P. W., Beattie, M. C., Noel, N., & Stout, R. (1995). Matching treatment focus to patient social investment and support: 18-month follow-up results. *Journal of Consulting and Clinical Psychology, 63*, 296–307.

Luborsky, L. (1984). *Principles of psychoanalytic psychotherapy: A manual for supportive-expressive treatment.* New York: Basic Books.

Luborsky, L., & Barber, J. P. (1993). Benefits of adherence to psychotherapy manuals, and where to get them. In N. E. Miller, L. Luborsky, J. P. Barber, & J. P. Docherty (Eds.), *Psychodynamic treatment research: A handbook for clinical practice* (pp. 211–226). New York: Basic Books.

Luborsky, L., & Crits-Christoph, P. (1990). *Understanding transference: The CCRT method.* New York: Basic Books.

Luborsky, L., Crits-Christoph, P., Mintz, J., & Auerbach, A. (1988). *Who will benefit from psychotherapy? Predicting therapeutic outcomes.* New York: Basic Books.

Luborsky, L., & Mark, D. (1991). Short-term supportive-expressive psychoanalytic psychotherapy. In P. Crits-Christoph & J. P. Barber (Eds.), *Handbook of short-term dynamic psychotherapy* (pp. 110–136). New York: Basic Books.

Luborsky, L., Mintz, J., Auerbach, A., Christoph, P., Bachrach, H., Todd, T., Johnson, M., Cohen, M., & O'Brien, C. P. (1980). Predicting the outcome of psychotherapy: Findings of the Penn Psychotherapy Project. *Archives of General Psychiatry, 37,* 471–481.

Luborsky, L., Singer, B., & Luborsky, L. (1975). Comparative studies of psychotherapies. *Archives of General Psychiatry, 32,* 995–1008.

Magnavita, J. J. (1993). The evolution of short-term dynamic psychotherapy: Treatment of the future? *Professional Psychology: Research and Practice, 24,* 360–365.

Malan, D. H. (1963). *A study of brief psychotherapy.* New York: Plenum Press.

Malan, D. H. (1976a). *The frontier of brief psychotherapy: An example of the convergence of research and clinical practice.* New York: Plenum Press.

Malan, D. H. (1976b). *Toward the validation of dynamic psychotherapy: A replication.* New York: Plenum Press.

Malan, D. H. (1979). *Individual psychotherapy and the science of psychodynamics.* Cambridge: Butterworth.

Malan, D. H. (1986). Beyond interpretation: Initial evaluation and technique in short-term dynamic psychotherapy. *International Journal of Short-Term Psychotherapy, 1,* 59–106.

Mann, J. (1973). *Time-limited psychotherapy.* Cambridge, MA: Harvard University Press.

Mann, J. (1991). Time-limited psychotherapy. In P. Crits-Christoph & J. P. Barber (Eds.), *Handbook of short-term dynamic psychotherapy* (pp. 17–44). New York: Basic Books.

Mann, J., & Goldman, R. (1982). *A casebook in time-limited psychotherapy.* New York: McGraw-Hill.

Marmar, C. R., Gaston, L., Gallagher, D., & Thompson, L. W. (1989). Alliance and outcome in late-life depression. *Journal of Nervous and Mental Disease, 177,* 464–472.

Marmor, J. (1979a). Historical aspects of short-term dynamic psychotherapy. *Psychiatric clinics of North America, 2,* 3–9.

Marmor, J. (1979b). Short-term dynamic psychotherapy. *American Journal of Psychiatry, 36,* 149–155.

Marziali, E. A. (1984). Prediction of outcome of brief psychotherapy from therapist interpretive interventions. *Archives of General Psychiatry, 41,* 301–304.

Marziali, E. A., & Sullivan, J. M. (1980). Methodological issues in the content analysis of brief psychotherapy. *British Journal of Medical Psychology, 53,* 19–27.

Mattson, M. E. (1994). Patient-treatment matching: Rationale and results. *Alcohol Health and Research World, 18,* 287–295.

Maude-Griffin, P. M., Hohenstein, J. M., Humfleet, G. L., Reilly, P. M., Tusel, D. J., & Hall, S. M. (1998). Superior efficacy of cognitive-behavioral therapy for urban crack cocaine abusers: Main and matching effects. *Journal of Consulting and Clinical Psychology, 66,* 832–837.

McCallum, M., & Piper, W. E. (1993). *Psychological mindedness assessment procedure manual.* Unpublished manuscript.

McCallum, M., & Piper, W. E. (1997). The psychological mindedness assessment procedure. In M. McCallum & W. E. Piper (Eds.), *Psychological mindedness: A contemporary understanding* (pp. 27–58). Mahwah, NJ: Erlbaum.

McCallum, M., Piper, W. E., & O'Kelly, J. (1997). Predicting patient benefit from a group oriented, evening treatment program. *International Journal of Group Psychotherapy, 47,* 291–314.

McLachlan, J. F. C. (1972). Benefit from group therapy as a function of patient–therapist match on conceptual level. *Psychotherapy: Theory, Research, and Practice, 9,* 317–323.

McLellan, A. T. (1986). "Psychiatric severity" as a predictor of outcome from substance abuse treatments. In R. E. Meyer (Ed.), *Psychopathology and addictive disorders.* New York: Guilford Press.

McLellan, A. T., Luborsky, L., O'Brien, C. P., & Woody, G. E. (1980). Improved diagnostic instrument for substance abuse patients: The Addiction Severity Index. *Journal of Nervous and Mental Disease, 168,* 26–33.

Mendelsohn, R. (1978). Critical factors in short-term psychotherapy: A summary. *Bulletin of the Menninger Clinic, 42,* 133–149.

Menninger, K. (1958). *Theory of psychoanalytic technique.* New York: Basic Books.

Messer, S. B., & Warren, C. S. (1995). *Models of brief psychodynamic therapy: A comparative approach.* New York: Guilford Press.

Miller, W. R., Benefield, R. G., & Tonigan, J. S. (1993). Enhancing motivation for change in problem drinking: A controlled comparison of two therapist styles. *Journal of Consulting and Clinical Psychology, 61,* 455–461.

Mogul, K. M. (1982). Overview: The sex of the therapist. *American Journal of Psychiatry, 139,* 1–11.

Moncher, F. J., & Prinz, R. J. (1991). Treatment fidelity in outcome studies. *Clinical Psychology Review, 11,* 247–266.

Najavits, L. M., & Strupp, H. H. (1994). Differences in the effectiveness of psychodynamic therapists: A process-outcome study. *Psychotherapy, 31,* 114–123.

Nielsen, B., Nielsen, A. S., & Wraae, O. (1998). Patient-treatment matching improves compliance of alcoholics in outpatient treatment. *Journal of Nervous and Mental Disease, 186*, 752–760.

Nietzel, M. T., Russell, R. L., Hemmings, K. A., & Gretter, M. L. (1987). Clinical significance of psychotherapy for unipolar depression: A meta-analytic approach to social comparison. *Journal of Consulting and Clinical Psychology, 55*, 156–161.

Nolen-Hoeksema, S. (1987). Sex differences in unipolar depression: Evidence and theory. *Psychological Bulletin, 101*, 259–282.

Norušis, M. J. (1993). *SPSS for windows advanced statistical release*. Chicago: SPSS.

Novalis, P. N., Rojcewicz, Jr., S. J., & Peele, R. (1993). *Clinical manual of supportive psychotherapy*. Washington, DC: American Psychiatric Press.

Ogrodniczuk, J. S., & Piper, W. E. (1999). Measuring therapist technique in psychodynamic psychotherapies: Development and use of a new scale. *Journal of Psychotherapy Practice and Research, 8*, 142–154.

O'Neil, J. (1980). Male sex role conflicts, sexism, and masculinity: Psychological implications for men, women, and the counseling psychologist. *The Counseling Psychologist, 9*, 61–80.

Orford, J. (1999). Future research directions: A commentary on project MATCH. *Addiction, 94*, 62–66.

Orlinsky, D. E., & Howard, K. I. (1986). Process and outcome in psychotherapy. In S. L. Garfield & A. E. Bergin (Eds.), *Handbook of psychotherapy and behavior change* (3rd ed., pp. 311–381). New York: Wiley.

Paul, G. L. (1967). Strategy of outcome research in psychotherapy. *Journal of Consulting Psychology, 31*, 109–118.

Person, E. S. (1988, Feb.). Love triangles. *The Atlantic Monthly*, 41–52.

Pine, F. (1976). On therapeutic change: Perspectives from a parent-child model. *Psychoanalysis and Contemporary Science, 5*, 537–569.

Pine, F. (1984). The interpretive moment: Variations on classical themes. *Bulletin of the Menninger Clinic, 48*, 54–71.

Pine, F. (1986). Supportive psychotherapy: A psychoanalytic perspective. *Psychiatric Annals, 16*, 526–529.

Pinsker, H. (1994). The role of theory in teaching supportive psychotherapy. *American Journal of Psychotherapy, 48*, 530–542.

Pinsker, H. (1997). *A primer of supportive psychotherapy*. Hillsdale, NJ: Analytic Press.

Pinsker, H., Rosenthal, R., & McCullough, L. (1991). Dynamic supportive psychotherapy. In P. Crits-Christoph & J. P. Barber (Eds.), *Handbook of short-term dynamic psychotherapy* (pp. 220–247). New York: Basic Books.

Piper, W. E. (1996). Psychodynamic psychotherapy. In L. J. Dickstein, J. M. Oldman, & M. B. Riba (Vol. Eds.), & K. R. MacKenzie (Section Ed.), *American psychiatric press review of psychiatry* (Vol. 15, pp. 109–128). Washington, DC: American Psychiatric Press.

Piper, W. E., Azim, H. F. A., Joyce, A. S., & McCallum, M. (1991). Transference interpretations, therapeutic alliance, and outcome in short-term individual psychotherapy. *Archives of General Psychiatry, 48,* 946–953.

Piper, W. E., Azim, H. F .A., Joyce, A. S., McCallum, M., Nixon, G. W. H., & Segal, P. S. (1991). Quality of object relations vs. interpersonal functioning as predictors of therapeutic alliance and psychotherapy outcome. *Journal of Nervous and Mental Disease, 179,* 432–438.

Piper, W. E., Azim, H. F. A., McCallum, M., & Joyce, A. S. (1990). Patient suitability and outcome in short-term individual psychotherapy. *Journal of Consulting and Clinical Psychology, 58,* 475–481.

Piper, W. E., Boroto, D. R., Joyce, A. S., McCallum, M., & Azim, H. F. A. (1995). Pattern of alliance and outcome in short-term individual psychotherapy. *Psychotherapy, 32,* 639–647.

Piper, W. E., Debbane, E. G., Bienvenu, J. P., de Carufel, F. L., & Garant, J. (1986). Relationships between the object focus of therapist interpretations and outcome in short-term individual psychotherapy. *British Journal of Medical Psychology, 59,* 1–11.

Piper, W. E., Debbane, E. G., Bienvenu, J. P., & Garant, J. (1984). A comparative study of four forms of psychotherapy. *Journal of Consulting and Clinical Psychology, 52,* 268–279.

Piper, W. E., Debbane, E. G., de Carufel, F. L., & Bienvenu, J. P. (1987). A system for differentiating therapist interpretations and other interventions. *Bulletin of the Menninger Clinic, 51,* 532–550.

Piper, W. E., de Carufel, F. L., & Szkrumelak, N. (1985). Patient predictors of process and outcome in short-term individual psychotherapy. *Journal of Nervous and Mental Disease, 173,* 726–733.

Piper, W. E., & Duncan, S. C. (1999). Object relations theory and short-term dynamic psychotherapy: Findings from the Quality of Object Relations Scale. *Clinical Psychology Review, 19,* 669–686.

Piper, W. E., Joyce, A. S., Azim, H. F. A. & Rosie, J. S. (1994). Patient characteristics and success in day treatment. *Journal of Nervous and Mental Disease, 182,* 381–386.

Piper, W. E., Joyce, A. S., McCallum, M., & Azim, H. F. A. (1998). Interpretive and supportive forms of psychotherapy and patient personality variables. *Journal of Consulting and Clinical Psychology, 66,* 558–567.

Piper, W. E., McCallum, M., & Azim, H. F. A. (1992). *Adaptation to loss through short-term group psychotherapy.* New York: Guilford Press.

Piper, W. E., McCallum, M., & Joyce, A. S. (1993). *Manual for assessment of quality of object relations.* Unpublished manuscript.

Piper, W. E., Rosie, J. S., Azim, H. F. A., & Joyce, A. S. (1993). A randomized trial of psychiatric day treatment. *Hospital and Community Psychiatry, 44,* 757–763.

Piper, W. E., Rosie, J. S., Joyce, A. S., & Azim, H. F. A. (1996). *Time-limited day treatment for personality disorders: Integration of research and practice in a group program.* Washington, DC: American Psychological Association.

Pollack, J., & Horner, A. (1985). Brief adaptation-oriented psychotherapy. In A. Winston (Ed.), *Clinical research issues in short-term dynamic psychotherapy*. Washington, DC: American Psychiatric Press.

Project MATCH Research Group. (1997). Matching alcoholism treatments to client heterogeneity: Project MATCH posttreatment drinking outcomes. *Journal of Studies on Alcohol, 58*, 7–29.

Rado, S. (1925). The economic principle in psycho-analytic technique. *International Journal of Psycho-Analysis, 6*, 35–44.

Rank, O. (1978). *Will therapy*. New York: Norton. (Original work published 1929)

Razin, A. M. (1982). Psychosocial intervention in coronary heart disease: A review. *Psychosomatic Medicine, 44*, 363–387.

Reich, W. (1933). *Character analysis*. New York: Farrar, Straus, & Giroux.

Rockland, L. H. (1987). A supportive approach: Psychodynamically oriented supportive therapy—Treatment of borderline patients who self-mutilate. *Journal of Personality Disorders, 1*, 350–353.

Rockland, L. H. (1989a). Psychoanalytically oriented supportive therapy: Literature review and techniques. *Journal of the American Academy of Psychoanalysis, 17*, 451–462.

Rockland, L. H. (1989b). *Supportive therapy: A psychodynamic approach*. New York: Basic Books.

Rockland, L. H. (1992). *Supportive therapy for borderline patients: A psychodynamic approach*. New York: Guilford Press.

Rockland, L. H. (1993). A review of supportive psychotherapy, 1986–1992. *Hospital and Community Psychiatry, 44*, 1053–1060.

Rosenberg, M. (1979). *Conceiving the self*. New York: Basic Books.

Rosser, R., Denford, J., Heslop, A., Kinston, W., Macklin, D., Minty, K., Moynihan, C., Muir, B., Rein, L., & Guz, A. (1983). Breathlessness and psychiatric morbidity in chronic bronchitis and emphysema: A study of psychotherapeutic management. *Psychological Medicine, 13*, 93–100.

Sammons, M. T., & Gravitz, M. A. (1990). Theoretical orientations of professional psychologists and their former professors. *Professional Psychology: Research and Practice, 21*, 131–134.

Schilder, P. (1938). *Psychotherapy*. New York: Norton.

Schlesinger, H. J. (1969). Diagnosis and prescription for psychotherapy. *Bulletin of the Menninger Clinic, 33*, 269–278.

Shapiro, D., Barkham, M., Rees, A., Hardy, G. E., Reynolds, S., & Startup, M. (1994). Effects of treatment duration and severity of depression on the effectiveness of cognitive-behavioral and psychodynamic-interpersonal psychotherapy. *Journal of Consulting and Clinical Psychology, 62*, 522–534.

Shapiro, D. A., & Shapiro, D. (1982). Meta-analysis of comparative therapy outcome studies. *Psychological Bulletin, 92*, 581–604.

Shapiro, D. A. & Startup, M. (1992). Measuring therapist adherence in exploratory psychotherapy. *Psychotherapy Research, 2*, 193–203.

Shaw, B. F., & Dobson, K. S. (1988). Competency judgments in the training and evaluation of psychotherapists. *Journal of Consulting and Clinical Psychology, 56*, 666–672.

Shefler, G., Dasberg, H., & Ben-Shakhar, G. (1993). A randomized controlled outcome and follow-up study of Mann's time-limited psychotherapy. *Journal of Consulting and Clinical Psychology, 63*, 585–593.

Shoham-Salomon, V. (1991). Introduction to the special section on client-therapy interaction research. *Journal of Consulting and Clinical Psychology, 59*, 203–204.

Shoham-Salomon, V., Avner, R., & Neeman, R. (1989). You're changed if you do and changed if you don't: Mechanisms underlying paradoxical interventions. *Journal of Consulting and Clinical Psychology, 57*, 590–598.

Shoham-Salomon, V., & Hannah, M. T. (1991). Client-treatment interaction in the study of differential change processes. *Journal of Consulting and Clinical Psychology, 59*, 217–225.

Shrout, P. E., & Fleiss, J. L. (1979). Intraclass correlations: Uses in assessing rater reliability. *Psychological Bulletin, 86*, 420–428.

Sifneos, P. E. (1972). *Short-term psychotherapy and emotional crisis.* Cambridge, MA: Harvard University Press.

Sifneos, P. E. (1972–1973). Is dynamic psychotherapy contraindicated for a large number of patients with psychosomatic diseases? *Psychotherapy and Psychosomatics, 21*, 133–136.

Sifneos, P. E. (1984a). The current status of individual short-term dynamic psychotherapy and its future: An overview. *American Journal of Psychotherapy, 38*, 472–483.

Sifneos, P. E. (1984b). Short-term dynamic psychotherapy for patients with physical symptomatology. *Psychotherapy and Psychosomatics, 42*, 48–51.

Sifneos, P. E. (1985). Short-term dynamic psychotherapy of phobic and mildly obsessive-compulsive patients. *American Journal of Psychotherapy, 39*, 314–322.

Sifneos, P. E. (1987). *Short-term dynamic psychotherapy: Evaluation and technique* (2nd ed.). New York: Plenum Press.

Silberschatz, G., & Curtis, J. T. (1986). Clinical implications of research on brief dynamic Psychotherapy. II. How the therapist helps or hinders therapeutic progress. *Psychoanalytic Psychology, 3*, 27–38.

Silberschatz, G., Curtis, J. T., & Nathan, S. (1989). Using the patient's plan to assess progress in psychotherapy. *Psychotherapy, 26*, 40–46.

Silberschatz, G., Fretter, P. B., & Curtis, J. T. (1986). How do interpretations influence the process of psychotherapy? *Journal of Consulting and Clinical Psychology, 54*, 646–652.

Silverman, W. H. (1996). Cookbooks, manuals, and paint-by-numbers: Psychotherapy in the 90s. *Psychotherapy, 33*, 207–215.

Sjödin, I., Svedlund, J., Ottosson, J.-O., & Dotevall, G. (1986). Controlled study of psychotherapy in chronic peptic ulcer disease. *Psychosomatics, 27*, 187–200.

Sloane, R. B., Staples, F. R., Cristol, A. H., Yorkston, N. J., & Whipple, K. (1975). Short-term analytically oriented psychotherapy versus behavior therapy. *American Journal of Psychiatry, 132,* 373–377.

Smith, B., & Sechrest, L. (1991). Treatment of aptitude-treatment interactions. *Journal of Consulting and Clinical Psychology, 59,* 233–244.

Smith, M. L., Glass, G. V., & Miller, T. I. (1980). *The benefits of psychotherapy.* Baltimore: Johns Hopkins Press.

Snow, R. E. (1991). Aptitude-treatment interaction as a framework for research on individual differences in psychotherapy. *Journal of Consulting and Clinical Psychology, 59,* 205–216.

Sotsky, S. M., Glass, D. R., Shea, M. T., Pilkonis, P. A., Collins, J. F., Elkin, I., Watkins, J. T., Imber, S. D., Leber, W. R., Moyer, J., & Oliveri, M. E. (1991). Patient predictors of response to psychotherapy and pharmacotherapy: Findings in the NIMH Treatment of Depression Collaborative Research Program. *American Journal of Psychiatry, 148,* 997–1008.

Spielberger, C. D. (1983). *Manual for the State-Trait Anxiety Inventory.* Palo Alto, CA: Consulting Psychologists Press.

Stanton, A. H., Gunderson, J. G., Knapp, P. H., Frank, A. F., Vannicelli, M. L., Schnitzer, R., & Rosenthal, R. (1984). Effects of psychotherapy in schizophrenia: I. Design and implementation of a controlled study. *Schizophrenia Bulletin, 10,* 520–563.

Steinberg, P. I. (1989). Two techniques of supportive psychotherapy. *Canadian Family Physician, 35,* 1139–1143.

Stiver, I. P. (1986). The meaning of care: Reframing treatment models for women. *Psychotherapy, 23,* 221–226.

Stone, M. H. (1989). Individual psychotherapy with victims of incest. *Psychiatric Clinics of North America, 12,* 237–255.

Strachey, J. (1934). The nature of therapeutic action of psychoanalysis. *International Journal of Psychoanalysis, 15,* 127–159.

Strupp, H. H. (1980a). Success and failure in time-limited psychotherapy: A systematic comparison of two cases (Comparison 1). *Archives of General Psychiatry, 37,* 595–603.

Strupp, H. H. (1980b). Success and failure in time-limited psychotherapy: A systematic comparison of two cases (Comparison 2). *Archives of General Psychiatry, 37,* 708–716.

Strupp, H. H. (1980c). Success and failure in time-limited psychotherapy: A systematic comparison of two cases (Comparison 3). *Archives of General Psychiatry, 37,* 831–841.

Strupp, H. H. (1980d). Success and failure in time-limited psychotherapy: A systematic comparison of two cases (Comparison 4). *Archives of General Psychiatry, 37,* 947–954.

Strupp, H. H. (1993). The Vanderbilt psychotherapy studies: Synopsis. *Journal of Consulting and Clinical Psychology, 61,* 431–433.

Strupp, H. H., & Anderson, T. (1997). On the limitations of therapy manuals. *Clinical Psychology: Science and Practice, 4,* 76–82.

Strupp, H. H., & Binder, J. L. (1984). *Psychotherapy in a new key: A guide to time-limited dynamic psychotherapy.* New York: Basic Books.

Strupp, H. H., & Hadley, S. W. (1979). Specific versus nonspecific factors in psychotherapy. *Archives of General Psychiatry, 36,* 1125–1136.

Strupp, H. H., Schacht, T. E., Henry, W. P., & Binder, J. L. (1992). Jack M.: A case of premature termination. *Psychotherapy, 29,* 191–205.

Suh, C. S., Strupp, H. H., & O'Malley, S. S. (1986). The Vanderbilt process measures: The Psychotherapy Process Scale (VPPS) and the Negative Indicators Scale (VNIS). In L. S. Greenberg & W. M. Pinsorf (Eds.), *The psychotherapy process: A research handbook* (pp. 285–323). New York: Guilford Press.

Sullivan, H. S. (1953). *Interpersonal theory of psychiatry.* New York: Norton.

Svartberg, M., & Stiles, T. C. (1992). Predicting patient change from therapist competence and patient-therapist complementarity in short-term anxiety-provoking psychotherapy: A pilot study. *Journal of Consulting and Clinical Psychology, 60,* 304–307.

Svartberg, M., & Stiles, T. C. (1994). Therapeutic alliance, therapist competence, and client change in short-term anxiety-provoking psychotherapy. *Psychotherapy Research, 4,* 20–33.

Tarachow, S. (1963). *An introduction to psychotherapy.* New York: International Universities Press.

Thase, M. E., Reynolds, C. F., Frank, E., Simons, A. D., McGeary, J., Fasiczka, A. L., Garamoni, G. G., Jennings, R., & Kupfer, D. J. (1994). Do depressed men and women respond similarly to cognitive behavior therapy? *American Journal of Psychiatry, 151,* 500–505.

Thompson, B. J., Gallagher, D., & Breckenridge, J. (1987). Comparative effectiveness of psychotherapies for depressed elders. *Journal of Consulting and Clinical Psychology, 55,* 385–390.

Tingey, R. C., Lambert, M. J., Burlingame, G. M., & Hansen, N. B. (1996). Assessing clinical significance: Proposed extensions to method. *Psychotherapy Research, 6,* 109–123.

Tukey, J. W. (1949). Comparing individual means in the analysis of variance. *Biometrics, 5,* 99–114.

Ursano, R. J., & Hales, R. E. (1986). A review of brief individual psychotherapies. *American Journal of Psychiatry, 143,* 1507–1517.

Wallace, E. R. (1983). *Dynamic psychiatry in theory and practice.* Philadelphia: Lea & Febiger.

Wallerstein, R. S. (1986). *Forty-two lives in treatment: A study of psychoanalysis and psychotherapy.* New York: Guilford Press.

Wallerstein, R. S. (1989). The Psychotherapy Research Project of the Menninger Foundation: An overview. *Journal of Consulting and Clinical Psychology, 57,* 195–205.

Waltz, J., Addis, M. E., Koerner, K., & Jacobson, N. S. (1993). Testing the integrity of a psychotherapy protocol: Assessment of adherence and competence. *Journal of Consulting and Clinical Psychology, 61*, 620–630.

Weiss, J., Sampson, J., & the Mount Zion Psychotherapy Research Group (1986). *The psychoanalytic process: Theory, clinical observations, and empirical research.* New York: Guilford Press.

Weissman, M. M., Paykel, E. S., Siegel, R., & Klerman, G. L. (1971). The social role performance of depressed women: A comparison with a normal sample. *American Journal of Orthopsychiatry, 41*, 390–405.

Werman, D. S. (1984). *The practice of supportive psychotherapy.* New York: Brunner/Mazel.

Werman, D. S. (1988). Technical aspects of supportive psychotherapy. *Psychiatric Journal of the University of Ottawa, 6*, 153–160.

Wierzbicki, M., & Pekarik, G. (1993). A meta-analysis of psychotherapy dropout. *Professional Psychology: Research and Practice, 24*, 190–195.

Winston, A., McCullough, L., Pollack, J., Laikin, M., Pinsker, H., Nezu, A. M., Flegenheimer, W., & Sadow, J. (1989). The Beth Israel psychotherapy research program: Toward an integration of theory and discovery. *Journal of Integrative and Eclectic Psychotherapy, 8*, 344–356.

Winston, A., Pinsker, H., & McCullough, L. (1986). A review of supportive psychotherapy. *Hospital and Community Psychiatry, 37*, 1105–1114.

Winston, A., Pollack, J., McCullough, L., Flegenheimer, W., Kestenbaum, R., Trujillo, M. (1991). Brief psychotherapy of personality disorders. *Journal of Nervous and Mental Disease, 179*, 188–193.

Wolpe, J. (1969). *The practice of behavior therapy.* New York: Pergamon Press.

Woody, G., Luborsky, L., McLellan, A. T., O'Brien, C., Beck, A. T., Blain, J., Herman, I., & Hole, A. V. (1983). Psychotherapy for opiate addicts: Does it help? *Archives of General Psychiatry, 40*, 639–645.

Woody, G. E., McLellan, A. T., Luborsky, L., & O'Brien, C. P. (1985). Sociopathy and psychotherapy outcome. *Archives of General Psychiatry, 42*, 1081–1086.

Worchel, J. (1990). Short-term dynamic psychotherapy. In R. A. Wells & V. J. Giannetti (Eds.), *Handbook of the brief psychotherapies* (pp. 193–216). New York: Plenum Press.

Yalom, I. D. (1975). *The theory and practice of group psychotherapy* (2nd ed.). New York: Basic.

Yeaton, W. H., & Sechrest, L. (1981). Critical dimensions in the choice and maintenance of successful treatments: Strength, integrity, and effectiveness. *Journal of Consulting and Clinical Psychology, 49*, 156–167.

Zettle, R. D., Haflich, J. L., & Reynolds, R. A. (1992). Responsivity to cognitive therapy as a function of treatment format and client personality dimensions. *Journal of Clinical Psychology, 48*, 787–797.

Zettle, R. D., & Herring, E. L. (1995). Treatment utility of the sociotropy/autonomy distinction: Implications for cognitive therapy. *Journal of Clinical Psychology, 51,* 280–289.

Zlotnick, C., Elkin, I., & Shea, M. T. (1998). Does the gender of a patient or the gender of a therapist affect the treatment of patients with major depression? *Journal of Consulting and Clinical Psychology, 66,* 655–659.

Zlotnick, C., Shea, M. T., Pilkonis, P. A., Elkin, I., & Ryan, C. (1996). Gender, type of treatment, dysfunctional attitudes, social support, life events, and depressive symptoms over naturalistic follow-up. *American Journal of Psychiatry, 153,* 1021–1027.

Zitrin, C. M., Klein, D. F., & Woerner, M. G. (1978). Behavior therapy, supportive psychotherapy, imipramine, and phobias. *Archives of General Psychiatry, 35,* 307–316.

Zitrin, C. M., Klein, D. F., Woerner, M. G., & Ross, D. C. (1983). Treatment of phobias. I. Comparison of imipramine hydrochloride and placebo. *Archives of General Psychiatry, 40,* 125–138.

AUTHOR INDEX

Numbers in italics refer to listings in the reference section.

Abraham, K., 35, *281*
Addis, M. E., 211, 213, 219, 221, *299*
Alexander, L., 16, 35, 36, 41, *281*
Allen, J. A., 123, *281*
Allen, J. G., 141, *286*
Anderson, E. M., 92, 119, *281*, *290*
Anderson, T., 210, 219–220, *298*
Andrews, G., 101, *281*
Annis, H. M., 29, *281*
Appelbaum, A., 34, 64, *281*, *289*
Auerbach, A., 24, *291*
Avenarius, H.-J., 43, *286*
Avner, R., 64, 73, *296*
Azim, H. F. A., 5, 30, 66, 74, 80, 82, 83, 85, 107, 115, 119, 135, 137, 146, 216, 217, 225, *294*

Bachelor, A., 135, *281*
Bachrach, H., 24, *291*
Badgio, P. C., 222, *282*
Baer, B. A., 100, *287*
Balint, E., 16, *282*
Balint, M., 16, *282*
Barber, J. P., 25, 29–30, 73, 138, 141, 142, 211, 220, 221, 222, *282*, *284*, *291*
Barkham, M., 23, 63, 75, *295*
Beattie, M., 70, 72, *290*
Beck, A. T., 41, 42, 68, 101, 106, 107, 127, 209, *282*, *299*
Beck, R. W., 101, *282*
Bellak, L., 17, *282*
Benefield, R. G., 70, *292*
Benjamin, L. S., 27, *282*
Ben-Shakhar, G., 22, *296*
Bergan, J., 63, 72–73, *282*
Bergin, A. E., 63, 91, *288*, *290*
Berstein, E., 74, *289*
Beutler, L. E., 5, 62, 63, 65, 72–73, 122, *282*, *283*
Bibring, E., 35, 214, 215, *283*
Bienvenu, J. P., 18, 23, 85, 98, 137, 138, *294*

Binder, J. L., 5, 17, 23, 27, 28, 30, 35, 144, 209, 211, 212, 214–215, *283*, *287*, *298*
Bisighini, R. M., 69, *284*
Blain, J., 41, 42, 68, *299*
Blatt, S. J., 73–74, *283*
Bloch, S., 36, 42, *283*
Bond, M., 101, *281*
Bordin, E. S., 134, *283*
Boroto, D. R., 135, *294*
Breckenridge, J., 23, *298*
Buckley, P., 33, 42, *283*
Budman, S. H., 91, *290*
Burke, J. D., 18, *283*
Burlingame, G. M., 106, 107, *298*
Butcher, J. N., 23, *290*
Butler, S. F., 14, 28, 211, 212–213, 214–215, *283*, *287*, *290*

Calvo, N., 222, *282*
Campbell, D. T., 211, 212, *283*
Carpenter, W. T., 43, *284*
Carroll, K. M., 65, 66, 69, 71, *284*
Castonguay, L. G., 148, *284*
Chevron, E., 209, *289*
Christensen, L., 106, *284*
Christoph, P., 24, *291*
Clarkin, 62, 72, *282*
Cohen, J., 105, *285*
Cohen, M., 24, *291*
Collins, J., 136, *290*
Collins, J. F., 75, 121, *288*, *297*
Colson, D. B., 141, *286*
Connolly, M. B., 138, 141, 142, *284*
Connors, G. J., 65, 66, 71, *284*
Cooney, N. L., 65, 66, 69, 71, *284*, *289*
Cooper, A., 25, *284*
Coyne, L., 74, 141, *286*, *289*
Crago, M., 62, 72, *282*
Creed, F., 92, *287*
Cristol, A. H., 23, *297*
Crits-Christoph, P., 23, 25, 29–30, 138, 141, 142, 220, *282*, *284*, *291*
Cronbach, L. J., 5, 64, 66, 224, *284*

Cross, D. G., 23, 284
Crown, S., 33, 56, 284
Curtis, J. T., 27, 296

Daldrup, R. J., 63, 72–73, 282
Dance, K. A., 5, 63, 66, 285
Dasberg, H., 22, 296
Davanloo, H., 15, 17, 18, 20–21, 30, 31, 137, 209, 285
Davis, C. S., 69, 281
Dawson, D., 92, 287
Debbane, E. G., 18, 23, 85, 98, 138, 294
de Carufel, F. L., 18, 82, 98, 138, 285, 294
Denford, J., 40, 41, 92, 295
Derogatis, L. R., 101, 106, 124, 285
Dewald, P. A., 34, 36, 40, 41, 44, 51, 285
Dewitt, K. N., 23, 26, 74, 92, 288
Dickter, D., 23, 285
DiClemente, C. C., 65, 66, 71, 284
Diguer, L., 23, 285
Dobson, K. S., 211, 296
Donovan, D. M., 65, 66, 71, 284
Dotevall, G., 41, 42, 296
Duncan, S. C., 80, 281, 294

Eisenstein, S., 16, 285
Elkin, I., 75, 121, 122, 123, 136, 211, 221, 222, 228, 282, 287, 290, 297, 300
Emery, G., 209, 282
Engle, D., 63, 72–73, 282, 283
Evans, M. D., 221, 287

Fasiczka, A. L., 121, 122, 298
Faude, J., 222, 282
Felsen, I., 73–74, 283
Ferenczi, S., 15, 17, 35, 285
Fine, R., 123, 285
Finney, J. W., 68, 70, 285
First, M. B., 95, 285
Flegenheimer, W. V., 12, 19, 39, 46, 285, 299
Fleiss, J. L., 224, 279, 296
Floyd, F. J., 228, 285
Follette, W. C., 106, 288

Frank, A. F., 40, 43, 287, 297
Frank, E., 121, 122, 298
Frank, J. D., 61, 63, 286
Freeman, E. H., 17, 287
French, T. M., 16, 35, 281, 286
Fretter, P. B., 27, 296
Freud, S., 14–15, 17, 34, 286
Freyberger, H., 40, 43, 286
Frieswyk, S., 141, 286
Frosch, J. P., 43, 287

Gabbard, G. O., 141, 286
Gallagher, D., 23, 136, 291, 298
Garamoni, G. G., 121, 122, 298
Garant, J., 18, 23, 85, 137, 294
Garfield, S. L., 62, 121, 122, 210, 286
Gaston, L., 134, 136, 286, 291
Gawin, F. H., 69, 284
Genack, A., 121, 122, 289
Getter, H., 69, 284, 289
Gibbon, M., 95, 285
Gill, M., 39, 48, 286
Gill, M. M., 35, 137, 286
Glass, D. R., 75, 121, 288, 297
Glass, G. V., 23, 63, 297
Glover, E., 35, 36, 286
Goheen, M. D., 73, 288
Goldfried, M. R., 148, 284
Goldman, G. S., 36, 286
Goldman, R., 21, 291
Goldman, R. L., 209, 286
Gordon, L. T., 69, 284
Gordon, S., 123, 281
Gravitz, M. A., 91–92, 295
Greaves, D. W., 91, 288
Greenberg, J. R., 15, 30, 286
Greenberg, L. S., 209, 286
Gretter, M. L., 106, 293
Grinker, R. R., 17, 287
Gunderson, J. G., 40, 43, 287, 297
Guthrie, E., 92, 287
Guz, A., 40, 41, 92, 295

Haas, G., 221, 290
Hadley, S. W., 23, 28, 298
Haflich, J. L., 74, 299
Hales, R. E., 19, 298
Hall, S. M., 69, 292
Hannah, M. T., 61, 65, 73, 296

Hansen, N. B., 106, 107, *298*
Hardy, G. E., 23, 63, 75, *295*
Hare-Mustin, R. T., 122, *287*
Harris, M. R., 17, *287*
Hartman, L., 70, *287*
Hauser, S. T., 121, 122, *289*
Havens, L. L., 18, *283*
Hayes, A. M., 148, *284*
Hellerstein, D. J., 34, 42, 46, *287*
Hemmings, K. A., 106, *293*
Henry, W. P., 28, 144, 211, 214–215, *283*, *287*, *298*
Herman, I., 41, 42, 68, *299*
Herring, E. L., 74, *300*
Heslop, A., 40, 41, 92, *295*
Hill, C. E., 211, 221, 222, 228, *287*
Hoglend, 138, *287*
Hohenstein, J. M., 69, *292*
Hole, A. V., 41, 42, 68, *299*
Hollis, F., 38, *287*
Hollon, S. D., 221, *287*
Holmes, J., 34, *287*
Horner, A., 28, *295*, *299*
Horowitz, L., 74, 100, 141, *286*, *287*, *289*
Horowitz, M. J., 16, 17, 21, 23, 25–26, 31, 74, 92, *287*, *288*
Horvath, A. O., 63, 73, 134, 136, *288*
Howard, K. I., 5, 23, *288*, *293*
Humfleet, G. L., 69, *292*

Imber, S. D., 75, 121, *288*, *297*

Jacobson, N. S., 106, 107, 211, 213, 219, 221, *288*, *299*
Jarlow, P., 69, *284*
Jennings, R., 121, 122, *298*
Jensen, J. P., 91, *288*
Johnson, M., 24, *291*
Jones, E., 14, 15, 35, *289*
Jones, E. E., 121, 122, 131, *289*
Jordan, J. V., 122, *289*
Joyce, A. S., 5, 22, 30, 66, 74, 82, 83, 85, 100, 107, 115, 119, 216, 135, 137, 146, 216, 217, 225, *281*, *289*, *294*

Kadden, R. M., 69, *289*
Kadden, R. R., 65, 66, 69, 71, *284*

Kalis, B. L., 17, *287*
Kalreider, N., 16, 17, 25, 26, *288*
Kaplan, A. G., 122, 130, *289*
Karasu, T. B., 39–40, 43, 53, *289*
Katz, H. M., 43, *287*
Kaufman, E., 53, *289*
Kerig, P. A., 122, *289*
Kernberg, O. F., 40, 45, 74, 221, *289*, *290*
Kestenbaum, R., 21, 28, *299*
Khan, J. A., 23, *284*
Kiesler, D. J., 62–63, *289*
Kinston, W., 40, 41, 92, *295*
Kirschner, L. A., 121, 122, *289*
Klee, S., 34, 42, 46, *287*
Klein, D. F., 40, 42, 92, *289*, *300*
Klerman, G., 100, 124, 209, *289*, *299*
Knapp, P. H., 40, 43, *287*, *297*
Knight, R. P., 36, *290*
Koenigsberg, H. W., 221, *290*
Koerner, K., 211, 213, 219, 221, *299*
Kopta, S. M., 5, *288*
Koss, M. P., 23, *290*
Krakauer, I., 222, *282*
Krause, M. S., 5, *288*
Krupnick, J., 16, 17, 25, 26, 122, 136, *288*, *289*, *290*
Krywonis, M., 70, *287*
Kurcias, J. S., 25, *284*
Kusebeck, H.-W., 43, *286*

Laikin, M., 39, 46, *299*
Lambert, M. J., 63, 92, 106, 107, 119, *281*, *290*, *298*
Landau, C., 122, *290*
Leber, W. R., 75, 121, *288*, *297*
Lemkau, J. P., 122, *290*
Lempa, W., 43, *286*
Leong, A., 26, *288*
Levenson, H., 14, 91, *290*
Levine, M., 35, *290*
Lindemann, E., 17, 41, *290*
Litt, M. D., 69, *284*, *289*
Longabaugh, R., 65, 66, 70, 71, 72, *284*, *290*
Lotterman, A., 221, *290*
Lowery, H. A., 221, *287*

Luborsky, L., 23, 24, 25, 30, 31, 37, 38, 41, 42, 44, 63, 68, 134, 137, 138, 141, 142, 220, 282, 284, 285, 288, *291, 292, 299*

Machado, P. P. P., 73, 122, *283*
Macklin, D., 40, 41, 92, *295*
Magnavita, J. J., 13, 15, 19, *291*
Mahler, G., 14
Malan, D. H., 5, 15, 17, 18, 20, 30, 31, 42, 49, 137, *291*
Malloy, P., 70, *290*
Mann, J., 17, 21–22, 30, 31, 137, *291*
Maracek, J., 122, *287*
Mark, D., 24, *291*
Marmar, C., 16, 17, 23, 25, 26, 74, 92, 136, 288, *291*
Marmor, J., 13, 14, *291, 292*
Marziali, E. A., 18, 137, *292*
Mattson, M. E., 64, 67, *292*
Maude-Griffin, P. M., 69, *292*
McCallum, M., 5, 30, 66, 74, 82, 83, 85, 100, 107, 115, 135, 137, 146, 216, 217, 225, *292, 294*
McCullough, L., 21, 28, 37, 38, 39, 46, *293, 299*
McGeary, J., 121, 122, *298*
McLachlan, J. F. C., 69, *292*
McLellan, A. T., 41, 42, 68, *292, 299*
Mendelsohn, R., 13, 14, *292*
Mendoza, J. L., 106, *284*
Menninger, K., 18, *292*
Meredith, K., 63, 72–73, *282*
Merry, W., 63, 72–73, *282*
Messer, S. B., 15, 17, 23, 24, 30, *292*
Miller, T. I., 23, 63, *297*
Miller, W. R., 70, *292*
Minty, K., 40, 41, 92, *295*
Mintz, J., 24, *291*
Mitchell, R., 72, 73, *283*
Mitchell, S. A., 15, 30, *286*
Mogul, K. M., 122, *292*
Mohr, D., 63, 72–73, *282, 283*
Moncher, F. J., *292*
Moos, R. H., 68, 70, *285*
Morrison, E., 70, *287*
Moyer, J., 121, *297*
Moynihan, C., 40, 41, 92, *295*
Muenz, L. R., 73, *282*
Muir, B., 40, 41, 92, *295*

Najavits, L. M., 143–144, *292*
Nathan, S., 27, *296*
Neeman, R., 64, 73, *296*
Neufeld, R. W., 5, 63, 66, *285*
Neufeldt, S. A., 122, *283*
Newsom, G., 141, *286*
Nezu, A. M., 39, 46, *299*
Nich, C., 69, *284*
Nielsen, A. S., 69, *293*
Nielsen, B., 69, *293*
Nietzel, M. T., 106, *293*
Nixon, G. W. H., 30, 80, 83, *281, 294*
Noel, N., 70, 72, *290*
Nolen-Hoeksema, S., 122, 130, *293*
Norůsis, M. J., 107, *293*
Novalis, P. N., 34, 37, 49, *293*

O'Brien, C. P., 24, 41, 42, 68, *291, 292, 299*
O'Neil, J., 122, *293*
O'Grady, K. E., 211, 221, 222, 228, *287*
Ogrodniczuk, J. S., 215, 218, *293*
O'Kelly, J., 83, 85, 100, *292*
Oliveri, M. E., 121, *297*
O'Malley, S. S., 145, *298*
Orford, 71, *293*
Orlinsky, D. E., 23, *293*
Ornstein, P. H., 16, *282*
Ottosson, J.-O., 41, 42, *296*

Paul, G. L., 63, *293*
Paykel, E. S., 100, 124, *299*
Peele, R., 34, 37, 49, *293*
Pekarik, G., 221, *290*
Person, E. S., 177, *293*
Pilkonis, P. A., 72, 75, 121, 122, 123, 136, *283, 288, 290, 297, 300*
Pine, F., 34, 44, 46–47, 48, *293*
Pinsker, H., 34, 37, 38, 39, 42, 46, 47, 49, 50, *287, 293, 299*
Piper, W. E., 5, 18, 22, 23, 30, 57, 66, 74, 80, 82, 83, 85, 98, 100, 107, 115, 119, 122, 135, 137, 138, 146, 215, 216, 217, 218, 222, 225, *281, 285, 289, 292, 293, 294*
Pollack, J., 28, 39, *295, 299*
Prinz, R. J., *292*

Quinlan, D. M., 73, *283*

Rado, S., 35, *295*
Rank, O., 15, 17, 21, *285*, *295*
Raue, P. J., 148, *284*
Razin, A. M., 41, *295*
Rees, A., 23, 63, 75, *295*
Reich, W., 15, 17, *295*
Reil, J., 34
Reilly, P. M., 69, *292*
Rein, L., 40, 41, 92, *295*
Revenstorf, D., 106, 107, *288*
Reynolds, C. F., 121, 122, *298*
Reynolds, R. A., 74, *299*
Reynolds, S., 23, 63, 75, *295*
Rockland, L. H., 34, 37, 40, 41, 42, 44, 45, 46, 47, 48, 49, 53, 221, *290*, *295*
Rojcewicz, Jr., S. J., 34, 37, 49, *293*
Rosenbaum, R., 23, 26, 74, 92, *288*
Rosenberg, M., 101, *295*
Rosenberg, S. E., 100, *287*
Rosenthal, R., 34, 37, 38, 40, 42, 43, 46, *287*, *293*, *297*
Rosie, J. S., 83, 85, 119, 216, *294*
Ross, D. C., 42, 92, *289*, *300*
Rosser, R., 40, 41, 92, *295*
Rounsaville, B. J., 65, 66, 69, 71, 209, *284*, *289*
Rush, B., 34
Russell, R. L., 106, *293*
Ryan, C., 121, 122, 123, *300*

Sadow, J., 39, 46, *299*
Sammons, M. T., 91–92, *295*
Sampson, J., 17, 23, 26–27, *299*
Saunders, S. M., 5, *288*
Schacht, T. E., 28, 144, 211, 214–215, *287*, *298*
Schilder, P., 35, *295*
Schlesinger, H., 44, *295*
Schmidt, K. A., 23, *285*
Schnitzer, R., 40, 43, *297*
Sechrest, L., 63, 65, 66, 67, *297*, *299*
Segal, P. M., 30, 80, *281*
Segal, P. S., 83, *294*
Selzer, M., 221, *290*
Settle, R. D., 74, *299*, *300*
Shaffer, C., 138, 141, 142, *284*

Shapiro, D., 23, 63, 75, *295*
Shapiro, D. A., 222, *295*
Shappell, S., 138, 141, 142, *284*
Shaw, B. F., 211, *296*
Shea, M. T., 72, 75, 121, 122, 123, *283*, *288*, *297*, *300*
Sheehan, P. W., 23, *284*
Shefler, G., 22, *296*
Shiang, J., 23, *290*
Shoham-Salomon, V., 61, 64, 65, *296*
Shrout, P. E., 224, *279*, *296*
Siegel, R., 100, 124, *299*
Sifneos, P. E., 15, 17, 18, 19–20, 30, 31, 43, 49, 137, *296*
Silberschatz, G., 27, *296*
Silverman, W. H., 210, *296*
Simmens, S., 136, *290*
Simons, A. D., 121, 122, *298*
Singer, B., 23, 63, *291*
Singh, M., 101, *281*
Sjödin, I., 41, 42, *296*
Sloane, R. B., 23, *297*
Small, L., 17, *282*
Smith, B., 63, 65, 66, 67, *297*
Smith, M. L., 23, 63, *297*
Snow, R. E., 5, 63, 64, 65, 66, *284*, *297*
Sotsky, S. M., 75, 121, 136, *288*, *290*, *297*
Speed, J. L., 91, *290*
Spiegel, J. P., 17, *287*
Spielberger, C. D., 101, 106, 127, *297*
Spitzer, R. L., 95, *285*
Stanley, H. H., 211, 212, *283*
Stanton, A. H., 40, 43, *297*
Staples, F. R., 23, *297*
Startup, M., 23, 63, 75, 222, *295*
Steer, R. A., 101, 106, 127, *282*
Steinberg, P. I., 41, *297*
Stiles, T. C., 20, 220, *298*
Stiver, I. P., 122, 123, *297*
Stone, M. H., 53, *297*
Stout, R., 70, 72, *290*
Strachey, J., 137, *297*
Strupp, H. H., 5, 17, 23, 27, 28, 30, 31, 143–144, 145, 209, 210, 211, 212–213, 214–215, 219–220, *283*, *287*, *292*, *298*
Suh, C. S., 145, *298*
Sullivan, H. S., 27, *298*
Sullivan, J. M., 18, 137, *292*
Supfer, D. J., 121, 122, *298*

Surrey, J. L., 122, *289*
Svartberg, M., 20, 220, *298*
Svedlund, J., 41, 42, *296*
Symonds, B. D., 63, 134, 136, *288*
Szkrumelak, N., 82, *294*

Tarachow, S., 36, *298*
Thase, M. E., 121, 122, *298*
Thompson, B. J., 23, *298*
Thompson, L. W., 136, *291*
Tingey, R. C., 106, 107, *298*
Todd, T., 24, *291*
Tomenson, B., 92, *287*
Tonigan, J. S., 70, *292*
Truax, P., 106, *288*
Trujillo, M., 21, 28, *299*
Tukey, J. W., 108–109, 113–114, *298*
Tusel, D. J., 69, *292*

Ureno, G., 100, *287*
Ursano, R. J., 19, *298*

Vannicelli, M. L., 40, 43, *287*, *297*
Villasenor, V. S., 100, *287*
Voth, H., 74, *289*

Wallace, E. R., 37, *298*
Wallerstein, R., 16, 17, 25, 26, 37, *288*, *298*
Walter, B., 14
Waltz, J., 211, 213, 219, 221, *299*

Warren, C. S., 15, 17, 23, 24, 30, *292*
Watkins, J. T., 75, 121, 136, *288*, *290*, *297*
Weiss, D. S., 23, 26, 74, 92, *288*
Weiss, J., 17, 23, 26–27, *299*
Weissman, M. M., 100, 124, 209, *289*, *299*
Wellmann, W., 43, *286*
Werman, D. S., 34, 36, 37, 40, 42, 44, *299*
Whipple, K., 23, *297*
White, H. S., 18, *283*
Widaman, K. F., 228, *285*
Wierzbicki, M., 143, *299*
Williams, J. B. W., 95, *285*
Wilner, N., 16, 17, 25, 26, *288*
Winston, A., 39, 46, *299*
Wirtz, P. W., 65, 66, 70, 71, 72, *284*, *290*
Wiser, S., 148, *284*
Woerner, M. G., 40, 42, 92, *289*, *300*
Wolpe, J., 209, *299*
Woody, G., 41, 42, 68, *292*, *299*
Worschel, J., 17, *299*
Wraae, O., 69, *293*

Yalom, I. D., 77, *299*
Yeaton, W. H., 66, *299*
Yorkston, N. J., 23, *297*

Zitrin, C. M., 40, 42, 92, *289*, *300*
Zlotnick, C., 121, 122, 123, *300*
Zoppell, C. L., 121, 122, 131, *289*
Zweben, A., 65, 66, 71, *284*

SUBJECT INDEX

Abreaction, 35
Active therapy, 15
Adaptation, 38
Adaptive defenses, 39, 261
Addiction Severity Index, 68
Adherence
 defined, 210–211
 measures, 211–216, 218–219, 238
Adjustment disorder, 174
Adult Children of Alcoholics (ACOA), 187, 188
Advising, 196–197, 264–265
Affect regulation, 80
Alcohol-dependent aftercare, 72
Alcoholics Anonymous (AA), 72
Alcoholism treatment, 66–72
Alexithymia, 40, 43–44
Alliance, 134. *See also* Therapeutic alliance
American Psychiatric Association Commission on Psychiatric Therapies, 37
Anaclitic characteristics, 73–74
ANCOVA (analysis of covariance), 125
ANOVA (analysis of variance), 65, 125
Antecedents, 80
Antidepressants, 99, 155, 182, 190, 198
Antisocial personality disorder, 68
Anxiety-provoking interventions, 17, 19–20
Approval, 264
Aptitude, 5, 61
Aptitude–treatment interaction research
 case illustrations, 173–206
 clinical significance, 106–107, 115
 conclusion, 114–120
 design, 94, 95
 follow-up findings, 110–114, 117
 interpretive and supportive variables, 91–120
 limitations, 119–120
 magnitude of effect, 105–106, 115
 medication, 99–100
 objectives, 93
 outcome variables, 100–101, 103, 108, 109
 patient personality variables, 100
 patients, 94–96
 procedure, 94
 referrals, 94
 settings, 93–94
 statistical analyses, 101–102
 statistical significance, 104–105
 therapies, 97–99
 therapists, 96–97
 therapy process, 133–150
Aptitude–treatment interactions (ATIs)
 anaclitic–introjective patients, 73–74
 aptitudes and theory, 64–65
 development, 62–64
 externalization–internalization, 72–73
 goal, 61–62
 impairment level, 74–75
 methodology–66, 67
 optimal patient-treatment matching, 66–72
 QOR characteristic, 74, 79
 reactance, 73
 research guides, 5–6
 self-concept levels, 74
 sociotropy–autonomy dimensions, 74
ATI psychotherapy research, 61–75, 133, 239
Auto-SCID (Structured Clinical Interview for *DSM-III-R*), 95
Auto-SCID II (Structured Clinical Interview for *DSM-III-R*), 95
Axis I diagnoses, 95, 96
Axis II diagnoses, 95, 96

Beck Depression Inventory, 101, 106–107, 127
Behavioral manifestations, 80
Benefiting, 86
Benign delusions, 266

Benign introjection, 36
Benign projection, 36
Bereavement therapy, 74
Beth Israel Psychotherapy Research Program, 21, 46
Borderline disorder, 21, 44
Boston University School of Medicine, 21
Brief adaptive psychotherapy (BAP), 28
Brief broad spectrum behavioral treatment (BBS), 70
Brief crisis intervention model, 17
Brief dynamic therapy models, 17, 22
    control–mastery theory, 23, 26–27
    stress-response syndromes, 23, 25–26
    supportive–expressive, 23
    time-limited, 23
Brief therapy of stress-response syndromes, 23, 25–26
Broad-focused, short-term dynamic therapy, 20

Center for the Study of Neuroses, 25
Change categories, 111–113
Character resistances, 15
Chicago Institute for Psychoanalysis, 16
Chronic obstructive airways disease, 41
Clarification, 35, 40
Clarifying interventions, 266–267
Clinical significance, 106–107, 115, 127–128
Clonazepam, 162
Cocaine abuse, 69
Cognitive–behavioral therapy (CBT)
    for alcohol dependency, 71
    contextual factor, 213
    counseling versus, 68
    insight therapy versus, 73, 74, 75
    STI versus, 23
Collaboration, 262–263
Community Mental Health Centers Act, 17
Competence
    defined, 210–211
    measures, 211–216, 219–220
    as intervention, 264
Completers, 94
Concentration, 137, 139
Concentration of transference interpretations (CTI), 139, 140–141, 142

Conceptual level (CL), 69
Configurational analysis, 25
Confrontation, 40, 267
Contractual agreement, 251, 257–258
Controlling relations, 80
Control–mastery theory, 23, 26–27
Coping, 69, 123
Coping skills training, 69
Core conflictual relationship theme (CCRT), 25
Corrective emotional experience, 16, 36
Cost-effective treatments, 245
Countertransference, 24, 31–32, 40
Cronbach's alpha, 224
Cyclical maladaptive pattern (CMP), 27–28

Decatastrophizing, 38
Decliners, 94
Defense mechanisms, 261
Defensive Style Questionnaire, 101
Dependent personality disorder, 190
Depressive disorders, 24, 68
Differentiated drinkers, 69–70
Dodo bird verdict, 63
Double depression, 152
Drive–structural model, 17, 20
Dropouts, 7, 94, 102–104, 116, 241
Dropping out, 143–148
    clinical illustrations, 153–171
    early session findings, 147
    findings summarized, 147–148
    last session qualitative findings, 141–147
    last session quantitative findings, 145–146
    pretherapy indicators, 143, 144
    therapeutic alliance, 143–145
Drug counseling, 68
Dynamic component, 218
Dynamic expression, 275
Dynamic therapies
    basic tenet, 216
    described, 13–28
    general classes, 4
    historical development, 4, 237
    individual, 46
Dynamic work, 145
Dysphoria, 161–169, 189
Dysthymia, 190

Edmonton Comparative Study, 30, 47–48, 67
Edmonton controlled study of day treatment, 83, 85, 86, 87
Edmonton controlled study of short-term group therapy, 85
Edmonton Controlled Study of Short-term Individual Therapy, 82
Edmonton predictor study of evening treatment, 83, 85
Education, 265–266
Effect size, 105
Ego-gratification, 262
Ego-strength, 262
Emotional re-education, 16
Environment, 70
Environmental interventions, 265
Expressive therapy. *See* Short-term interpretive psychotherapy
Extended cognitive–behavioral therapy (ECBT), 70
Extended relationship enhancement therapy (ERE), 70
Externalization–internalization, 73

Factor structure, 226–227, 228–229
Features, 49, 51, 52
Flexibility, 55, 243–244
Focal conflict, 16
Focal psychotherapy, 16, 18
Follow-up assessments, 110–114, 117–118
Free association method, 14
Frequency of transference interpretations (FTI), 139, 140–141
Full transference neurosis, 14–15

Gender, 121–132
    effects on outcomes, 8, 122–124, 131–132, 242
    follow-up outcome, 128–129
    form of therapy and, 125
    patient, 121–122, 129–130, 243
    patient–treatment matching, 131–132
    posttherapy outcomes, 125–128
    study limitations, 131
    in therapeutic alliance, 124–125
    therapist, 122, 127, 130–131

Global Severity Index, 106, 107, 124, 127
Group therapy, 69

Health care costs, 3
Health care reform, 245
Hierarchical regression analysis, 113–114, 132

Individual dynamic supportive therapy, 46
Informing interventions, 265–266
Insight therapy, 73, 74, 75, 237
Insurance providers, 22
Interactional group therapy, 69
Interaction effects, 113
Internal consistency, 224, 226, 228
Internal validity, 211
Interpretations, 35, 250, 253, 271, 274
Interpretive accuracy, 32
Interpretive and Supportive Technique Scale (ISTS), 98
    assessment, 229–230
    characteristics, 270–271
    comparative trial functions, 230–231
    conversion scales, 271–272
    described, 222–224, 238
    future implications, 231–232
    item descriptions, 272–278
    objectives, 269–270
    psychometric properties, 224–229
    rater manual, 269–279
    rater reliability, 225–226, 227–228
    training recommendations, 278–279
Interpretive approach, 250, 253–254
Interpretive (expressive) therapy
    described, 3–4
    developments, 237
    dropouts, 116, 144, 153–171, 241
    good match illustrated, 174–181
    personality variables, 173–181
    poor match illustrated, 182–189
    primary objective, 51
    QOR, 86, 116–118
    secondary objective, 51
    supportive therapy versus, 35, 46–47, 49–57
    time-limited individual, 79

Intraclass Correlation Coefficient (ICC), 2, 100, 101, 145, 224, 279
Introjective characteristics, 73–74
Inventory of Interpersonal Problems, 100

Joint Commission on Mental Illness and Health, 17

Links, 272, 276
Locus of control, 70

Magnitude of effect, 105–106, 115
Main effects, 113
Maladaptive defenses, 39, 40, 261
Management, 265
Manipulation, 35
Manual for Time-Limited, Short-Term, Interpretive Individual Therapy, 32, 217, 249–258
Manual for Time-Limited, Short-Term, Supportive Individual Therapy, 48, 217, 259–267
Matching Alcoholism Treatments to Client Heterogeneity (MATCH), 70–71
Matching factors, 64, 131–132
Mature defenses, 39, 111
Mature relations, 80
McGill University study, 20
Medication, 99–100, 247
Menninger Psychotherapy Study, 37
Meta-analysis, 23
Methadone maintenance program, 68
Mini-SCID (Structured Clinical Interview for *DSM-III-R*), 95
Modeling, 266
Montreal Comparative Study, 82, 85
Morale, 263
Motivation, 15, 29, 64
Mount Zion Psychotherapy Research Group, 26

Narcissistic personality disorder, 198
National Institute on Alcohol Abuse and Alcoholism, 70
Nefazadone, 155, 182, 198
Negative transferences, 260

NIMH Treatment of Depression Collaborative Study, 73, 123
Noninterpretive interventions, 271

Oedipal victory, 175, 178
One-person psychology, 15
Opiate addiction treatment, 24
Optimal matching
    ATI designs, 61–75
    future designs, 245–247
    prescriptive therapy, 62
Outcome factors and variables, 111, 240, 241, 242
Outcome predictors, 64
Overall objectives, 51
Overinclusion, 49–50, 237

Paroxetine, 162, 190
Passive–aggressive personality disorder, 198
Passive–receptive approach, 250, 252–253
Pathogenic beliefs, 26–27
Patient characteristics
    assessment, 62
    in brief therapy, 29–30
    coping style, 69–70
    gender, 121, 129–130
    as matching factors, 64
    measures, 246–247
    motivation, 29, 64
    as outcome predictors, 64
    PM, 6–7, 77–79
    QOR, 5, 6–7, 30, 77–79
    research implications, 88–89
    research recommendations, 78
    research reviews, 78
    in short-term therapy, 6
    types, 77–78
Patient coping style, 69–70
Patient-rated alliance, 124, 134–136
Patient selection
    interpretive therapy, 28–30
    short-term, anxiety-producing therapy, 19–20
    STI therapy, 13
    supportive therapy, 40–44
Patient selection criteria
    alexithymia, 43–44

characteristics, 40–41
chronic patients, 42–43
physical conditions, 41–42
Paxil, 162, 190
Pearson correlations, 135
Penn Psychotherapy Project, 24–25
Peptic ulcer disease, 42
Permission, 263–264
Personality disorder, 24, 68
Phobia, 42
Plan formulation method, 27
Posttherapy outcomes, 125–128
Posttraumatic stress disorder, 17
Prescriptive therapy, 62
Primary objectives, 51
Primitive defenses, 45–46
Primitive relationships, 80
Problem focus, 251, 256–257, 259–260
Project MATCH, 67–68, 70–72
Psychiatric severity, 68–69
Psychoanalysis
   early goals, 14–15
   history, 14–16, 34–35
Psychodynamically oriented supportive therapy (POST), 44–45
Psychodynamic theoretical model, 3
Psychological mindedness (PM)
   contrasted with QOR, 6–7, 77–79, 87–89, 118–119, 243
   defined, 83
   dropouts, 153
   form of therapy and, 109–110, 239–240
   levels, 83–84
   outcome-related, 242
   scoring criteria, 246
   treatment criteria, 87–89, 173
Psychological Mindedness Assessment Procedure (PMAP), 177, 201
Psychosomatic character pattern, 43
Psychotropic medication, 247

QOR Assessment Interview, 81
Quality of object relations (QOR), 80–83
   contrasted with psychological mindedness, 5, 6–7, 77–79, 87–89, 118–119, 243
   described, 5, 30, 80
   dropouts, 153
   form of therapy and, 107–109

in interpretive therapy, 132
levels, 80
as matching variable, 74
scoring criteria, 246
in supportive therapy, 116–118, 239–240
transference interpretation and, 138, 139–143
as treatment criteria, 87–89, 173
Quality of Object Relations Scale, 82

Rater Manual for the Interpretive and Supportive Technique Scale, 269–279
Rater reliability index, 224
Reflection, 38
Regression techniques, 65, 66, 113
Relapse prevention therapy, 69, 70
Reliable change, 127–128
Remaining, 86
Reverse triangle, 177
Rivotril, 162
Role relationship schemas, 25

Schizophrenia, 42–43
SCL-90-R global severity index, 106, 107, 124, 127
SCID-II PQ, 95
Searching relationships, 80
Secondary objectives, 51
Self-esteem regulation, 80
Self-Esteem Scale, 101
Separation anxiety, 21
Serzone, 155, 182, 198
Session objectives, 52
Short-term, defined, 3
Short-term anxiety-producing psychotherapy, 19–20
Short-term interpretive psychotherapy (STI)
   beginnings in psychoanalysis, 14–16
   contractual agreement, 251, 257–258
   drive–structural model, 17, 20
   effectiveness, 92
   first wave, 16–22
   general themes, 235–247, 258
   identifying characteristics, 13–14
   implications for therapist activity, 251–252

STI psychotherapy, *continued*
    interaction effect, 240
    patient selection, 13, 28–30
    second wave, 22–28
    shared characteristics, 30–32
    theoretical approach, 240–251
    therapist interest in, 91–92
    time-limited approach, 21–22, 23
Short-term supportive individual therapy
    concepts and implications, 259–262
    contractual agreement, 259
    theoretical approach, 259
    therapist interventions, 262–267
Social Adjustment Scale interview (SAS), 100, 124
Sociotropy–autonomy interaction, 74
Split-object triangle, 176–177
SPSS program, 107
Statistical significance, 104–105, 115, 125–127
STI therapy. *See* Short-term interpretive psychotherapy
Stress-response syndromes, 23, 25–26
Structural Analysis of Social Behavior (SASB), 215
Substance abuse therapy, 66–72
Suggestions, 35, 264–265
Suicidal ideation, 174
Superego problems, 42
Supportive–expressive (SE) psychotherapy, 23, 24–25
Supportive psychotherapy
    appropriate patients, 40–44
    compared to good parenting, 34
    contemporary approaches, 44–47
    described, 33–34
    distinguishing features, 3, 4
    dropout rate, 7, 144, 241
    goals, 34
    good match illustrated, 189–197
    guidelines, 35–36
    historical overview, 34–37
    interpretive therapy versus, 35–37, 49–57
    overinclusion, 49–50
    poor match illustrated, 198–205
    prevalence, 92
    primary (direct) objective, 51
    secondary (indirect) objective, 51
    shared characteristics, 37–39
    short-term characteristics, 47–48
    technique modifications, 39–40
    time-limited individual, 79
Symptom Distress Checklist-Revised (SCL-90-R), 101, 124

Tavistock Clinic, 18
Technical eclecticism, 62
Termination date, 19
Themes, 235–247
Therapeutic alliance
    corrective–supportive techniques, 170–171
    defined, 124, 134, 217
    dropping out, 143–144, 154–161
    gender effects, 124–125
    outcomes, 63, 135–136
    patient-rated, 124, 134–136
    perceptions, 135
    QOR-related, 5, 86, 239–240
    in STI, 249, 251–252
    strengthened, 161–169
    therapist-rated, 124, 134–136
    transference interpretations, 139–140
Therapeutic focus, 23, 251, 256–257
Therapeutic relationship, 34. *See also* Therapeutic alliance
Therapeutic technique, 35, 136–143, 169–170
Therapist flexibility, 55, 243–244
Therapist interpretation, 4
Therapist Intervention Rating System (TIRS), 98, 138–139, 218
Therapist interventions
    advising, 264–265
    categories, 262–267
    clarifying, 266–267
    confronting, 267
    environmental, 265
    informing, 265–266
    supportive, 262–264
Therapist–patient (T–P) linking interpretation, 18
Therapist-rated alliance, 124
Therapist training, 214–216, 231–232
Therapy manual
    adherence to, 210–216, 218–219, 221
    competence and, 210–216

described, 209, 246
negative effects, 210, 238
research component, 4–5
uses, 209–210, 238
Therapy process, 133–150
Third-party payer systems, 22
Time-limited dynamic psychotherapy (TLDP), 27–28, 212–213, 214
Time-limited, defined, 3
Time-limited, interpretive individual therapy, 79
Time-limited, short-term therapies, 3, 5
Time-limited, supportive individual therapy, 79
Time-limited therapy (TLLP)
    described, 21–22
    predictive patient characteristics, 77–89
    psychological mindedness, 77–79, 83–86, 87–89, 92–93
    QOR, 77–79, 80–83, 87–89, 92–93
    selection, 22
    substance-abuse, 68–72
    termination, 22
Training, 214–216, 231–232
Trait Anxiety Scale (TAS), 101, 106–107, 127
Transference cure, 35
Transference interpretation, 136–143
    defined, 218
    findings summarized, 141–143
    general effects, 136–137
    ineffective, 7
    long-term therapy, 4
    outcome and, 140–141, 241
    short-term therapy, 4

STI, 24, 31–32
therapeutic alliance and, 139–140, 241
Transference relationship, 14, 15, 250–251
Transference role, 16
Transferential reactions, 250–251, 255–256, 260–261
Treatment adherence scale, 4–5
Treatment manuals, 209–220
Trial interpretations, 16
Trial therapy, 20
Triangle of conflict, 17
Triangle of insight, 17, 18
Triangular relations, 80
12-step facilitation therapy (TSF), 69, 71–72
Two-person psychology, 15

Universalizing, 38

Vanderbilt I study, 28
Vanderbilt II study, 28, 214–216
Vanderbilt Psychotherapy Process Scale (VPPS), 145, 215
Vanderbilt Therapeutic Strategies Scale (VTSS), 214
Ventilation, 38

Will therapy, 15
Working relationship. *See* Therapeutic alliance

ABOUT THE AUTHORS

William E. Piper, PhD, is a professor in the Department of Psychiatry, University of British Columbia. His primary research interests include process and outcome research for both individual and group forms of psychotherapy, and he has been the recipient of many research grants. He has published more than 120 journal articles and book chapters, and three recent books, including *Psychological Mindedness: A Contemporary Understanding*, *Time-Limited Day Treatment for Personality Disorders*, and *Adaptation to Loss Through Short-Term Group Therapy*. He is past president of the Society for Psychotherapy Research and is currently editor of the *International Journal of Group Psychotherapy*.

Anthony S. Joyce, PhD, is an associate professor in the Department of Psychiatry, University of Alberta, and coordinator of the Psychotherapy Research Centre, University of Alberta Hospital Site, in Edmonton. His research interests include the interaction of patient, technique, and process variables in short-term forms of dynamically oriented therapy and the treatment requirements of patients with personality disorders. He has been involved in studies of individual and group therapy, partial hospital treatment, and continuing care for patients with chronic forms of mental illness. He is a former president of the Canadian Group Psychotherapy Association. An advocate of the scientist–practitioner model, he maintains a private psychotherapy practice.

Mary McCallum, PhD, is an associate clinical professor and research associate with the Psychotherapy Research Centre, Department of Psychiatry, University of Alberta. She also conducts a half-time private psychotherapy practice and supervises psychiatry residents in psychotherapy. Her research interests include the assessment of patient characteristics associated with successful process and outcome of individual and group forms of psychotherapy. She has published numerous articles in the psychotherapy research field. This is her third book.

Hassan F. Azim, MD, is a psychiatrist, an honorary professor in the Department of Psychiatry, University of British Columbia, and a training and supervising psychoanalyst in private practice in Vancouver. Previously, he has held professorships in the departments of psychiatry at McGill University and the University of Alberta, where he was also codirector of the Psychotherapy Research Centre. He has been dedicated to rigorous research, teaching, and supervision in the areas of personality disorders, program development, and the various forms of psychoanalytic psychotherapy, including individual, group, and partial hospitalization. He has authored or coauthored approximately 50 articles and chapters, as well as two books.

John S. Ogrodniczuk, PhD, is a clinical assistant professor in the Department of Psychiatry, University of British Columbia. His research interests include identifying matches between patient characteristics and types of short-term, time-limited psychotherapies (individual, group, partial hospitalization) and studying the underlying mechanisms of change through the examination of the processes of psychotherapy. Other interests include the use of psychotherapy for medically ill patients.